TRINITY WORSHIP

BECOMING LIKE CHRIST IN HOW WE RELATE, HOW WE DO THINGS, HOW WE ORGANIZE, HOW WE LEARN, AND HOW WE LEAD

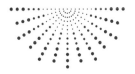

DAVE YAUK

GARDEN CITY

CONTENTS

Endorsements   v

Part I
INTRODUCTION

1. My History   3
2. Imago Dei   13
3. Unity & Glory   21
4. The Fall   27

Part II
THE TRINITY IN PERSON & TIME

5. The Father   39
6. The Son   49
7. The Holy Spirit   59
8. The Trinity in the Old Testament   71
9. Trinitarian History   85
10. Biblical Worship   95

Part III
C: HOW GOD RELATES

11. Types of Community   109
12. Baptism   135
13. One Another   147
14. The Trinity Answers Community   161

Part IV
R: HOW GOD DOES THINGS

15. Our Temple Home   173
16. A Family of Families   187
17. The Lord's Supper   195
18. Liturgy & Rhythms   219
19. The Trinity Answers Reasoning   233

Part V

O: HOW GOD ORDERS LIFE

20. PPK Household   251
21. Church Polity   275
22. A Brief on Governance   295
23. The Trinity Answers Organization   313

Part VI

S: HOW GOD TEACHES AND EXPECTS US TO
LEARN

24. Hermenuetics   321
25. Creative Transformation   353
26. The Trinity Answers Scripture   373

Part VII

S: HOW GOD LEADS

27. Everyone is a Church Planter   383
28. Synergetic Worship & Mission   403
29. The Trinity Answers Mission   419
30. Circle Resources   427

Part VIII

APPENDICES

31. Appendix 1: PPK Assessment   431
32. Appendix 2: Using the PPK Plans   435
33. Appendix 3: CROSS Prophet   441
34. Appendix 4: CROSS Priest   445
35. Appendix 5: CROSS King   449
36. Appendix 6: Trinitarian Diversity   453
37. Appendix 7: Spiritual Ministries List   457

Endnotes   463

ENDORSEMENTS

Trinity Worship is an inspirational, rational, creative, and deeply missional work that the church needs to experience. As an academic and professional creative person, I resonate with the dogged commitment to God the Father, Son and Holy Spirit, and the centrality of the cross. This work is a new challenge to live, create, work from, and worship within a Trinitarian paradigm. Dave Yauk drives home simplicity of awe towards God and his creation, while going deeper beyond platitudes of Sunday messages into a creative, transformational, pictorial, and truly missional living. I applaud this book's grounded scope and circular simplicity.

~ Ken Steorts, *President of Visible Music College*
Founder of the Band Skillet

In this day and time, we need a loud grace-filled call back to a Biblical wisdom around worship as a fully orbed experience of God as Trinity. The people of God need the Father's heart, the work of Jesus, and the experience of the Holy Spirit. Trinity worship is that call to the Church.

~ Charlie Hall, *Worship + Liturgy Pastor*
+ Singer-Songwriter at Frontline Church

Trinity Worship is an engaging personal story, a readable and relatable life journey. Such a multi-faceted theological reflection that treats the topic of the worship of the Triune God as an asset, not a liability, is much needed in this age of religious pluralism. For the reader interested in heeding the exhortation of whole life worship urged in Rom 12:1-2, this book will help you get there.

~ Andrew Hill, *Professor of Old Testament at Wheaton College*

PART I
INTRODUCTION

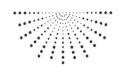

1

MY HISTORY

BEGINNING A BOOK ON THEOLOGY with the author's personal history may seem a little strange to you. But in this case, a brief exploration of my past will do much to explain why this book came to be. So indulge me for a moment while I tell you who I was, who I am, and why it matters.

My early life is summarized in the following phrases: Certain but clueless. Solid yet sinking. Skilled without wisdom. Opinionated but insecure. Contemporary and relevant yet without any solid foundation. Exalted, but for no good reason. Prepared for the stage and lacking any posture bent toward service. Creative? Sure. But to what end and for what purpose?

Loving? Not at all!

Worship? What's that?

Humble learner? Not at first; I was just a newborn, but I didn't realize it.

I'm not attempting to wield a punishing stick of judgment on myself or anyone else in acknowledging my clumsy tromp through the forest of God over the years. Rather, I'm setting the stage to explain why I've written this book, *Trinity Worship*. This work is not an opus drawn from my expertise. It contains relics of desire to learn and uncover my own anemic understanding of worship in hopes that I may become a wise and mature lover of our Triune God.

I first realized my own immaturity concerning the topic of worship when I came to faith at the age of eighteen. Up to that point I had given sole allegiance to sex, money, pride, and self-preservation. I was the master of my own destiny. I bought into the delusion that I was the Alpha and Omega, and was controlling the joystick in this game we call existence.

Maybe a description of the state of my faith at that time is captured in the language of sociologists Christian Smith and Melinda Lundquist Denton. They've coined the phrase *Moral Therapeutic Deism*. I believed loosely in a divine mind that created the world (theism) and that this *being* desires humanity to be good and nice to each other (moral); but to be good by my standards, this being must prioritize my comfort, entitlement, and pleasure (therapy).

Despite my disbelief in any genuine idea of God, and my willing idolatry of my own comforts, I went to church begrudgingly with my family. Some of the church leadership saw in me natural abilities for speaking and leadership. Most of all, they saw that I was a musician.

Because I was musical, I was immediately exalted, even before I became a Christian. I was put on stage in front of the lights. I was given responsibilities in a spiritual world that I had no right filling, and because of my ability to "keep up appearances," I was able to fly under the radar while encountering firsthand the immaturity of the church concerning the topic of worship. Like a dummy, I participated blindly in the magic game of smoke and mirrors.

One might find it almost humorous that I could fill a role in worship at that time. To me, the whole idea of worshipping God seemed a hoax and a giant waste of time. The sad tragedy is that the title of "Worship Leader" actually perfectly described me in a negative sense. I led worship all right! I drew all the attention to me. On stage, I found myself at the center of everything.

And then it happened…

In a downhill spiral of sex, abuse, suicidal thoughts, and in the darkest depression I've ever known, Jesus met me right after I turned eighteen. Christ awakened my dead heart. He breathed on me. I came alive by his choice and chose him. I underwent what can only be described as a transfer of worship. My allegiance changed. My king changed. My honor and my posture were forever altered. And yet amidst the beautiful hurricane of my salvation experience, the next ten years of my Christian life further exposed my inner-hypocritical oxymoron.

I became a pastor. Yes, I no longer worshipped myself, and I recognized that Jesus was the Savior and the object of all worship and satisfaction. Yet I resisted the path of discipleship. Nothing about me changed in any drastic sense. Why should it? Even before becoming a Christian or having any semblance of maturity, I was affirmed in my natural abilities. It seemed logical to me that I could keep doing life as usual. I now had a sidekick in Jesus that would work to get me where I wanted to go and in record time.

To make matters worse, the people around me didn't seem to change much either. They kept mistaking gifting in craft for growth in character. They continued to give me credit for being a godly man just because my talent seemed a bit extraordinary. Like them, I fell right into the trap of believing in magic tricks, and I acted like I was a disciple who had arrived. The irony is that *disciple* means "learner," and I had been led to believe that I was in need of anything but learning.

The leaders around me unwittingly uttered lies about me time and time again in reference to my expertise. One of my favorites is this one: "He has wisdom beyond his years." This lie inflicted the most damage. I was affirmed for my skill as a speaker and performer, and people assumed my Christlikeness was just as intact. Wrong. People merely misconstrued me as being mature and wise. I'll admit, I believed the hype.

It's fascinating to me the damage that hype can do. According to Proverbs, "The crucible for silver and the furnace for gold, *but people are tested by their praise*" (27:21 italics mine). The Scripture is clear that the praise and approval of men remains one of the most mine-riddled testing grounds of life. The wrong kind of appreciation, affirmation, and exaltation, given or accepted, can actually build into someone a god-complex. The half-truths that the Body of Christ fed into my soul sank deep into me like contaminated food. Every bite was killing me.

My pride kept inflating.

When it came to the practices of worship, Christian maturity, and Christlikeness, I considered myself to be the guru. The Shaman. The Dalai Llama. Deep down I operated in the pride of life and thought everyone else to be less than me and in need of my spiritual wisdom.

I am thankful that our Triune God has been extremely gracious in redeeming me out of my god-complex, one step at a time. In those days God met me and let me fall. I fell deep. For the last fifteen years, I've been wallowing. I scrub like a pig every day to remove the muck of my own inadequacy, and the funny truth is that it's from the slop that I've discovered tiny morsels of worship. Now twenty years after becoming a Christian, I feel for the first time since being saved that I've become a disciple. I've begun to realize that I'm anything but a leader on the topic of how to worship God. I'm merely a learner who is investigating.

A MIRROR IN WHICH WE CAN SEE OURSELVES

If you're a human, then you can probably relate to my story at least in part. You can relate to the self-centeredness. You can relate to the pride, and if you've grown up in the church over the last hundred years, you can most certainly relate to how anemic the church's definition of worship has become. Worship has become all about the gifting. Music. Leadership. Stage. Performance. Style. Preference. Experience. Relative. We have created a persona and caricature through our models for ministry that exalt music and the worship leader (whatever that means) to a place of unbiblical primacy, and yet we've never taken the time to really think through the job description we've formed.

It only takes a quick search through the Internet job postings on "worship" to see that a shallow understanding of the topic is pervasive. Even the fact that worship is now seen as a job should be clue number one. Most job postings pertaining to worship can be summarized in this way; "we need a tall, handsome, talented, musician, who fits into, can execute, and replicate our style, preference, and genre of music. We need one who has the sweet tenor voice of a Chris Tomlin, the unique and brandable look of a David Crowder, and let's be honest, if this person has swoopy bangs, a faux-hawk, tattoos, wears skinny jeans, and loves Converse shoes, he's hired." Job offers for worship leaders today sound like something Israel might have posted on the village walls when looking to anoint Saul as king.

The story of Saul in the Bible reveals the human tendency to exalt personality based on our own external stipulations and expectations. We often choose leaders based solely on non-leadership qualities. It's part of our fallen DNA.

As a result of our misshapen structures for worship, our study of worship over the recent century has attempted to scratch the service of praxis and pragmatics, particularly within the isolated gathering of God's people, and has altogether ignored the Scripture's emphasis on *ontology*, or *being* within the scattered surrounding world.

When all is said and done, the saddest reality that I've observed in the last twenty years is that our faulty ideas of worship birth whole structures, methods, and systems that actually promote and engrain unhealthy understanding. We have constructed and normalized environments that undermine our message of the gospel (*more on this later*).

THE JOURNEY OF LEARNING AND ASKING BETTER QUESTIONS

The concepts in this book represent my crawling from the depths. This book is a manifesto that has emerged in me over the last ten years as I've become a learner of worship. Once I admitted that I was not wise beyond my years and stopped equating natural talents with Godly maturity, I attempted to bow my knee to those who know more than I. I've tried to listen intently to the plethora of denominations and traditions, the biblical storyline, theological giants, and our countless historical legacies. I've pulled up a chair and desk and become a student of our Sovereign God. He knows more about worship than we will ever comprehend. Since the dawn of time, he's smuggled countless treasures about worship into the cosmos, the church, and the culture. It's about time we find the gold. We must avail ourselves to the Scriptures, the creation, the "great cloud of witnesses" throughout the physical and heavenly millennia, and to the God beyond time, and invite them to teach us. If we don't commit ourselves to learning more deeply, I'm afraid history will keep repeating itself.

A great starting place is to ask better questions of ourselves and our surroundings. As C. S. Lewis says (and I'm paraphrasing), "what the world needs now is not smarter people, but deeper people." Let's think deeply.

EVERY ISSUE IS A WORSHIP ISSUE

Don't make the mistake of thinking this is a book written for those on your worship teams or praise bands—whatever those titles even mean. This book is about the making and shaping of all of our being, skill, vocation, and calling. When boiled down to a basic principle, I believe every issue in life is a worship issue. Scripture reveals that **worship is a world word**. It encompasses everything. Who we choose to erect at the center of our life and our commitment will feed into everything we become and do. The object of our worship will undoubtedly appear in every decision, brand, logo, business name, vehicle driven, house built, curriculum designed, food eaten, drink consumed, scheduled commitment made, parenting style applied, political view embraced, budget line items dotted, and much more. Day to day, our worship will shine most brightly in our checkbook, cabinet and cupboard, date book, text log, and to-do list. Everything to which we apply sight, smell, touch, taste, and hearing, becomes a barometer into our worship life.

THE UNIQUENESS OF THIS WORK

In this book, I will contemplate the Trinity from every angle of which I'm currently aware in hopes to expand our discussion of worship beyond just our gathering as a people. I will discuss all that it means to become like our Triune God in order to take worship out of the confines of only stages and buildings and explore what worship might look like from a holistic viewpoint on the level of our *being* not just our *doing*.

The subtitle attempts to describe the angles of my exploration. It reads: *Becoming Like Christ in How We Relate, How We Do Things, How We Organize, How We Learn, and in How We Lead.* In the pages to follow, I will explain what all these categorizations mean and how they fit into the overall landscape of worship. For ease of comprehension and retention, I will also attempt to file the main ideas into the memorable acronym C.R.O.S.S.: Community, Reasoning, Organization, Scripture, and Signature Mission.

Finally, as I close this introduction I will introduce my one big goal for this book and for my life in studying worship. My bottom line is simple: *"to prepare myself and others for real life."* Let me share a couple of responses from close friends that will help you unwrap the meaning of this statement.

One friend was asked this question in front of a panel of today's most famous worship personalities: "What's your goal when you 'lead worship?'" His response was to say, "to prepare people to go and die." When compared to the watery responses of the other people on the panel, this man's answer was quite shocking to most people. It grieved me that no one asked him why he said what he said. There's a lot of wisdom that was overlooked in his statement, and many failed to chew on its meaty depth because they simply had forgotten to put in their teeth that day. My other friend, when asked about his philosophy on picking songs for worship, gave this answer: "I want to put lyrics on people's lips that help them to suffer well unto God's glory if and when the darkest persecution comes."

Both of these responses are powerful, and I say a hearty "Amen" to both.

Many of those contemplating the topic of worship today have undoubtedly failed to factor in the necessity we have in preparing people to live as Peter says in his Epistle—as sojourners. Exiles. Suffering is our reality and we must prepare people for a life of abundance within it.

However, death is not the ultimate reality. Life is. When we help others to explore and follow God in worship, we want to form in them an expectation for what a capital "R" reality is like. True realness is the kingdom of God, and many worship paradigms today don't tap into biblical, theological, and historical logic for equipping people for life within God's perfect kingdom. Too often we're seduced by the cult of cool, and by any creative fancy we may desire to insert into our "*setlist*."

We must prepare people better for both pain and praise. Both pain, in the kingdom of the world, and God's praiseworthy and perfect kingdom rhythms, grow up from within our midst, and interact together in this life. Both are necessary for ushering us into the life of Christ. I don't think there's a contradiction here. Paul in Philippians 3:10 lofts up both concepts in one prayer: "that I may know Christ and the power of his resurrection, and may share his sufferings, becoming like him in his death." In one statement Paul prays for the discernment to *live* in Christ's life—the resurrection—and at the same time to *live* in abandon to Christ's suffering. Both are essential to what? To becoming like him.

On one hand we prepare people to become like Jesus amidst the suffering we encounter in the fallen world—which is an inevitable truth—but in another and more profound sense, we want the people we shepherd to walk into the doors of heaven and utter, "This is greater than I ever dreamed, but I recognize this place—the rhythm, the liturgy, the form, and the expectation are similar to what I experienced within my church family on earth." I want to give those around me such a grand, nutritious diet of *life* that it eclipses suffering; that their worship-palette is equipped to live "life and life abundant" both in the present pain and in the next life that is absent of it (John. 10:10).

I'm convinced that our stage-centric, coliseum-businesslike approaches to church are neither helpful toward the aforementioned end, nor biblical. I am looking for something more sustainable and real, such as what may develop in us the fortitude-of-soul that Job demonstrates.

Consider Job. After his body, his family, his wealth, and his livelihood are all stripped away, the Scripture tells us the first thing Job does is "erect an altar to worship the Lord." This shows us that Job is an emotional, theological, doxological, and fortified giant of faith. Is our worship making us into this type of people-in-crisis? Can we find life in the deadliest moments? Do we understand this strength of soul?

ANY TIME, ANY PLACE, AND UNDER ANY CIRCUMSTANCE

Is our worship today fortified? Is it a bulwark that catches the biggest of waves? In the spirit of considering men like Job, I will seek to use a very repetitive phrase throughout this book to help you as the reader continue to revisit my primary aims in equipping to *experience the truest reality of our Life in God, both future and present, amidst the complications of the life in the world now.*

Here's the phrase:

WE MUST SEEK A WAY OF BELIEVING AND OF DOING LIFE TOGETHER THAT WORKS IN ANY TIME, IN ANY PLACE, AND UNDER ANY CIRCUMSTANCE.

Let's be honest; most of what we've dreamed up in the realm of worship methodology today gives rather slim answers to my phrase and to a holistic definition of **life**. I've become particularly tired of mankind's assumptions pertaining to worship because they are so timely. They fail to be timeless. They fail to answer the deepest and darkest struggles with the most robust sense of life. Though we've become very busy at the table of invention in our denominations, businesses, families, and in all realms of culture, trying to dream up better ways to create deities and create "togetherness," we've only seemed to become more and more void of things that actually accomplish those aims.

With every new invention of the church or culture, we amplify a recipe for growing apart. We attempt to come up with ways to be healthier in worship and more social in community, and all that happens is that suicide rates skyrocket. We try and invent ways to do things better than God, and we end up ripping people away from the simplicity of a table, the home, a marriage, and a family.

We need to flesh out the topic of worship and how our communal Triune God "does life together" in order to arrive at some convincing and scrumptious conclusions that empower God's honor, and our best, in any time, place, and circumstance.

A Prayer and a Hope

The journey toward investigating the slew of questions regarding worship has only begun. Thank you for the privilege of inserting some of my thoughts into your travels as you walk this road of faith. We're in this together. I pray that this book will be a blessing, and that it will help you explore, be satisfied in, contemplate, worship, adore, and become more like Jesus within the context of his Triune image.

2

IMAGO DEI

WHERE DID ALL THIS TALK ABOUT WORSHIP START?
I ended the introduction with a peculiar phrase—*Triune image*. It sounds fancy. It sounds confusing. What on heaven and earth does such an elevated, theological term have to do with worship? I'm glad you asked.

When introducing the topic of worship, the Bible begins differently than most would expect. Most books on worship today begin with our actions, our liturgy, our work, and so on. In other words, what we are to *do*, over what we are to *be*. Nevertheless, we are called human-*beings* rather than human-*doings* for a reason. Scripture's emphasis seems to lean first toward what we are *becoming* in Christ—Christ being the one who is already doing the work that deserves our worship—before discussing our actions.

The Bible begins with *image*. God's image. Right out of the gate, in Genesis 1:1, God answers two questions: "Who is to be worshipped," and "Who should be doing the worshipping." I would say this verse also answers the question: "into whose image are we to be *becoming conformed* in our worship?"

Genesis 1:1 reads, "in the beginning, God *created*..." This is a fascinating opening line on many levels because it establishes everything about what *image* is. It speaks first of the only *being* existent in the beginning. God! If he was there to author the beginning of our reality as we know it, then that means he's part of a bigger "R"eality that we have yet to encounter. God's reality is timeless. It's eternal. It's foreverness. When discussing worship, we must keep in mind what relates to forever and is not merely temporal. We must weigh all definitions of worship in light of kingdom realities, not earthly puppets.

Second, this verse establishes that God is the Master over all that has been created. He's the source. The designer. Inventor. Planner. Therefore, the authority. Everything we see and experience points back to his likeness, mind, imagination, character, and nature, and can only be rightly understood as he would prescribe and describe. We humans, always balking at authority, might grimace at the notion of God establishing his right to be King over us. We might glower at the idea of control being foundational to his image, but it's something we by nature understand.

For example, when the inventor of the pencil markets it for purchase, he or she does so in a manner that defines the pencil's destiny and function. It's for writing. The consumer writes with a pencil. He is free to grip it in any way that best expresses his language and personality. But if the consumer tries to unlock a car door with a pencil, it fails. Why? The inventor's authority is infused into the created object. That is to say, it's made for the purpose the inventor intends. When we write with a pencil, we are obeying the authority of its inventor.

Our relationship to God should be as simple as the pencil's relationship to its inventor, and yet we twist matters. We are like pencils that want to perform any function but write. We strive hard to define ourselves on our own authority, and we waste time attempting to fit ourselves into purposes and rhythms that are simply not for us. We attempt to jam pencils in keyholes.

Authority is true and foundational to God's image. His attributes are woven into the fabric of all that he creates. Though he's altogether separate from his creation—like the inventor is separate from his pencil—there's much of his desire, creativity, and personality infused in the objects he makes. God is the timeless authority toward which all creation points.

In simple ...

Worship.

Created things worship. They point. They ascribe a direction back to their source. The universe has the all-supreme good as its founder. It's God. All things are made good because the Creator in his goodness spent time and resources to give us tools to thrive, flourish, and express ourselves in beauty.

God's creation worships him. It is good. Bottom line: It is because God is good that we worship.

Third, Genesis 1:1 establishes the motive by which our God operates as we worship him. He's clearly not in need of anything. He's clearly not demanding anything. He doesn't need our work. He's self-sustaining, so only one word can resolve for us the foundational question, "What motive did God have in creatively extending his all-sufficient reality into our needy existence?" If he didn't need us, why did he make us?

The answer is *multiplication.*

Let me unpack what I mean.

Think about it. Our God is "love," right? Theologians such as Augustine, wrote down many things regarding the love of our One-and-Three Trinity. Augustine penned that our God is Lover, Beloved, and Love simultaneously. Without a Beloved (Jesus), there can be nothing for the Lover (the Father) to Love, and without two or more together, the Spirit of Love (Holy Spirit) cannot exist. Simply stated, God is Love. Love is simply who God is over and above his actions. Love is his *being.* His loving nature and experience is what he wanted multiplied.

In comparing God's nature to love, let us not make the mistake of thinking that Augustine is trying to make God into an emotion or chemistry. He's grounding God's essence into a concept beyond time and space. Love. In doing so, he is also demonstrating why a relational universe demands a relational inventor. He gives us adequate language to express the manner of our existence. To understand ourselves, we must understand the Trinity.

Love, from a scientific standpoint, is not a necessity to existence. It's chemical, not logical. The scientist will hypothesize that love is not essential to life. Love is just genetics in a non-relational, evolved universe. Yet the scientist will ignore the glaring facts that a non-relational universe is incapable of evolving into what we now experience as reality. Despite the claim that love has no evolutionary function, we do love and we need love. There's no sensical explanation for our need of love if the universe began without loving potential. Love is not factual if it is purely chemical. But love does exist. Because it exists and often acts in a manner that defies any logic, we have to assume that something relational and loving caused it.

I first encountered this logic of love when I was an atheist. A friend posed this question to me: "Do you have a desire to be perfectly loved?" My response, of course was, "No, that's impossible." My friend rebutted by saying, "I didn't ask you if it's possible; I asked if you desire it." My response was, "Well, of course everyone wants to be loved in a way that upholds you best and never hurts you, but that doesn't exist." This friend then went on to quote C. S. Lewis: "If I find in myself a desire that nothing in this world can satisfy, the only logical explanation is that I was made for another one."[1]

My friend stumped me. I indeed found in myself a desire for perfect love, and yet this world could not fulfill that need. The simple fact that we need something other in such a perfect manner that the world cannot supply demanded a conclusion that unsettled my self-constructed hypothetical world: "There is a loving being out there from which we all come."

The only thing that *multiplies* in the view of Augustine, Lewis, and now myself, is God's ability to express more love. It's basic to his *image,* his *being.* Again, he doesn't need anything. He's perfect, but out of his love, he's compelled to love more. Love multiplies. Relationship multiplies. Love proves why humanity has much more than mere social needs.

Social media preys on our search for love. It attempts to fulfill our need but leaves us empty. It pretends to meet our desire to be whole and "liked" on a global and ever-multiplying level, and yet fails to live up to its own hype.

Genesis 1:1 has revealed to us a God that is unmatched, relational, loving, timeless, and is unparalleled as the supreme object of worship because he is love. He's the only object worthy of our allegiance. In worshipping him, we become what we were created to be. We become lovers in the purest sense of serving the other, and we become loved. To pay homage to anything lesser will lead us down a wandering hallway of dead ends and moral nothingness.

Finally, wrapping up all we've already discovered in Genesis 1 about image is the fact that God creates. This is foundational to the image of God. All his creation actually explains everything else about him. By simply looking at his inventions we can get a glimpse into his mind, his nature, and what he's like. Nature is like a photograph. Just as a photo isn't actually the reality it captures, nature is likewise not what we worship, but we see within it a picture of the real One that created it. We honor the Creator not created.

Creation is similar to a hyperlink. Anyone who searches the web knows what a hyperlink does. To the user of the Internet, the link appears simple. It comes in the form of a highlighted word, a button, or an image to be clicked on. The link opens the user up to a world filled with information, knowledge, and multi-sensory experience. All of creation is God's hyperlink. When we ponder all that we see (click on it), we come to the inevitable conclusion that there's knowledge, information, and a multi-sensory world that lies beyond each object.

It's the hyperlink-nature of God's creation that drives every vocation. It drives humanity to invent, to explore, to create, to innovate, and to hold an insatiable and unquenchable thirst to keep learning, keep clicking, and keep making.

MANKIND AND THE GARDEN

If we are relationally created beings that project our Inventor (*the imago Dei*), then how are humans to best serve like hyperlinks—pointing toward the reality of a world that tells of our timeless, loving, and creative God? Much debate still surrounds what actually constitutes the *imago Dei*, so bear with me as I get a little heady with you in trying to examine the topic.

The three most prominent views attempting to describe how we as humans display God's likeness is the *substantive view*, the *relational view*, and the *functional view*. The *substantive view* proposes that humanity is somehow physically or psychologically made to resemble God. But if a person only substantively consists of the reasoning or cerebral and mental capacities of God, this would imply that the smarter someone is, the more of the image of God they have.[2] Such a description would clearly call into question the value of humanity and our distinctive attributes beyond just our minds. Assuming God just made us for knowledge alone would put God on trial and put us in grave danger. We would have to assume that our value and worth as humans is measured solely by how intellectual we are. Such conclusions prime the pump for another Hitler to rise up and be praised for killing those deemed intellectually inferior. Also, if God based our inherent value on our varying degrees of intelligence, we would have to assume he has played favorites from the beginning. It would appear that he used preferential treatment both in the Creation and in the Fall. The smarter ones are of more value than those of lesser intelligence.

We can rejoice in the fact that God did not create in such a way. The Bible makes it clear there is no "favoritism with God" (Rom. 2:11; Acts 10:34). His nature keeps him from handicapping an individual's value based simply on the level or his or her I.Q.

The *relational view* of how we reflect God's image proposes that the *imago Dei* is best seen in the experience and ability a person has to build relationships between other humans and with God. This view gets us closer to our goal, yet does not reach it completely. It explains why we need each other and why we are sustained by knowing God intimately. But on the other hand, this view can imply that social interaction is our measure of value. It insinuates that those who are extraverted rather than introverted hold greater worth. If we're not careful we can start measuring human life by things like hygiene, manners, etiquette, cultural norms, the ability to pick up on subtle social cues, and much more.

We correctly describe humans as relational when we use the term positively to show how we reflect the nature of our relational *Triune* God. But we can miss this kingdom perspective by negatively defining "relational" in the narrow ways we earth dwellers understand. We can veer into the realm of what a human does rather than what a human is. We teeter when we suggest that a greater variety of God's image dwells within those who are more socially adjusted. The relational view must not be synonymous with relational skills, but considered on the level of our being. Whether we're good at relationship or not, we all need togetherness to survive. It's who we are. It's the very substance of us.

Lastly, the *functional view* of how we reflect God's image says that the *imago Dei* is found in the human's ability to have dominion, to produce, to make, to wield resources, etc. In one sense, this concept is correct. Our God is a relational and creative multiplier. He's a Father, Son, and Spirit, and bestows on creation the ability to be fathers and mothers, and to multiply through children. But our image does not simply boil down to human work or to mere experience.[3] To believe only in a functional view implies that a varying degree of image resides in a person based on how well he or she functions. It implies that the more efficient people are, the more value they possess.

To swing hard in any of the above viewpoints of the *imago Dei* leads to Marxist and humanistic conclusions that call us to treat humans as evolutionists do—as objects. Objectifying humans based on their efficiency or utility has led to the scientific religion of Darwin and men like Hitler who decided who was "naturally selected" and who was not.

All the above views fall short it defining what is human. It's detrimental to measure our image, self-esteem, identity, or whatever one may call it, by elements of *doing* before *being*. Allowing humanism into our debate over image has kept us from considering God's Triune image first when drawing conclusions about ourselves.

Millard Erickson begins with contemplating God, not humanity, in order to define our image. We must also. His observations begin with none other than the Son of Man—Jesus. Jesus is in perfect fellowship with the Father,[4] obeys his Father's will perfectly (Lk. 22:42), and displays love at all times (Matt. 9:36). Jesus portrays the perfect form of what it is to be a Son, and he does it while remaining fully God. We should pattern our lives and ourselves after Jesus, the complete revelation of the image of God,[5] and the fullness of his image is embodied and displayed in the complexity of the Trinitarian harmony.

Within the Trinity, there is a role,[6] relationship,[7] and resemblance[8] among the three persons of the Godhead, and human creations are meant to bear these attributes. We cannot measure our identity solely in "me and I" ways. We cannot say "*I'm* relational," "*I'm* functional," or "*I'm* smart." A more accurate way to measure our value is to view ourselves in the context of community. If God draws his identity from the internal relationship of the members of the Trinity, then we reflect his image by drawing our identity from our relationship with others. We are relational, we are functional, and we are smart, *together.* We grow, mature, and produce via our creative image, *together*. He desires that we be *one* in the same way that he is, a way that is best for us.

Since the Garden, God's relational unity within himself is projected in the man and woman's relationship with each other. His theological unity is cast correctly when men and women walk with God together. His philosophical and missional unity is sketched most clearly in Adam and Eve's untarnished desire to live for the purpose and ways of God.

But the problem of image and the idea of "good" goes deeper than marriage or togetherness. Even in the Trinity, all that is within his nature is married and fused together by one thing. What is it? The one thing is *glory*. I suggest that the one common denominator of glory describes the nature of our image better than anything else. We are to bear witness to God's glory. Glory summarizes, and at the same time explores, all we need to know about worship.

God's glory is a complex term throughout Scripture but can refer to his reputation, weightiness, dwelling, presence, and exaltation. His glory is the binding agent of togetherness. Adam and Eve walked *with* him in the Garden. The root word for *with* connotes us being face-to-face with God as if in a dance. Our oneness with God and each other is what most deeply glorifies God. The glory of God is the beginning of our discussion on worship.

God's motive in all his willing and acting is to exalt his own name. In

3

UNITY & GLORY

A FTER GOD CREATED HUMANITY in his likeness, he uttered the words; "It is good." Though he defined all creation as "good," there's a particular flavor and heft to what he established in humanity. Unlike all other created creatures and features in the cosmos, we humans can worship out of choice, will, volition, and action. We can erect altars of worship. We can relate beyond the realm of animal tendency. We can be intimate beyond sexuality and instinct. Humans far outweigh what some would reduce us to: mind, function, utility, consumeristic passion, and efficiency.

God gave humanity the ability to reflect the glory and unity of God. His image within humans is what brings him the utmost pleasure. Before sin entered the world, humans not only knew good but could also choose good. By definition, humans were the most free of any of the other creatures. We could comprehend and contemplate God's definition of perfect. We could move toward his purposes volitionally and desire nothing but him. These abilities separated us from the likes of lions, tigers, and bears.

Our ability to know God's glory kept us in oneness with God. When I refer to *oneness*, I'm not talking about a brand of unity that is pantheistic, New Age, Buddhist, or a concept of world unity that Green Peace might teach. I'm not talking about a physical or emotional unity like that which binds husband and wife. I'm not talking about a unity of substance in which the distinction between God and people is lost; as is often the case in Eastern philosophical concepts of unity. I'm also not talking about what the Early Church Fathers taught as *theosis*, or becoming divine in the same manner as God, or even that we become gods. As 2 Peter 1:3-4 clearly explains, we aren't one with God in equality or power, but rather that our only godlike qualities come from Jesus, giving us the ability through his death, resurrection, and ascension to overcome corruption and death.

What kind of unity, oneness, and glory am I talking about?

A hint resides in Jesus' prayer in John 17 about the *unity of love*. Jesus prays for us to experience a oneness of love: "I [Jesus] have given them the glory that you [Father] gave me, that they may be one as we are one." God welcomes us into his Triune life of love with and toward one another—Father, Son, and Holy Spirit. He lets us share in his life and his qualities. We get to partake in his immortal life (live forever). He causes us to become sons and daughters. Family. And in the words of Cyril of Alexandria, those who were alien from God the Father and slaves, he raises up to the nobility of our Lord on account of his warm love toward us.[1]

Notice the emphasis on love in Cyril's description, as well as in Jesus' prayer. The perfect unity of love and fellowship that the Father and Son enjoy is ours to partake in. Augustine speaks about oneness and love in the same manner:

> Jesus declares his divinity, consubstantial with the Father ... that is in the consubstantial equality of the same substance, and he wants his disciples to be one in him, because they cannot be one in themselves, split as they are from each other by clashing wills and desires, and the uncleanness of their sins. Just as the Father and Son are one not only by equality and substance but also by identity of will, so these men, for whom the Son is mediator with God, might be one not only by being of the same nature but also by being bound in the fellowship of the same love.[2]

Jesus' emphasis regarding oneness is placed on the idea of love, but it also pertains to salvation. His prayer in John 17 reflects something of the tone of losing the paradise God intended for us to have. He prays that we may be one as if we've somehow lost what we once had. Jesus acknowledges that he came to earth to restore something that we humans gave up. We lost the ability to enjoy and express pure love. The Garden reality vanished. We waived the wand. We made the bunny jump out of the hat. We sealed our own doom as a result of our own cleverness, and we can measure the loss.

Jesus affirms that the loss of the Garden can be felt today. In his prayer, he purposes to restore two things: our *oneness* so that we may partake once again in his *glory*. Christ prays for the very thing that the cross accomplishes! The cross bridges the gap—the void caused by our sinning. Christ closed the chasm caused by our forsaking his perfection (Rom. 3:23). Jesus' work affords us the chance to come back into the fold; back into a place of recognizing him; back into a place of having him; back to the garden. Being restored to God through justification, remission of sins, redemption, reconciliation, and adoption are not separate things that happen when one begins to trust Christ. Rather, all of these restorative acts derive from and revolve around the same reality. The believer's union happens with Christ through the Holy Spirit, and thus the believer shares in the Trinitarian relationship. Our coming back has less to do with our individual salvation and more to do with the whole of God's family being reunited.

The idea of a family as a "we" is huge. Because we live in a very individualistic world where we focus on my time, my things, and my territory, we tend to individualize love. We individualize everything in Scripture. We believe that he is our personal God who meets us in our personal quiet times in order to cultivate our personal relationship with him. Christ's verbiage, on the contrary, is always familial. He's a Triune God. God is family. He came to establish and connect a grouping of people, and he did it in a very ancestral way.

In the day and age in which Jesus prayed the prayer in John 17, it was actually illegal to group those not related by blood by using family terms to refer to them. To call someone a brother or sister that wasn't one by DNA violated the government's definition of family. But Christ came to unite and set up a household in the most inclusive sense. Galatians 3:20 says that "he became a mediator not for one, but for many …" He came in order to call us brothers and sisters. Christ's very ministry modeled his heart toward family. Being grafted into him was to accept involvement in a counterculture—something not sanctioned by the world. Something illegal.

The picture of unity and oneness in Scripture covers a much broader spectrum than just liking each other. Unity goes much deeper than just "getting along," and it is much bigger than people merely working together and staying together. We must recognize the nature of what the cross did and the family unity that proceeded as a result of Jesus' work. The unity that all humanity can now experience is what Paul refers to in 1 Corinthians 10:17 and 12:26. He calls us a body. We are many but one. If one suffers, the whole suffers. If one member is honored, the whole body is edified with it. Our body-connection goes deeper than something we merely do. It's something we *are* in Christ. Paul refers to it as "Baptism of the Holy Spirit." It's being added into God's household. It's enjoying and living for and in his glory. This is the storyline of worship. It is the story of redemption.

In light of the above, consider the Hebrew concept of *yachad*, the concept of "all together alike." Consider the Greek concept of *heis*, or the oneness nature of the family of God. To see how pervasive this concept of the bonded nature of God's kingdom is in Scripture, consider the following selected examples:

- **Matthew 5:18** speaks of the oneness of God's Word.
- **Matthew 5:30** speaks of the detriment one person's sin can have to the whole of the body.
- **Matthew 6:24** speaks of maintaining unity within ourselves by trusting, serving, and worshipping only one master.
- **Matthew 10:42** speaks of recognizing our unity with one another by giving of our surplus to the less fortunate among us.
- **Matthew 18:6** speaks of our need to remain aware of the children who watch us, lest we cause them to fall.
- **Matthew 18:16** speaks of our need to hold each other accountable in matters of justice and correct ruling.
- **Matthew 19:6** speaks about maintaining the oneness of marriage.
- **Matthew 19:17** speaks of Jesus being the only good.
- **Romans 3:10** speaks to the fact that all humans are one in their fallen condition and in their need of Jesus.
- **Romans 5:12,16-19** speaks to how we are no longer one with Adam's sinful legacy but are now one with Christ's legacy.
- **I Corinthians 10** speaks to the family supper as being the picture of our oneness.
- **I Corinthians 12** speaks to our uniqueness in serving the body of Christ with our gifts.
- **Galatians 4:22** speaks to our oneness with Abraham and all those with whom God covenanted.

- **Philippians 1:27** and **Colossians 3:15** speaks of our single-mindedness in Christ.
- **Philippians 2:2** speaks to our one purpose in Christ.
- **I Timothy 2:5 & Hebrews 2:1** speaks to the fact that only in the Trinity are we truly unique, yet truly part of a family.
- **James 2:19** and **Hebrews 6** indicates that we can buy into the world's fake imitations of true unity and never find the real thing.

The world knows we are Christian's by our love. Our embrace of others in Christ's body provides an alluring picture to others. When we value each other and our roles in the body of Christ, the world sees the complete picture of him. When we come together—the hands, feet, face, eyes, nose, brain, etc. of his body—we are declaring and portraying the fullness of Christ by reflecting who he is.

What's tragic is that when we get away from centralizing the cross and our commonality as the body under one head, Jesus (Eph. 2), we become like the Corinthian church. We begin to covet and be jealous of one another (1 Cor. 3:2). We begin to devalue each other in relationships, marriage, or through sexual exploration falsely labeled as freedoms. We also begin to put extra-biblical laws and regulations on each other (e.g. believing that people should eat certain foods, observe certain days, etc.). We divide when we centralize above Christ things such as morality, human freedom, spiritual gifts, famous personality, intelligence, pet theologies, denomination, polity, hobby, affiliation, vocation, preference, worship music, marriage, finances, relationships, success, class, race, politics, and the list goes on and on. Our lack of understanding concerning the centrality of the cross, and its bond, persuades us toward division.

Wouldn't we solve all our issues today if we simply presented the story of the cross—that of humanity being restored to a place where God is rightly understood as the only satisfier and sustainer? If we understood that through Christ's cross, he befriended us even while we were his enemies and restored us to him as family, wouldn't we befriend and "be-family" our foes? If such was the case, no longer would we have to plead and prod for people to act according to Scripture, for people do not act on the cross of Christ until they understand who they've become in the cross of Christ.

Shouldn't the work of Jesus be the central theme of all that we do and every service we provide? The mystery of its power will always drive us one step deeper. The more we understand the cross and view everything through it, the humbler we'll be. Our humility will fuel our worship.

A NEW CREATION IN GLORY AND ONENESS

Jesus correlates our seamless union with how his glory is most fully known. When Jesus prays in John 17—"I [Jesus] have given them the glory that you [Father] gave me, that they may be one as we are one," he says that the glory he gives us is his unbroken bond.

In the Garden of Eden, Adam and Eve knew God's glory in the truest and most tangible sense. They dwelled literally in God's presence. His weightiness was not a fright to them but a protective and vaulted canopy of protection. His acclaim was all they lived for. In his house, they were most satisfied, most safe, and at peace. The concept of peace in Hebrew is captured in the word *shalom*. Perfect resonant completeness. Humans reveled in the forever along with the stars, sea-fowl, and creepy critters of the muck and mire. All creation was afforded the opportunity to live in complete bond. Symphony. Peace. Agreement. Amen.

God's intends for us to dwell in his Triune reality. It is what he intentioned and defined as good, and it is also what he calls free. The Scripture tells us that where God is, freedom is (2 Cor. 3:17). Adam and Eve knew the true representation of freedom. They knew no division. They knew no right and wrong. All they knew was grandeur.

Biblical worship begins here. Oneness. Beauty. It is perfected around the opulence, celebrity, and fame of one—God.

4
THE FALL

WE ARE NOT IN THE **G**ARDEN OF **E**DEN ANYMORE.
Our image has been marred. What our *being* naturally points to now, without the intervention of God, is the reality of sin. All creation is groaning. We no longer understand the shalom or flourishing peace of all things—a norm in God's kingdom. We no longer willingly aim our worship and honor at God without a new being. A new heart. A new creation. Our willing worship has been redirected at lesser loves.

In our world, the expression and worship of our will, choices, desires, and wants are prized above all else under the facade of "freedom." Free will. People will say that we're most free when allowed to choose between what we deem right and wrong. Freedom has become subjective. The validity of the choices we make in the name of freedom have been left to the eye of the beholder. Freedom has toppled us into a humanistic waste pool. Freedom has become so incessantly based on individual preference, bias, comfort, entitlement, entertainment, greed, and any one of a hundred other me-centered sins, that we need to rediscover the word's original meaning before we can even discuss the difference between freedom and fallenness. As Bruce Ware would has said:

> … freedom is not my deciding, from the urges and longings of my sinful nature, to do what I want to do, when I want to do it, how I want to do it, with

whom I want to do it. According to the Bible, that is bondage, not freedom. Rather, true freedom is living as Jesus lived, for he is the freest human being who ever lived. In fact, he is the only fully free human being who has ever lived, and one day we will be set free fully when we always and only do the will of God—freedom is submitting.[1]

Even most Christians today have bought into the moralistic and relativistic nature of what freedom and fallenness really mean. I've heard many mature and well-meaning Christians say that God must preserve our choices and wants in all matters in order to preserve any sense of love. They claim that a world without free will is a world inhabited only by programmed robots. On the coattails of this same notion, many Christians also hold to the idea that humans are basically good apart from God, not inherently bad. They carry within themselves a cancerous obsession to believe that because we're good we can trust our choices. We can follow our hearts, because at heart, we are convinced we're intrinsically good.

Scripture teaches otherwise. Jeremiah says, "The heart is deceitful above all things, And desperately wicked" (Jer. 17:9 NKJV).

In futility we dive down deep into the muddy waters of our own inner confusion to find "our best self." Our worship turns inward. We classify ourselves as good and view humanity through a lens of *deserving*. Then when trouble hits us, we wonder why bad things happen to good people, and we play the victim card because we failed at proving that we are in fact mini-gods. We often fail to hear the Bible say, that without God, "there's no one good, no not one" (Rom. 3:10).

Please don't hear me wrong as I write of the problem inherent in our concept of freedom of choice. I do not believe that the world is deterministic, and devoid of human choice. But it seems that in our attempts to make our nature good and our freedom of choice paramount, we have overlooked one subtle detail. We must remember that God did not originally want us to know right and wrong. The unveiled division of our will (separating good from bad) is what corrupted us, not what freed us.

Our fall into right and wrong corrupted our love. Many have convinced themselves that choice is necessary for love to exist, and it is, but whose choice? We assume that love depends on preserving our own freedom to choose. However, we must remember that the Bible says, "This is love, *not that we have loved God, but that he has loved us*" (1 John. 4:10, italics mine).

God's loving choice toward us is all that's necessary for love to be preserved because he is love. Within him, and without us, is choice. It's his choice that makes love continue. Not ours.

This leads us to an important question: If choice is an option to be exercised by God, what are we now to make of the human will pertaining to worship? What is its function?

WHAT HAPPENED TO THE HUMAN WILL?

Since the fall, our posture has changed. Paul in Philippians 2:15 describes this change in terms befitting worship. He says that the original intention of man was to be like shining stars. Beacons of worship. Called to shine. Then to describe the change, which we experience as a present reality, Paul couples the imagery of stars with the image of us living in a "crooked and perverse generation." The word in Greek here for *crooked* is a worship term meaning *bent*. It evokes a picture of two types of persons—one standing straight, the other hunched over.

God's perfect picture of honor is of humans standing upright. We stand correctly in all things only when our hands and eyes are lifted to the heavens looking for our meaning and definition from God. The picture of a bent man is one who is hunched over, with hands, eyes, and desires directed outward toward the world or inward on oneself. If God is removed from the centerpiece of our affections, our allegiance looks toward people, places, and things to define our identity and give us meaning.

Our human will and volition are corrupted by our change in posture. We've lost our ability to proclaim God's intentions as good. We no longer naturally choose and seek God, and thus we can't experience him willingly. God defined this ability to experience him willingly as being free. We forfeited that glory. We chose bondage, not freedom. Without a new heart and without God's intervention, all that is imperfect leaves us feeling the effects of our transfer. We're bent.

Our bentness reveals itself best in our human willing. To explain what this means, we must pause here and define the nature of human volition.

A purely systematic perspective on human will says willing can be classified into three categories: self-determination, determinism, and indeterminism.[2] Self-determination presents a humanistic approach to life, and is what some deem an apt solution to why humanity has fallen so far from the

Garden directives. From this humanistic and psychological approach, a "human can discover no divine purpose or providence for the human species. While there is much that we do not know, humans are responsible for what they are or will become. No deity will save them; they must save themselves."[3] Self-determination suggests that human reality is caused by our actions. To assume such a view requires us to take on humanistic beliefs. We must believe that our willing is not bad or bound, but rather good and free. John Owen concludes that our attempt to make humanistic willing a good thing is chasing of wind. He says that any "endeavor to prove that the will of man is absolutely free, independent, and uncontrollable of God, is an unfortunate attempt."[4]

In Scripture, we see that self-determinism is a joke, for even Eve's actions had a cause and were never truly self-determining. We could attribute her actions to Satan's temptation or blame them on Adam's passivity. Not only did the consumption of the apple determine Eve's fate, but also that of Adam and Satan, and vice versa all the way around. What happened in the Garden was a collective determining.

Notice how Adam and Eve responded once their self-determinism took root. They hid. They ran. They secluded themselves. Why? Their will was now being imposed upon by a different force. Shame. Sin. In hiding from God, for the first time in their existence they moved away from him. Before the Fall, when God moved toward them, they lovingly moved toward him. Freely. After their Fall, God still moved lovingly toward them, but now they moved away from him, playing hide-and-seek. They hid from God as he, their cause, brought about a different effect. They no longer moved toward love but away. They hid as a direct response to God moving toward them in love and concern.

Self-determinism does not expand human will. Even in the Garden we see that humanity is not by definition free in willing without the appropriate ability to react to God acting upon us. Post-Fall, we are incapable of exercising free will independent of outside influence. In fact, the only person we see in the Genesis scenario who is free in willing is God. The Scripture teaches choice,[5] but it also teaches foreknowledge and predestination, and that God is not dependent, but rather independent from human choice.[6] Freedom is only found in God. We were created to share it, but in our infinite foolishness we threw away the key in an attempt to unlock the safe.

The second explanation for human willing is called determinism. Determinism claims that free will is an illusion because all our decisions and actions are invariably shaped by external causes. Everything we do is the inevitable result of nature, stimuli, genetics, physiology, and the accumulation of previous influences. It says that the will and our actions are a result of precursor causes, both naturalistically and theistically. Theistically speaking, determinism seeks to blame God, Satan, and even the tree for human failing. However, the Bible makes it clear that God created people with the capacity to override external influences on their will and to make clear choices based solely on their freedom to choose. To blame the faulty choices made at Creation on a perfect God is incorrect. And shifting the blame to someone other than the true source of the offense—in this case, humanity—is foolish at best. God compelled the humans to take responsibility for their own sin rather than seeking to blame external causes.

Finally, inter-determinism seeks to define our will as having no determining causes. God is removed from the picture, which leaves humanity to do whatever he deems best for himself with no God-given moral law to bother with. This leads to the dismissal of any evil action, sinful nature, and Godly sovereignty. This view is easy for Christians to discount because we do not even see it operative in the Garden or in the world today. God sustains the creation and providentially intervenes in its affairs.[7] He designed the world to function with cause. Even science—the study of the natural world—is dependent on the fact of cause and effect.

Though many today try to explain the way in which our will interacts with the natural world, most fail to come to any satisfying conclusions. Even throughout history, the greatest minds are found wanting. Aristotle considered contiguity philosophically, and Pavlov tried to describe psychologically how behaviors and willing are paired with new stimuli. But even they could not explain how new behaviors are acquired or where they find their origin.[8] Thomas Hobbs and B. F. Skinner asserted that human behavior can be fully explained in terms of natural causes—otherwise known as "operant conditioning."[9] Skinner's theory is that if positive reinforcement is introduced to a subject's behavior, that behavior will occur again, whereas if negative reinforcement is all that is present, then the behavior will diminish.[10]

All of the above fails to explain the dissonance between what we know and what we show.[11] If theories like Skinner's were true, with all the current information available in our day, our logical choices and worldly affairs would be progressing, not digressing. The evidence shows that we're not evolving, but devolving. We didn't come from monkeys, but we're coming dangerously close to rooming with them. It seems that every act of our will breeds the invention of new ways, technologies, and devices to divide from and harm one another. We turn animalistic. We continue to arrive at conclusions that are degrading to humanity and pull us further from God's glory. We are not moving closer to God. The murderous and destructive nature of the world is the tragic result of what human willing and fallen decision-making does. All the horror before our eyes and in our news is the logical result of humankind living apart from dependence on the goodness and glory of God.

The human will is much more complex than mere psychology or science would suggest. The will is the seat upon which our worship sits. The will, as God created it, is the total expression of one's self and personality.[12] It expresses outwardly the greatest allegiances honored inwardly. Our will directs us toward the glory that we deem most valuable. The center of the human self and personality is located in what the Scripture calls the heart, which is mentioned over 726 times in the Old and New Testaments.

Jesus challenged psychology and philosophy by stating that bondage in the world originates in the sinful prison of mankind's fallen faculties: his heart. Where a person's heart is, his mouth, his actions, and his life will follow. Jesus made the observation that it is not what goes into a man's mouth that defiles him, but what comes from inside him. Man, losing his ability to do things unto God's glory, removed the possibility of doing anything good or free without the direct intervention of God himself.

God knew that if humans knew good and evil, they would never know glory.

THE PURSUIT OF OUR OWN GLORY

If you remain unconvinced that our own self-glory-seeking is harmful to us, consider where all our fame-grabbing attempts have led us. One of the paramount tragedies that occurred in Scripture because of humanity's selfish wants is the Tower of Babel.

At first glance, the Tower of Babel looks like a picture of what happens when we unite to seek glory. The people willingly built a tower to their name and their reputation. Though we may consider the unified construction of the tallest building in the world to be a success, God viewed it as the ultimate display of pride and disunity. The text tells us why God viewed the Tower through such a negative lens. The people were innovating to be noticed in the eyes of others. They wanted others to see how great they were. The people of earth were making themselves bigger. Exaltation. Worship.

God spoiled their fun—not to ruin them, but to help them. God knew that their greatest satisfaction and purest hope was found in realizing that their flawless fulfillment was in a perfect God. At the moment they started looking to others, they became imperfectly motivated toward the incompleteness of man's praise, and God knew that this would only destroy and leave them lacking in all things. Bent. God stepped in to make his celebrity known. He caused the splitting of nations.

A tragic comedy. The God of embrace intentionally created a situation of perceived disunity. We might interpret his actions as divisive, but God defines unity as found in himself, whereas we define unity as being found in anything else.

God stepped in and caused an impossible circumstance to develop because we as humans are about the possible. If we can do it, taste it, feel it, and touch it, we like it. God is about the impossible, and if he is to ensure that we come to him in dependence and trust, he must create impossibility. So he divided the world.

But his promise to Abraham still remained—that through One seed he would bring unity and blessing to all (Gal. 3:16). That seed, by which the whole world is brought together, is in the cross and resurrection of the person of Christ. He died to reconcile all things to himself (Col. 1).

The nations who were once divided were prayed for in Christ's High Priestly prayer—the one we've been discussing in John 17—and Christ's prayer was answered at Pentecost. The Apostles, with tongues like fire resting on their shoulders, spoke out in the various languages of the people as a sign that salvation had come to the Gentiles and to all nations. God was making a statement. He was redeeming Babel.

God wants us to see that unity is not about what we are or who we are to each other. Unity can never be built around our own visions of what we deem to be the good life. This is not biblical integration, as we see in Babel. This is not glory. This is not freedom. This is not God's image. This is not oneness. False unity gets us in trouble. Unity is realized in our oneness with Christ. Recognizing our place in the family and in the fellowship is where freedom lies. Our baptism into the death and resurrection of Christ leads us to a knowledge of our restored fellowship with the Creator. This is what Christ achieved at the cross.

As recorded in Genesis 11, the Tower of Babel perfectly illustrates humanity's current definition of what we would define as freedom and goodness. The story records for us what truly lies in the human heart apart from God. The people of Babel were thrilled at the idea of erecting a structure that would display their power throughout the land, as are we. In all reality, when we seek to exalt our own fame we become, as Johnathan Edwards says, "poor deluded wretches, who think they look so glistering in God's eyes, when they are smoke in his nose and are many of them more odious to him than the most impure beast in Sodom, that makes no pretense to religion."[13]

THE FALL FROM GLORY AND THE HUMAN WILL

Jesus agrees that our fall from the serene perfect image of God, the unity of God, and the familial fellowship and oneness with the Spirit in the Garden, happened with our belief that we could willfully find completeness and fulfillment elsewhere. Our spiritual death bound our bodies over to the grave and our spirits over to bondage. We became totally depraved in that we lost our sensitivity and ability to bring glory to God. We didn't lose our ability to choose what is right and wrong; rather, we gained that bondage, and became slaves to it. We've become enslaved to what we *want* to do, and we called it "God's plan."

OUGHTNESS

I think C. S. Lewis may resonate best with Jesus as he associates our bondage not with our ability to do what we want to do, but with our incapability to do what we ought. He calls it *oughtness*. Lewis implies that what makes us most human and most free is our ability to point to God in our choosing. It's what we ought to do. Remember, created things *point*. Our volition is most free when all it seeks is to put God on stage. Our posture is aimed at making much of God, not ourselves, and it's the sole quality of God's glory that makes possible the satisfaction of man. Without God's perfection as the aim of our affections, we are doomed to be let down by lesser things. Tumbling into the ravine of inadequate loves is how we define the Fall.

The Scripture describes the Fall of Humanity as happening around the one concept of *glory*. Romans 3:23, one of the most memorized, quoted, and misunderstood verses in all of Scripture, describes this phenomenon perfectly;

"For all have sinned and fallen short of the glory of God." Our broken nature is prone to sin in our choices. Our plummeting condition means that we are forever imprisoned and bound in a holding cell. Choice remains, and yet any choice we make lacks keys. All decisions are made behind bars, and we can't unlock our confinement. A prisoner in chains may make choices between this or that—to sit or rise, to sleep or exercise, to eat or read—but the prison walls still remain.

Our sin took away our ability to point back to, worship, and pay allegiance to our King. Sin is in and of itself, treason. It's a violation against a kingdom. We are rogue criminals. When we attempt to transfer supremacy away from what God desires to what we desire, we make ourselves into tiny little deities lacking any of God's ability to help ourselves. Our tectonic shift in worship brings a seismic fault into everything. All that we deem fit becomes our new object of worship.

Oughtness and glory operate on a higher plane. *Oughtness* enables us to perceive a situation correctly and travel a higher road than mere right and wrong. God does not see in black and white moral dichotomy, nor should we. He is concerned about the preservation and display of his name. Love. This is not a selfish desire on God's part, mind you. He commits to his own supremacy in all things because he's perfect. For him to allow anyone to seek satisfaction in anything not perfect would be to deprive humanity of true fulfillment. If God allowed humans to find ultimate satisfaction apart from him, he would be committing idolatry and making something else higher than himself—as if that were possible. For God to provide us with the option of finding his glory is not an attempt to aggrandize himself in his own eyes, but a way to preserve our greatest good. We praise him for our sake; not his. In seeking to have his own creatures praise him, God demonstrates that he is the greatest and most selfless servant of all. He is urging us to do what we ought to do for our own good.

God's oughtness is what makes Jesus the servant Savior. Jesus displayed perfection in Gethsemane in Luke 22:42 when he "cooperated with God's revealed purpose"[14] amidst the gravest of evils. He was tempted to find a way out of the predicament. His disciples perceived "good" for him in attempting to help him escape the situation. Satan sought to dissuade Jesus from his mission by offering a way out. Here we see oughtness in operation because Jesus was free to choose something higher than mere mortal good or evil. He was free to choose the glory of God. He was free to gaze upon the harshest of the world's suffering and torment—the cross—and yet choose a higher reality. He stood steadfast in the exaltation and magnification of his beautiful Father.

WE MUST CONCLUDE ...

We humans cannot restore ourselves to a place of oneness, glory, and God-centered worship via our own volition, freedom, or goodness. Without God, we can only devalue and deprecate the truth of the gospel. Apart from salvation, we have lost our ability to choose what we ought, and we are bound to the pursuit of what we want. In our lost ability to choose what we were made for, God looks upon our current condition and cannot find the word "good" on his tongue. He sees a broken creation desperate to know goodness. That goodness is only offered through the redemptive and restorative work of Jesus upon the cross.

It is appropriate that we weigh freedom and the function of the will by one measure—the glory of God.

Our sole hope is summed up in the words of Johnathan Edwards:

"Saints of God do not first see that God loves them, and then see that he is lovely but they first see that God is lovely, and that Christ is excellent and glorious, and their hearts are first captivated with this view, and the exercises of their love are what begins here, and arise primarily from these views."[15]

As God's people, the church, we are thus called to worship God the Father, God the Son, and God the Holy Ghost—three persons, one Godhead, undivided in honor and glory and substance and kingdom.[16] If we as God's people begin to contemplate the glory of the three persons as they are and stop meditating on what we as God's people are doing, we will experience worship in a truly golden and saving chain.

PART II
THE TRINITY IN PERSON & TIME

5

THE FATHER

Not a Concept ... a Person

I assume that many of those reading this book have semi-solidified ideas of what the Trinity is, and is not. I use the word *what* factitiously, implying that many deal with the topic of the Trinity at a concept level. We've hammered the Trinity out in seminary as an idea. We've tried to explain the concept using various models, analogies, or word pictures. Yet in all our efforts to explain God, we've divorced concept from *personhood*. This *being* is an actual *being*. He's not a theorem. He's not a *what* but a *whom*. He's not best described modally separate as in liquid, gas, and ice. When we reduce God to a hypothesis or something concrete, we ignore the abstract and the grey. Let's remember first that we're dealing with a spirit-person.

It would absolutely bring me joy if after reading this book, one simple conclusion were to override and consume your soul. The Trinity is a person. He's a whom! The Way, the Truth, and the Life is not merely an apologetic or some kind of debate. The Way is a person. The Truth is a person. The Life is a person. Matter of fact, Love is a person. Love is not a force, chemistry, or a brain connection. The concept of Love is not relegated to individuals who find some make-believe soul mate or true love. Love is only found in finding Jesus.

The *Trinity* is a person.

Need I repeat?

In the next four sections, I will isolate our discourse concerning the personhood of God to the Scriptures alone. I don't want to voice what some pastor or professor said about the Trinity or the latest and greatest pop-radio McSermonizer's concept of deity. Before we address theological traditions and ideas, let's first consider what the Scripture reveals to us about him. We will look at the Father, Son, and Spirit predominantly in the New Testament first, and then we'll discuss the Trinity in the Old Testament.

AN EXPECTATION OF FATHER

When I began my understanding of "Father," I started like anyone might. I began by considering the nature of my Dad. Knowing very little of theological or biblical thought, I simply laid my assumptions about Dad onto the concept of Father. Quickly, as most do, I turned the Father into an idea. I began breaking God down into a concept. I amplified the problem because the truth of the matter is, I grew up knowing my Dad as an idea. I never really knew a Dad-type figure on an intimate level as some have. Though my Dad has been largely redeemed over the years and we share a growing relationship that is in its infancy today, my experience of my Dad growing up was one defined by distance. He was quiet, worked twenty hours a day, and didn't really speak to us kids much.

I will say this; my Dad never raised a hand to us in anger, and he largely righted the wrongs of his Father by avoiding becoming a mean drunk. But nonetheless, there were many times when I dreamed of grabbing him by the collar and screaming; "just tell me what you think of me." The distance I felt growing up registered in me the same as abuse. Bottom line, a kid wants to be known by and to know his Father. This desire is put in us by God. When we're deprived of closeness in any manner (through distance, abuse, absence, or otherwise), we may not be able to articulate our sense of incompleteness in words, but we lash out in ways that communicate it nonetheless. Many find an outlet for the distance they feel from their Fathers through drugs, alcohol, sexual exploration in all its perverted forms, anger, depression, extreme introversion, reclusion, narcissism, distrust, and many other behaviors that tend to isolate them from others or alienate others to the point of keeping them at arm's length. All these behaviors are desperate grasps for attention. they are internal screams that cry, "please acknowledge that I exist."

I brought the idea of distance into my thinking regarding my Heavenly

Father. For years I struggled to understand all the "child of God" language in Scripture because I felt that there was a missing bone in my spiritual body. It wasn't that I doubted that we are God's kids; I simply had nothing in my spiritual anatomy that resonated with the idea. I remember asking God to simply "grow a new bone in me where one had never existed."

For me, learning to understand the Father has become a voyage of miracles. The fact that I can in some manner understand intimacy with God and others today is because my Father in heaven has been good to lead me along in my handicap.

Those of you who grew up with Dad's defined not by distance but by closeness are the minority. To have a Dad be intimate, known, and transparent, is a gift. I have many friends who have Dad's that are still their heroes. I know people who speak of their Dad's as a known person. Though it's hard for me to relate, I still find myself rejoicing in their blessing.

ALL BELIEVERS CAN KNOW THE FATHER

All of us have an equal ability to understand God as Father. It's part of the package deal of grace. Our Father is close. Knowing the Father is one of the primary privileges of being saved. Paul says in Ephesians 2:18-19, "Through him [Christ] we both [Jew and Gentile] have access in one Spirit to the Father. So then you are no longer strangers and aliens, but you are fellow citizens with the saints and members of the household of God." Did you hear that? We all have access to the Father. One of the primary acts of salvation was to connect us back to him. One of the rights of God's people is to be in his household. All who believe have that privilege.

Whether we relate to the word "Father" with distance or with closeness isn't based on our experience with humanity. We must not mistake Father for Daddy. God is not of this world. He is supremely forever and supremely separate from us. He possesses qualities that are simply not human. Comparing Father to Daddy is like comparing an ant's relationship with his colony leader to that of a newborn baby's relationship with her loving parents. I've known many today who will read the word "Abba"—a name ascribed to God in various places in Scripture—and assume that this is equivalent to "Daddy." It is a word of intense affection. Nevertheless, though Abba is an absolutely normal and familiar way of addressing God,[1] it does not mean "daddy," as is popularly thought.[2]

When we form our idea of closeness or distance to God through a human lens, we risk making two common mistakes. First, we tend to make God too *eminent*. We see him as too big, too separate, too elevated and celebrated to be approachable. This approach can turn God into something only a Deist might recognize—a big force that created everything but is now hands-off. Or, to the other extreme, we tend to make God too *imminent*—too close, too cozy, too much a buddy rather than a Father. Process theologians are the best at this. Some have made God so personal—or close in the negative sense—that there's no room for reverence.

A better way to think is to bring our experiences, presupposed ideas, and relationships that form our idea of *Father* into the light of Scripture for adjustment and correction. What I've found is that my idea of Father over the years has grown beyond the simplicity of a human dad. Though a human dad is a representation of some of God's qualities as a lover of the family and household of God—from which we can and must draw parallels—I think we'll find that our ideas about worship will explode if we let God blow up our box. If we admit that dad's can't fill God's shoes because God doesn't have shoes, we may discover a borderless relationship with our Father that just flat-out shreds our nice theological ribbons.

In an effort to lay out something that is simple and yet can be as profound as one makes it, I underwent a study for my own benefit regarding the Father. As I began, I thought to myself *Who might be the expert on the Father?* Who might know him more intimately than anyone? The answer: Jesus.

Considering the fact that one can't have the title "Father" without an offspring, it makes sense that we can only understand the Father best in how he relates to the Son. Scripture tells us that Jesus is the "exact representation of the Father" (Heb. 1:3). Other translations replace "representation" with the word "imprint." The word imprint implies that when you see Jesus, you see the Father. If you want to know the Father, study everything Jesus does with a magnifying glass. Jesus and the Father are one.

In the spirit and joy of talking about the unity and oneness of our God, I felt the best way to get to know the Father is through the lens of Jesus. To do so, I went through the four gospels and recorded all the verbs (actions) and prepositions (words indicating relationship) concerning the Father. It was a tedious task, but it's important to recognize that language means something. God uses language to reveal himself to us, and it's very important to know exactly what he said.

In my analysis below, I first list Scriptures throughout the gospels that make mention of the Father. Second, I record words that bear action or relational implications. And lastly, I have crafted statements that summarize what I found:

Passages

Mt. 4:45; 5:16, 45; 6:4, 8-9, 18; 10:33; 7:11, 21; 10:20; 16:17, 27; 22:27; 26:53; Mk. 8:38; Lk. 9:26; 11:32; Jhn. 5:18-19; 5:22; 6:40; 8:16; 14:6, 10-31; 16:10, 15, 26, 32.

Actions and Prepositions

Actions: The Father sees, makes, sends, seals, knows, comes, lives, is before, and judges.
Prepositions: through, of, with, to, in, at, on, and before.

Relationship and Role

- The Father's location is **in** heaven, and all glory is given **to** him. From heaven, he dispenses all his resources through Jesus. Jesus represents and **comes in** the Father's name and glory. Jesus stands with the Father **at** his side and has life **in** himself, just as the Father does. Jesus also proclaims himself equal **with** God—claiming he is **in** the Father, and the Father is **in** Him.
- The Father gives all things **to** Jesus as Christ appeals, prays, asks, and returns everything **to** the Father. No one comes **to** the Father except through Jesus, and not everyone who calls Jesus Lord enters the kingdom, but only those who do the Father's will **in** heaven. The Son therefore acknowledges or denies us **before** the Father.
- The Father also gives and dispenses sound judgment **to** the unjust. Likewise, Jesus is going to come in judgment—for the Father also judges no one but gives judgment **to** the Son and judges **through** the Son. Jesus comes **with** his angels, and **with** the Father, and **in** his Father's glory to judge and reign.

- The Father **knows** all our needs **before** we ask. The Father **takes** all that's from Christ and declares it and gives it **to** us. At the same time, he also **sees** how we use his resources. He sees all our giving and fasting done **in** secret. He works his resources together with the Spirit's power, who is **of** the Father, in an effort to speak **through** humanity and also creation. The Father not only has made humans and uses them, but he also **makes** and **sends** rain and sunshine, and all that's been created bears his voice. All that he provides is bestowed **on** those just and unjust, and he **sets** his seal of eternal life **on** the Son of Man.

PASSAGES

Mt. 11:25; 18:10, 14; 20:23; 25:34; Lk. 11:13; 12:32; 22:29, 42; 23:46; Jhn. 1:14; 3:35; 5:17-18; 6:32, 57, 65; 10:15, 20-21, 32, 37; 8:27-28, 38; 10:30; 11:41; 12:50; 11:41; 13:3; 15:1-24; 17:25; 20:21.

ACTIONS AND PREPOSITIONS

Actions: The Father grants, commands, gives, assigns, sends, honors, loves teaches, raises, draws, glorifies, looks, sees knows, lays down, dwells among, lives, and works.
Prepositions: from, up, through, by, about, of, until, with, to and into, all things are heard and learned from, and for.

RELATIONSHIP AND ROLE

- The Father **gives** the Holy Spirit and all things into Christ's hands —the true bread from heaven—and assigns the kingdom and all things **to** Jesus and those that ask. The Father also **loves** the Son. We abide **in** that **love**.
- The Word (Jesus) became flesh and **lived, worked,** and **dwelt among** us as the Son **sent from** the Father. Jesus receives his authority to lay down his life and take it **up** again **from** the Father. The Father **commands** Jesus, telling him what to speak. Jesus

speaks **about** what he's seen **with** the Father. Jesus gives thanks to the Father, and the angels always face the Father and call him Lord **of** heaven and earth. Jesus does nothing **of** his own accord but only what he **sees** the Father doing. Jesus attributes his will to being **of** the Father, even to the point of entrusting his suffering and Spirit **into** the hands of his Father's will. Jesus and the Father are **One**. Jesus and the Father **know** each other, and this causes them to lay their lives down **for** the sheep. Jesus says that his Father is working **until** now, and so He too is working.

- The Father **draws** people to the Son, **sends** the Son, **gives** the Son up as a sacrifice, **glorifies** the Son, and **shows** Jesus what he's doing—even unto **raising** the dead. He **teaches** Jesus what to say and **gives** all things **into** the Son's hands; even the **honor** the Father himself receives.

- All who **look** on the Son receive the will **of** the Father—eternal life. Jesus notes that rewards and blessings in the kingdom are prepared **by** his Father and that **by** our bearing fruit, the Father is glorified. No one can come to a blessing or to Jesus except if it's granted **by** the Father.

PASSAGES

Lk. 10:21-22; 24:49; Jhn. 4:23; 14:2; 15:26.

ACTIONS AND PREPOSITIONS

Actions: The Father sends, is worshipped, comes, proceeds, bears witness, is truth, and owns.
Prepositions: of, in, from, to, about, and upon.

RELATIONSHIP AND ROLE

- Jesus rejoices **in** the Holy Spirit over the fact that God the Father hides the truth of Jesus **from** those that think themselves to be wise, and gives authority to Jesus **to** reveal himself to whom he wishes. Jesus **sends** the Holy Spirit, the promise **of** the Father, **upon** us.

- We **worship** the Father **in** the Spirit and **in** truth, and the Father seeks people **to** worship him. But when the Helper **comes**, whom the Father **sends to** us **from** the **truth**, who **proceeds from** the Father, he **bears witness about** Jesus.
- Lastly, the Father **owns** the house Jesus speaks of preparing for all who believe.

IF YOU SPEND some time meditating and soaking in the various Scriptures and realities of what's mentioned in the examples above, I think you'll come to a few conclusions. One conclusion might be that this *Father-Son relationship is much more extraordinary and seamlessly integrated than we can fully understand.* When Jesus calls the Father, *Father*, the implications go far beyond what is meant by the term Daddy. There is a complete centripetal (moving toward) and centrifugal (moving away) spin that's going on. They mirror each other in a perceived paradox, and all the while they remain altogether separate. It's interdependence, trust, transparency, leaning on, and submitting to one another of the highest kind. It's a naked relationship at the core. It's complete.

The second conclusion one might reach is that the Father can be considered complete only when standing in direct relationship to what is other than he. Verbs and prepositions can't really exist without something other about which they express action or relationship. The complete identity of the Father is wrapped up in *whom he is within his community of the Godhead.*

To help understand this intertwined relationship, consider the structure of an orange. Oranges are composed of rind, juice, and pulp. Three different components; one entity. If you separate one from the other, they become something else altogether. Pulp without juice becomes coarse, hardened threads. Juice without rind becomes a drippy mess. A rind with nothing inside becomes a meaningless, dried-up shell. An orange is an orange only when all parts are acting together in relationship to the whole.

The orange also illustrates the fate of our physical bodies when their parts are separated. Remove the brain, the heart, or the blood, and not only do those parts become meaningless, the body dies. Just as human body parts and orange pieces must remain unified in order to realize their truest purpose, we as the worshipping people of the church can't either. We are one body as a believing people, but we're made up of many parts and systems that spin in concert to make us one though we are many.

The relationship of *Trinity* becomes more intuitive when we realize the collective nature of almost everything. It's when we start to isolate parts and view components as standalone entities that the concept of united oneness becomes confusing—much like a pinky toe viewed apart from a foot. Without the foot, or body for that matter, for which that little guy provides balance, a pinky toe is just an odd-looking, meaningless creature.

IMPLICATIONS

The worship of God is at stake in our view of the Father. Our likeness to him is at stake. If we fail to ponder the way in which Father is imperative to Son, we may miss the fact that we are imperative to each other. You need me in order to embrace the title *friend*. A child needs a parent to embrace the identity of son and daughter. A husband needs a wife, a nephew needs an aunt, and a grandparent needs the grandkids. Just as the idea of employee would not exist without employer or music would not exist without a musician, we must see that the togetherness of the world is due to the togetherness of its source. The Father-Son-Spirit world. Our preconceived ideas regarding what constitutes closeness or distance revolves around how we view the Trinity and his nature in the world. If we seek out the other as a means to uncovering the beauty of what God's instilled in us, we'll find closeness. Anything other than service to others will bring isolation and the bondage of individualistic identity.

Our quick look at the Father sheds light on him relationally, but many of the words used in our examples previously are not solely intimacy words. We must resist the urge to make Father and Daddy synonymous. He is intimate and close and a deep lover, but also so much more. The Father is couched in words of deployment, vocation, function, ability, capacity, and nature. Everything the Father is and does is compacted into Jesus and explodes from Jesus. The Father and Son's closeness is alongside and face to face closeness. They work together and accomplish each other's goals and desires, and yet they never get too busy at their work to sit down for a heart-to-heart joyous celebration.

What a blessing it is to consider that the same explosive power of the A-Bomb-of-Heaven is compacted into us. God slams into us like a cataclysmic hug. His fatherly rhythm of service, celebration, and identity bring us peace when we grab hold. Embrace. When magnet hits magnet at the right poles, it has no choice but to move closer to the other. Rightly positioned, magnets hold fast to one another. Wrongly turned, magnets repel into eternity. They run. The Father, like a rightly positioned magnet, pursues us, attempting to draw us to him. We either repel or attract his advance. Idle neutrality is not an option. This Father pursues on a steed. As he runs toward us, it strikes into us either notions of fear or of joyous rescue.

Keep in mind the brilliance of the Father as we now consider the Son.

6

THE SON

KINGDOM OF KINSHIP OR COMMUNITY OF COMPETITION?

A s the Father is much bigger than our understanding of our earthly fathers and yet is influenced by our experience of closeness or distance with them, the same is true of the Son. As sons and daughters of God, the believer's relationship to Jesus our Savior is that of brotherhood. Kinship. Siblings. Our view of the Son is shaped by how we relate to the idea of a sibling and yet greatly exceeds our understanding of that relationship because he is also our Savior.

The church of God is called the household, the family, and the bride of Christ. We must realize that all of these are family images. How one relates to a family will determine how one postures him or herself in the kingdom.

Like many others, I bring a handicap to the area of kinship. I was raised in a divorced family. My younger sister and I are biologically linked to each other directly, but my Dad sired another daughter with his previous wife. Because of that, I was well acquainted with step-siblings. It's a crude idea, the notion of step-siblings. We assume they'll be a step up or a step back, but we degrade them by assuming they are a step at all. My older sister entered our home in every way a "step." She was walked on, and for this I'm sorry. She also did her fair share of walking on us as well. I loved her, and still do, but her position within the family was far more complicated than mine. She came into a battle.

She instantly felt the need to wage war with her new mom and yet to remain civil to us as siblings.

My biological sister and I were never taught the meaning of *together*. We were only trained in the art of war. The formula for warring was perfect in my upbringing. My Dad willingly withheld love, which caused all of us to constantly compete with each other for affection. In contrast, my mom held us up on golden pillows in praise, to the point of idolatry. This caused us to believe we were entitled to whatever we wanted. All in all, the environment provided the perfect recipe in forming full-blown narcissists. On one hand we became the center of the universe and occupied the throne, and on the other hand, we knew we didn't deserve it. We knew intuitively that Mom was compensating for Dad's neglect. We were reminded every day on the inside that something was wrong with us—not in the healthy sense of sinners needing a Savior, but the in the sense of thinking we were unlovable.

As a result, the paradox of competition and cowardice defines how I naturally relate to the idea of a sibling. It's how all of us relate to each other apart from God's grace. Why else would we desire to tear someone else down but that we perceive them higher than ourselves? Why else would we desire to flatter and falsely elevate another but to bring them into our fold to make them a blind cheerleader for us?

I grew up knowing that I needed to outbid my other siblings in order to be accepted. I set out to out do them in accomplishments, and though I was overtly praised by my Mom in an unhealthy manner, I held my trophies in the air for Dad to see. His silence convinced me that I knew nothing. In one regard I was a fighter, and on the other, I knew I could never win. This built into me the perfect ingredients for a what I call *identity in wandering*. I grew up never knowing who I was.

Because I knew only a community of competition in relation to blood-family, I brought the same posture into the church. My kingdom family. Because Jesus' blood runs thicker than ancestry, my time with God's people only amplified my mess. I began hitting people with intimidation instead of comforting them in love. My perpetual glory-seeking and self-worship stepped me up higher in leadership while making everyone lower than me a servant. I was so blind. The honest words of those who openly confronted my arrogance sounded to me like the ravings of lunatics.

I had grown up swimming in the reality of rejection, so I was a pro at being unloved. I embraced rejection. I accepted the fact that no one would ever like me as a lord and master, but in my mind that didn't mean I wasn't perfect for the job.

I thought my world secure, and yet it was crumbling. Any world built by a false lord is destined to crumble because at its foundation is insecurity, cowardice, and fear. Luckily, I was in a new family now. Slowly I began to realize that sibling relationships in God's family are built on *kingdom kinship*. The more I tried to push in competition, the more I saw that God's gracious family was not interested in the contest.

I started to meditate on what God says of his family—namely, that "There is neither Jew nor Gentile, neither slave nor free, nor is there male and female, for you are all one in Christ Jesus" (Gal. 3:28). I began reading through Acts and seeing how atrocious the racism and cultural pride were between the Jew and Greek, and the Jew and Samaritan. In the culture of today, I saw the hostility growing between races, cultures, and even religious sects of Christianity. I read 1 Corinthians and saw what hero worship and personality-driven ministry had done in dividing the Christians of history. I looked out and saw the same cult-of-personality driving church and culture today.

Competitive cowardice is the way the world works. It's the world's training ground. The world's system of sin began with a competitive servant wanting to be God. Satan attempted to devour the angels in heaven. He never loved them. Satan's whole goal in stealing humans away through lies had one aim: to put God on trial. His anthem is; "did God say…?"

Satan has built his empire on competitive cowardice. He aims at God with an AK-47 and puts the gun in our hand armed with the same doubts: Is God good? Is God true? Is this all God wants? Satan entitles us. He flatters us. He puffs us up, and yet he never affirms us. He is a magician at conjuring insecurity and fear. He makes a person feel bulletproof as his puppet. He pulls the strings as we march into battle. Right when we need his false promises most, he pulls the hand out from the back of our puppeteering clothing and we fall lifeless and empty to the ground without anyone to make our mouth move.

He has disrupted our view of God and each other. Races compete against race, and their only reward is pride in their pigment. Culture aims at culture and the only trophy is bragging rights. Class belittles class and calls it evolution. Satan pits husbands against wives and leaves them thinking that they just "fell out of love." He shrouds us from the truth that it's impossible to fall out of love. The very definition of love knows only to *fall in* over and over again, to give and give without expectation of return, even to the detriment of the lover. But Satan tells us that love means we need to "get ours." We buy it. We buy into the illusion that God is withholding something. We buy into the illusion that we're missing out, or that somehow others are better because of their class, their job, their materials, their boob job, or their fast car. It's sick really.

All of our anarchy comes down to competitive cowardice. It comes down to the fact, that without Jesus, we know nothing of kingdom kinship.

SIBLING RIVALRY AND JESUS

Though we must not make the mistake of humanizing the Father's relationship to Jesus and comparing it to our relationship with others, we must also be wise enough not to miss the parallels. Jesus did relate to the Father as a human, all while being fully God. His art of relating unveils for us principles to be applied, both in our interactions with people and with God.

In our comparison, however, let's not overlook one crucial fact that makes us different from Jesus. We entered into war against heaven in the Garden. Jesus was never at war with the Father. They are one.

Because of sin, we now live in a world competing with Jesus. Sibling rivalry. There's a reason why people hate the Christian message to the degree of wanting to do nothing more than crucify the Christian Savior. The world today reacts toward Jesus in the same manner as King Herod. When sweet, innocent baby Jesus slid through the birth canal, we are told in Matthew's gospel that Herod's response, along with all of Jerusalem, was to be overcome by "disturbing fear." Imagine that! A little baby igniting fear?

As Jesus arrived, out came the insecurity. Everyone from Herod to the Sanhedrin knew they couldn't beat him, so they needed to exterminate him while he was weak. They knew his kingdom had arrived, and their defeat was at hand—for all the prophesies had pointed to this moment—and they still rose up with a sword to fight a losing battle.

Meanwhile, back at the humble stable, Jesus' entrance stands in stark contrast to the picture of any other warrior—of which he is the fiercest. He began his life in our world in the feeding-trough bassinet of Mary. He became a sibling and a son. He entered into the strife of the human family. He drank the venom first spit out in Cain and Abel in order to turn it to sparkling water.

Cain's hate is the murderous undercurrent to all human history. The same cancer that eats at us attempted to feast on Jesus' family.

In John 7:5 we are told that his own brothers were reluctant to follow him. Why? Because they didn't believe he was God? Maybe at the time, but it can't be true forever because in the Acts account we see that his family—his mother and brothers—are among the first members of the church. James, his half-brother, even wrote about Jesus being God in his letters. So we must ask, why were they hesitant to believe at first?

The brothers of Jesus (James, Joses, Simon, and Judas are all named in Matthew 13:55, *and no not that Judas*), had grown up with the very Son of God living under the same roof. Some of them were old enough to remember their older brother Jesus at the age of twelve going to the temple and teaching the religious leaders (Luke 2:39-52). They were also likely among the invited guests at the same wedding in Cana where Jesus performed his first miracle of turning water into wine (John. 2:1-11). Some of them would likely have been present or at least aware of when their older brother turned the tables in the temple and how this act carried with it the bold messianic statement that the temple was "his father's house." They would also have known that Jesus healed an official's son (John. 4:46-54), healed the man on the Sabbath at the pool of Bethesda (John. 5:1-17), fed 5,000 people with five loaves of bread and two fish (John. 6:1-14) and walked on water (John. 6:16-21). All of the above took place before Scripture says, "his brothers did not believe him" (John 7:5).

The brothers of Jesus had grown up with perfection. They couldn't beat him at soccer. They lost to him on math tests. I'm kidding of course, but maybe not much. All throughout his growing up, Jesus' actions and behavior convinced his family of his flawlessness. Deep down, they saw the difference. Jesus' perfection awakened his brother's insecurity. It challenged their own notions that they were gods—a notion that has inflected every human since the Fall.

We are all like Jesus' earthly siblings. We do not relinquish our own sense of superiority readily. Worship is the heart of our problem as humans. Deep down, we want to worship ourselves and we resent having in our presence someone who deserves worship more than we think we do. The same animosity that drove Cain to kill Abel dwelled in Jesus' own family. Jealousy.

So jealous and competitive were they that they attempted to get rid of Jesus. He was outshining them and embarrassing them with his grandiose claims. The text tells us that Jesus was becoming kind of a nuisance in his home region—going around telling everyone that he is God. So his brothers in John 7:3-5 say, "leave here and go to Judea, that your disciples also may see the words you are doing. For no one works in secret if he seeks to be known openly. If you do these things, show yourself to the world. *For not even his brothers believed him*" (italics mine). Catch the subtle undercurrent. His brothers attempt to send him away to another town like a drug addict's mother sends away her son to rehab. Jesus was embarrassing them. At this time, they deemed him a lunatic, and it was not on the basis of perfection. They knew Jesus was perfect. Herod knew Jesus was perfect. The whole world knew Jesus was the sole subject worthy of our worship and allegiance, and they hated him for it.

JESUS' ACTIONS

The world today hates Jesus for his claim to be God. It's this very claim and his rising from the dead to back it up that make people angry. People can deal with him as a good guy, a prophet, or an even a wise teacher, but for him to lay down "God" as his one card causes people to make Jesus their enemy in greater fashion than when a gamer yells "UNO!" A UNO player knows that an opponent's "one card" in hand means his own doom—he is on the losing side. Jesus playing the "God-card" reminds the world of the same reality. We are on the losing side when the worship of self is pitted against the worship of the Savior.

The point is, we're broken in our understanding of how to relate to God, and this has brought havoc into our relationships with each other. The very reason we punch, kick, and fight for a position within families and between siblings is that we are fighting a deeper war within our heart. If we choose not to believe that Jesus is Lord, we are at war with the Son. Our sin boils in rage even as Jesus dares to call us to his table as our brother.

Graciously, by the Spirit's saving power, our temper tantrum turns to rejoicing. When God brings us into his home, and we bring all our competitive cowardice and its insecurities with us, God turns it to good. He uses and shapes us within his family in a way that reveals our weaknesses to each other. The church, when functioning properly, is entangled with sibling rivalry. The only difference between the church and the world is that our rivalry raises the white flag. We raise the sign of surrender to Jesus and each other and choose to lay down our need to be bigger or better when compared to someone else in God's family. We begin comparing ourselves to Jesus.

There is no other comparison worth making.

When we all look at Jesus, we realize we've been duped, and in the best way. We've been outlasted, bested, and the thought of it just brings joy. When we finally take our place as *lesser than* others, we begin to learn how to treat others as *more than* ourselves. So how do we as the church learn to love each other well? How do we learn to embrace the mess? The best way I can think of is to get to know Jesus as Savior and Lord.

I can't think of anyone who may be able to testify to knowing Jesus more closely than two of his dearest and most prominent leaders. Peter and Paul understood the reality of Jesus as Master and Mentor. Savior and Sibling. Researching their words about our Brother-Savior instructs us in how this Son relates to his brothers and sisters. He loves us not in competition or cowardice but with a love that bleeds so we can be saved:

PETER'S WRITINGS

PASSAGES

1 Pt. 1:1-3, 7, 13; 3:21; 2 Pt. 1:1; 1:16; 3:18.

ACTIONS

The Son is of, to, in, for, with, through, and by.

RELATIONSHIP & ROLE

- Peter proclaims himself to be an apostle **of** Jesus Christ and calls all people **to** obedience to Jesus according **to** the Father's foreknowledge, **in** the sanctification of the Spirit, **for** obedience **to** Jesus Christ, **for** the sprinkling **with** his blood. Peter seems to teach that it is only **through** the knowledge of Christ that we can overcome the defilement of the world.
- Peter bases his conclusions and his message on his eyewitness account **of** Jesus' Majesty.
- Peter claims that all praise and honor for our faith is a result **of** the

revelation of Jesus Christ and that it is only **through** the resurrection of Jesus that we—the body of Christ—can be built up into a spiritual house and a spiritual priesthood that offers acceptable sacrifices **to** God. It's only **through** Jesus, and learning more about and **of** Jesus, that we can grow, that God can be glorified, and only **by** his righteousness can we be acceptable **to** God.

PAUL'S WRITINGS

PASSAGES

Rom. 1:1, 6-8; 2:16; 3:24; 5:1, 11-17; 6:3, 11, 23; 7:25; 8:2, 11, 39; 13:14; 15:5-6, 16-17.

ACTIONS

The Son is of, to, by, from, by, and through.

RELATIONSHIP & ROLE

- Paul gives himself a title: A Servant and Minister **of** Jesus Christ. In his letter to the Romans, he considers himself to be one amongst the many who are called **to** belong to Jesus. He not only writes his letter with the authority of God the Father, but he also is clear that his letter is **from** Jesus Christ.
- His affirmation of Christ as Lord—the one true God equal to the Father—is not based in wishy-washy journalism, but he claims that Jesus is the Son of God in power according **to** the Spirit of holiness **by** his resurrection **from** the dead.
- He thanks God **through** Jesus. He claims that God judges the secrets of men **by** Jesus. He claims that all those who are justified and made right and at peace with God, are made so **through** the redemption of Jesus.
- We rejoice **in** God **through** our Lord Jesus Christ, **through** whom we now have reconciliation and eternal life **by** his grace. Those who were once dead **in** sin are now alive **in** Christ Jesus and

therefore have no condemnation. The law **of** the Spirit—the same Spirit that raised Jesus **from** the dead—sets us free **in** Christ. We now have been added into love, and the person that no longer allows us to be separated from the love of God is Christ Jesus.

- Believers are called to put **on** Jesus in order to experience victory over the flesh. Putting on Christ is the only way to experience harmony **with** God and one another. Putting on Christ is the only manner in which Paul finds any meaning to his own work.

LOYAL TO JESUS

Paul and Peter's relationship with Jesus is not one of competition. It is a surrendered resolve to serve. Clearly, they both acknowledged Jesus to be more than human. Although human, they also affirmed him as God. Like John, Jesus' most beloved disciple, Peter, and Paul were eyewitnesses to Jesus in every way. Their response to Jesus' nature and to what he taught them about our relationship to God is found in 1 John 1:1-4:

> That which was from the beginning, which we have heard, which we have seen with our eyes, which we looked upon and have touched with our hands, concerning the word of life—the life was made manifest, and we have seen it, and testify to it and proclaim to you the eternal life, which was with the Father and was made manifest to us—that which we have seen and heard we proclaim also to you, so that you too may have fellowship with us; and indeed our fellowship is with the Father and with his Son Jesus Christ. *And we are writing these things so that our joy may be complete* (italics mine).

We have no greater evidence of Jesus's life, death, resurrection, ascension, and testimony of truth than through the mouths of his followers. They touched, saw, heard, and exercised all their senses while with him. For them, it was not faith, but sight. They wrote down their *sight* so we could see with faith. They wrote, not to dismiss this heretic who would call himself God, but to do exactly the opposite. They wrote to confirm to us that Jesus is the only way to become friends with the Father. Their writing informs us today, which makes their joy complete.

Much ink has been spilled proving that Jesus is God and Savior, and one of my intentions in the above sentences is to spill a little more making the same point. The Bible teaches us not only who Jesus is as God and as the Son of the Father, but also who he is to us as a sibling. He restores our lost way back to heaven, but he also repairs the damage we've done to the earth.

Very little ink has been spilled on what Jesus has done for us by way of a sibling relationship. We've spent too little time pondering how he works as a brother to us. I believe this because I see the church today killing its own. Jesus said the world would know us "by our love," and yet I see the opposite. The world often sees us fighting the same turf wars that they know all too well.

In order for us to truly become like Christ and to experience worship on the personhood level, rather than just the practical side of what we do for God, our surrendered flag has to be waved at each other. We must stop competing. We must stop comparing. We must stop trying to prove ourselves through our own version of sorority initiation. We must stop trying to assert ourselves, our methods, and our ways. We've got to resign from the war to be king of the hill.

7

THE HOLY SPIRIT

Nothing describes the Holy Spirit's nature better than the Greek word *paraclete*. The word means to be "called alongside." He's the Helper. An Advocate. Though his help to humanity is assuredly beyond measure, the Bible seems to sum up his service in these encompassing three terms: he comforts, he counsels, and he convicts. He does all that he does in a manner that brings everyone to Jesus.

Any hurt needing comfort exists because of something we've believed, done, or encountered, that is contrary to the loving nature of Jesus. Every ill-mannered decision or wrong way taken resulting in failure occurred because we have come up short in our attempts to do something in a better way than Jesus. Any violation of conscience or attempt to skirt the absolutes that are woven into the fabric of creation can only mean one thing: We believe ourselves better or smarter than Jesus, and thus the Spirit convicts us of our mistake.

The Holy Spirit is the complete mother of heaven, and when I say *mother*, I'm not referring to gender. I'm not making God into a female because gender is too small a category for the Trinity. I'm also not going to delve into the heresy of books like *The Shack* or movies like *The Matrix* and tell you that the container for all wisdom comes in the form of a black woman baking cookies. When I liken the Spirit to that of the properly tender persona of a mother, I'm not trying to humanize God to make sense of him. To do so is scandalous.

What I am saying is that much of the paracletic nature of the Spirit is woven into the tapestry of everything good that we may call *motherly*.

I will get more into how the Trinity affects our view of the sexes and roles later in this book, but for now, I want to cast the paracletic role of the Spirit into the light of helper and servant, not sexes. I want to assume that what makes the Spirit most helpful is his personality. He's a servant.

JESUS RECOGNIZES THAT WE NEED HELP

The Spirit is a servant to Jesus. One of the main occurrences where the Spirit shows up is at Jesus' Baptism. As Jesus comes up out of the water the Spirit descends on him like a dove, and Jesus hears a voice from heaven saying, "This is my Son in whom I'm well pleased." Jesus' baptism is one of the most astounding Trinitarian events in the Bible, but let's not stop quite yet to ponder why; let's jump quickly to consider what the next verses tell us. Luke says that the Spirit immediately leads Jesus into the wilderness to be what: tempted by the Devil. After Jesus emerges in victory from the war in the desert, Scripture says he begins the work of ministry in the *power of the Holy Spirit*.

There are three pivotal scenes in the timeline. The Spirit is there when Jesus is affirmed in his *identity* in his baptism, he's there when he's *challenged* in that identity in the temptation, and he's the reason Jesus operates *victoriously* in that identity in his ministry. Jesus was affirmed by the Father as a Son. He received the Father's affirmation in the form of pleasure. The identity of Jesus brings pleasure to the Father, and it's all made possible by the Spirit.

The Spirit directs his counsel, conviction and comfort toward sonship, pleasure, and identity. In the timeline, Jesus is first affirmed as a Son and as pleasing. Identity. His identity is confirmed as a Son of the Father.

Coming up fresh from his baptism and affirmation as the Father's Son, Jesus is immediately attacked. Satan's first sword slices at identity, sonship, and pleasure. Satan's arrow flies: "If you are the Son of God ..." Satan proceeds to offer Jesus *provision* (turning stones to bread), *power* (the kingdoms of the world), and *protection* (angelic help from a suicide attempt off the walls of the temple), and he tries to make Jesus fall for such temptations by first attempting to get Jesus to doubt who he is. The doorway through which Satan seeks to gain access into Jesus is through Jesus' identity.

He knows if he can get Jesus to doubt whose he is, he can get him to fall for anything. This is how all temptation works.

In the final scene, Jesus turns to Satan, points his finger in his face, and says, "Remember, I AM (Jesus) the Lord, YOUR (Satan) God." All of Satan's false attempts to offer Jesus things that are already Jesus' to begin with, came from Satan's empty pockets. Jesus knows who he is and who Satan is not. Jesus is Satan's Lord, not the other way around.

The Spirit's counsel, conviction, and comfort hold us fast in the kinship, pleasure, and identity of our Father. As with Jesus, Satan will show up in a variety of ways, but will always enter through one door—identity. If he can get us doubting whose we are, he can get us to fall for anything.

Jesus needed the Spirit, and so do we. In John 14:16-17, 26-27, Jesus himself prays that the disciples would also be sent the gift of the Spirit. Note carefully why he prays for such a thing:

> And I will ask the Father, and he will give you another Helper, to be with you forever, even the Spirit of truth, whom the world cannot receive, because it neither sees him nor knows him. You know him, for he dwells with you and will be in you ... the Helper, the Holy Spirit, whom the Father will send in my name, he will *teach* you all things and *bring to your remembrance* all that I have said to you. *Peace I leave with you; my peace I give to you.* Not as the world gives do I give to you. Let not your hearts be troubled, neither let them be afraid. (Italics mine)

The same ministry of teaching (counsel), conviction (helping us remember our beliefs and the reality that the enemy has been judged), and peace (comfort) that Jesus experienced in the Spirit, he prays upon us. Notice also that he says that this Spirit *who is with you* will now *be in you*. Jesus promises the disciples even greater things, and this is it. The Spirit had only descended *on* Jesus, and when Jesus went to heaven to take the throne, he granted the power that the Spirit could now live *in*, not just *on* us. To live in is much greater than to live on.

The Spirit, as seen thus far, is not just some kind of magic trick that knocks us down, convulses, and makes us ecstatic. The Spirit calls us to remember our identity as sons and daughters, and that through Jesus' life, death, resurrection, and ascension we've been made pleasing to the Father. When the Father looks at us, Jesus is all he sees. We're eclipsed and engulfed by Jesus, and therefore we benefit from being mistaken for him. We are absorbed in his likeness. Christians. Little Christs. We are in Jesus and he is in us. One.

A TABLE FOR THE SPIRIT

It is clear that the Spirit is the connecting agent between heaven and earth. He's the conduit and piping through which the love between the Father and Jesus flows into our being. He's the wellspring of life welling up within our hearts.

It would be a fair statement to say that no one quite understood the Spirit's work so originally and personally as those early disciples. Though I'm not saying the early believers had a front-row seat to things you and I can never touch now, which is obviously not true, I am saying that the Spirit in those days went public for the first time, so to speak. Never is the hype over anything higher than when something first is unveiled. Never was the iPhone's promise of possibility ever as profound as the moment it was first released.

Though we feel the effects of the Spirit today, we must acknowledge that the initiatory experience of the original disciples gave them special clarity and insight into the descent of the Holy Spirit.

To understand the Holy Spirit, we must listen to the words of these early disciples. They are unclouded, while we today must glean through generations upon generations of confusing misunderstandings regarding the Spirit's work. The disciples give us the clearest by which to filter out any heresies that have developed over time. In the examples below, I studied the prepositional and verbal language that is ascribed to the Spirit throughout Acts at the inception of the church, as well as in Romans and 1 Corinthians where the doctrine of the Spirit is most widely discussed. My findings were helpful to me, and I hope they will be of help to you:

PASSAGES

Acts 1:2, 5: 2:4; 4:8, 31; 5:32; 6:10; 8:15, 17-19; 9:17; 11:16, 24; 13:9; 13:52; 15:8; 21:4; Rom. 5:5; 8:11; 1 Cor. 2:10; 12:8. 1:5: 2:4; 4:8, 31; 5:32; 6:10; 8:15, 17-19; 9:17; 11:16, 24; 12:3; 12:13; 13:9; 13:52; 14:2; 15:8.

ACTIONS

Actions: The Spirit gives, speaks, receives, fills, baptizes, and anoints, *Prepositions:* with, to, and in. It is through the Spirit that God's nature, gifts, commands, life, and love are given.

RELATIONSHIP AND ROLE

- God's nature, gifts, commands, life, and love are given **through** the Holy Spirit to all those chosen. Believers are **baptized, receive**, are **filled with**, and walk according **to** the Holy Spirit, and are **given** the ability to speak boldly **in** the Spirit. The Father gives the Holy Spirit **to** those that obey him, and the Holy Spirit can be **seen** in a person's life. Acts records that God **anointed** Jesus **with** the Holy Spirit and **with** power, and in similar fashion, he fills us **with** that same power.

PASSAGE

Acts 1:6; 4:25.

PREPOSITION

The Spirit is *upon.*

RELATIONSHIP AND ROLE

- The Holy Spirit comes **upon** us to give us the power to witness for and about Jesus.

PASSAGES

Acts 1:16; 11:28; 16:6; 20:22; 28:25; Rom. 2:29; 8:13-15; 15:16,19; 1 Cor. 2:13-15, 6:11; 12:9, 11.

ACTIONS AND PREPOSITIONS

Actions: The Spirit foretells, speaks, sanctifies, empowers, leads, teaches, washes, and justifies.
Preposition: by.

RELATIONSHIP AND ROLE

- Scripture was spoken and foretold **by** the Spirit through King David and Isaiah. The Spirit still has the power to send people **by** his authority, **sanctify** them, **teach** them, **wash** them, **justify** them, or to forbid people to say and do things **by** that same authority. Salvation, victory over the flesh, leading, gifts, and the authority of the believer only comes from within the heart **by** the Spirit.

PASSAGES

Acts 2:17, 18; Acts 10:44; 11:15; 19:6; 1 Cor. 12:4.

ACTIONS AND PREPOSITIONS

Actions: The Spirit falls, gifts, and pours.
Prepositions: on, out.

RELATIONSHIP AND ROLE

- God **pours** out his gift, the Spirit, **on** all flesh, and the Spirit can **fall** or be **poured out on** those who hear the word of God. The believer can also set their mind **on** the Spirit to receive gifts, life, and peace from the Spirit.

PASSAGES

Acts 2:33; 6:3, 5; 7:55; Acts 16:7; Rom. 7:6; 8:2, 6, 11; 8:27; 15:30; 1 Cor. 2:11-15; 6:19; 7:40; 12:7; 14:12.

ACTIONS AND PREPOSITIONS

Actions: The Spirit comforts, loves, and serves.
Prepositions: from, of.

RELATIONSHIP AND ROLE

- The Holy Spirit is the promise **of**, love **of**, and is received **from** the Father at baptism. The Holy Spirit is also spoken of as being **of** Jesus. Believers are the temple **of**, can be full **of**, can bring forth manifestations **of**, know the mind **of**, are made alive through the law **of**, and can **serve of** the Spirit and his **comfort**.

PASSAGES

Acts 5:3, 9; 7:51.

PREPOSITIONS

We can do things To the *Holy Spirit* to Test or Resist his work …

RELATIONSHIP AND ROLE

- The Holy Spirit is a person **to** which we can lie and test. The Holy Spirit can be resisted.

PASSAGES

Acts 8:29; 10:19; 11:12; 13:2; 20:23; 21:11; Rom. 8:16.

ACTIONS AND PREPOSITIONS

Actions: The Spirit speaks and bears witness.
Prepositions: with, through.

RELATIONSHIP AND ROLE

- The Holy Spirit **speaks through** us and **bears witness** with our spirit that we are children of God.

PASSAGE

Acts 8: 39.

ACTIONS AND PREPOSITIONS

Actions: The Spirit carries.
Prepositions: with, through.

RELATIONSHIP AND ROLE

- In the case of Philip, the Spirit **carried** him away.

PASSAGES

Acts 19:21; 20:28; Rom. 8:1,9-10; 9:1; 14:17; 15:13; 1 Cor. 2:4; 3:16.

ACTIONS AND PREPOSITIONS

The Spirit is *in,* and so are we.

RELATIONSHIP & ROLE

- Paul is said to have resolved **in** the Spirit to make decisions upon his journey. It is **in** the Spirit that believers receive authority and wisdom, have the Spirit **in** them, and belong to Christ. This Spirit is the believer's life, joy, righteousness, hope, and peace, and can give life, or even fill a believer with the power to become an overseer of God's people—the church.

PASSAGES

Rom. 1:4; 8:5.

ACTIONS AND PREPOSITIONS

Actions: The Spirit accords.
Preposition: to.

RELATIONSHIP AND ROLE

- The Son of God's power is **according to** the Spirit of holiness.

PASSAGE

Rom. 8:26.

ACTIONS AND PREPOSITIONS

Actions: The Spirit helps and intercedes.
Prepositions: in, for.

RELATIONSHIP AND ROLE

- The Holy Spirit **helps** and intercedes **for** us **in** our weaknesses.

PASSAGE

1 Cor. 2:10.

ACTIONS AND PREPOSITIONS

Action: The Spirit searches.
Preposition: of.

RELATIONSHIP AND ROLE

- The Spirit **searches** the depths **of** God.

What is most profound about the Spirit, is that he is almost a person and a non-person at the same time. When the Spirit is most active is often when he's profoundly overlooked. He does many things, but he only has one finger. His one finger is always pointing back to Jesus. He's the willing COO of heaven; always taking the second chair and enjoying the task of carrying out the CEO's affairs. If one were to ask what the Spirit is doing, he will only answer, "Let me ask Jesus."

He's the pipeline that brings to us the life of Jesus as life moves up and down the stairway to heaven. If a conduit cracks, fails, or is removed, we most certainly know it immediately. One knows when the Spirit of God has withdrawn from a people, rendering them no longer a church. We hear the lack of Jesus in the singing, the comfort, counsel, and conviction. We see the loss of identity in a people becoming all consumed with competitive cowardice and attention grabbing. Gossip abounds and lays people low. Flattery multiplies to keep people artificially close. People walk around with their eyes to the ground, not to the heavens, inwardly obsessed with themselves. People hide like Adam and Eve, afraid to come out and expose their greatest struggles for fear of ridicule. Yes, we know very well the unmistakable signs of the Spirit's absence because we know so well the evidence of his presence.

When he's amongst his people we are filled with Jesus, just as when a BBQ is present people are filled with meat. The love between the Father and the Son somehow makes its way into our midst when we're in the Spirit's grip. People mutually submit when he's around. We serve. We humble ourselves. We become Holy. We take the back seat. In other words, the self is put on the shelf. No greater love is there than this: that a man lays down his life for his friends.

In the safety of all that Jesus has given up, naked souls expose themselves without fear of shame. I'm not talking about a nudist colony, but a world of personal and spiritual openness where people feel free to be the most human. Incomplete. Fallen, and yet free. Saint and sinner—the glorious tension between what we are currently and where we want to be in the future. Sojourners on a journey toward home.

THE GIFT AND THE GIVER

Consider once again John 14:16. Jesus is praying, "And I will ask the Father, and he will *give* you another Advocate, to be with you forever, even the Spirit of truth" (italics mine). This marvelous text gives us yet another glimpse into the way the Trinity talks. Jesus is praying to the Father, the Father is listening, and the Father is gifting to Jesus the rights to give away the greatest power of heaven, the Spirit. The Spirit is willing to go. Notice also that Jesus isn't praying here for the body of Christ to know more about the Giver, or about the gifts, though this is important in other Scriptures. Jesus' emphasis is on the *gift*. There's only one gift. The Spirit. He's a person. Heaven's greatest ribbon is wrapped around one being, and that is the Holy Spirit. Likewise, the affections of our hearts should be wrapped around one desire, to be filled more with this gift of heaven.

The gift of heaven is not about what one gains, but about who one knows. When we pray for the Spirit to fill us more deeply, we pray not that the Spirit will somehow make himself more than he is—that's impossible—but we pray that heaven would have more of us. We want the kingdom to grab hold of more of our will, more of our affections, and more of our worship. We surrender all our closed doors and keys to our off-limits closets unto the Spirit and ask him to unlock us.

In highlighting Jesus's reference to the Holy Spirit as a gift, I'm making a small distinction, but it's a crucial one. It's a point I've never read in a book about God, gifts, and much less the Trinity. The glorious secret of heaven has now been made known to us in the mystery of the gospel. God dwells with mankind. His home is in our hearts through faith, by the power of the Spirit. That's it. The ultimate.

Amongst all the silly nonsense we pray for throughout the day, the Spirit is the greatest of all prayer requests. In every situation, what is needed most is not more comfort, ease, fixing, fortune telling, lack of adversity, justice, balance, stability, or a greater power from our ability. What is needed is one thing. The Spirit. The conduit of heaven. He connects hearts to thrones. He connects temporal to eternal. He makes worthless dross into gold. He makes useful the useless.

As we press on to consider the Father, Son, and Spirit in the Old Testament, pause and ask the Spirit once again to "fill you afresh."

8

THE TRINITY IN THE OLD TESTAMENT

Is God Bi-Polar or Does He Have Multiple Personalities?

O ne of the primary emphases of the Old and New Testaments is that God is one.[1] Yet the New Testament seems to spend more time in revealing God as three with greater intentionality.[2] Why is this? Is God bi-polar about himself, or does he merely have multiple personalities and modes that he transforms into when the mood is right? What are we to believe?

To address this apparent contradiction between the Old and New Testaments, we must first state obvious truths. First, God is unchanging,[3] and there's no shadow of confusion in him. Any perceived problem in resolving the issue lies with us, not in God. Second, Jesus claims to be unchangeable in the New Testament and therefore links himself to the God of the Old and New.[4] Discussing Jesus' personhood is going to be very helpful in bringing unity to the Old and New Testaments. Third, thinking across the whole of Scripture will help bring clarity. Too often we isolate texts from one another and treat the Bible in a manner we wouldn't dare treat any other book. We forget that it's a cohesive story. It presents an unfolding storyline, including red herrings, scapegoats, incomplete endings, and a final resolve. It has all the elements that make for a good story and then some. The only difference between the Bible and fable would be as C. S. Lewis states, this fable is true. When we must isolate one section of the Bible for a particular study, we must keep in mind how it fits into the overarching storyline. Otherwise, we might miss the purpose of what that portion intends to say in relation to the whole.

IN THE BEGINNING

Scripture doesn't reveal God's three-in-one nature across every line of Scripture explicitly, but it absolutely does implicitly. We meet the Triune God at the beginning of the storyline in Genesis and the unified-plural nature of God is threaded through the tapestry of the whole Bible—making its way through to the final book of Revelation.

The most commonly cited verse in Trinitarian thought is found in Genesis 1:26. God makes Adam and Eve and says, "Let *us* make man in *our* image, after *our* likeness" (italics mine). God is presented as a *we* and a family. Everything created is presented in terms of *ours*. An *us*. So why don't we just assume that this god is some pantheistic plethora of gods? Is every religion correct? Can all gods be part of the Bible God's *we*? The answer is, no!

We must not overlook God's oneness as presented also in Genesis 1:1-25. As God is creating the heavens, the seas, and the land, and then filling them with orbs and stars, birds and clouds, and animals and vermin, the Hebrew term used for God is *Elohim*. Though Elohim is a plural noun for gods, when used in Hebrew, it is usually understood to be grammatically singular. The word the text uses for God actually confirms that our God is a *one multiple*.

Similarly, all that Elohim creates in the Genesis account are called *thems*, not *its*. As a one multiple, God creates everything, calls things good, and assigns *them* to their proper places. The word "them" is important on a variety of levels. First, God is not what pagans and mystics might think—that he infuses himself with creation. He is separate from creation. It's he and us. It is he and them. Second, we cannot invent a pantheon of gods and call ourselves pantheists because the God of the Bible prioritizes his oneness in making us. No matter how many of us there are, there is still one of him. Up until Genesis 1:26, where God reveals his plural nature in creating male and female, God is portrayed as a unity. A one-in-three (v. 25). Even in the creation account, God reveals his unity and his *threeness*.

What is striking about God's sovereign, multi-colored order is that randomness and calculated certainty dwell together in harmony. The harmony plays out in a threefold chord. In his book, *The Holy Trinity: In Scripture, History, Theology and Worship*, Robert Letham says that,

First, God issues direct commands. He says, "Let there be light," and there is light (v. 3). By seemingly effortless command, he brings into being the expanse (v. 6), the dry ground (v. 9), the stars (vv. 14-15), and the birds and fish (vv. 20-21). It is enough for him to speak; his edict is fulfilled at once. *Second, he works.* He separates light from darkness (v. 4). He makes the expanse and separates the waters (v. 7). He makes the two great lights, the sun and the moon (v. 16), setting them in the expanse to give light on the earth (v. 17). He creates the great creatures of the seas and various kinds of bird (v. 21). He makes the beasts of the earth and reptiles (v. 25). Finally, he creates man— male and female—in his own image (vv. 26-27). The thought is of focused, purposeful action by God, of divine labor accomplishing his ends. *Third, God uses and works in and through the activity of the creation.* God commands the earth to produce vegetation, plants, and trees (vv. 11-12). He requests the lights to govern the day and night (vv. 14-16). He commands the earth to bring forth land animals (v. 24). Here the creatures follow God's instructions and contribute to the eventual outcome. This God who created the universe does not work in a monolithic way. His order is varied—it is threefold, but one. His work shows diversity in its unity, and unity in its diversity. This God loves order and variety together.[5]

The unified-other nature of God and his words are infused in creation. It's what inspires humans even thousands and billions of years later to continue to acknowledge the brilliant cohesion and variety throughout the universe. In John's gospel, he acknowledges that Jesus is on the scene when our ordered symphony plucked its first note. Not only does John believe Jesus to be the one God spoken of in Genesis 1, but he also believes Jesus to be part of the Trinitarian "us." He writes, "In the beginning was the Word [Jesus], and the Word was *with* God, and the Word *was* God. He was in the beginning with God…. And the Word became flesh and dwelt among us, and we have seen his glory, glory as of the only Son from the Father, full of grace and truth" (John 1:1,14 italics mine). John's words connect the unified diversity of the God of Genesis with the New Testament presentation of Father and Son. The word translated *with* in John's gospel is a Greek word that creates a picture of two people dancing face-to-face. John's understanding of Jesus' divinity with the Father is one of intimate and joyful connection. Later in chapter 1, he introduces the Holy Spirit as being present right along with Jesus and the Father. Genesis confirms the Holy Spirit as well. The text tells us in the creation account that, "The Spirit of God hovered over the waters" (Gen. 1:2).

We will speak more of the Spirit when we talk about Jesus' Baptism being a link between the Old and New Testaments in just a moment, but for now, let's jump to the end.

THE BOOK OF REVELATION

Let's discuss the end of all of history. We must assume that if God's Triune nature is revealed in the beginning, he will also be unchangingly the same in the end. We look at the symmetry of Scripture to avoid inserting an understanding of the image of God into the story that it does not intend to convey.

What we see in The Book of Revelation is very convincing. Revelation presents the greatest evidence of God's Trinitarian nature. God's archenemy attempts to take on trinitarian form. Satan actually admits, of his own accord, that God is one and three by trying to become the same. God's rival asserts his belief in the Triune God by attempting to counterfeit his own version. His parody of the Trinity appears in chapter 12 of Revelation.

Let's first set the stage for where we are in Revelation. There's a lot that leads up to chapter 12, and scholars all agree that something unique happens in chapter 12. In chapters 1–3, God addresses the seven churches about his pending judgments that are to come upon the world. He asserts in chapters 4–8 that those judgments will come first in the form of seven Seals and in 8–11 through seven trumpets. In following the logic, one might think that the very next thing listed would be the seven bowls of wrath spoken of in chapter 16. However, the four chapters relating to the seven bowls are postponed in order to take us on a bit of a rabbit trail.

The jump throws a clog into the entire flow of the book and a wrench into people's conclusions that Revelation is an exact timeline for the end of the world. Up until chapter 11, there's remarkable cyclical repetition. It's unified. For example, there are three sets of seven in a row; each one takes us to the end of the world, and each is separated by interludes. They parallel each other. (Actually, Revelation brings us to the end of the world a total of seven times.) But chapter 12 brings to the foreground a character that's been forever behind the scenes—Satan.

In this chapter, Satan comes to center stage. He's depicted as having authority in the form of a red dragon attempting to consume a baby. In chapter 13 he calls for the assistance of his two other helpers. He calls the beast of the sea and the beast from the earth. The dragon, the beast of the sea, and the beast of the earth parody the Father, Spirit, and Son. They attempt to imitate the Trinity.

In the text, Satan's false attempt at sovereignty is compared to that of the true God actually sitting on the throne. The beast of the sea fakes a resurrection from a "fatal wound" and mocks the crucifixion and victory of Jesus. The beast of the earth chimes in to breathe life into his followers, and in all his works attempts to point back to his master, the dragon. The attempts of the beast at pretending to give life parrot the genuine power the Holy Spirit has in giving breath unto new life.

In chapter 17, the unholy trinity brings forth an unholy people. Babylon. Babylon is a symbol of unsaved humanity and its systems and is personified as a prostitute. On the other hand, the holy Trinity brings forth a holy people. In Revelation 19, the true Trinity reveals the city of their creation, which is called the New Jerusalem and is personified by the bride of Christ. Believers. God's people.[6]

Satan's attempt to end God's creation with trickery demonstrates his lack of inventiveness. He's a copycat. He can pervert but never create. He can twist but never make. He's the world's greatest puppeteer and magician, and he serves humanity only toward its own death by fashioning deadly counterfeits of godlike ideals to fit our liking. The one thing that Satan and all false religions can't be is good and true.

At the end of time, the reality of our three-in-one God is confirmed by the most unlikely and therefore the most convincing spokesman of all—the being that wants nothing more than to harm God's ends by destroying God's reputation and his people. Satan! He's the greatest antagonist in the story of life, and at the climax he aims at God but ends up shooting himself in the foot. He exposes himself as a fraud, and because of it, we have one of the truest accounts of the validity of the Trinity at our disposal.

THEOPHANIES AND HOW GOD REVEALS HIMSELF

There you have it. The Trinity in the beginning and the end. But what about the middle? To answer the question, let's separate the middle portions of Scripture out into what I'll call the Middle-A and Middle-B sections.

Everything before Jesus' Baptism is Middle-A, and everything after it is Middle-B. I'll explain why I believe that Jesus' baptism is the hinge point.

To tackle the Middle-A section (everything from the Fall to Jesus' baptism), we must first discuss the word *theophany*. It's a fancy word that comes from the Greek word for "God" (*theos*) and the Greek verb "to appear" (*phainein*). Theophany refers to an appearance of God, and the Old Testament is riddled with them.

Throughout the Bible, God has a tradition of appearing to his servants throughout the course of his redemptive plan. For example, one might think of how he revealed himself to mankind in the Garden,[7] or to Noah[8] and his sons.[9] One might consider the smoking fire pot and flaming torch of Genesis 15 when God appeared to Abraham, or later to Abraham and his wife Sarah.[10] God revealed himself in the burning bush to Moses[11] and on Mount Sinai through lightning,[12] earthquakes,[13] fire,[14] smoke,[15] clouds,[16] and trumpets. Joshua later meets one whom he acknowledges as a commander and Lord[17] before entering the Promised Land. Isaiah catches sight of God.[18] David sees God riding on the wind like a cherub,[19] and prophets such as Amos had visions,[20] along with Jeremiah,[21] Ezekiel,[22] Zechariah,[23] and even the false prophet Balaam.[24]

God manifests in angelic form[25] in prophetic visions, and is pictured upon a throne[26] attended by angels and other heavenly beings.[27] All these appearances serve to reveal his glory,[28] to bring about his judgment,[29] to ignite the fear of God in humankind,[30] and to bring about the commissioning[31] and authentication[32] of God's servants.

Despite all these glorious appearances, one thing is missing in all the Old Testament's theophanies. In the Old Testament, all we're given are shadows of real things. God's perfect reality peeks through created things.

When the New covenant emerges, everything changes. Jesus becomes the pivot point by which God communicates. Unlike anyone before, Jesus is perfect. Sinless. Uncreated. Alive. He's not a puppet. He's not a walking zombie. He's fully God and fully man, and as the writer of Hebrews demonstrates, Jesus is better than the angels,[33] flesh and blood,[34] Moses,[35] the symbol of the law, Aaron[36] and the sacrificial[37] system of the priesthood, Abraham[38] and the old covenants,[39] Melchizedek, all kings, and the Sabbath,[40] and the temple.[41] He is the founder, perfecter, originator, and completion to all faith.[42]

Jesus is the ultimate *theophany* and appearance of God.[43] In the words of

Jesus himself, when we see him, we see the Father.[44] Jesus needed to come to earth to reveal God's heavenly nature through our earthly means of apprehending truth. Now that we have Jesus—the ultimate appearance of God—bringing to a close the *theophany* appearances in Middle-Section-A of the Old Testament, what follows in the Middle-B section of Scripture changes everything.

THE BAPTISMAL LINK

At last, we can speak of Jesus' baptism in light of his appearing at the beginning (creation), the Middle-A (theophanies), and the end (the second coming). Jesus' baptism is a theophany that links Middle-A and Middle-B. It's a connective ligament that binds the Trinity's ministry of heaven to the people of earth.

It is at Jesus' baptism in our earliest gospel, Matthew, that the Trinity is first revealed to us in all three persons at once. As the Spirit of God hovers over the waters in the creation event, so Jesus enters Jordan's waters and is met by the Father and Spirit. Their affirmation and power descend on him. Jesus' baptism signifies the beginning of a new kingdom and a new creation event. In fact, in Matthew's gospel, he begins his writing to his Jewish audience with the phrase *bibles geneseos*, which is a form of the word *genesis* or *beginning*. Matthew knows his Jewish audience. Anyone who has studied Matthew knows that the book begins with five discourses from Jesus—mirroring the five books of the Pentateuch (Genesis, Exodus, Leviticus, Numbers, and Deuteronomy)—and proceeds into speaking of Jesus. He structures his book intentionally. He places the Baptism of Jesus where he does to cause the reader to see that this man is not just a man, but he is the new creation. He's the Genesis of all humanity, both for Adam and for you and me.

Matthew tells us that as John the Baptist is baptizing people and readying them for what he calls "The Kingdom," a man appears from the crowd and requests to be baptized. John recognizes Jesus, and says "Behold, the Lamb of God." As John catches his breath upon seeing the Messiah, Jesus readies himself to be immersed in the water of the Jordan. The question must surface in our mind, as it must have in the mind of John the Baptist, "Why in the world would Jesus need to get baptized?" It doesn't make sense. The narrative tells us through Jesus' own lips that it's to "fulfill all righteousness," but that's pretty ambiguous. What righteousness? Is he saying he needs to do it to be righteous? Is he referring to the fact that we need to be made righteous and forgiven of our sins, and therefore he too must identify by doing baptism with us? Is Jesus somehow making himself a servant to sin in baptism?

I do not believe it's any of these options.

As Jesus rises from the watery depths, everyone hears a voice from heaven saying, "This is my Son in whom I'm well pleased." Heaven opens up and the Holy Spirit descends on Jesus like a dove. For the first time, heaven connects to earth—not through the temple or the priesthood, but via the man, Jesus. Until now, no one was able to enter the sacred conversations held within the holy of holies lest they die, but here we see the Trinity colliding with earth. The mystery is appearing. Theophany. Revealing. People hear God speak unhindered.

The communication is clear. Jesus has a Father. Jesus is a Son. The Spirit is the Helper. Jesus has authority from the Father in the power of the Spirit to now bring about the bridge between ages. Whereas in Genesis the unified Spirit of God hovered over the waters and spoke into being a united creation and a human race that very quickly fell into division, here we have a new Genesis creation. A reversal. God gives us a front row seat as we gaze upon his "unified-multiple personhood." The baptism of Jesus is all about a Trinity revealed. A kingdom. A new family. A new creation.

LIFE BEYOND THE JORDAN

Consider also where this Triune-revealing is taking place. The Jordan River. The Jordan is a significant symbol in the life of Israel. After coming out of slavery under Egyptian rule, the people of God wandered in the desert and were brought to the edge of the Promised Land. The one thing that blocked their entrance into all God had promised was the Jordan River. The river is a symbol of the barrier that only a miracle of God can overcome.

If you do a word study on the Jordan River in the Scripture, you'll find that a popular phrase emerges. In Jewish thought, there is a concept of *life beyond the Jordan*. The Jordan is a symbol of living in or outside of the Promised Land. In other words, the Jordan symbolizes crossing from one kingdom into another. To live beyond the Jordan, for the Jew, is to live in the Promised Land. To cross the Jordan is to pass from one land into the next—from the temporal into the eternal. Slavery into freedom. To cross is to "pass over" from a life that feels void of God's presence into a life full of God's presence.

Jesus' baptism is far more robust in symbol than meets the eye. He's saying something profound in being baptized. He speaking to all those on "the wrong side of heaven" that he is the bridge into everyone's deepest hopes and dreams.

To make sense of the Jordan's meaning in the life of Israel, think back to the timeline of the Jewish exile out of Egypt:

- ISRAEL IS CAPTIVE TO THE KINGDOM OF EGYPT—A PLACE OF SLAVERY.
- ISRAEL COMES UP OUT OF EGYPT AND IS SPARED DURING THE TIME OF INFANT SLAUGHTER AND GOD'S JUDGMENT IN THE 10TH PLAGUE.
- ISRAEL FIRST ENCOUNTERS THE RED SEA. GOD PARTS THE WATERS, THE PEOPLE WALK ACROSS, AND THEIR ENEMIES DROWN IN DEFEAT.
- GOD TAKES ISRAEL TO MOUNT SINAI AND GIVES THEM THE LAW— THE TEN COMMANDMENTS.
- THE PEOPLE COMPLAIN AND REBEL, AND BECAUSE OF THIS, GOD SENTENCES ISRAEL TO WANDER IN THE DESERT FOR FORTY YEARS.
- JOSHUA ENCOUNTERS THE JORDAN. AFTER FORTY YEARS, THEY COME TO THE RIVER AND ARE LED THROUGH THE WATERS INTO THE PROMISED LAND BY JOSHUA.
- THE PROMISED LAND REPRESENTS STARTING OVER—*LIFE BEYOND THE JORDAN.*

The Jordan imagery brings to life the idea of "kingdom-transfer" in the timeline of Israel—the nation's transfer from the kingdom of slavery to the kingdom to the kingdom of freedom. It evokes the same transfer in the life of Jesus. Jesus' journey brings him to the Jordan River for baptism, but with Jesus, the progression of events occurs in reverse order.

- JESUS IS CAPTIVE TO THE KINGDOM OF HEAVEN—A PLACE OF FREEDOM.
- JESUS, AS A BABY, COMES UP OUT OF EGYPT AND IS SPARED DURING THE INFANT SLAUGHTER IN BETHLEHEM BROUGHT ABOUT BY THE JUDGMENT OF HEROD.
- JESUS FIRST ENCOUNTERS THE JORDAN RIVER. GOD PARTS THE HEAVENS, JESUS COMES OUT OF THE WATERS AND PREPARES TO

DROWN HIS ENEMIES (SIN, SUFFERING, SATAN, AND DEATH) IN
DEFEAT.

- **GOD, THE SPIRIT, TAKES JESUS TO WANDER** IN THE DESERT FOR
  FORTY DAYS TO FULFILL THE LAW IN PERFECTION.
- **JESUS WINS THE BATTLE IN THE DESERT** THAT ISRAEL LOST. HE
  SUCCEEDS IN SECURING THE PROMISED LAND AND BEGINS HIS
  MINISTRY BY TEACHING AND HEALING. ONE OF HIS FIRST ACTS,
  MUCH LIKE THAT OF MOSES AT SINAI, IS TO ASCEND THE
  MOUNTAINSIDE AND GIVE THE LAW OF THE KINGDOM IN THE
  SERMON ON THE MOUNT (MATT. 5–7).
- **GOD'S PEOPLE ARE NOW CALLED TO BAPTISM.** GOD PARTS THE
  SYMBOLIC WATERS OF THE RED SEA IN SEARCH OF US; OUR ENEMY
  DROWNS IN DEFEAT, AND WE ARE LED BACK TOWARD THE PROMISED
  LAND, NOT BY MOSES, BUT BY JESUS.
- **THE PROMISED LAND** REPRESENTS A STARTING OVER—LIFE
  BEYOND THE JORDAN.
- **AS BELIEVERS, WE LIVE IN LIFE BEYOND THE JORDAN** AND ARE
  COMMISSIONED AS CHRIST'S CHURCH TO DO AS JESUS—TO GO BACK
  INTO A WORLD FULL OF ENEMIES AND SLAVES, MUCH LIKE CROSSING
  BACK OVER THE RED SEA, IN ORDER TO SEE GOD SET CAPTIVES
  FREE THROUGH US.

Jesus' baptism isn't about the *mode*—sprinkle vs. immersion—nor is it
merely about our individual purity or salvation from sin. I think we've missed
the meaning of baptism entirely. Historically, baptism is a transfer of kingdom.
It's being added into a family through an act of war. This is what Paul has in
mind when he talks about the baptism of the Holy Spirit. It's a family transfer.
We are taken out of the darkness and brought into a family of light.

Moses led the Israelites up out of Egyptian slavery and infant slaughter to
Mount Sinai to receive the law of God; then through forty years of rebellious
wandering in the desert to finally bring God's people to cross the Jordan into
the Promised Land (led by Joshua). Jesus provides the perfect reversal. Jesus
comes *from* the Promised Land—heaven—crosses into his *life beyond the
Jordan,* which is our fallen world or desert wandering, and enters his
children's life of poverty and sin. Where we have failed, he succeeds and gives
us his perfect law of the Kingdom. He invites us out of slavery through
baptismal waters into his family once again. We get to start over in life beyond

the Jordan. We now have the Promised Land in Jesus. We are now afforded the same journey of reversal. We join Jesus as ambassadors of the kingdom. We smuggle slaves one by one into their freedom home via the gospel.

This Trinitarian baptism bridges heaven and earth once again. It provides a bridge between enslaved life beyond the Jordan and free life beyond the Jordan.

Since the Garden's Fall, God could only communicate from heaven with us through *dead* shadows in a theophany. He could only share with us his rescue mission from up beyond the stratosphere. Eminence. Once Jesus' baptism took place, God's rescue mission found itself headquartered on earth and empowered by our ascended commander and Lord Jesus, seated on his throne. Immanence. The kingdom is now among us.

The line of sight has changed. The camera angle moved. No longer is the zoom lens aimed at God looking down. Now God has come down to us so that we now can clearly see what's been hidden to us. We're invited to see the brilliance of how the Father, Son, and Holy Spirit act because the heavens have been torn open. We can see what's been hidden behind the veil because Jesus' life reveals it.

FATHER, SON, SPIRIT, AND ISRAEL … SAME GOD, SAME PEOPLE

I think we are beginning to understand why the Old Testament uses Trinitarian language so sparsely. It's purposeful. God waits patiently in the Old Testament to lay out his story.

To be fair, the Old Testament is full of Trinitarian imagery. It would be a mistake not to take notice of that specifically before closing this chapter. We will see that God does reveal himself as Father, Son, and Holy Spirit in the Old Testament, but only when there's a specific purpose.

Let's begin with the idea of God being a Father. The Old Testament only uses this term for God in reference to Israel[45] and individuals[46] fifteen times, as opposed to the distinctive covenant name of God, YHWH, which is used nearly 7,000 times. At times, father imagery is present though the term itself is not used.[47] One might explain the absence of Father language by the fact that it was frequently used amongst sexual fertility religions in the Near East, or by a myriad of other reasons. But I think its avoidance has a more intentional purpose.

Let's look at the phenomenon through the lens of Jesus' baptism. Consider how all the Fatherly language in the Old Testament relates to the nation Israel. They are personified as a "son." God's use of the title "Father" in the Old Testament refers to the covenantal relationship of Yahweh to Israel,[48] and Jesus is the fulfillment and ultimate revealing of that covenant. It makes sense that God uses the word 'Father' sparingly in the Old Testament if he knows all along that his ultimate plan is still to come in Jesus. Not only did Jesus live out, mirror, complete, perfect, and reverse the path of Israel (becoming the New Israel), he brought about the new kingdom.

In 2 Samuel 7:14 we find a curious use of the title, Father. It occurs when God is making a covenant with King David. The context is kingdom. God is making a promise to Israel's king, and yet the language suggests a replacement that is to come. I do not mean that Israel is going to get replaced by a new people—the church—but rather, Israel is going to be replaced by a new "kingdom son"—Jesus. The promise to David makes the flogged and suffering son a *greater-than* bearer of our sins and a replacement to the people of Israel. Jesus, as the new nation, brings with him something that Israel could never bring. Forever. Eternity. A kingdom beyond time and space.

Here's what God says in 2 Samuel about these people of God that come from him, the true Israel:

> I will be to him a father, and he shall be to me a son. When he commits iniquity, I will discipline him with the rod of men, with the stripes of the sons of men, but my steadfast love will not depart from him, as I took it from Saul, whom I put away from before you. (2 Samuel 7:14)

God promises David a kingdom despite the fact that David himself and all people after him commit iniquity. Jesus comes to bear up a lineage that is seeped in sin in order to grant a kingdom that is perfect and will never end. He promises David a kingdom legacy that will stand even in heaven. There's only one kind of kingdom that can cause our Father to cry out "Son!" It's nothing that you and I would or even could build. It's a kingdom not made by us. It's the man Jesus.

The Father imagery is given explicitly to David as the kingdom's king to describe to us the nature of the coming kingdom. It is a kingdom family. It's a kingdom of sons and daughters. We are knee deep in brother and sister language. No one is better at bringing together kingdom and family language than Jesus, our brother-Savior.

The promised Son is cloaked in a greater promise of One who will rule in unending peace, security, and justice. Isaiah promises that this forever-King will sit on David's throne.[49] Not only this, but this King, like David, will be from Bethlehem and have a superhuman origin.[50] This Son of Man[51] brings with him everlasting and ever-growing dominion.

The dominion of Jesus is present, powerful, and was promised from the beginning in Genesis 3:15 when God cursed the serpent: "I will put enmity between you and the woman, and between your offspring and her offspring; he shall bruise your head, and you shall bruise his heel."[52] Though this promise is fulfilled by Jesus—one born of a woman and one dealing the mortal blow to the devil—we must see how the promise connects Middle-A, Middle-B, and the ending. The whole story together reveals the same God. He is God of a kingdom, and he comes from a family. The story of this kingdom home unfolds like any good book. The characters are revealed slowly by intention, but they have always been fully known by the author before the book was ever penned.

What about the Holy Spirit in the unfolding?

B. B. Warfield believes the work of the Spirit connects the cosmos, the kingdom of God, and the individual, concluding that he is at work in the Old Testament in all the ways that he works in the New Testament.[53] Whereas the Spirit in the New Testament is spoken of as the messenger and the power that enables God's works to flourish, we see in the Old Testament that over 400 times Yahweh acted through the Spirit. As in the New Testament, the Spirit guides, instructs, and is grieved. He gives life and breath[54] and makes alive dead bones.[55] He empowers people for kingdom service[56] and is the protector of God's people.[57] He rested on men like Gideon, Samson, Saul, and Joseph, and gave them divine wisdom as they loved God's people in the like manner that he rested on and empowered the Messiah.[58]

From the beginning, the Spirit has assisted the Father in his work and will,[59] including his creation of the world[60] and the redemption of sinners.[61] He will continue to do so all the way up to the ultimate consummation at the end of the world.[62] In the same way that the Spirit breathes[63] in the men and women of old—*theopneusto,* he breathes in us. We're told in 2 Peter 1:20-21 that prophets of the Old Testament "speak from God as they were carried along by the Holy Spirit," and the same is true today with one exception. John 14:12 captures Jesus saying this about New Testament believers: "Whoever believes in me will also do the works that I do; and greater works than these will he do because I am going to the Father."

To reiterate, in the Old Testament the Spirit rested *on* people not *in* people. Through Christ's work today, we not only have the promise of the Spirit's power, but even greater, we have the promise of the Spirit's salvation. God now lives inside of us. We are one in the same manner he and the Father are one. Though we're not God, we are his temple. We are the connection point between heaven and earth.

Today the Spirit's work and words continue to speak one message through us as messengers. The Spirit exists to glorify Jesus.[64] He is still telling the world about the Messiah and he is still doing it through us, his people. No longer do we proclaim the Messiah to come. We proclaim the same Messiah who is now here and who is coming again.

His voice and power center around the work of Jesus done upon the cross. To make central anything else but the life, death, resurrection, and ascension of Jesus is to become a false teacher, heretic, an apostate,[65] and thus ignore the legacy we have in the Trinity.

We must draw one conclusion from our look at the trinitarian nature of our God. Though to some, God appears to be bipolar and have multi-personalities, to believe that the Trinity resembless a psych-ward patient is absolutely preposterous. God's consistent appearances in both Old and New Testament, linked together by the Kingdom-Son, Jesus, speak only of one person and one kingdom in utter diverse harmony.

9

TRINITARIAN HISTORY

How has the Triniatarian tradition of the Old and New Testaments carried through into church history?

The human timeline shows that the idea of the Trinity has been accompanied by much debate and bloodshed. Today we may enjoy how simple it is to discuss the topic, but we must remember that the freedom to do so was not always available. We must also remember the glorious family-members in God's kingdom who have risked life and limb to preserve the vital truth of his nature.

DEFINING AND DEBATING THE TRINITY

Though it is clear that the concept of a triune God has never been new to the Bible, the word "trinity" never appears in Scripture. Tertullian, a Latin theologian who wrote in the early third century, is credited as being the first to use the term. Tertullian lived and worked in North Africa between AD 160 and 220. Tertullian was a lawyer by profession, but he also had some learning in medicine and literature and probably some knowledge of military affairs. He emphasized the oneness of God, and he asserted the distinction between the Father and Son. He also worked out the terminology that the church needed in order to express its beliefs clearly. He coined the word trinity, or tri-unity, meaning three-in-one. Unfortunately, many even in Tertullian's time were confused about what he was trying to say about God. Tertullian writes:

> I testify that Father and Son and Spirit are unseparated from one another. ... Understand then, I say that the Father is one, the Son another, and the Spirit another—every untrained or perverse person takes this saying wrongly as if it expressed difference, and as the result of difference meant a separation of Father, Son, and Holy Spirit.[1]

Ever since coining the title, and I would suggest even before, the debate about God's nature has centered around three ideas: Christ as deity, the personhood of the God, and the substance of God. To make our examination of these big ideas easy, I've included below the four major councils in which the Trinity was discussed. I've also listed the predominant heresies that were prevalent surrounding the Trinity during each time period so that you can understand why each council felt the need to meet. I've also attempted to list what I believe to be the main point of each council's agenda:

JESUS WAS FULLY GOD

- **First Council**: Nicea (AD 325)
- **Was Counteracting the Heresy of**: Arianism (the idea that Christ is a supernatural being, but not divine)
- **What Principle Were Biblical Scholars Trying to Defend**: Only God Can Save.
- **Main Point**: Christ Was and is Fully God.

JESUS WAS FULLY HUMAN

- **Second Council**: Constantinople I (AD 381)
- **Was Counteracting the Heresy of**: Apollinarianism (the idea that the Divine Logos merely used a human body to appear to be human—"God in a bod"—but was not human in actuality).
- **What Principle Were Biblical Scholars Trying to Defend**: Only that Which is Assumed Can be Healed.
- **Main Point**: Christ Was and is Fully Human.

JESUS WAS ONE PERSON

- **Third Council**: Ephesus (AD 431)
- **Was Counteracting the Heresy of**: Nestorianism (the idea that Christ was bi-polar—that his human and divine natures were not united or integrated)
- **What Principle Were Biblical Scholars Trying to Defend**: There's No Division, and No Separation.
- **Main Point**: The divine and the human natures are so united in Christ that he is one fully integrated Person — the goal for us is, likewise, integration of personality (shalom).

JESUS POSSESSED TWO NATURES

- **Fourth Council**: Chalcedon (AD 451)
- **Was Counteracting the Heresy of**: Eutychianism (the idea that Christ's divine nature eclipses the human nature — the human nature withers in the presence of the divine).
- **What Principle Were Biblical Scholars Trying to Defend**: There's No Confusion, and No Change.
- **Main Point**: Christ's divinity joins his humanity without destroying it — the goal for us isn't the loss of our humanity, but its restoration.

Nicea's Council first met to address the wrongful teaching of Arianism. During Constantine's rule, Rome was becoming Christian, but as everyone was debating theology, they were settling on the view of Arius, a popular pastor in the day. Arius taught that there was no unity between the Father and Son. He believed Jesus to be a created being and not eternal at all. Arians claimed that Jesus was inferior to and of lower rank than the Father. He was a middle creature, neither God nor man.[2] Though Arius was eventually declared a heretic, people still believed him.

Wrong thinking about God was multiplying. Even before the Council of Nicea met, in and around the same time as Tertullian, men like Origen argued for subordination in the Trinity. Only later did men like Athanasius teach differently. If we couple Arianism together with the heresy still lingering from around 100 years prior in Sabellianism (as called in the East), and Patripassianism (as called in the West), the problem compounds. Sabellianist's suggested that claiming Jesus as God is to attack the Father. They objected to the fact that the Son could in some way be equal with God the Father because that would mean that the Father suffers, and did so on the cross.

The increasing debate over the Trinity disrupted Constantine's ability to rule using Christianity as a unifying force, and so he called the Council of Nicea in AD 325 to discuss the debate raging between Arius, Athanasius, and Alexander. The core underlying issue to the Nicea Council had to do with the nature of salvation. Can Jesus save? The only way God can perfectly save us is if he brings the full weight of heaven together with the full weight of the earth. If Jesus was not fully man and fully God, the whole Christian message is useless.

Christianity was being threatened. The assault aimed to neuter Jesus. Even Cyril of Alexandria later said that if Christ was not fully human it would "bankrupt" salvation.[3] Athanasius said salvation would be incomplete.[4] For Jesus to save us, it is essential that he become what we are in order to obtain the riches and deliverance that he desires to give us. Just as in Moses' day God united with the bush without consuming it, God can inhabit humanity and not consume us.

Embracing the God-man is essential to show that God doesn't leave us alone in our struggles but is also fully able to transcend them. He himself passed through all the things we experience and shared in them with us. He surpassingly conquered everything, training and teaching us not to be anxious about any of our trials. The Council of Nicea fought for the saving nature of the God-man in Christ.

If Jesus is not fully God, and somehow subordinate to the Father, then Paul was wrong in Colossians 1:15-20 in his reference to Christ as equal to the Creator, *Elohim*:

He is the image of the invisible God, the firstborn of all creation. For by him all things were created, in heaven and on earth, visible and invisible, whether thrones or dominions or rulers or authorities—all things were created through him and for him. And he is before all things, and in him all things hold together. And he is the head of the body, the church. He is the beginning, the firstborn from the dead, that in everything he might be preeminent. For in him all the fullness of God was pleased to dwell, and through him to reconcile to himself all things, whether on earth or in heaven, making peace by the blood of his cross.

Nevertheless, despite the council's attempts, people continued to discuss Jesus in a way that separated him from the Father. Many were still asking, "Is there anything that the Father does that the Son does not do?" Augustine's answer was No.[5] Calvin later replied that deity could not be subordinate, neither could it owe its existence to someone else. Christ, if he were God, could not owe his being to any superior divinity. He must be God "from his very self." In terms of his eternal nature, status, and independence, he must be fully the Father's equal.[6]

Despite many best efforts, the belief that Christ is lesser than the Father continued to spread and led to greater and greater heresy. Thinkers of that day began to explore the idea of *modalism*, which is the belief that the Father, Son, and Holy Spirit are successive modes of active and revelation of the One God. Again, this clearly goes against the concept of *logos* which explains that the Godhead consists of simultaneous distinctions[7] and is not "one or the other" at various times. Gregory uses the word *motion* to help us understand how the working of God and the being of God are altogether unified. The idea of motion manages to convey, at least partially, the eternal movement of love between Father, Son, and Holy Spirit. He says;

> The Father is the begetter and the emitter; without passion, of course, and without reference to time, and not in a corporeal manner. The Son is the begotten and the Holy Ghost is the emission. The Father begets the Son, but not in a human manner and not in time. The Son is begotten, but has always been begotten. And the Spirit is emitted and always has been emitted. Thus we have an eternal movement of love grounded in the essence of God Himself.[8]

Modalistic thought removes the possibility of love because it prioritizes the individual far too much. It's a humanistic approach that fueled many cults in their formation and built up load-bearing walls upon which countless false religions built their structures. Modalistic thinking is what led Joseph Smith and the Mormons to declare Jesus a "distinct personage"—meaning that each person is separate and that the Godhead is polytheistic and made up of three gods.[9] It led Mohammad to create separation in Jesus' birth: "the father, the virgin, and their child."[10] To this day Muslims do not believe that Jesus claimed deity. The Qur'an is unrelenting in its antagonism toward the Trinity.[11]

The same fundamental issues drive Gnosticism. Gnostics believed that not only is separation inherent in the nature of God; it is also inherent in the nature of humans. Therefore, Godhood cannot merge with humanity in Jesus because the spiritual can't dwell with matter. They believed the body to be of no enduring value, which led them to openly mistreat their bodies in rampant perversion, sexual immorality, and abuse. Similarly, Docetism, which stems from the word *dokeo*, "to seem," said that Jesus seemed to have a human body, but was in reality Spirit. And Eutychianism suggested that Jesus was a blend of God and man like cherry syrup poured into a cherry Coke, which led ultimately to the next debate of Constantinople 1 (AD 381).

Constantinople 1 likely emerged in the midst of all the compounding chaos of the past 200 years. As you can see, the ideas spinning around makes one dizzy. Around the time of the convening of the council, a specific collision of all the ideas was looming in what is known as Apollinarianism. It was spreading, and people were teaching that Jesus had a human body and a "sensitive soul," but his spirit was God. In other words, he was one-third human and two-thirds divine. Crassly put, he was a "God in a bod."

Similar issues remained in play regarding Christ's divinity, God's personhood, and the substance of the Trinity. People were just not able to accept Jesus' divinity, nor were they able to articulate the oneness and threeness of God.

Nestorianism provided the exclamation mark to it all. This doctrine surfaced around fifty to sixty years later. It put the cherry on top of the long-running heresies and led to conclusions by men such as Cyril of Alexandria that could be summed up like this in today's terms: "Let's just call it what it is, Jesus is schizophrenic, bi-polar, and belongs in a psych ward." Positively, Nestorianism summed up the stupidity of the debate by pointing out that people were trying to mix heathenism with Christianity.[12] Negatively, Nestorianism played into the long string of false debates and failed to offer any solutions.

UNIFIED SUBSTANCE AND ONE PERSON

The good news is that amidst all the swirling falsehood, a joyous conclusion to the matter exists. Good Christian thinkers fought relentlessly during the first 400 years of the church to preserve crucial truths about God, arriving at helpful solutions that are still impacting us today.

Around the time these issues were peaking—all of which ultimately led to the Council of Ephesus and Chalcedon—a man by the name of Apollinaris of Laodicea first uttered the word *hypostasis* in trying to understand how our fully God deity could have become fully man. It turns out that this one, simple word mines from Scripture what had been there all along.

At the Council of Chalcedon, the word paid reference to the fact that in Christ there are two natures, each retaining its own properties, and together united in one person and in one single subsistence (εἰς ἓν πρόσωπον καὶ μίαν ὑπόστασιν, eis hèn prósōpon kaì mían hypóstasin).[13] This means that God's being matches with God's personhood. It preserves the one person of Jesus amongst the three (*hypostasis*), but also maintains the one essence of God (*ousia*). God is a me and a we.

The beginning of these ideas was present as early as the Nicene Creed, but now they were becoming more concrete. Whereas the Nicene Creed first used the word *homoousios* to define Christ as being "of the same substance" as God and alludes to the fact that Jesus was begotten not made, the Hypostatic Union (hypostasis) defined God as being also one in full with humanity. The conclusion that Jesus is fully man and fully God would undoubtedly bring pleasure to men like Cyril of Alexandria who simply says, "Doesn't Immanuel mean 'God with us?'"

Hypostasis also suggests something of what we are to be as a community of believers. We are like the Trinity. We cannot "exist without communion," nor can we thrive in any form of "communion that denies or suppresses us as a person."[14] Neither hierarchy nor anarchy work in community. We are *ecstasis* (free in the community of togetherness) and *hypostasis* (uniquely individuals). We can't live without one another, nor can we live under one another. The Trinity dwells together alongside one another in mutual submission and in a perfectly loving dance. So should we.

CONCLUDING THOUGHTS

For most people, and sadly, for most Christians also, the Trinity is the great unknown. He's viewed as a riddle wrapped up inside a puzzle and buried in an enigma. Even if the Trinity could be understood, of what practical value—even what spiritual value—would it have for ordinary people?"[15]

Many in our history have found it comfortable merely to say, "We'll never know."

But clarity is available. We don't have to answer the above questions in the same manner as Kant and Jefferson. They saw the Trinity as inconsequential.[16] Such faulty logic is much too simplistic. The Trinity is of great consequence, and the image of our God impacts everything we know, do, think, taste, smell, feel, see, hear, and touch in this life and the next. The Trinity is the greatest topic of discussion. Perhaps the Trinity is the only person worth discussing.

Instead of remaining confused or indifferent, let's honestly assess what this Trinity has to do with us. What can the Trinity teach us about community? What can God's very nature teach us about how we are to do things in our home, churches, work, play, and beyond? What does this saving God have to do with the absolutely broken world in which we live?

John believes there are satisfying answers. In 1 John 5:7-8 he considers the proof of the Trinity as it relates to our personal testimony and story:

> For there are three that testify: the Spirit, the water and the blood; *and the three are in agreement. We accept man's testimony, but God's testimony is greater* because it is the testimony of God, which he has given about his Son. Anyone who believes in the Son of God has this testimony in his heart. Anyone who does not believe God has made him out to be a liar because he has not believed the testimony God has given about his Son. And this is the testimony: God has given us eternal life, and this life is in his Son. He who has the Son has life; he who does not have the Son of God does not have life. (italics mine)

We must flesh out abstract concepts and make them concrete by utilizing the acronym C.R.O.S.S. We will examine the five ways in which the Trinity is united in an attempt to give an all-encompassing and relatable form to worship. In examining the Trinity in Scripture and C.R.O.S.S., we will more fully understand what is already present in the family and the community; the being and the doing; the cosmic and the personal; the prescribed and the described; the inward and the outward; the hierarchy and the submission; the completed alongside of obedience; the joy because of suffering; the believed truths and the enacted truths; the theological and the biographical, and the doxological and the missional.

For too long our categories for worship have remained far too skinny because we've neutered our Triune God into something he isn't. We've defined worship from one angle at the expense of the other. Not so anymore. An apt definition of worship should address all aspects of life. Real Life. Kingdom life. The Trinity does just that.

BIBLICAL WORSHIP

Worship is: to understand the Triune nature of the Godhead as seen in covenantal history, and to understand the Father's mission and action upon the earth so as to respond both individually and corporately to his being and willing through imaging Jesus' nature in character, and by accomplishing the Holy Spirit's work in carrying out the Great Commission.

The first letter in our C.R.O.S.S. acronym is C. It stands for community. In Genesis 1:26 God says, "Let us create man in our image." The Godhead is a we. They are joined in community, family, friendship, and in how they relate. For a human image-bearer of God to rightly project his nature, God deemed it not good for man to be alone. One must start his or her journey into worship with community. Not solely with idea of "hanging out," but with an understanding of God as a unified we. The *Shema* says, "I the Lord God am One."

Since the day Adam and Eve decided that the Triune community was found wanting, all humanity has struggled to commune with and like the God that created them. Seeing our wound, God unsheathed his scalpel like a skilled surgeon. He covenanted to heal the division.

Throughout Old Testament history, God brought about covenant plans of restoration with his people as illustrated in the Adamic,[1] Noahic,[2] Abrahamic,[3] Mosaic,[4] and Davidic covenants[5]—ultimately culminating in the once-and-for-all sacrifice of Jesus upon the cross. In giving the covenants, the Lord delivered instructions for worship. He made a way that all being and action could be directed toward him.[6] His promises reinitiate relationship and family with his rebellious creation.

His covenants are acts of divine love worthy of adoration. Worship revels in and exalts the greatness of our covenant Lord.[7] His covenant is not only great in that he reaches beyond our human depravity to continue to extend the riches of his perfection and promises to us, but he also calls us to this same type of covenant-community toward each other.

One of the Hebrew words for worship, 'abad, speaks of our service and slavery in loving each other and obeying God. Edification of God's body is an essential ingredient to Christian life and worship.[8] We must prioritize how to build each other up in the corporate pursuit of God. Ephesians 4:12-13 calls us "to equip his people for works of service, so that the body of Christ may be built up until we all reach unity in the faith and in the knowledge of the Son of God and become mature, attaining to the whole measure of the fullness of Christ." In other words, Paul in Ephesians is telling us that Gathered Worship is more than just music.

Mentioning music at this point is crucial because Paul associates music with community-building. Though the Bible does not syncretize music and worship as being one and the same, Colossians 3:16 links this idea of rich community and discipleship with that of song. One of the core purposes of music is to teach. Song is not meant to be merely a vehicle to express and process our own emotions, as it has become today, though it does include that. When we sing, our whole selves get involved, and the lyrics must teach us about the Trinity so we know the target at which to aim our whole selves.

Ironically, as one of my dear friends did an exhaustive word study of the top songs of this generation, as compared to the Psalms and Hymns of old, he found one glaring difference between them. In the songs of today, we have all but lost a Trinitarian language. The "we and us" language that is so predominant in the songs of our ancient past have turned to "I and me."

We've lost the ability to think about the *other* in our singing. It's exposed in the lyrics we write. The church is anemic and dying on the altar of the majority of our modern-day songwriting. Singing has become less about edifying our neighbor and meditating on our life together in God, and more about meditating on self. I call it "song psychology." We must learn to think like God in song all over again. We must feel like him in song. Via song, we must be driven to act like him, see like him, hear like him, etc.

Paul calls believers to sing to God and to each other in psalms, hymns, and spiritual songs. These three songs of biblical history, human history, and personal history establish a sound and deep theology within biography and emotion for us all to enjoy. Our singing is to emerge from God's people in response to God's love in, for, and through us together.

Emerging sound from within the heart of the people is an art that has largely been put to death in local churches today due to the rise of large music production companies. They are based on individualistic models and therefore they eclipse the local voice with mega personalities and popular tunes. The voice of God's people is now formed more by studios and business models than from within community. This travesty is not only true of singing, but also of all creating, producing, and bringing flourishing to our surrounding environments together. The church as an entity has become a consuming beast, not a producing family that images our God's creative synergy.

R.easoning

God is not only united in how he relates, but also in how he does things. Dictated by covenant and driven by what most upholds God's own glory and the satisfaction of his people, God set precedents in the beginning for how we are to proceed in carrying out of the Great Commission.

Covenant insists that we take God's purposes seriously. Covenant and kingdom are like two sides of the same coin. They evoke the same reality in slightly different ways. If we are to enter the story, we must look backward and forward. We look backward because the kingdom mission of Jesus is the climactic chapter of Israel's story. Kingdom comes through covenant. We also look forward because the New Testament depicts the early church as it continues the kingdom mission of Jesus.[9] Kingdom preserves covenant.

Through Christ's saving work at Calvary, he gave us the pinnacle example of how true *imago Dei* living should commence. He reasoned that the life of the Christian would be one of sacrifice, suffering, and great joy. Jesus' ministry clearly shows how a life lived in this way takes place in simplicity. He came "eating and drinking!" He gathered in homes around tables and in support of families. He embraced the plight of the human at the most grassroots level.

Jesus' whole ministry is home- and family-shaped. Because of the simplicity of his way of life, we're now a family bound together in unity.

God's reasoning in family is not done in methods; he's a God of *paradigms*. Methods and models are manmade. As grass withers and flowers fall, they fade. Paradigms are timeless. They are God-made. Paradigms are stationary and unchanging pieces God sets in place to anchor us to eternal realities. They are like the sun that we forever orbit. God's paradigms are simple. God moves like a satellite around family, meals, marriage, home, and image—particularly in the man Jesus.

To make more sense of how paradigms work as opposed to methods, picture a magnet placed in the middle of everything that's spinning in your life. The magnet is God's main focal points for life: family, meals, marriage, home, Jesus. These actions and institutions are the essence of how he does things. When we begin whirling around in our various schedules, budgets, ambitions, vocations, and vacations, they either cling to the magnet of God's focal points or they fall to the ground and go nowhere.

The magnet analogy helps us assess how paradigms differ from method. We enjoy inventing our own central magnet and determining through models of ministry how family, church, and life should work best, but God doesn't leave that up to us. We may stubbornly want to complicate his simplicity by adding huge corporate church structures to his way of doing things, but our creative inventions will never produce his results.

God works principles and paradigms into his family that transcends time, place, and circumstance. He does so to keep us on course. To meditate on his paradigms rather than devising what we believe to be new and improved methods for ministry will result in greater unity among believers and churches, even amidst our great diversity.

God provides some helpful indicators to evidence whether a community is reasoning like him or not. He says we are called to live in peace with each other; we are called to show kindness, speak truth, and not devise evil in our heart toward one another. These pieces of evidence reveal God's nature amidst his people. We are called with a pure heart to encourage each other, bear each other's burdens, forgive and love one another, hold up a brother who falls, serve each other, and even to share each other's consequences in seeking justice for one another. As one body with many different parts and gifts, we serve and accomplish tasks together. We teach each other. Our living in this way fulfills God's hope that we be like him in the manner of his prayer in John 17—that we may be one.

God's people interact with him and his created world in oneness beyond the words that one sings. Our actions play a reverent and sober role in exemplifying the true call of Christian worship—to project the Creator onto the screen of culture so that all people can understand Christ as applicable and saving to their circumstance. The Hebrew words *yare*, *hawah* or *shahah*, and the Greek words *proskunéo* and *sébomai* collectively display how all our acts of love should be done with sober and reverential fear and humility, and thus be carried out in corporate and holistic life within the family of God.

We must all ask ourselves, to what extent has God already laid down the paradigm and reasoning for worship? To what extent can our own preference and creativity interact with what he's already established? If he makes clear how he does things, then in following his being with more deliberate intent we will find ourselves becoming more greatly unified as a global Body of Christ?

Many guide their way through the adventure of the above questions with what is called the Regulative and Normative Principles.

The Regulative Principle suggests the Scripture prescribes everything that should and should not be involved in the life of worship. The Normative Principle focuses on the Scripture's role in describing the general desires of God in worship while leaving certain aspects of it open-ended for us. The Regulative Principle gives a red light to everything not in Scripture, and the Normative Principle gives a green light to any and all of our creativity that would not violate or take the place of what God already mandates.

Determining the reasoning behind what we can and can't do is important. If we don't find an intersection between God's mandates and our creativity, nothing will be considered off limits. Such a course is dangerous. We can veer into some unwanted form of relativistic and humanistic worship. We can presume that how to honor God is up to us. It is not!

John Frame in *Worship in Spirit and Truth* helps us to see the grey area. Frame observes that God regulated the sacrificial worship of the tabernacle and the temple in detail, but when it came to the synagogue meetings, he "left the arranging largely up to the discretion of the people."[10] One knows from the New Testament language that the believer's Spirit-filled heart becomes the temple and God's residence. Within the heart, God still holds strict and regulative commands for worship. We are to be slaves not to sin, but to righteousness. However, when it comes to the corporate gathering of the church, God leaves it fairly normative yet governed by constant paradigms and principles of conduct that are timeless.

My apparent rabbit trail concerning how God does things, which led us to a brief look at the Regulative and Normative Principles, is not a divergence at all. The worshipper of the true God must note that worship goes far beyond just gathering together, though it most certainly includes that. In gathering, we assemble together a mere small amount of hours weekly, but the majority of our life is lived in the spaces of home, work, and play. The majority of our lives are lived within the form and function of the world that is constantly attempting to shape and mold us into its image rather than God's image. To battle against the opposing forces as Spirit-filled believers (the temple-filled church), and the Body (the temple-equipped church), our worship training must go far beyond music's walls. We must engage in a discussion about how God does all of life.

God is much more interested that a **regulative heart** of love *in all of life* dictates our actions in all our encountered time and spaces. It leads toward the **normative edification** of all, in all places and situations.

We'll see in forthcoming chapters, that to R.eason like God in our worship, necessities that we become like him in **much** broader categories.

O.rganization

The Trinity is united in how they relate and how they do things, and they also clearly maintain an aspect of how they order life. Their interaction is a dance between authority and submission.

Let's review in brief the unique organization of the Trinity. The Father is the grand architect. He is the wise designer of creation, redemption, and consummation.[11] He plans and implements everything that the Trinity has chosen to do. He determined that Christ would be the focal person of the story[12] and the one who is said to be the *eschaton* (the end) of human history. Jesus comes according to the Father's will.[13] Jesus brought all the plans of the Father to fruition. He is the giver of every gift.[14] He is for us,[15] he draws men to himself,[16] sends the Holy Spirit,[17] answers prayer, accepts worship, and his calling is sovereign.[18] Jesus is even shown as speaking of the temple as his "Father's house,"[19] and at his baptism, the Father declares Jesus as his Son.[20] The Father seals Jesus,[21] and Jesus directs the Samaritan women to worship the Father as God.[22] Jesus asserts the Father as the "sender," the raiser of the dead, and the judge of the world.[23] Jesus prays to him[24] and the Father accepts prayers from Jesus.[25]

IN SOME MANNER, JESUS AFFIRMS THE FATHER AS HIS OWN AUTHORITY WHILE THE FATHER IS ALSO IN SUBMISSION TO THE OTHER MEMBERS OF THE TRINITY.

Hebrews 1:3 declares Jesus as being "the radiance of the glory of God, and the exact imprint of his nature." Hebrews 1:6 implores us to "let all God's angels worship Him," and Luke 4:8 declares Jesus as God and equal to the Father when it says, "You shall worship the Lord your God, and him only shall you serve." Jesus then is the immutable (unchanging) God over all.[26] He sits at the right hand of God,[27] rules in all authority over the nations[28] and is in charge of building a church that is under his command and ownership.[29] He alone can save[30] as he correlates himself with God as the object of faith.[31] He can give life,[32] create,[33] and exercise judgment[34]—even as the judge at the last judgment.[35] He, as Yahweh, can calm raging storms, ride on waves, and command nature.[36] We should pray in his name, as he is our mediatory agent and priest before God the Father.[37]

Matthew 11:25-26 portrays Jesus as claiming mutual sovereignty and knowledge with the Father. This is described as the most important passage for Christology in the New Testament.[38] Though Jesus claims a voluntary ignorance to what the Father knows while in his human and incarnate state,[39] Jesus in his fully God state claims to have sovereign knowledge like the Father over who is saved and who is not. In Philippians 2:5, Paul refers to Christ's pre-incarnate form, saying that he did not regard his status of being "in the form of God" as something to be exploited for his own advantage, but instead "humbled [or emptied] himself." The present participle, "being"—*hyparchon* —denotes continuance. Christ's being in the form of God neither ends nor is shortened by his incarnation (becoming man), but rather continues. This is important because Jesus was fully God and fully man. Jesus mediates between God and man, as he stands as the perfect representation of the human form in heaven.[40] He is directing all things until all his enemies submit,[41] at which time death will be eliminated, and he will hand everything back to the Father.[42] Jesus is worthy of our worship along with the Father[43] and Holy Spirit.

IN SOME MANNER, JESUS IS AFFIRMED AS AN AUTHORITY, BUT ALSO IN SUBMISSION TO THE OTHER CHARACTERS IN THE TRINITY.

The Spirit is a person. He comforts, convicts, and abides.[44] He can be lied to,[45] grieved,[46] quenched,[47] resisted,[48] and he can be blasphemed.[49] He is the Spirit of Holiness,[50] the Spirit of Knowledge,[51] the Spirit of Life,[52] the Spirit of Might,[53] the Eternal Spirit,[54] and the Spirit of Truth.[55] In his power he is sent to indwell the believer, and he can be known in the same way a person can be known.[56] Whenever Christ speaks of the Holy Spirit, he speaks of *him* as a person—a noun.[57] He is the Spirit of Christ, the Spirit of God, the Spirit of Glory, the Spirit of the Lord, the Spirit of the Father, the Spirit of the Son, and the Power of the Highest,[58] and even in his greatness, he, like the Father and the Son, is humble.

The Spirit never draws attention to himself in a loud display, for he is always looking to serve the gospel.[59] He's always looking to empower the work of Jesus.[60] The Spirit works through the word of the gospel of Christ for the salvation of sinners, and not independent of it.[61] He is quenched when the message of salvation is neglected. The gospel of Christ that he fights for is also the gospel to which he conforms us. He never seeks to bring the believer into alignment with his own image, but rather to the image of Christ.[62]

Evidence of the Spirit's personal involvement in an individual's life is reflected in the life and service of Christ. The very nature of the Spirit of God is a servant. We can thus quench the Spirit of God in our life by refusing a life of service.

IN SOME MANNER, THE HOLY SPIRIT IS AFFIRMED AS AN AUTHORITY, BUT ALSO IN SUBMISSION TO THE OTHER CHARACTERS IN THE TRINITY.

One of his most important verses regarding how the Trinity works together in the power of the Holy Spirit is found in 2 Corinthians 3:18: "And we all, with unveiled face, beholding the glory of the Lord, are being transformed into the same image from one degree of glory to another. For this comes from the Lord who is the Spirit." Paul bows before the *Father*, pleading for the *Spirit* to do his work, in order that *Christ* may dwell in our hearts (Eph. 3:14-19).

There is a clear pattern of linear and circular movement, governance, and strategy within the Godhead. Though the Father clearly is the conductor and "first among equals," Jesus provides humanity access to the Father's counsel.

The Spirit submits to Jesus' instructions upon the earth but carries out the Father's will. The Father carries out his own will but clearly submits all things under Jesus' command.

Organization exists in the Trinity. The three are united in worth and yet differ in function. Their nature flows down into God's people. We, like the Trinity, are bound in unity, equality, dignity, and worth, and yet we voluntarily submit to each other and lead each other in different areas. We recognize different levels of function, not worth.

As a result, it is absolutely necessary and unavoidable that our worship be embedded in physical structures. It is impossible for us to avoid theology in how we pattern worship in the church.[63] How we meet together matters! Our structure preaches. The gospel is not only heard in the words sown, it is also *shown* in the visual manner in which God's people connect. More simply stated, the environment can either support or undermine the message.

Not only do worshipping communities merely give ear to the gospel, but also as an act of worship they should seek to model every facet of their life and church after the truths that they hear. The Godhead's organization brings implication on the Headship and submission roles of the man and woman in marriage. It brings implication on the roles of pastors and deacons within the community. It brings implications down into every Trinity-shaped, triperspectival[64] (more on this word to come), prophet, priest, or kingly role that has played out in all of church and cultural human history. It stems into the authority and submission roles of every human being walking the earth. There is clearly a chain of command in hierarchy, equality, and submission that is present in the Trinity, and so should there be in our service and worship.

S.cripture

The members of the Trinity are united in how they relate, how they do things, how they organize, and also in how they believe. They are also united in how they expect us to learn and teach. The Trinity lays out all we need to know in a treatise of their affections known as the Holy Scriptures. These penned documents of fact testify completely to the nature and story of God himself as he works and lives amongst his people. The Scriptures are much more than doctrinal statements to be believed. They instruct the body of Christ on how to function under Triune charge and within Triune closeness. Scripture is the concise way in which God teaches and the precise way in which we are to learn. The Great Commission likewise records Jesus telling us to learn to obey all that is taught and commanded. The Greek words for worship, *latreúo* and *latrefeia*, reinforce such patterns by implying that discipleship is ritual action and form bound up in the rhythm of God's command and our obedience.

The first aim of Scripture is to awaken our senses to the story of God. He awakens our connection to him. He awakens our connection to the characters within his narrative that went before us and are currently walking with us and after us. W. Temple says "To worship is: to quicken the conscience by the holiness of God, to feed the mind with the truth of God, to purge the imagination by the beauty of God, to open the heart to the love of God, to devote the will to the purpose of God."[65]

At the fall, our connection to each other within God's story became individualized and tarnished in beauty. John D. Witvliet puts it, "When worship is concerned only with inward, subjective, individual, and ultimately incommunicable truths, then it is in danger of losing its *raison d'eire* (reason of existence) as a result of the extreme subjectivizing of faith."[66] We lost beauty. We turned inward and became lonely. As a result, many worshipping communities today turn off the lights, personalize the atmosphere, and everyone connects to God like separate atoms floating meaninglessly around a room, never to bump into each other. God has to recalibrate our brains through repentance to once again live by the Spirit as a people, not by the flesh as individuals only. The Scriptures clearly teach us how to transform into his community likeness once again and how to avoid being conformed to the pattern of this world.

The Scripture is the story of a supernatural name, our willing and arrogant forfeit of that name, and God's supernatural journey to help us reclaim our friendship with his fame. God renames us and recreates us, changing us from rebel to disciple; from sinner to saint; from dead in sin to alive in Christ; from a prisoner of darkness to a citizen of heaven. The Scripture clearly teaches us the doctrine and dogma of the kingdom. It re-tunes our minds in repentance, enabling us to think as we ought to think and to perceive God's story, as well as our own. This is worship. In thinking rightly, we live rightly.

S.IGNATURE MISSION

Fortunate for us, in the redemption plan of the Great Commission, the

Triune Godhead beckons us, along with original disciples, to "go into all the world." Christ incarnated himself into creation to reveal to us his sending nature—or being—and in our partnered action and obedience, we rehearse his being in the *misseo Dei*.[67] Joining God's mission enacts the Hebrew word, *darash*—to seek as in a quest. It brings to life the principles in worship words like *nagash* or *qarab*, which mean to draw near to an approachable God, and the Greek words *leitourgéo* and *leitourgia*—meaning liturgy and the performing of this said plan of redemption.

In God seeking and finding us as lost sheep gone astray, we are now brought near to him to join in his quest to seek and find others. We are afforded the pleasure of performing his actions of gospel evangelism and ministry to those in the hurting and broken world around us. Salvation is not an escape from creational life into a "spiritual" existence. It is the restoration of God's rule over all creation and all of human life.[68] Worship must converse with the cosmos, the church, and the culture in order to understand what it truly means to become like Christ—our Triune Savior. We all must participate in the liturgy of God in every realm of human existence—at home, in all work, and in all play—and demonstrate how God's effects on character differentiate the true experience of God from what is false.[69]

Worship is the very soul of the believer, and it infiltrates into the very heart of civilization. If a person truly grasps God's family, reasoning, organization, and precepts, it will only be a matter of time before this understanding transforms lifestyle, relationship, and message. The gospel is not simply the restoration of individuals; it is the rectifying of families, methods, structures, educational aims, governmental structures, media, culture, and the like.

May all creation dance rightly under the authority of God.

PART III
C: HOW GOD RELATES

COMMUNITY

TYPES OF COMMUNITY

I t's fair to say that everyone in the world is searching, grasping, and clawing at relationship just trying to understand and experience the idea of community. Our search is innately in us because we are made in the Trinity's image. Yet no one seems to be finding satisfaction. The world desperately seeks to ground friendship in mutual hobbies, sexuality, efficiency, self-service, vocation, political parties, TV shows, and a hundred other things. Does that mean the church is just another community among many? Aren't we to be the only true example of "many as one"?

To become the Body of Christ is to first ask, "What makes God's community different from any other group of people?" Christian community is distinct in that it's beyond time, and yet it works in any time, in any place, and under any circumstance. Today the church's primary vehicle for cultivating community is a practice that most churches call small groups. That's where we will begin our study.

HOW THE CHURCH TYPICALLY APPROACHES COMMUNITY

Group work has become increasingly important in the church today. The church makes use of many types of groups: church staff, deacons, church councils, leadership groups from organizations, committees, and boards. Small groups (also called cells, home groups, life groups, or other names) are generally organized for lay members, enabling them to relate to each other on a more intimate and personal basis than in the larger congregational assembly.

The book of Proverbs has several verses that emphasize the importance of believers being together in this manner:

- **11:14** – "Where there is no guidance, a people falls, but in an abundance of counselors there is safety."
- **18:17** – "The one who states his case first seems right, until the other comes and examines him."
- **20:18** – "Plans are established by counsel; by wise guidance wage war."
- **28:26** – "Whoever trusts in his own mind is a fool, but he who walks in wisdom will be delivered."

The Bible states that individualism simply doesn't jive. A life of isolation, hiddenness, and performance is a life fraught with sin. Sin makes things confusing. It divides. Where there's confusion in a relationship of any kind, it's because we're bringing our Adam-and-Eve-centric selfishness to the table. The only way to gain wisdom is *with* one another. We must step out from behind the masks and allow our hidden selves into the light if we hope to find any freedom in Christ and the Trinity of Love.

To remedy our shameful and fleshly desire to retreat inward—becoming self-sufficient and detached—the people of God have historically developed ways of being together. In the last 100 years, in particular, new models have emerged and claimed patents on what is "best" for how we are to become our fullest communing selves. We must examine the inventions we've come up with in order to be wise. What kind of models has the church put in place to try and help grow a distinctive community?

Let's dive into a brief birds-eye summary of each model that's prevalent in church communal life today. I will offer a short critique of each approach pertaining to how it fulfills the mission of the gospel. At the end of each tidbit, I will suggest possible paradigm-shifts needed to confront anything that's gone wrong in our approaches. I will attempt to encourage us and not flatter in order that we may make deep the thinking that has recently been made shallow. Much of these summaries, minus the discussion surrounding the gospel, are paraphrased and adapted from a posting made by *Christianity Today*.[1]

Keep the following three things in your mind as you read through:

1. Ask yourself, can this model succeed in any time, in any place, and under any circumstance?
2. Does this model reveal and show the gospel in the truest and fullest sense? If not, what might go wrong if we keep viewing community in this way?
3. Do any of these models give people a way to commune that's any different than the way of the world?

MODEL 1: OPEN SMALL COMMUNITY

DESCRIPTION: Open small communities have space available for visitors and new members. Most of these groups generally remain open all the time, meaning there is no limit to the number of new people who can join.

Advantages to Christian Community

- **Strength 1:** Open communities are outreach-friendly and a proven tool for multiplication.
- **Strength 2:** They help members stay focused on evangelism and encourage regular prayer for unbelievers.
- **Strength 3:** They allow for greater flexibility within a small-groups ministry.

Disadvantages to Christian Community

- **Weakness 1:** Some feel that open groups limit the potential for deeper accountability and trust.
- **Weakness 2:** If not controlled, open groups can grow to a size that damages the community feel of a small-group experience.
- **Weakness 3:** Open groups often do not inspire a high level of commitment.

GOSPEL-CENTERED RAMIFICATIONS:

In thinking through open groups, consider the nature of the gospel in Jesus' illustration of the Great Banquet in Luke 14:12-24. Jesus says:

"When you give a dinner or a banquet, do not invite your friends or your brothers or your relatives or rich neighbors, lest they also invite you in return and you be repaid. But when you give a feast, invite the poor, the crippled, the lame, the blind, and you will be blessed, because they cannot repay you. For you will be repaid at the resurrection of the just."

When one of those who reclined at table with him heard these things, he said to him, "Blessed is everyone who will eat bread in the kingdom of God!"

But he said to him, "A man once gave a great banquet and invited many. And at the time for the banquet he sent his servant to say to those who had been invited, 'Come, for everything is now ready.' But they all alike began to make excuses.

"The first said to him, 'I have bought a field, and I must go out and see it. Please have me excused.'

"And another said, 'I have bought five yoke of oxen, and I go to examine them. Please have me excused.'

"And another said, 'I have married a wife, and therefore I cannot come.'

"So the servant came and reported these things to his master. Then the master of the house became angry and said to his servant, 'Go out quickly to the streets and lanes of the city, and bring in the poor and crippled and blind and lame.'

"And the servant said, 'Sir, what you commanded has been done, and still there is room.'

"And the master said to the servant, 'Go out to the highways and hedges and compel people to come in, that my house may be filled. For I tell you, none of those men who were invited shall taste my banquet.'"

Jesus invites everyone to join in his life; however not just anyone can stay.

Jesus is certainly the most inclusive being in that he freely extends his grace through the gospel to all people. This is a claim unique only to Jesus. But the only prerequisite for the *all* is that anyone desiring to participate in his kingdom must repent of sin and believe. This is why 1 Timothy 4:10 says that God is the "Savior of *all* men ..." but it is then followed by the words, "... *especially* of those that believe" (italics mine). Apparently, there is a limited and unlimited nature to Jesus' grace. He's merciful enough to feed, clothe, and sustain the whole cosmos in a banquet that provides for all plants, man, and beast—even those that mock and spit at him—and yet he saves eternally only those who believe.

Open groups tend to negatively enforce values opposite to the gospel. They extend an invitation but neglect the hand of commitment. Negative implications hide beneath such invites. Human systems form groups around what feels welcoming. Open groups are naturally bent to serve those in their own defined proximity—namely family, friends, and those nearby. They lean toward attracting a uniform demographic. Everyone ends up being relatively the same, overlooking the wide variety of types in Jesus invitation list. Jesus opens his group to those we would consider the most offensive and distant.

Secondly, Jesus is a covenant-making and covenant-keeping God. Any attempt at community must strive to model his character and commitment. Open groups tend to exalt the loving and gracious aspects of Christ's invitation to come but struggle in producing a real commitment to the cause of Jesus in the call of repentance that requests our willingness to go and die for this King. The laissez-faire approach to the seriousness of the cross and Christ's mission is negligent in creating loyalty. Open groups tend to fail in an effort to establish a Christianity all about service and generosity.

A consumer mentality forms. Long-term transformation fails to take root because responsibility beyond just coming to the group is not a given.

We must ask ourselves, is our idea of openness representing the embrace and serving generosity of our Triune God?

MODEL 2: CLOSED SMALL COMMUNITY

DESCRIPTION: Closed small communities limit the number of participants in order to focus on building trust, intimacy, and accountability between group members. Once a group starts, new members and visitors are generally discouraged from attending meetings. Closed groups usually convene for a specific period of time before opening back up to welcome new members.

Advantages to the Christian Community

- **Strength 1:** The members of a closed small group generally have a high expectation for discipleship and spiritual growth.
- **Strength 2:** Closed groups provide an opportunity for deeper levels of trust and accountability.

- **Strength 3:** Closed groups require a high level of commitment from their members.

Disadvantages to the Christian Community

- **Weakness 1:** Closed groups can hinder the practice of relational evangelism, as seeking friends and family are prohibited from joining.
- **Weakness 2:** Some believe that closed groups have a tendency to become inwardly focused, which can eventually lead to cliques, gossip, bitterness, etc.

GOSPEL-CENTERED RAMIFICATIONS:

There is nothing wrong with holding a closed group for a short period of time. This can be beneficial. Even the Trinity reserves private confidences within themselves that they do not divulge in full with us. However, the oneness love of the Trinity is anything but closed. Love is always spinning inward on itself between Father, Son, and Spirit. It simultaneously speeds up as it is hurled outward toward as many as possible.

True biblical discipleship and Christlike character develop within environments of both meditating *and* mission. Closed groups tend to focus on meditating on God's Word and talking over pertinent issues apart from any outside influence. Prolonged and isolated study vanquishes joy, as does exhaustive outward sacrifice with no refill. As disciples, we don't simply learn by sitting or by only moving. We become like Jesus most when we encounter an enemy outside our ranks with the strength that comes from holding hands in the bunker.

Consider the fruit of the Spirit list in Galatians in pondering the true nature of discipleship. To be like our Triune God, we must bear the fruit of love, joy, peace, patience, goodness, kindness, gentleness, faithfulness, and self-control. None of these attributes can plummet to such complete depths as when we are called into empty canyons of adversity surrounded with enemies. True love is shown when an enemy is the recipient of it. Fullest Joy is only experienced when facing sound defeat. Patience is only truly tested in the tension of waiting. Goodness shines only in the midst of the darkest evil. Kindness is made complete when one chooses not to retaliate when spit on and bullied. The purest depths of gentleness shine in the face of Jesus on the cross, "who when reviled, he did not revile in return; when he suffered, he did not threaten, but continued entrusting himself to him who judges justly" (1 Pt. 2:23). Faithfulness is measured when one keeps plodding along the journey, even through the desert while resting in self-controlled trust that God.

We must ask ourselves, "Is there any way in which being *closed* to the outside world can help us to take on the fullness of a fruitful Triune Christlikeness?"

MODEL 3: CELL COMMUNITY

DESCRIPTION: The cell group model views the small community as the basic unit of a whole, much like an organic cell is the basic unit of a human body. Thus, small communities are not treated as one program among many, but are necessary to the survival of the whole. Four key items make up the DNA of a cell group: worship, edification, relational evangelism, and discipleship. And if operating properly, each cell group will grow and multiply on its own, transferring this DNA from group to group.

Advantages to the Christian Community

- **Strength 1:** Cell groups are intentional about creating full-bodied disciples of Christ.
- **Strength 2:** Cell groups are a practical and effective way to build a culture of discipleship within a local church.
- **Strength 3:** Cell groups focus on relational evangelism and are a proven way to grow the kingdom of God.

Disadvantages to the Christian Community

- **Weakness 1:** Elevating the importance of small groups beyond other ministries sometimes causes cell groups to withdraw from the rest of the church and become isolated.
- **Weakness 2:** The cell structure lacks flexibility and can be rigid within an overall small-groups ministry.

- **Weakness 3:** The emphasis on evangelism and numerical growth can potentially limit the level of trust and intimacy within a group.

GOSPEL-CENTERED RAMIFICATIONS:

Cell structures reveal a particularly negative theology regarding "doing church." The cells themselves are not viewed as churches, as would be more typical to the early Church's view of the home life of God's people. Cells become as satellites—orbitting the church proper, rather then becoming the sources of life themselves.

In church life today everything orbits the one-hour a week services and all things centrally located in the church building. Every cell becomes an add-on program utilized to sustain, build, or nourish the church-central. It's like a satellite. A space satellite's sole purpose is to orbit the earth and serve it as the main hub. In church life, the cells become the satellites orbiting the congregation as a whole.

The church of the New Testament seems to be very different. Not merely different, but completely reversed from this model. Households of Christians were considered full-blown churches. They were the sources. Central. Any central hubs and larger gatherings that grew up and formed only did so in a manner to resource these households. The central hubs were the satellites. These household churches were places that originated the multiplying and spinning of Christ's life out into the surrounding community.

The discipleship centers, "earths," or what we might call Sunday Church today, were considered outgrowths of the cells. Not the other way around. The cells didn't orbit, they were orbited. Homes were churches (small) within the church (central). All elements of growth in worship, community, mission, and oversight flourished. They developed their own voice, their own ethic, and cultivated their own personality, trade, artistic expression, vocational target, and uniqueness within the community. Thus, when the greater outcroppings all connected to gather as one, the gathering became an expression of the curated lives within the smaller homes. The larger gathering never attempted to take on a life of its own, which it absolutely has today.

Today, the central hub of church takes on such a dominant life of its own that everyone is then expected to come and consume the entities' vision and meld in their own giftings to that construct in order to keep building it. In essence, the church equips the body to build a consuming entity rather than to become a producing family.

We must ask ourselves, "Is there something detrimental to our presentation of the likeness of Christ when we view cells as being secondary to the church-central?"

MODEL 4: FREE MARKET COMMUNITY

DESCRIPTION: Communities form around specific interests, topics, or affinities. The goal is to transform an interest group into a spiritual community through relationships and spiritual practices. Groups may be large or small, and topics are developed by the leader. A key assumption behind this model is that people don't want to be told what to do. They want choices.

Advantages to the Christian Community

- **Strength 1:** Starting a group is easy, and groups are ideally formatted for fellowship and relational development.
- **Strength 2:** The groups are effective for evangelism because they are organized around hobbies or common interests.
- **Strength 3:** Leaders form the vision for their groups based on their own individual passions and skills, rather than adapting to the church's vision.

Disadvantages to the Christian Community

- **Weakness 1:** A broad definition of small groups can over-inflate the number of people actually participating in meaningful discipleship.
- **Weakness 2:** Groups may not be focused on spiritual formation and growth.
- **Weakness 3:** Groups are often transitory, which can be a detriment to any genuine intimacy and connection between members.

GOSPEL-CENTERED RAMIFICATIONS:

It can be a difficult balance, living in an entertainment and consumer-based society while trying to become like Christ. On one hand, we need to reach people through the various means to which they are accustomed. On the other hand, the means through which most people are accustomed to relating to each other counteracts and distracts from the simplicity of the gospel. So which is it? Do we meet people where they are, and through the use of free-market groups prioritize the wants of people? Or, do we ignore these various aspects altogether?

The answer is both/and. We choose the cross. The cross of Christ is where Jesus met every need, split every idol, and defeated every darkness. It is on the cross that he identified and fulfilled every human's deepest longing for fellowship and belonging. True fellowship is formed between people who make the humble cross and resurrection of Jesus their center. Entertainment models and consumer-based programming reinforce the already looming sense of entitlement that people carry.

Centering around the personhood of Jesus brings us into a truer fellowship with each other because it reveals us far more deeply. Comparing what we do to what Jesus has done levels the playing field. It exposes the lie of our own false hopes placed in what we can accomplish. It exposes the temporal nature of hobbies and all other aspiration of vocation by placing them against the backdrop of heaven. The Kingdom unveils how trivial and flimsy our pursuits for escape and comfort really are. Kingdom perspective places hobbies in their proper place as benefits to us. When we remove them from an exalted place, we find ourselves enjoying them more by no longer finding identity in them. Our real roots anchor to the life found in God. It's a more secure and unifying bedrock from which to gather our water source.

Hobbies and interests are not bad things, but they are not the main thing. Jesus is. Who we are—our identity—and who we actually need to become is resolved far deeper in Trinitarian thinking than in hobbies. Free market interests do not define us, but we have let them do it.

Model 5: Neighborhood Community

Description: This model is centered on the belief that community happens more deeply and naturally when people do life together on a regular basis. Thus, small groups are assembled based on geography, with people of different ages and social affinities forming groups within their neighborhoods. A church's coaching/shepherding structure is also based on geography, with each coach supervising a specific region (often based on elementary school districts).

Advantages to the Christian Community

- **Strength 1:** Geographical proximity provides more chances for group members to spontaneously interact and develop intimacy.
- **Strength 2:** Geographical proximity also removes the commuter mentality from a small-group ministry, which can save a lot of time for group members.
- **Strength 3:** This model can help group members connect with an early-church view of community, such as the one described in Acts 2. Cell groups focus on relational evangelism and are a proven way to grow the kingdom of God.

Disadvantages to the Christian Community

- **Weakness 1:** A church's rigid application of this model can produce negative consequences for groups that are strongly influenced by affinity, such as young adults.
- **Weakness 2:** This model severely limits choices for small-group members.
- **Weakness 3:** A return to an early-church mindset can be jarring for people who are thoroughly entrenched in a twenty-first-century mindset.

GOSPEL-CENTERED RAMIFICATIONS:

Loving our neighbor is second only to loving God in the Great Commandment. The ability to love the ones closest ignites in us the fire of the priesthood of the believer. Suddenly everyone is a helpful Christlike servant to those in their neighborhoods. The voice, DNA, and makeup of each community begin to surface in group expression as those meeting together find their uniqueness in living together. It promotes the sharing of goods, services, time, and talents, amongst one another in an even and organic way.

Similar to the other models, neighborhoods still begin to become subservient to the central hub (the Sunday church and all its programs). Don't hear me wrong by thinking my statements reflect an anti-authority bias. I embrace authority rather than reject it. But what begins to happen is that the neighborhood voice is brought into the corporate makeup of the church and is shaped to reflect that one central entities' personality rather than seeking to cultivate the unique expressions of the component groups. Uniformity is again the conclusion. Uniquenesses become sameness.

If the neighborhood is the sole model for relationship then uniformity will ultimately define the group. Why? Usually, neighborhoods are made up of people from the same basic class. Nothing shapes us more than class. Class has less to do with financial status and more with a way of seeing life. Our class shapes the way we respond to politics, race, work, needs, and countless other things. If we are all uniform in our class system, over the long haul we lose the multi-colored nature of God. What is even more profoundly lost is his nature of being with and across from people in true fellowship. If a class that is middle tries to reach out to one lower or higher, then ministry forever takes on the shape of hierarchy, not friendship.

We must ask ourselves, How do we envision a better way forward that loves our neighbor, but ensures that we maintain our personality alongside of our group's reflection of God's Trinitarian color and variation?

MODEL 6: PURPOSE-DRIVEN COMMUNITY

DESCRIPTION: The purpose-driven small groups model evolved from Rick Warren's experiences at Saddleback Church, which is detailed in his book *The Purpose-Driven Church*. This model seeks to intentionally deepen five areas in each small group: fellowship, discipleship, ministry, evangelism, and worship. This model does not stress multiplication as a way to grow the ministry but relies instead on regular church-wide campaigns. Within these campaigns, new leaders are initially recruited as hosts and then trained as spiritual leaders over time.

Advantages to the Christian Community

- **Strength 1:** A focus on five purposes of the Great Commission carries the potential for more full-bodied disciples of Jesus Christ.

- **Strength 2:** Initiating new leaders as hosts lowers the threshold of expectations, making more potential leaders available.
- **Strength 3:** Growth through campaigns allows individual groups to deepen trust and intimacy without worrying about an eventual split.

Disadvantages to the Christian Community

- **Weakness 1:** The use of regular campaigns requires a more involved administration effort for churches and ministry directors.
- **Weakness 2:** The use of campaigns creates a high amount of turnover, with large numbers of groups both forming and disbanding.
- **Weakness 3:** Lowering the threshold for new leaders can create problems if those who respond aren't ready for the responsibility— or aren't even disciples of Christ themselves.

GOSPEL-CENTERED RAMIFICATIONS:

I applaud the purpose-driven approach for identifying the elements of the Great Commission: worship, discipleship, fellowship, ministry, and evangelism. Nevertheless, it compartmentalizes everything. It's like telling someone to work on arm strength without simultaneously working the core. If the arm is worked without recognizing it's association with all the other body parts, the arm gets overdeveloped and out of sync with the whole. We as people are not compartmentalized. We are whole.

I've personally witnessed how compartmentalized thinking impacts people. It produces a faith in "to-do" lists. We so categorize and schedule everything, including our quiet time with God, that we disconnect from where God is in the not so quiet moments of our driving, walking, working, playing, and any of the other hundreds of thousands of things we do each day.

We must also consider that God did not call us first and foremost to find *our* purpose. He called us to first and foremost find *his* purpose (Eph. 1). For fun, read Ephesians 1 and notice how Paul uses the word purpose in reference to Christ. He frames the Father as the writer and originator of our entire story and concludes that the main point of all of history is Jesus. When we make our purposes, dreams, and aspirations central in our focus, Jesus becomes the add-on side-kick that helps us reach toward our goals. It's not that we lose worship, discipleship, fellowship, ministry, and everything else; it's that a flavor of humanism taints it. We begin placing our satisfaction in the realization of our own ends. Our own tasks completed. Our own dreams realized. Our own personal best self. Our own fulfillment. It's a quick jump right into man-centered theology.

We must ask, will a purpose-driven mentality aimed at the gifts Jesus gives shape us differently as believers than if we are person-driven and aimed at the Giver as a *being*?"

MODEL 7: SERMON-BASED COMMUNITY

DESCRIPTION: This model links a church's small-groups ministry with the weekly sermon and worship service. Group members study the same topic or passage of Scripture that was covered in the sermon, often delving deeper into areas not covered in detail by the preacher.

Advantages to the Christian Community

- **Strength 1:** Combining the weekend sermon with a small-group Bible study provides repeated exposure to the material covered, which can help it stick with group members.
- **Strength 2:** Group leaders are freed from the burden of hunting down new curriculum ideas (or writing their own).
- **Strength 3:** Having all small groups study the same material creates a wider sense of unity and common direction.

Disadvantages to the Christian Community

- **Weakness 1:** The pastor must finalize his sermon material at least six weeks in advance in order to properly develop the curriculum resources.
- **Weakness 2:** Some group leaders may chafe at having curriculum assigned to them rather than realizing part of their nature as a follower of God is to produce and be creative.
- **Weakness 3:** The potential exists for small groups to turn the Bible study into a critique of the pastor's sermon.

Gospel-Centered Ramifications:

To apply Mark Driscoll's apt phrase—"There's the air war and the ground war"—the sermon provides the air war to the masses, and the small groups mobilize the ground offensive. This model ensures great unity for the church as a whole regarding what is believed. This model is very Western in thinking. We are a literate culture, and so we sum up our beliefs about discipleship by recording them in writing. In this view, it is essential that a central "church headquarters" of some kind designs the manner of believing to which we all conform and communicates that design via the printed page.

The above is not how oral culture predominantly operates, and oral culture is the predominant posture in Bible times. Perhaps only 2 percent of those in the believing community, and upwards of 22 percent in the Roman world as a whole were even literate. Most information traveled through the arts (poetry, acting, music, story, limerick, parable, etc.) Even today, 80 percent of our world still operates in an oral mindset. We see an explosion of artistic desire from world-sized businesses like Apple and Amazon, and it must stir us to ask: "if it is the artists and creators that are positioned to be most influential in our world, then why is the church so anemic in focusing on the arts as a predominant way of preaching the Gospel?" We must consider how spreading belief and sound doctrine might change amidst such realities.

Now, don't get me wrong, I absolutely believe in literacy and in orthodoxy (the unchanging tenets of the faith that have been handed down, proven, and tested in that they are true). We must hold in a closed hand that which is essential to faith (e.g., Jesus' life, death, resurrection, and ascension), and hold in an open hand issues that are free for continued discussion. Nevertheless, we must also pay attention to how Paul views what doctrines should be taught in passages such as Titus 2:1-10. We might assume Paul would urge Titus to launch into a sermon on the church's core beliefs. However, notice where Paul goes instead:

> ... *teach what accords with sound doctrine.* Older men are to be sober-minded, dignified, self-controlled, sound in faith, in love, and in steadfastness. Older women likewise are to be reverent in behavior, not slanderers or slaves to much wine. They are to teach what is good, and so train the young women to love their husbands and children, to be self-controlled, pure, working at home, kind, and submissive to their own husbands, that the word of God may not be

reviled. Likewise, urge the younger men to be self-controlled. Show yourself in all respects to be a model of good works, and in your teaching show integrity, dignity, and sound speech that cannot be condemned, so that an opponent may be put to shame, having nothing evil to say about us. Bondservants are to be submissive to their own masters in everything; they are to be well-pleasing, not argumentative, not pilfering, but showing all good faith, so that in everything they may adorn the *doctrine of God our Savior* (italics mine).

Paul immediately connects doctrine to the *being* aspects of older and younger men and women. He connects the idea of sound doctrine, not only to what is believed, but what is "seen" in the visual community. He makes doctrine an art-form.

He uses a literary device called an *inclusio* to heighten his point. He begins the section by introducing the primacy of sound doctrine. Then he defines sound doctrine and ends the passage by reasserting his opening idea that this is the doctrine to be taught. The doctrine concept bookends the argument. An *inclusio*. The bookends tell us how to understand the in-betweens. Inside the *inclusio* of Titus 2:1-10, Paul talks more directly about what is shown amongst the community over and above what is believed. What is shown reveals what is truly embraced. Paul yearns for a visual community; a community that people see and then say to themselves, "They must have a different king." Paul focuses much more on the "show" than the "tell." His emphasis is not only on what is believed; he wants the community of God to *look like our Savior*. We must use Paul's measurement to determine the authenticity of Christlike community.

If you wonder why Paul did not go into a didactic presentation of core theological beliefs after urging Titus to preach sound doctrine, you must remember that in New Testament times, people did not think as much in linear sermons and platform delivery like we do today. Take Jesus' words for example. For every statement he makes in the gospels, he asks four questions. He uses story, dialogue, parable, and questions to teach truth. Yes, we do have longer sermons on record for Jesus (the Sermon on the Mount) and the apostles (Peter's sermon in Acts 2) that are more didactic. But overall, notice the presentation of story. Open ended questions. The framework for teaching is hung on scaffolding that doesn't always answer life's deepest questions with tightly sewn-up three-point conclusions for practical application.

Modern sermonic thinking has really done more damage than good, in my opinion. It has postured people to think about truth (which is a *person*, by the way[2]) more as a consumer than a participant. Truth comes *at us* instead of *amongst us*. Modern sermonic form has taught us what to think but not how to think. As a result, I hear more congregants talking about what the pastor thinks than what the Bible says.

People now think of preaching as a performance on a stage. Truth is no longer something we interact with; it's something that's shouted down at us. It has caused a division between what some call "head and heart." The Jewish way of training knows no such division. For people to properly know anything, they must know it in their affections. The mind and heart are not divided; they dwell in absolute combination.

Even though sound teaching and doctrine is crucial, we must consider whether uniting around a sermon is the best way to shape Trinitarian community,

MODEL 8: ORGANIC COMMUNITY

DESCRIPTION: In many ways, organic small groups are a reaction against highly programmed and structured models of community. They seek to move away from such structures in favor of a more natural method of building community.

Advantages to the Christian Community

- **Strength 1:** Organic groups provide an alternative where traditional small groups have not worked—especially in communities with more postmodern members.
- **Strength 2:** Organic groups allow church and group leaders to minister and connect in ways that best match their gifts and passions.
- **Strength 3:** Success is not dependent on getting a certain percentage of a church's congregation into small groups.

Disadvantages to the Christian Community

- **Weakness 1:** This model may seem chaotic and confusing to those who have been satisfied in a traditional small-groups ministry.
- **Weakness 2:** The model's lack of programming and control can sometimes lead to a lack of accountability.
- **Weakness 3:** In reacting heavily against programming and control, organic groups can sometimes lose sight of many benefits derived from traditional small groups.

GOSPEL-CENTERED RAMIFICATIONS:

God is a God of structure, as we'll discuss more in our organization section of C.R.O.S.S. The only question is, What kind of structure? What is seemingly organic is always planned. Even the organic craze in the produce industry is driven by structure in the form of scientific growth methods. Many think that plans, futures, structures, and the like hinder and break creativity that's real, authentic, and organic. The truth is, structure actually enables creativity to flourish with purpose.

God makes structure essential. It is prescribed and commanded. Structure is in the very "DNA" of God, so to speak. Structure within the Trinity doesn't kill relationship; it amplifies it. Though we may attempt to deny structure, we defeat our own argument, for we have to use structured propositions based on laws of logic to do so. God laid the foundations of the earth, and within those foundations are absolutes that we cannot avoid even if we try.

I'm not attempting to say that things in God's kingdom shouldn't happen naturally. I'm merely exposing the true nature of *naturally*. I'm convinced that what many are calling "natural" is foreign to God's order for life. Many have begun to buy into lies as being the truth. I'd much rather ask, How does God plant, water, grow, trellis, prune, and harvest in his kingdom? He does all things in a very Trinitarian manner. We'll consider more of what this means in the pages to come.

MODEL 9: HOUSE COMMUNITY

DESCRIPTION: Similar to the cell group model, house churches view small groups as the basic unit of a congregation. Taken to the next logical step, small groups then become churches in and of themselves. This does not mean that members of a house church automatically abandon corporate worship with other groups and believers—although sometimes that is the case. But it does mean that the primary burden of ministry falls on the house-church leader and members—not on paid church staff members.

Advantages to the Christian Community

- **Strength 1:** House churches represent a return to early church ideals of community and doing life together. They present the best atmosphere (around a table) to experience the face-to-face nature of the Trinity within the oversight of Trinitarian leadership and church leadership.
- **Strength 2:** They provide a successful platform for intergenerational ministry and learning.
- **Strength 3:** They produce high levels of intimacy, accountability, and trust.

Disadvantages to the Christian Community

- **Weakness 1:** House churches can be vulnerable to poor teaching and heresy when not connected and accountable to an established body.
- **Weakness 2:** House churches are often disconnected from the financial resources of larger churches, which can limit opportunities for ministry.
- **Weakness 3:** House church leaders often lack established overseers who can assist with the sometimes-volatile nature of group dynamics (e.g., handling a difficult group member).

GOSPEL-CENTERED RAMIFICATIONS:

God is about the small and the large. God is all about an order as well, for it preserves the upholding of his precious truth. House churches seek to provide the community that people search for, but it is often short-sighted. We cannot make the mistake of assuming that because we meet in a home, we are the *household* of God that Paul talks about. Home church models, when they seclude, miss the forest for the trees and fall into heresy around the failed assumption that if they meet like the early church met, the same results will follow. Laziness regarding orthodox truths can sneak in, and individual groups disconnect from the traditions that have sustained the family of God for millennia. True Christian development cannot thrive without the presence of the big and small; air and ground war; structure and free-wheeling. All sides have to function rightly so we can grow up into all things, which is Christ our Head.[3]

We must consider what makes a typical *house* different than a *household* and *home* in the truest sense of New Testament thinking—one that represents the Triune image of the God we serve.

MODEL 10: HOST GROUPS

DESCRIPTION: Small-group leaders are recruited as hosts, meaning they do not carry the responsibility for the spiritual development of group members. Instead, hosts carry the responsibility of running a group meeting—including providing a location for the group to meet, managing a pre-packed curriculum (often in the form of a video or DVD), and providing snacks. Hosts are often recruited in conjunction with a church-wide campaign.

Advantages to the Christian Community

- **Strength 1:** Because the threshold for becoming a host is low, many new small groups can be formed quickly.
- **Strength 2:** This model provides a way for potential leaders to ease into the responsibilities of a small group.
- **Strength 3:** If the pre-packaged curriculum is of high quality, the teaching time can be as good as or better than a traditional small-group Bible study.

Disadvantages to the Christian Community

- **Weakness 1:** Because the threshold for becoming a host is low, the potential exists for churches to recruit leaders who are not ready for the responsibility.

- **Weakness 2:** Host groups are often dependent on the quality of the pre-packaged curriculum, which may not turn out well.
- **Weakness 3:** The number of host groups are often up-and-down. A church sometimes loses as many groups as they gain in the course of a campaign.

GOSPEL-CENTERED RAMIFICATIONS:

Obviously, someone has to host any gathered event, whether large or small. It's a no-brainer. Simply defining a church by the host—a "provider of couch and concessions"—is far too shallow. In doing so, we dumb down the function of a true host and the nature of authentic hospitality. True transformation within groups comes not only at the hands of information but also through some semblance of restoration. A host should be presenting truths that they too are already coming in contact with themselves. How God has moved in them for their restoration becomes the groundwork for powerful transformation in the other members of their group. Group leader simply viewing themselves as hosts is incomplete. It seems to exempt them from the true task of growing up into a disciple of Jesus. It also handicaps them in seeing their role in how Jesus sees their role. Hosting is not just a task of form and function, but a truly pastoral and priestly work. It's helping people transform into God's image.

We must consider the nature of hospitality and fellowship in God's household from the perspective of the Trinity.

WHY ALL THE FUSS IN SEMANTICS?

It's important to dissect all we do as a church because the show speaks louder than the tell. Our Heavenly Father knew that in order for us to understand the invisible God (the tell), he would have to make him visible (the show) in the God-man, Jesus.

How we commune with each other and God greatly impacts the image into which we are formed. Every time we meet together as people, we lay our body, mind, soul, and spirit on the worldview, shape, and model we come in contact with. Once the clay pot is spun, we have to ask ourselves, Toward whom does this image point? If we are spinning ourselves into a frenzy over things that aren't quite central, we may be making idols out of our own images and therefore create mountains that stand in our way.

In all of the above models, what I believe to be lacking is a paradigm surrounding what unites us. Some believe gender affiliation is the uniting paradigm. Some believe it's politics, polity, or purity. Some believe it's our hobbies and habits. Some believe it's our search for purpose, or even communal neighborhoods or demographics. All of us fall into the trap that unity and true oneness among many can be found in proximity, class, race, creed, nationality, cultural upbringing, affiliation, status, vocation, articulation of belief, structure, and the ability to follow one sole leader at the top. All our models attempting to define what unites us have resulted in one thing: churches continuing to remain divided. By placing the wrong "emPHAsis on the wrong sylLAble," as Mike Myers would say, we make the language of God hard to understand.

I'm suggesting that C.R.O.S.S. is most impactful to shaping how we do community. It leads us to unite around the *being* of the Trinity and also to *do* as the Trinity does. It keeps us from making central in our communing, issues like hobby, purpose, affinity, preference, agenda, etc. We set those lesser things aside and conclude that it's the person and work of Christ that brings us together. But its more than that. He teaches us not just about a moment, but about a way of life. Our God has a very specific way in how he relates (C.ommunity), how he does things (R.easoning), how he organizes life (O.rganize), how he teaches and expects us to believe (S.cripture), and how he leads (S.ignature Mission). His truth, way, and life are the same in every person, church, and culture. In living his way of life together, we magnify his unity and his diversity. We draw all people to consider the same fundamentals while never overriding their uniqueness with our own pet visions.

PRESENCE AND PERSON DRIVEN

The simple truth is that we do not unite around any of the things highlighted in the models we've examined. One thing makes Christian community different than any other community in the world. That one thing is the presence of the person of Jesus. By placing anything incomplete in the middle of the room and uniting our life together around it, we may get small dividends of the real thing, but not the full share. It's my absolute conviction that all the language of group life today emphasize good things but they are not ultimate things.

To truly form Biblical community, we need to contemplate, unite around, and hone in on one thing and one thing alone—the Trinity. Trinitarian life includes all the aspects of the community in the group modes listed above, but the person and presence of Jesus is the thing that holds them all in balance and authority. We can be open and proactive in sharing the gospel with anyone, and at the same time closed and/or diligently protective against those who would seek to divert us from our central focus on Jesus. We must go beyond hearing the Word to embodying it and letting it embody us. The Bible says we are in Christ and he is in us. We must be organic enough to sustain the direction of the Holy Spirit and hospitable enough to provide transformative spaces with meal and drink for people to commune with each other and God.

AT THE BEGINNING of this chapter, I asked you to keep a few things in your mind as you read it. I will now repeat those items so we can build on them a bit:

1. Can the Trinity-centered model of community succeed in any time, in any place, and under any circumstance?
2. Does this model reveal and show the gospel in the truest and fullest sense? If not, what might go wrong if we keep viewing community this way?
3. Do any of these models give people a way in which to commune that's any different than the world?

We're beginning to learn that Jesus' definition of a church is far different than ours. What some might conclude makes a church a church from our methods today is sound systems, staff, an elder (in terms of a staff or position), buildings, programs, and on and on it goes. No! We've complicated it all. Our basis for unity is found in the reality that Jesus continues to remain present amongst us. This is what makes us different. We unite not around his works, not our own works (buildings, agendas, community enrichment programs), but around his being. He's fashioning into us his likeness, not his trade as a carpenter.

Not only is Christ's personhood comprehensively different in how it forms bonds; it is also different in how it forms us spiritually. His personhood forms not merely on focused parts of us, but our whole being. Vocation is too narrow.

Race is too narrow. Class is too narrow. Closed and Open is too narrow. Purpose is too narrow. Sermon-slant is too narrow. Denomination is too narrow. Theology is too narrow. Personality is too narrow. Neighborhoods, gender, interests, etc. It's all too narrow. It slenderizes the soul. It makes Jesus skinny and void of full sustenance and nutrition. It makes us as humans one dimensional. It dumbs us down and makes us valuable only when measured by one standard.

When Christ told us to follow the narrow way, he certainly did not mean this.

If we seek to conform ourselves to Christ's image rather than confining him into our boxes and preferences, we begin to dream in better forms. We imagine better paradigms to think in. In meditating on the Trinity, I believe we arrive less at *what* to think, and discover better *ways* to think. There is an enormous difference.

C.R.O.S.S.

I must say it again. The C.R.O.S.S. is the most profound uniting agent. Not only is the work of the cross where true oneness is found, but unity is found in the personhood of the one who died on it. Paul says in 1 Corinthians 2:2 that the cross and personhood of Christ are the bases for unity. Amidst all his experience, hobby, learning, and background, he says, "I resolved to know nothing while I was with you except Jesus Christ, and him crucified."

The cross is simply where we all cross paths. It's the only place where we can all agree. We all have to answer to its sermon, not our own. In dying for us as the perfect human, God humbles the loudest and proudest. He silences anyone who thinks they're something. It's at the cross that Christ also exalts those who are the lowest and poorest. He gives voice to anyone who thinks they're nothing. It's a level playing field at the feet of Jesus. We're all forced to lay down our crowns and take up our cross. The cross exposes our deepest pride and extensive shames. In both cases we stand at its base and struggle, either looking down at those around us with a proud a haughty eye and continuing to compete for first place, or equally as destructive, staring in humiliation at ourselves and realizing that nothing can come of us. The cross confronts and crushes both the humiliated and the haughty. The cross heralds a King while also being the emblem for the scum of the world. It's the truest art we have. On Christ's cross hung the greatest treasure and the lowest tragedy ever painted by any artist.

The cross is the only thing to which we all can relate. It's simply the only statement in the history of the world to which every human must come to grips. This crucified Christ claimed to die for all creation and the entirety of human existence. He claims that it is solely he to whom we must compare ourselves. If we unite around anything but the personhood and cross of Jesus, we risk making something else our ultimate. We risk fashioning for ourselves another form that may be good (purpose, affinity, gender, culture, hobby) but not great.

Only when the cross and Christ come together can the things of the world fade as the dominant objects of our appetites. The proper placement of the cross and Christ in our affections equips you and me to commune with the world. We can now dine with saints and sinners of all gender, preference, affiliation, interests, and proclivity. It's our honor as a community now to commune like our King. In meals. Amongst sinners. With the scum of society both high and low; with the prostitute and homosexual and also with its highest and most corrupt gangsters and crooks.

When we commune in this way, we do not preach acceptance, but we teach embrace. Acceptance sees the person as they are and never takes them to the cross. Acceptance leaves any person in their filth and requires nothing of them. Embrace sees the person as they are and takes them straight to Jesus. His cross confronts all of our vice and any supposed virtue. We hold each other's hands in friendship and let the work of Christ burn away the dross—letting the true gold of who we are created to be emerge within the flame.

We truly get rolled up into the bliss of the Trinity. We cling to each other in utter need of each other's humanity—good and bad—and in looking upon our family King together, we begin to contemplate a better person to follow than ourselves. He supersedes our choices and offers a better path to take.

We've definitely said a lot in this chapter. There's much to think about. Luckily, God gives us easy symbols through which to look in order to condense all our information into digestible food. The most profound symbol we have in learning how we are now to *commune* because of what Christ has afforded to us is …

Baptism.

BAPTISM

I n discussing how to rightly form and fashion Christian community going forward, we absolutely need to revisit the idea of baptism again as a place of origin. If we leave baptism on the table and only engage it as the once-and-for-all goal and conclusion of evangelism, never speaking of it again when a believer encounters temptations, life's challenges, and the world in all its flavors, we are absolutely shooting our faith in the foot.

Proper conversations about baptism are just not being had, and it's adding to our anemic view of how to form close-knit community. In the theological circles I tend to travel in due to my vocation, I find that all our chatter orbits the mode or method of baptism while ignoring the actual meaning. Our debates center around immersion or sprinkling. People simply want to know whether they should dunk or drizzle. People also want to know whether we're supposed to wait until we get older to profess *personal* faith in Christ, or whether *padeo-baptism* (infant baptism) professes *corporate* faith in Christ on behalf of the child before he or she can believe.

There's no shortage of differing viewpoints on baptism. Three have risen to prominence among theologians. Some say baptism is to be understood in light of *The Sacramental View*: Baptism is a means of saving grace; others *The Covenantal View*: Baptism is a sign and seal of the covenant, and others *The Symbolic View*: Baptism is a token and witness to our salvation. We lose sleep over the "right" way of thinking and doing things, and in prioritizing rightness we miss the point.

IT'S ABOUT A MESSAGE

We have spent inordinate time on methods and modes of baptism and missed its message. Remember back to our discussion about Jesus' baptism. Matthew affirms the focus of meaning. He lays out his gospel in a way that highlights Jesus reliving the life of Israel, but in reverse. Matthew hones in on what is symbolized above whether or not Jesus is being dunked or drizzled.

If you disagree and want to get down to brass tacks, we can solve the issue right now. Jesus was an adult and was dunked. Issue resolved. If I'm going to get into it over baptismal praxis, at the end of the day I'm going to land and camp on how Jesus did it.

What is clear is that the primary reason for Jesus' baptism was to usher in a *new creation—a life beyond the Jordan*. His baptism was about a kingdom-family transfer. Not only did he act out and demonstrate an old kingdom utterly destroyed and a new Israel and people of God erected in his personhood, but he also confirmed a new reality in receiving the pleasure of his Father, and his Friend, the Holy Spirit.

A DIFFERENT VIEW

I would like to throw into the fray of historical debate a fourth view on the meaning of baptism. I call it the *Message of the Kingdom-Family*. Baptism reveals the individual's new personhood to the community as a member of God's Triune family.

Jesus makes his family through water, not hobby, predilection, interest, orientation, or anything else. Baptism indicates a transfer of community based on the right criteria. Water is something that is forever. It is timeless. We emerge from the water as a new creation that is not of this world. We are born into a separate reality.

The church today generally uses the word membership to denote one's entrance into the kingdom's new reality. I fear that most church approaches to membership turn out to be trite and trivial and yet another way to link our unity in Christ to something lesser. Many have boiled membership down to mere attendance or the dutiful signature on a piece of paper that says "covenant." The meaning of baptism exceeds a signed piece of paper, a class, or a way of thinking as rights toward membership, as many in the West would understand today. Baptism affirms one's *personhood* as a valuable member in God's household apart from his or her correct doctrine, maturity, or ability to fulfill a ledger of responsibilities in order to be part of his family.

I'm not undercutting the need for each member in God's Body to serve out his role for the good of the whole, but I am saying that baptism shifts the way in which we go about things. Baptism prioritizes the fact that we are reborn into a family and kingdom life with an attitude of working *from* love not trying to live up to any external add-ons that may give the impression that we work *for* love. Baptism makes the statement that we are well pleasing to God from the moment we slide down the birth canal.

Family and Kingdom membership is how Paul understands "the baptism of the Holy Spirit." And contrary to the thoughts of many in the church today who try to turn baptism in the Spirit into a never ending cycle of supposed add-ons to salvation, Paul only uses this phrase three times. He speaks of our baptism in the same way as Jesus. Our salvation and our affirmation as Christ's family members happens at the same moment. Salvation and baptism in the Holy Spirit are the same things. God saves us, and the result is we come out of the family of darkness and into the family of light. Baptism is a video display of what's already happened in the sound waves.

We must resist the temptation to turn baptism into a Christian badge that only marks the beginning of all we need to acquire, pursue, have, or do, *after* salvation. Our add-on mentality is based in the way the flesh thinks, not the spirit. We are perpetually prone as humans to making ourselves "more than" the rest of the field in some way.

Baptism silences any attempt to judge some Christians as being better or worse than others. It preaches the same message to all. Jesus is the gateway into a family of unity. To add *anything* to Jesus is insanity and only leads to confused chaos. Baptism preaches the opposite of a family of competition, fear, and endless rainbow-chasing. It preaches a faith of confident resolve and utters peaceful convincing. Baptism assures us, despite what gifts we may or may not have been given, that we are his and we have his pleasure. We are his kids, and because of Jesus, the Father is well pleased with us.

I'M SADDENED THAT WE DO NOT START HERE

Over the years, I've been in thousands of churches around the world. I'm deeply grieved at the absence of meaningful engagement with baptism. What I've observed, in myself and others, is that profound insecurity relating to identity and community plagues God's people as a result. People are still walking around in the church trying to one-up each other. People are still trying to pick anything out of the air as their cry and cause for unity. People are still embracing hidden shames. Competition and seclusion are opposite sides of the same coin. They are signs of immaturity, not secure identity.

Baptism is absolutely essential to producing **worshipping** Christlike followers that have a sure sense of who and whose they are and where they belong.

Martin Luther, the man to which we credit the Protestant Reformation, understood the connection that exists between baptism and the believer's stability as pleasing sons and daughters of the King. Luther was asked how he withstood the constant attacks from the enemy throughout his life—attacks that often left physical markings on him. His response was to say, "I remember my baptism." Luther's stability in life was anchored in baptism. Baptism wasn't just a one-time event for Luther; it was a daily source of contemplation and spiritual nourishment.

Martin Luther understood baptism. He understood that in Jesus' baptism, the Father and Spirit's pleasure rests on the Son. Having the Father's unlimited pleasure prior to and apart from any work is what kept Jesus steadfast throughout his ministry. It's what anchored Luther in his faith. It's what anchors us.

The struggle for identity is a real issue for all believers, and I'm convinced it's a battle we're losing. We are wrestling with powers and principalities at the level of identity and personhood, and we stand without the tools to fight. Baptism arms us with our sword.

Theologians refer to the battle over identity as a constant wrestling between *positional* and *practical* holiness. Scripture tells us that we are positionally "in Christ," but that practically Christ is "in us" in the day-to-day. What such a distinction suggests is that we've been perfected, and yet we haven't. We've arrived, and yet are still traveling. We are saints and sojourners simultaneously struggling with sin.

Paul actually stresses that we're in Christ over 270 times in Scripture compared to the meager 70 times he says that Christ is in us. The imbalance tells us something. Thinking upon where we're hidden *in Christ* is the absolute secret to how we win the war of being exposed to the elements in the world as Christ is living *in us*.

Paul writes in Colossians 3:2-4: "Set your minds on things *that are above*, not on things that are on earth. For you have died, and your life is *hidden with Christ in God*. When Christ who is your life appears, then you also will appear with him in glory" (italics mine). Why does Scripture emphasize our place in Christ?

To understand the wrestling between who we are positionally and where we are practically, picture water and an empty thermos. In your mind, describe them both. The water is wet, clear, formless to a degree, vapid, etc. The thermos is tall, cylindrical, metal, and hollow. Each of these things has its own properties and each is different from the other. Now picture me putting the water inside the thermos. Now describe the water. Trouble is, you can't see it anymore. The water is inside the thermos. If you were to put into words the current situation, you'd have to say that all you see is something tall, cylindrical, metal, etc. The water has now taken on the same shape as the thermos.

This is how being *in* Christ affects us. We are swallowed up in his attributes. Life. It happens as we are buried in his death. The book of Romans says that baptism is where all this takes place:

> Do you not know that all of us who have been baptized into Christ Jesus were baptized into his death? We were buried therefore with him by baptism into death, in order that, just as Christ was raised from the dead by the glory of the Father, we too might walk in newness of life. For if we have been united with him in a death like his, we shall certainly be united with him in a resurrection like his.

When set apart from Christ, we have our own properties. We are unloving, depressed, unfaithful, harsh, anxious, and worried. Dead. Christ is loving, joyful, peaceful, patient, kind, good, gentle, faithful, and self-controlled. The miracle of us being *in* Christ is that we (the water in our analogy) get placed inside of our God (the thermos). When the Father or anyone in the family of God looks at us, all that is seen is Christ. Death is swallowed in victory. If you were to ask the Father to describe you, he would look into Jesus and say that you are loving, joyful, peaceful, patient, kind, good, gentle, faithful, and self-controlled.

We have such difficulty seeing ourselves through the *positional* eyes that baptism affords us because we still wrestle with sin and flesh every day in the present. We begin to doubt our "forever nature" in Christ because our living faith in the present may have just fallen into temptation for the umpteenth time.

Our struggle with identity centers around what we see in ourselves practically when compared to who we are positionally. Positionally we are whole. Practically we are still in process.

There's a different mentality that emerges depending on the order in which you arrange your thoughts. If you emphasize the practical side and think of yourself as unloving, mean, harsh, impatient, etc., your thinking will skew your real place *in Christ*, and you will never feel good enough to be an authentic member of the community of believers. You won't approach the throne of grace with confidence, but you'll only feel despair. You'll also pray like this: "God make me patient, loving, and kind," and you'll forget that you *already are*. You don't need to ask for more of the fruit of the Spirit. In thinking you need more, you embrace an *identity* that lives in incompleteness, and the struggles that come from living this way are obvious and exponential. You will always fall for add-ons.

I'm sure you can identify with the struggle I'm describing through the lens of your own worry-ridden, anxious, stress-filled, impatient, unloving, and selfish shortcomings. In the reality of our baptism, and our kingdom transfer into a new family and new personhood, we already possess it all. We don't need to ask for more. We don't need to be more. We merely need to ask for perspective. We need to pray and seek rest in what we are and in whose we are. When we rest, all our work transforms. Shalom.

Practically, our position *in Christ* helps us to struggle with sin and shortcomings through a more powerful line of sight. We don't work *for* love in order to grab hold of things we don't possess. We work *from* love, and revel in all Christ has already done. I love how Paul describes this back-and-forth dance between positional and practical holiness in Philippians 3:12, 16: "Not that I have already obtained this or am already perfect [practically], but I press on to make it my own, because Christ Jesus has made me his own [positionally]… only let us hold true [practically in the now] to what we have attained [positionally]." Paul recognizes how his growth is constantly on the upswing in Christ. He sees that he's transforming even amidst failure. What's causing his forever upswing is his recognition that Christ has already finished him in holiness. Paul recognizes that all he aims to be—namely perfect—is already at rest in Jesus.

Oh, how this changes everything! Baptism is the symbol of heaven meeting earth. Baptism affirms Jesus' identity as perfect, even as Jesus goes into the depth of the imperfect desert to battle Satan. Baptism is the resolve that helps us manage the stress of the positional and practical holiness dancing together.

IDENTITY WITHIN THE FAMILY

Baptism bursts our isolated, individualistic, and insecure bubble. It's the first time we see clearly. Baptism helps us continually see clearly. It's the looking glass we must keep looking through all our days. We must break our habit of thinking about baptism as only a starting place. By divorcing it from our spiritual growth throughout our entire Christian journey, we leave ourselves open to attack. Very quickly we begin trying to devise other methods by which to affirm a person's dignity or membership within the community.

Our foundation for unity begins not with a series of classes, denominational handbooks, slogans and statements, and to-do's to be accomplished. It begins with God proclaiming, "This is my son and daughter, in whom, I'm well pleased."

Oh, how I mourn all the disciples of Christ I've met over the last twenty years who still do not understand God's pleasure over them. They are still working *for* love, not *from* love. They are still checking off discipleship spreadsheets to get one step holier and failing to realize that in some manner they already are. Joy is zapped in the dance to be holy like Christ because we embrace the journey as a chore. We see holiness as something we're constantly falling short of—and it is. We're not remembering that holiness is also something that is secure and something Christ is constantly meeting on our behalf. Such a realization makes us better. As Paul says, we are "striving toward what we've already attained."

Maybe you identify with the problem I'm describing. You've never embraced who you already are in Christ. Maybe you've been given a list of things to do to be acceptable to the community, and like all humans with a propensity toward the fear of man, you and those around you have fallen right into the same old tricks of comparing, competing, and creating expectations for involvement in the Kingdom that not even Jesus would adhere to. My invitation to you, oh little precious babe in Christ, is to rest. Come unto him who knows that you're weary. His burden is easy, and his yoke is light. Come to him as a helpless, suckling infant and watch how you begin to grow.

BABIES ARE DIFFERENT

Baptism provides a better way forward for understanding the family of God as it works at any time, in any place, and under any circumstance. Not all people have pens, paper, or literacy by which to sign a membership covenant. Not all people have healthy physical, mental, or social abilities to embrace logic, systematic ordered doctrines, or to act out commands. We must allow the kingdom to be offered to all. The family of God extends the same dignity to the unborn, the handicapped, the disabled, the delusional, the PTSD vet, the bed-ridden, the paraplegic, the elderly that may have graduated past any point of self-functioning, the orphan, the widow, the fatherless, etc.

Again, baptism utilizes water. Timeless. It's a symbol common and accessible in every place and era, and to every person. It extends the kingdom equally to all, past and present, in exactly the same way. Water is the essential element of birth. Timeless. Birth is something to which any man, woman, and child can relate. Baptism is a new birth. When we go under the water, we symbolize death, and when we emerge, we symbolize being reborn or regenerated. Baptism is passing through the birth canal.

Baptism produces new infants, not full-grown experts. Babies interact within community very differently from doctrinal and theological studs. Babies don't know the codes of conduct, all that's required of them, and the norms dictating how they're to dress, act, and behave to blend in. Babies stand out. They cry. They wet themselves. Their sheer cuteness makes even the angriest parent melt amidst the most violent tantrum of immaturity.

Babies just know pleasure. They know safety simply by the embrace of a tender nipple. Babies are completely surrendered to the work of the parent, and they lay no claim to know any to-dos that could somehow qualify them as family members. A baby's resting in a parent's love is actually what causes the healthy baby to grow.

Newborn language is why the word regeneration only appears twice in the Bible (Mt. 19:28, Ti. 3:5) but is accompanied by a constellation of birth-related images in both testaments (e.g., circumcision). The primary image used for entrance into God's kingdom is that of being reborn. The image of rebirth suggests a total overhaul of one's inner and outer self, just as Jesus explained to Nicodemus (Jn. 3:1-21. See also Dt. 30:6; Jer. 24:7; 31:31–33; 32:39–40; Ez. 11:19–20; 36:26–27). In being reborn, one becomes a "partaker of the divine nature" (2 Pt. 1:4), a "new creation" (2 Cor. 5:17), a "new man" (Eph. 2:15; 4:24), "alive together with Christ" (Eph. 2:5; Col. 2:13), and "created in Christ Jesus" (Eph. 2:10). A work of this magnitude is based on the work of the parent, not the baby. Babies do not know how to bring themselves into the world. Likewise, we do not know how to birth ourselves anew, and that's why it's a work of the Holy Spirit (Jn. 3:5-8).

Just to make the impossible seem even more impossible, consider what the effects of regeneration are. They are numerous and beyond any humans ability:

REGENERATED people have the Trinitarian Creator God of the Bible as their new Lord, thereby displacing all other false and functional lords who had previously ruled over them (1 Jn. 5:18).

REGENERATED people are a new creation, transformed at the deepest levels of their existence to begin living a new life. People being renamed at their conversion, Saul becoming Paul and Cephas becoming Peter, illustrates that we are new people in Christ (2 Cor. 5:17; Gal. 6:15).

REGENERATED people have a new identity from which to live their new life because their old identity no longer defines them (Eph. 4:22–24).

REGENERATED people have a new mind that enables them to enjoy Scripture and thus to begin to think God's truthful thoughts after him (Rom. 7:22; 1 Cor. 2:14–16; 1 Pt. 2:2).

REGENERATED people have new emotions so that they love God, fellow Christians, strangers, and even their enemies (1 Jn. 4:7).

REGENERATED people have new desires for holiness, and no longer is their deepest appetite for sin and folly (Ps. 37:4; Rom. 7:4-6; Gal. 5:16–17).

REGENERATED people enjoy a new community and fellowship with other Christians as members of the church (1 Jn. 1:3).

REGENERATED people live by a new power to follow God by the Holy Spirit's enabling (Rom. 8:4–13).

REGENERATED people enjoy a new freedom to no longer tolerate, manage, excuse, or accept their sin, but rather put it to death and live free from habitually besetting sin (Rom. 6:6; 7:6).

The culmination of the effects of regeneration is a new life of worship that is markedly different from how life would otherwise be (Gal. 5:19–23).

Conclusions

The Trinity builds a community around ways of relating that are different than we do. We can't continue to build commonality around all things physical. Race. Cultural background. Hobby. Trade. Worldview. Purpose. Vision. We'll only succeed in keeping all our definitions of friendship anchored to temporal things that only last as far as the universe can stretch. Things like identity, personhood, water, and the cross, on the other hand, ground us at the core of where worth and value are forever found. These things are timeless. They transcend all the boxes we've made. When this life is over, we'll carry these things with us into the kingdom eternal. We will be together as a bride of the King (identity), surrounding one like the Lion of Judah and a sacrificed Lamb (images of the victorious cross), and will know God as he fully knows us (personhood). Running through the city of God will be rivers of life. All this has been made possible by the sacrifice of the one that John sees in his vision in Revelation 5:6-10:

> Then I *saw a Lamb, looking as if it had been slain* [the cross links eternity to earth], standing at the center of the throne, encircled by the four living creatures and the elders. The Lamb had seven horns and seven eyes, which are the seven spirits of God sent out into all the earth. He went and took the scroll from the right hand of him who sat on the throne. And when he had taken it, the four living creatures and the twenty-four elders fell down *before the Lamb.*

Each one had a harp and they were holding golden bowls full of incense, which are the prayers of God's people. And they sang a new song, saying:

"You are worthy to take the scroll and to open its seals, *because you were slain*, and with your blood *you purchased for God persons from every tribe and language and people and nation. You have made them to be a kingdom and priests to serve our God, and they will reign on the earth*" (italics mine).

If the sacrifice of our risen King Jesus—his personhood, his Trinitarian unity, and his identity—is what truly causes us to love God and enjoy an anchored spot in his family lineage, we must turn our attention now toward how we are to love one another in light of these truths.

13

ONE ANOTHER

There is no better description of how we are to love our fellow brothers and sisters than Paul's words in 1 Thessalonians 2:7b-9. Please don't just breeze over the words. Dwell on the absolute depth of Paul's heart toward Christ's family. He says:

> Just as a nursing mother cares for her children, so we cared for you [those in Thessolonica]. Because we loved you so much, we were delighted to share with you not only the gospel of God but our lives as well. Surely you remember, brothers and sisters, our toil and hardship; we worked night and day in order not to be a burden to anyone while we preached the gospel of God to you …

Paul likens his care for God's people to that of a mother nursing a baby and even takes it a step further in verse 17: "But, brothers and sisters, when we were orphaned by being separated from you for a short time (in person, not in thought), out of our intense longing we made every effort to see you."

In Paul's mind, the family vein runs deep in God's baptized people.

Revisit the image of the nursing mother. Ponder the dependence, the physical affection, the bonding, the embrace, and the closeness. Science even acknowledges the unique relationship that exists between mother and baby. When the brains of those orphaned and left without intimate touch are compared with those of babies who experience constant touch and bonding, something horrific becomes apparent. Neglected brains fail to turn on. They show very little synapse firing. Connections are left open-ended, and the brain dies away. The long-term effects of motherlessness affect education, cognition, identity, psychosis, and all matters relating to a human growing up into a healthy adult. The infant experiencing embrace and acceptance reveals a brain lit up with vibrancy.

Paul's analogy of a mother nursing an infant goes far beyond just a feeling. Paul recognizes what science confirms. The embrace of God's family is essential for any newborn in God's kingdom to grow, learn, and understand the height, depth, and width of God's love. We're lying to ourselves if we believe that faith can be forged in isolation. It's not just a lie, but Scripture tells us its an oxymoron.

Paul also likens his relationship within the community to that of labor and toil. He describes his agony and anguish in relieving the community of any burden. Paul doesn't church shop. His affections for God's people exceed just showing up to services to "get fed." For Paul, the church is not just a place of entitlement, observation, consumption, and a locality where we coddle the seeker and call it being sensitive. Paul's not just a tourist. Paul is not just a global church traveler trouncing around the earth collecting stories to tell. Paul's toil and labor are real. He is a man that takes up responsibility rather than avoiding it. He's a family member.

In a church age today where many want the church to program us to death with services that meet our needs and fancy, Paul's insights are quite honestly stabbing. Like a knife to the lung, Paul reveals our absolute anemia in comprehending the full cost of community. We fail to grasp that the household does not exist first and foremost to *meet our needs*. Community, if anything, adds pain, pressure, and less margin to our lives.

Sacrifice is the example of the Trinity. God laid down everything. God was perfectly content in heaven. He was like one living high in the hills of Switzerland eating curds and cream and enjoying skis and skates in the glassy beauty of rolling hills and white-capped peaks. This God, living in a kingdom far exceeding Switzerland, chose to come into our pain. What crazy person would lay down perfection to add pain to their life? Quite possibly only a sane God might do such a thing.

God's sacrifice proves most sound because of Paul's third image. Paul likens being apart from God's people to being orphaned. Before Jesus was delivered up to be crucified, he said the same thing to the disciples in John 14:18. When the disciples revealed their growing despair over Christ going away, He said to them, "I will not leave you as orphans; I will come to you." God promised them the Holy Spirit to comfort their wound. Paul and Christ equate being apart from God's Triune family as being orphaned.

With such an image at the forefront of their minds, we can understand why it proves the sanity of God to lay down everything to love the other. If we fail to love, we leave each other in the trash heaps. Orphaned. There's nothing psychologically correct about ignoring the leper reaching out for healing or a trafficked child reaching out for rescue. Without God, we all wallow in the reality of the dying and the trafficked slave.

The abandoned infant in all of us includes both rich and poor. Though we compensate for our isolation in different ways, without God as our parent, we all are enslaved by a vicious adversary who sells us into slavery or we're infected with the incurable disease of mortality. We are outside the secure walls of warmth, love, and protection offered by family.

THE KINGDOM FORGED IN US AND AMONG US

Like me, you may be feeling pretty small after coming in contact with the robustly passionate heart of Paul. We are all culpable for our own smallness of heart toward community, and the typical church gatherings and their structures today have served to reinforce our dwindling heart. The environments we've invented in which to gather as God's bride often undermine the very image of community that should draw us together.

Churches are filled with stages, lights, rows, and things that make isolation and distance possible.

As we press forward in our investigation of the Trinity, I pray we'll all start to re-envision better ways of shaping our affections and our life lived together. My prayer is that of 2 Thessalonians 1:3: "We ought always to give thanks to God for you, brethren, as is only fitting, because your *faith is greatly enlarged*, and the *love of each one of you toward one another grows ever greater*" (italics mine).

The greatest evidence that kingdom-baptism is taking shape in us is that we each feel the burden of the mother, the orphan, and the toil toward our own growth in love. The kingdom affections can't grow in us merely through online sermons, books, music, social media, podcasts, and the countless other programs mediated by non-profits. Love can't grow in distance. Our love is a family affair.

To focus on positive ways to improve our togetherness, let's look into Scripture's many uses of the phrase "one another." In the chart below I lay out all Scriptures making reference to "one another" along with a brief description of what takes place in love. I also suggest what each verse might imply for our communities of love today:

SCRIPTURE(S): Neh. 4:17
DESCRIPTION: The people come together to make brick.
COMMUNITY PRINCIPLE: IN COMMUNITY, WE ACCOMPLISH TASKS TOGETHER.

SCRIPTURE(S): Gn. 42:21; 37:19
DESCRIPTION: Joseph's brothers grow in bitterness together and come to forgiveness together.
COMMUNITY PRINCIPLE: IN COMMUNITY, WE EXPERIENCE THE POWER OF HOLY OR UNHOLY PEER PRESSURE.

SCRIPTURE(S): Ex. 18:16; Jgs. 6:29
DESCRIPTION: Moses' people come with disputes, and he helps solve and search out the matter together.
COMMUNITY PRINCIPLE: IN COMMUNITY, DISPUTES ARE FORMED AND RESOLUTIONS ARE FORGED TOGETHER.

SCRIPTURE(S): Ex. 25:20
DESCRIPTION: The Cherubim face each other on the Ark of the Covenant.
COMMUNITY PRINCIPLE: IN COMMUNITY, WE EXPERIENCE UNITY ONLY WHEN STARING AT JESUS' FACE IN HIS PRESENCE.

SCRIPTURE(S): Lv. 19:11; 25:17; 25:46; Col. 3:9
DESCRIPTION: Don't lie, ruthlessly hurt, or steal from one another.
COMMUNITY PRINCIPLE: IN COMMUNITY, WE LEARN HOW TO LOVE EACH OTHER AS WE OURSELVES ARE BEING LOVED.

SCRIPTURE(S): 2 Chr. 25:21; Jas. 5:16

DESCRIPTION: Various matters are handled face to face.
COMMUNITY PRINCIPLE: IN COMMUNITY, WE LEARN THAT GOSSIP, SLANDER, AND BACKSTABBING IS DESTRUCTIVE. WE LEARN TO GO TO ONE ANOTHER, NOT AROUND ONE ANOTHER.

SCRIPTURE(S): Ps. 75:7; Mt. 25:15; Mk. 9:34; Jn. 13:14; Gal. 5:26; I Pt. 5:5
DESCRIPTION: God exalts and humbles, and God gives talents as he wills.
COMMUNITY PRINCIPLE: IN COMMUNITY, WE LEARN THE FULL MEASURE OF OUR PRIDE AND GROW IN HUMILITY FROM ONE ANOTHER.

SCRIPTURE(S): Prv. 11:24; 13:7
DESCRIPTION: How we handle our wealth and poverty impacts God's family.
COMMUNITY PRINCIPLE: IN COMMUNITY, WE LEARN TO BE GENEROUS IN SHARING OUR NEEDS AND OUR BLESSINGS OPENLY.

SCRIPTURE(S): Eccl. 4:10
DESCRIPTION: It is our job to lift up the brother who falls.
COMMUNITY PRINCIPLE: IN COMMUNITY, WE EXPERIENCE THE LIVES OF OTHERS ABOVE OUR OWN. WE WEEP WITH THOSE WHO WEEP AND REJOICE WITH THOSE THAT REJOICE.

SCRIPTURE(S): Is. 6:3; Eph. 5:19; Col. 3:16
DESCRIPTION: We learn from heavenly beings how praise is amplified. By experiencing God's presence together we grow in wisdom.
COMMUNITY PRINCIPLE: IN COMMUNITY, WE GATHER WITH HYMNS, SONGS, AND SPIRITUAL SONGS THAT EDIFY AND AMPLIFY PRAISE.

SCRIPTURE(S): Is. 13:8; Jer. 7:5; Mt. 18; I Tm. 6; I Cor. 6:1
DESCRIPTION: Justice is seen both in sharing in consequences together and seeking justice with one another.
COMMUNITY PRINCIPLE: IN COMMUNITY, WE LEARNING JUSTICE AND CONSEQUENCE.

SCRIPTURE(S): Jl. 2:8

DESCRIPTION: Only together do we advance.
COMMUNITY PRINCIPLE: IN COMMUNITY, WE'RE UNSTOPPABLE IN OUR GIFTINGS TOGETHER.

SCRIPTURE(S): Zec. 7:9; 8:16-17; Jms. 4:11
DESCRIPTION: We are to show kindness, speak truth, and not devise evil in our hearts.
COMMUNITY PRINCIPLE: IN COMMUNITY, OUR INDIVIDUAL MEDITATION ON TRUTH BRINGS A BLESSING TO THE WHOLE.

SCRIPTURE(S): Mk. 9:50; 11:31
DESCRIPTION: Be at peace with one another. Discuss issues openly in this spirit.
COMMUNITY PRINCIPLE: IN COMMUNITY, OUR PRIORITY IS TO BE PEACEMAKERS.

SCRIPTURE(S): Mk. 15:31
DESCRIPTION: Jesus is mocked on the cross.
COMMUNITY PRINCIPLE: IN COMMUNITY, WE GROW IN OUR DELUSION OR IN OUR RECOGNITION OF TRUTH.

SCRIPTURE(S): Jn. 5:44
DESCRIPTION: We can seek glory in God or in each other.
COMMUNITY PRINCIPLE: IN COMMUNITY, WE LEARN TO HONOR GOD'S GLORY TOGETHER.

SCRIPTURE(S): Rom. 1
DESCRIPTION: Together is where sin or righteousness is birthed.
COMMUNITY PRINCIPLE: IN COMMUNITY, RIGHTEOUSNESS AND WICKEDNESS ARE DIFFERENTIATED.

SCRIPTURE(S): Rom. 12:5; 1 Cor. 12:8, 25
DESCRIPTION: We are one body.
COMMUNITY PRINCIPLE: IN COMMUNITY, EVERYTHING WE DO AFFECTS THE WHOLE.

SCRIPTURE(S): Rom. 12:10; 15:5; 2 Cor. 13:11

DESCRIPTION: We honor and love each other in, healthy competition, harmony, and comfort.
COMMUNITY PRINCIPLE: IN COMMUNITY, LOVE CAUSES EVERYONE TO GET BETTER.

SCRIPTURE(S): Rom. 13:8
DESCRIPTION: We are givers and not lenders, owing nothing.
COMMUNITY PRINCIPLE: IN COMMUNITY, ALL MATTERS ARE HANDLED DEBT-FREE SO THAT LOVE IS UPHELD.

SCRIPTURE(S): Rom. 14:5, 13; 15:7; Eph. 4:2, 32
DESCRIPTION: Don't judge or make someone stumble and be welcoming, with all patience.
COMMUNITY PRINCIPLE: IN COMMUNITY, WE HAVE THE MIND OF CHRIST, AND ALL OUR THINKING SHOULD BE COLLECTIVE THINKING.

SCRIPTURE(S): Rom. 15:14
DESCRIPTION: Teach each other.
COMMUNITY PRINCIPLE: IN COMMUNITY, EVERYONE IS A PASTOR IN SOME RESPECT.

SCRIPTURE(S): Gal. 5:13; 6:2; Col. 3:13; 1 Pt. 4:8, 10; 1 Jn. 4:7, 11
DESCRIPTION: Serve; bear each other's burdens, forgive, and love.
COMMUNITY PRINCIPLE: IN COMMUNITY, WE DISCOVER THE ONLY THING THAT CAN CAUSE A PEOPLE TO FLOURISH—SERVING.

SCRIPTURE(S): Eph. 5:21
DESCRIPTION: Submission
COMMUNITY PRINCIPLE: IN COMMUNITY, WE LEARN GODLY ROLES AND AUTHORITY.

SCRIPTURE(S): 1 Thes. 4:18; 5:11; Eph. 4; Heb. 3:13; 10:24-25
DESCRIPTION: Encouraging motives with words
COMMUNITY PRINCIPLE: IN COMMUNITY, WE AFFIRM VIRTUE AND DISPEL VICE.

SCRIPTURE(S): 1 Pt. 4:9

DESCRIPTION: Hospitality
COMMUNITY PRINCIPLE: IN COMMUNITY, PEOPLE ARE WELCOMED IN EVERY SENSE.

SCRIPTURE(S): 1 Jn. 1:7
DESCRIPTION: Learn to walk in the light
COMMUNITY PRINCIPLE: IN COMMUNITY, WE HOLD TOGETHER ONLY IN CONFESSION AND OPENNESS.

KEY PASSAGES

1 PETER 1:22
HAVING PURIFIED YOUR SOULS BY YOUR OBEDIENCE TO THE TRUTH FOR A SINCERE BROTHERLY LOVE, LOVE ONE ANOTHER EARNESTLY FROM A PURE HEART.

1 JOHN. 4:12
NO ONE HAS EVER SEEN GOD; IF WE LOVE ONE ANOTHER, GOD ABIDES IN US AND HIS LOVE IS PERFECTED IN US.

The listings above may make it seem that becoming like our Triune God brings on a lot of heavy responsibilities. But with these responsibilities come enormous blessings. Think of them as Jesus thinks about the cross. Hebrews tells us that for the joy set before him Jesus endured the cross. We are to think about community through the framework of joy. On the tail end of all that's required of us, there is an exponential blessing that comes our way. The ultimate prize is not each other. The ultimate reward is not having our needs met. The crown is not won by how many friends, likes, connections, followers, or tasks we've accomplished. The true joy of community is that we, and I emphasize *we*, get to become like our God. Our Christlikeness as individuals comes together when we learn how to interact with our brothers and sisters and mothers and fathers.

We press into the family. The Bible tells us how.

We are called to live in peace with each other;[1] we are called to show kindness, speak truth, and not devise evil in our heart toward one another.[2] We are called with a pure heart[3] to encourage each other,[4] bear each other's burdens, forgive and love one another,[5] hold up a brother who falls,[6] serve each other, and even to share each other's consequences in seeking justice for one another.[7] We hold a duty to rebuke and confront one another[8] face to face,[9] and at the same time we are called in our openness10 to honor each other in harmony, peace, and mutual submission.[10] We are perfected in our walk together.[11] As one body with many different parts and gifts,[12] we serve and accomplish tasks together,[13] we teach each other,[14] and thus our salvation fulfills the prayer of Christ that we may be one.[15]

We became one with Christ not in equality, divinity, or essence, but through the simultaneous event of regeneration and of the baptism of the Holy Spirit; which is given when we are added to the Trinitarian family through Christ by the power of the Holy Spirit.[16]

We are now to extend this grace in fellowship to other believers and extend it through hospitality to all those that don't believe.[17] We are to share our time,[18] our talents,[19] and our treasure[20] with all those in need, especially with widows and orphans, for they represent the fatherless and husbandless condition of humanity apart from God. Our unity is bound together in a family and spiritual covenant with a loyalty that cannot be broken.[21] It is beyond preference or hobby, race or creed, difference or indifference, comfort or discomfort, feeling or want, male or female. We are held together by the unity of God's word,[22] brought together under one name that is perfect—Jesus,[23] loved by one Father,[24] and empowered to proclaim one message through the empowering of one Spirit.[25]

Unforgiveness is the Thief of being One Another

We live in a world bound in unforgiveness. It's the common denominator in every situation that divides. It's the reason we can't be together. We create separation between ourselves and God because we choose not to forgive or receive forgiveness.

When we refuse to forgive, it's like drinking poison and then waiting for inflicting person to die. When we dwell on the hate that boils within us when we have been wronged, we allow the person who has wronged us to dominate our thoughts. Disproportionately, they stand out in our mind. Our unforgiveness creates idols. Our enemies become all we see. They become objects of undue attention, making them akin in a negative way to worship.

When forgiveness is restrained, we allow people to take on roles in our hearts and minds they were never meant to fill. As a result, anything said or done to us is interpreted through lenses that are skewed. We become suspicious of people's motives and intentions. We see everyone as a potential gun just waiting to shoot and kill us. We become a perpetual victim. Everything and everyone gets bigger and we shrink more and more.

When we refuse to forgive, we turn ourselves into king's occupying thrones. Though God has said "it is finished" in the matter of forgiveness, we still carry on the plague of bitterness. We won't let God forgive people. We won't let his cry of mercy sound until we're vindicated. We will occupy the throne and determine who gets grace and who gets mercy.

The inevitable result of unforgiveness is separation. Divorce. Our isolation pulls us back into self-protection from the bullies looming three-times their actual size in our minds. We withdraw from all those seeking to love us. Our retreat begins to evidence itself most clearly through our speech and our inability to be "with" each other.

I call it with-ness.

We've lost it.

In a world where people are perpetually crook-necked down toward their iPhones and device screens, we no longer can look at each other eye-to-eye. We hide behind the glass of devices that enable us to reveal ourselves solely on our terms. We let people see only what we show them, and we die on the inside knowing that the person we're revealing on social media is just a lie.

On the inside, we know our brokenness, but just as we can't forgive someone else, we determine it right not to allow God to forgive us as well. We flip him the middle finger and hold onto our shame like a life raft when it's really an anvil.

When people encounter us on the bottom of the sea in our shame, we attempt to convince them that "we're okay" by performing. We put up a front. We create an alter-ego. We invent a self that we most want people to see. We cast our false perception of ourselves mainly through how we dress, our affluence and influence, but most assuredly through our speech.

We're divided inside, and so our speech divides. We invent for ourselves a persona that keep us from getting too close to others, or worse … prevents them from getting close to us. I call the characters we invent for our self-protection "verbal villains." Below is a list showing how I classify them:

- **The Robber** fills in the blank or completes your sentence when you are struggling to process what you think, feel, or believe about something. It's the Robber's way of maintaining distance through supposed expertise.

- **The Historian** has a story for every occasion, and his brother the Teacher has a lesson for every occasion. They both take most of the "air time" from the conversation. It's the Historian's way of diverting attention away from their person, and onto the story.
- **The Interrogator** asks a lot of questions, but only to prosecute his case! It's the Interrogator's way of covering up their wrongs by exerting how right they are.
- **The Doctor** has a diagnosis and treatment for whatever you say. It's their way of diverting attention away from their own sicknesses and insecurities, and propping up their need to fix what they can't fix in themselves.
- **The General** takes charge of the conversation to make you fall in line. It's the General's way of keeping things predictable and hiding from things that might require what is unpredictable like faith, trust, hope, and love.
- **The Cardist** is adept at the sleight of hand needed to make the topic suit his needs. It's the Cardist's way of controlling you into what they desire, and away from what they don't want you to see.
- **The Wallflower** is barely noticeable, and so deprives everyone of her insights. It's the Wallflower's way of dominating the room and seeking people's pity and attention in a warped form of worship.

Each villain reveals an inner bitter root. Each villain is built on an internal idol of worship that's being held onto for dear life. The Robber is a know-it-all and anchors identity to certainty. Robbers can't enter into the unknown of anyone else's thoughts or feelings because it would obliterate everything they hold true inside themselves. A Robber can't get close to people because he has assessed that no one else is good enough to associate intimately with him.

The Historian maintains bigness through "big fish" stories. Historians maintain the seat of glory and attention. Meanwhile, they flit about in worldwide travel, collecting stories that inflate their self-importance, but they can't seem to acquire a true artifact of love.

The Interrogator likewise deflects attention from his real self by putting all the attention back on other people. His work is not a charitable one mind you. It's not loving! His inner bitterness doesn't want to know people, but rather to expose people for who they really are. The Interrogator takes pride in the fact he gets to uncover someone's inner demons all while hiding his own.

The Doctor holds the answers. The savior complex. The General holds the directions and control. The lord complex. The Cardist will only allow you to play his or her game, and the wallflower won't play at all.

Which one are you? What false version of yourself have you created out of a fight for survival? What character have you invented so people will like you and not see the real you?

Let's face it, we all have inner bitterness that we refuse to water with forgiveness. When we neglect forgiveness, it requires us to build up false "fakebook" characters constructed only from the information we want people to know. Our alter-egos become our idols. They grow into what is supposedly required to protect us. The only thing our unforgiveness really achieves is the forming of a personality that can never experience with-ness. We never feel close to anyone, nor can we accept embrace.

We collapse with our heads hanging over the glow of phones, mesmerized by the false worlds of games, movies, and entertainment galore, all the while hiding from the real loves, real conquests, and real battles to be fought in the real world.

MEDITATION AND QUESTION

What unforgiveness keeps us from more than anything is what I call "one-anothering," a term that should by now be so self-explanatory that it needs no further elaboration. As I close this chapter, I want to leave you with two things. First, don't move on from this chapter too quickly. Think on and pray over the Scriptures and thoughts included prior in our analysis of all the "one another" verses.

Second, consider the depth and span of Christ's household and what it means to play your role in the family of God. It may be helpful to consider these questions as you ponder:

1. How does the Trinity change the way I think about and live in community?
2. What's the ultimate goal to community, and how is Christian community different because of the Trinity?
3. What is the basis of unity in Christ's family? Are my expectations

of friendship based on personal preferences, biases, or interests that are not necessary for true unity?

4. Are my choices in Christ's Church causing me to grow in a motherly affection, a laborious toil, and the embrace of myself and others as adopted orphans now made into a family?

5. How have the environments of distance we've invented as churches today actually undermined the very message of closeness we hope to preach?

I pray that your time of contemplation is fruitful.

14

THE TRINITY ANSWERS COMMUNITY

D on't you wish you had a simple formula that could answer all of life's problems? This is what the Trinity gives us. A unified place to begin inquiry. We often overlook the most deeply helpful answers in many realms of study because we tackle them from a place of division. We compartmentalize subjects by looking at them through fractured lenses. We put religion over here. Science over there. We pit psychology against sociology. Archaeology is set apart from biblical history. Anthropology becomes cancerously natural because it doesn't adequately consult theology or philosophy. Literacy doesn't cross-pollinate with the arts. Math is separated from music.

Because we separate things into nice little boxes, we miss wholistic answers, and we end up creating a lot of false positives across disciplines. The Trinity provides a unified lens through which to view all things without destroying their interrelationships. In the closing chapter of each section on C.R.O.S.S. I'll demonstrate how deliberating on the Trinity can provide a thorough approach to giving answers to all realms of study. We'll do this by addressing some of what I call the "ics" and "als."

THE "ICS" AND "ALS" OF EXISTENCE

Just to clarify, "ic" is not referring to something icky, nor is "al" the name of a weird Muppet from the 70s. They are the endings that we add onto words to indicate various areas of learning. Some study the psychological, others study the biographical, the ethical, the sociological, the musical, or the historical. Some study rhetoric, logic, or the scientific. Adding "al" or "ic" to the end of a subject is the smart way to say that we are compartmentalizing our learning. We are choosing to hone in on one subject in isolation from all others.

The same practice of isolation happens all the time in church life. We might create a distinction between sacred and secular, even though there's absolutely no such distinction in how God's kingdom operates. We may dissect the human into pieces and call one part physical and the other part spiritual. That's just Gnosticism. We may create tidy bins for sin. We make homosexuality worse than white lies. We make pornography worse than overeating. Meanwhile, we have a church full of people who are fat without any concern of obesity, and yet are scared to death of the Internet.

Compartments. Levels. Ranks. We humans are great at inventing this stuff. And as we've seen in chapters previous, we fall into a wave pool of errors when we start trying to pigeonhole individuals in isolation from community.

Our error begins when we think solely in terms of what works in the West. Because the West is literate and pragmatic, all our ways of doing life together are boiled down to what works. What may work in a remote oral culture in the middle of the Amazon looks to us like primitive tribalism. We dismiss as inauthentic practices that differ from ours. We endorse only those that eat, sleep, and dream like us. It's isolating.

It's not gospel.

What has resulted is that our ways of "doing life" undermine the message.

The gospel is universal and equally applies to everyone. The gospel of Jesus is that our loving God provided a way forward that transcends time and space. There are absolutes in God's story that carry across all the differences between peoples that we may face. We must never allow our practices in doing church to limit God's paradigm for life to our time and space and understanding. If we do so, we'll come up with never-ending patterns and ways of relating that suit us. We'll lay these biases atop Scripture and skew its meaning.

It is my absolute conviction that the Trinity helps us solve what has become an epidemic. The Trinity forces us to think in unity. Because human history is made up of quite a lot of isolated thinkers that think in *timely* ways and not *timeless* ones, we are in need of more cohesive, transcendent, and inclusive ways of seeing life in a way that brings all disciplines under one roof for the best dissection and analyzation. The Trinity is the only person that can help us develop paradigms for how to view all of life consistently in every time, in every place, and under any circumstance.

It's only in and through Trinitarian lenses that we see true meaning. By contemplating the Trinity, we will arrive at the only means by which we as humans can experience the truest sense of peace, harmony, unity, and friendship with each other across all disciplines of thought and practice.

Regarding the topic at hand—C.ommunity, and how the Trinity relates—I will target some specific "als" and "ics." Take a look at Figure 3.1:

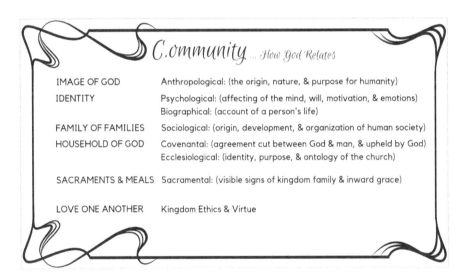

Community ... How God Relates

IMAGE OF GOD   Anthropological: (the origin, nature, & purpose for humanity)

IDENTITY   Psychological: (affecting of the mind, will, motivation, & emotions)
Biographical: (account of a person's life)

FAMILY OF FAMILIES   Sociological: (origin, development, & organization of human society)

HOUSEHOLD OF GOD   Covenantal: (agreement cut between God & man, & upheld by God)
Ecclesiological: (identity, purpose, & ontology of the church)

SACRAMENTS & MEALS   Sacramental: (visible signs of kingdom family & inward grace)

LOVE ONE ANOTHER   Kingdom Ethics & Virtue

Fig. 3.1

EVERY ONE OF the areas in the graphic is a topic of interest for the human race. Anthropological studies seek to know the origin, nature, and purpose of human societies and cultures. Those who dive into the biographical and psychological want to understand what makes a person a person in terms of both external and internal experience and influences. The sociological spins off of anthropology and psychology and tries to understand how the individual and collective peoples have all been formed by cultural evolvement because our varying cultures appear to influence our ethics, our morals, our sense of virtue, and our belief about how everything holds together.

Add to all that the exploits of the church and its approach to the above issues. Not only do we concern ourselves with the nature of individual and corporate identity, but we also desire to provide answers to how things sustain. Add into the mix our investigation into family, household, church, virtue, covenant, and personhood, and we recognize that we in the church are trying to provide consistent answers in our quest for knowledge of ourselves and our world just as are those outside the church.

So, the big question we want to address is this: Can the Trinity bring unity of thought and help us dig out real answers that unify all knowledge consistently under a single umbrella?

The Trinity Speaks a Better Word

The Trinity speaks a better word than anthropology. The anthropologist longs to know the biographical information concerning living things in order to know why civilizations develop. They seek to uncover why ethnocentrism is where we always seem to end up (i.e., cultures judging others based on their own societal and personal assumptions and preferences). It appears that humans have an insatiable need to judge others by their own rules of right and wrong.

Judging is the way our world works. Perhaps this is why Jesus said that he didn't come to judge the world, for it stands condemned already. He came to save it. Our world is already riddled with our human assessment of things. What we need is not more judgments based on what we think; we need more thought invested into what our God thinks.

We use our judgments as criteria to either unite or separate. Jesus' judgment operates differently than ours. Whereas our world pronounces verdicts via *contracts*, our Trinity acts in *covenants*. Contracts are self-serving. When a contract is written, it sets down rules based on parameters relevant to the issue at hand. Contracts are assessments. As a result, penalty and punishment come when expectations are broken. Contracts get business done, not relationships.

Covenants form around serving others. Our God is the only one ever worthy to cut a covenant. When God made a covenant with Abraham, it was a promise and a binding agreement made between two parties. In Genesis 15:9-

10 we observe a ritual common in the Near East when confirming a covenant. God promises Abraham land, seed, and blessing, and seals the deal by dividing animals. Their blood pools in the crevice of two adjoining hills. The two parties then walk through the blood, in essence saying, "If I do not hold up my end of the bargain, then do to me what was done to these animals." God's promise differed, however, in that he put Abraham to sleep and walked through the blood on his own behalf and on behalf of Abraham. The symbol is that God's promise to humanity depends not on our commitment to God, but rather on his commitment to us.

The Trinity's loyalty to humanity exceeds that of any human love toward another human. God's devotion to the preservation of anthropological life took him to the cross. Whereas anthropology dissects all of what makes us human using self-devised standards and viewpoints—holding everything and everyone under that magnifying glass—God sees humanity from a much fuller purview. God assigns rules and then audaciously makes himself liable for the penalty and punishment if the rules aren't met. He positioned himself to die in order to forgive and commune with us. He did so in order that love, grace, and mercy could remain.

The contractual nature of our world that exists between people, societies, cultures, and all kinds of cliques and groups produces restrictive systems like Marxism, Communism, and even thinking similar to Claude Lévi-Strauss' Structuralism (his belief that society springs from the human mind). Contracts have birthed historical world powers such as Rome and the United States. Covenants are foreign to human thinking because we expect everyone first to answer to us. We become, in our own minds, our own deity. We sit on the bench as judge and preside over our fellow man.

Our Triune God's desire to connect one to another reaches much deeper into the actual questions that studiers of humans face every day. Only the existence of a Triune God can explain why have any sense of justice with its attendant penalties and punishments. Deep down, we not only believe that there is a right way to do things but we believe that all people should know and adhere to this universal truth. Our desire to believe and to bring others along with us reflects the faint shadow of how all men still reflect the Trinity. We all recognize that we are *persons*, but few realize that we are only truly persons when we are together hand in hand with each other and the Trinity.

The same faint but often-distorted shadow of godlikeness within humans causes social changes, including new technologies, new societal standards and expectations, new governments, and revolutions. Add to this changes in the environment, including climate and adaptational changes in plants and animals, and you have encompassed the questions that anthropologists grapple with. What factors lead to the creation of culture and ideology as we now know them?

The Trinity answers all of the above in entirety. The desire of a dictator to control others demonstrates in a backhanded way that man has the image of God in him. If man had just evolved from some primordial soup, a desire to rule and reign would be foreign to humanity. We would have no need to invent the idea of a god if everything is random and our destiny lies within ourselves. The only way our desire to study anthropology, sociology, or culture in any form even makes sense is if there's a source from which our desires to create and rule originate.

The Bible tells us that our image to take dominion was placed in us by God. We were made to rule, conquer, steward, cultivate, and prune the Garden (Gn. 1–3). God made us to be culture creators. He assigned us the responsibility to care for and multiply everything on the earth. He made us servant conquerors, not communists, democrats, or republicans.

The cog in the machine that frustrates anthropological studies, ultimately affecting everyone's story and identity, is what we mentioned back in the introduction concerning the Fall of Humanity. The Fall of Humanity is what makes it possible for psychology and sociology to exist. These disciplines thrive on uncovering what motivates us and seek to explain why we do the broken things we do. The psychologist will attribute the cause of all our problems to the id or super ego that house our primitive instincts that drive us to negative ends. Psychologists explain adequately why we exalt our way of thinking as supreme and why we hold everyone accountable to us for pardon upon disobedience to what we deem right. We think only in contracts and cut ties with all those that don't do it our way. Even the non-Christian observes how our sinful nature has made us into demanding, make-believe deities.

We ultimately find that broken people build increasingly broken cultures because the nature of the heart became broken in the Fall of Humanity.

The Trinity speaks a better word to the sociologist and psychologist. Unlike them, the Trinity doesn't compare people to each other or evaluate them on a culturally devised scale to determine value. The Trinity is perfect, and says "Compare yourselves only to me." We can only understand culture when we identify to what degree it has either moved toward or away from

God. When we begin to examine God's likeness and image and sense how culture has either gotten closer or further away, only then can we start to determine what the idols are amongst a culture of people. Only then can we place our finger on what imperfect loves have captured a particular group's heart and begin turning it back to a place of perfect satisfaction in God.

Still, the psychologically minded will fight against a God centrality. They will try and explain that external forces have made us so internally perverted in our worship of self and created things. God identifies our problem as being internal. We are our own greatest enemy. We cannot self-examine to reach inner enlightenment. Can you believe the idiocy? Attempting to find perfect satisfaction by dreaming inside of ourselves. We're broken ruins.

Martin Luther would say that a type of yoga-esque self-intuition only leads us to half the answer. Self-examination leads only to one conclusion: We are not god, nor will we ever be god. Luther would describe sin as, "turned in ourselves." Self-examination can only lead us to deeper and deeper conclusions about how broken we are, but it can never bring us to perfection. Our constant state of self-reflection, whether it comes through psychosis, meditation, mantra, psychiatry, life coaches, or any other form of new age enlightenment, is all merely another way of chasing sin.

What many who study human nature can never realize is that the cause of culture and all things related, is a result of the heart. Man's broken heart grabs at broken things. Dead people do dead things, and we are dead in sin. That's why we take our newest technologies and newest discoveries and invent better ways to turn on each other, not love each other.

As seen in Figure 3.1, we must surrender our "als" and "ics" in relationship to community to the arms of the Trinity. If we start dreaming in God and not in fallen flesh, we'll start to come up with some real timeless solutions and the best discoveries.

R.easoning How We Do Things

Let me usher us into the next section and the "R" in our C.R.O.S.S. acronyms with some questions about church, meals, family, etc. I do so to demonstrate that there's a connection between how we understand community and how we've chosen to do things in the manner we have.

We must ask ourselves what the Trinity might speak into our images of church and family. If one were to ask Jesus or Paul to bring to mind their image of a meal, a church, a family, a pastor, a sermon, music, a gathering, and on and on, how would their answer compare with what we're doing?

Consider what they might think of our logic in rowed seating. If the nature of the Trinity is *with* each other (face to face as in a dance), then why do all churches have chairs that face the stage, not each other? Does architecture matter? Can it help or hinder the gospel? Is embrace and family connection strengthened in something as simple as a time in the service where we shake hands or listen to announcements? Are the only forms of art and media valuable to the sharing of the gospel public speaking, video, and music? If this is not our belief, why are these art forms the only created human things we showcase? Are the only vocations valuable to the kingdom missionary work and church staffing? If not, why are they the only ones the church prays for? Why are they the ones most often referred to as "doing ministry?" Do trades, craft, and worship-in-culture have ministerial value?

What about our worship? Is there a reason why congregations still associate worship with music and the presence of God with a worship leader, even though every Sunday one can hear a worship leader say, in essence, "It's not about me, the stage, or the music"? Is what we're showing in the environments and reasoning of our inventions elevating something that actually undermines what we're trying to say? Is the church supposed to be home-shaped or audience-shaped? Is there a difference? Even more to the point, are the messages we give more about practical living than about becoming like Christ? And if it's about Christ, does the theology preached tend to exclude even Jesus?

What about our homes? Is your home open, closed, or something in between? What is the nature of the home's flow? To what ultimate things does our worship in the home point? How do you lay out your mealtime? Is the Trinity a dominant focus in our eating or in how we express our with-ness to one another?

We must meditate on how to best dream in ways that press church and family life back toward, and not away from, the orbit of the table—being *with* one another as in a Trinitarian dance. We must consider our relationship to be a dance of closeness. We must do so because today many of our models have only driven more wedges between us. I find it sad that more often than not we dance around trying to solve issues that are keeping us far apart. Are the problems we're facing arising because of something we are doing?

I ask again, are our current environments that we've creatively invented for our time and space undermining the message? Ask yourself, Do I see ways of doing life in my family and church spaces that are shaping me toward or away from the closeness described in the Trinity? Are the environments we are fashioning actually promoting friendship on a "with each other" level, or do the stage and lights and programs and activities actually escalate separation?

If a Trinitarian relationship is one of authority and servanthood, and all believers are members of the priesthood of God, is an elevated platform and pulpit helpful in showcasing proper relationship, or is it further enforcing a divide between leader and laity? If all the words referring to the kingdom of God are family words, like son, daughter, bride, groom, household, meals, men, women, etc., then why are so many churches so businesslike today? Does the street preacher, hailing Christ's message from a concrete slab corner, match visually the familial words of the gospel being spoken audibly?

If the Trinity holds together in a bond of mutual submission and selfless service to one another, I find in myself a longing to know how and why this happens. Their ability to be intimate is not beyond us, and yet it is completely beyond us. The bond the Trinity exhibits with humanity exists in me through the Spirit and is completely absent of any of my effort. It's a covenant. I'm "covenantally indwelled" and can covenantally commit to the other, even to the point of death.

I dare say that covenant is not what holds the Trinity together, and yet it does. They do not need a sacrifice for sin, nor do they know what "death" without any connection to life is, but their service unto to one another is unyielding, and it is unending. One could postulate that since Jesus willingly went to the grave to maintain a relationship with us he would do the same for his Father the Spirit if that were ever an even conceivable option.

The bottom line is that God's family, household, provision, and kingdom-love is always spinning toward the other. The Trinity's gaze is always at the other member. They are forgetful of themselves within the whole, and they commit to each other perfectly because they consider only the wants and desires of the other. In this love, God is most famous. Distinct. Holy. Set apart. It is my desire that in this dance of love and worship we might find our greatest fame and connection to glory.

Let's turn our attention to bringing some practical answers to the questions we've raised in this chapter. How the Trinity relates is often opposite to how we naturally think, and more opposite still is how God does things. Let's discuss R.easoning.

PART IV
R: HOW GOD DOES THINGS

REASONING

OUR TEMPLE HOME

THE GENESIS OF HOME, NOT OF SCIENCE.

God has a philosophy of ministry. Better said, God has a *paradigm* for ministry. A philosophy changes from mind to mind, person to person, and place to place. A paradigm references a way of thinking that is universal and transcends time, space, and personal preference. We must repeat his paradigm over and over to ourselves so as not to fall prey to the glitz and glamor of what is contextually and culturally changing. We must avoid believing that somehow the foundations of ministry are creatively up to us. If we're not careful, we begin buying into the lie of "relevance." We forget that the gospel has always been relevant and always will be.

Three main categories are needed to properly discuss God's underlying logic to his paradigm. I introduced them at the tail-end of the last section on community. They are the concepts of the home, the family, and the meal.

Our first item of mention is the home. Paul calls God's family the kingdom household. Scripture's idea of home is far more profound than we might think. To build an understanding and unpack all that biblically goes into the word home, we must return to Genesis 1 and go on a bit of a rabbit trail. Bear with me!

"In the beginning …"

The author's priority in Genesis is not to deal with the primordial soup or the Big Bang. The central theme of the creation event is the making of an environment sufficient for habitation by humanity. A home!

Some textual items help us to arrive at such a conclusion. Who wrote the book of Genesis? Moses. To whom did he write it? The Israelites. And when did Moses write the book of Genesis? Most likely the book was written during the time of Israel's wandering in the desert. If all this is the case, we must ask ourselves: "Is Moses' primary goal in Genesis 1 to convince his original audience of the scientific harmony of creation?"

My answer is, no!

His intent in the Book of Genesis is much more about home than it is about a hypothesis. But before I go too far into the unsexy and unscientific purpose of Genesis 1, let me indulge you folks who have itchy ears and agendas pertaining to the age of the universe. If we're not careful to deal with your pre-conceived notions about what Genesis 1 is, and isn't, I feel you'll never be able to see through the scientific malaise down to the pastoral core of Genesis.

I believe that Genesis 1 leaves room for both Old and New scientific beliefs. Most debate jumps too fast into the aspects of what constitutes a day—in Hebrew the *yom*, or length of time and genealogy. In making this jump, we totally skip over the first three words. In Genesis 1:1, Moses says "In the beginning ..." Wait! Stop there.

Moses uses a very curious word for the beginning. It is the Hebrew word *reshit*. It has a very specific sense in Scripture. It refers to an extended yet indeterminate duration of time—*not* a specific moment.[1] It is a time before times. It's a span that falls before a list of events. This way of reckoning time in the Near East was common, particularly in counting the years of a reigning king. Scribes would begin dating the king's reign specifically only after the ruler had been serving as king over a general timeframe. *Reshit* alludes to a king that had been reigning over an indefinite length of time, only then to be followed by a specific numbering of literal days in increments of time.

Moses assumes the role of a scribe. His opening phrase, "In the beginning," implies the existence of a time before times. In doing this, he emphasizes his point. He draws our attention to the fact that God is Israel's King. Moses stresses to the people that God has been their forever King and is so specifically now. Why create such a distinction, and what does it have to do with the concept of home? Well, his logic makes sense if we picture Moses writing his letter to the wandering tribe of Israel. God had just delivered them from underneath the horrific rule of Pharaoh. They'd been enslaved for 400 years by a man claiming the authority of a king. In a way, their first days of wandering free from Pharaoh's grip is their first day walking beside their Trinity King. Though God had been ruling and reigning all along, the Israelites had forgotten their forever past. They needed a fresh reminder and a new start. They desperately needed governance under the helm of a good and gracious ruler, and Moses begins by assuring them that God is providing just that. He's doing a new creative work. He's remaking them into a people of freedom and promise under the oversight of a loving King. He's taking them out of exile and toward their new home.

The wording in Genesis 1 is also remarkably similar to how other Old Testament writers speak of the "preparation of an uninhabited land for habitation." Moses reminds the people, who presently felt they lacked a place of habitation, about the preparation of a Promised Land for them. He reminds them of the covenant.

Moses references the formless deep and unformed world poetically almost to allude to the very state of the people being led out of horrible slavery. He portrays the Spirit of God as "hovering" over the waters as he hovers over the Israelites in a cloud by day and fire by night.[2] Moses uses the phrase *tohu wabohu*. It likens the waters to what is "unseen" and "unformed." The typical use of this phrase in Scripture, as it is also used in Jeremiah 4:23-26, is not to describe a formless and empty chaos—evoking images of a Big Bang as is popularly thought amongst creation-scientists today—but rather to describe an uninhabited and inhospitable stretch of wasteland.[3] What Moses is describing is a piece of land that is unfit for life (a desert) and he's promising to make it fit for a home. The people understood Moses' literary and artful expression as they journeyed through the desert in their own version of a wilderness wandering.

Jeremiah also curiously uses the same language in speaking of exile. Jeremiah doesn't describe the land as void and empty, but as "deserted and uninhabited."[4] God communicates in wordplay. He's telling his people that he's making ready a habitat (a home) for them that will serve as a suitable living space. God's use of the word *tohu* ("deserted") and *tob* ("good") in response to his completed work, tells us the conclusion. God calls the home "good" in that it is ready to support life for his people, as opposed to bondage.

What follows Genesis 1:1 is not a description of the creation of the whole universe; it's a description of the preparation of a land for *a people*. A home!

Moses' reminder boasts of great encouragement to the Israelites because they were a kingless, landless, wandering, and homeless people.

Thus, it is concluded that Genesis is a pastoral document of God leading a homeless people toward home, and they understood it as such.

THE GENESIS OF A CREATION-TEMPLE HOME

What kind of home is being promised to the people of God?

No singular parcel of land is home. God's intention from the beginning is that the whole world is home for his people and his glory. The layout of Eden, the Garden, and the outer uninhabited wilderness beyond the outskirt boundaries tells of a God who desires to live with, in, and amongst his people wherever and whenever they are. It tells us of a God who fills all things and is cuddled up close to us as we sleep, rise, walk, dine, and lay down at night.

Unfortunately, human sin twisted knots into God's straight and narrow plan for dwelling with his people. God's holiness is too concentrated to dwell with weakened imperfection. His very presence would kill us. God's temporary remedy to the problem of sin was to live amongst his people in the construction of a tabernacle, and ultimately the temple. In Genesis 1–3, Moses intentionally uses tabernacle and temple imagery in his creation account. The language elicits in the minds of the Israelite how they are to think of home.

Let's first discuss the temple, which at the time of Moses' writing was prefigured in the more portable construction of the tabernacle. It is interesting to note that only one verse of Scripture records the creation of the heavens and earth (Genesis 1:1), while fifteen chapters are devoted to the tabernacle (Exodus 25 – 40), and a whole book (Leviticus) to the service of it.[5] Suffice it to say, the true design of the temple/tabernacle is pregnant with meaning far beyond that of simple architecture. The structure presents us with the hope of the anticipated day when "the tabernacle of God is with men, and he will dwell with them, and they shall be his people" (Rv. 21:3).

The temple was composed of three main parts, each of which symbolizes a major part of the cosmos: (1) the outer court represented the habitable world where humanity dwelt; (2) the holy place of the inner courts was emblematic of the visible heavens and its light sources, (3) and the holy of holies symbolized the invisible dimension of the cosmos, where God and his heavenly hosts dwelt.[6] On the outside, the large molten water basin was respectively called the 'sea' (I Kgs. 7:23-26), the altar was known as the "altar of the earth" (Ez. 43:16), and surrounding the basin were twelve bulls and a lily blossom that circled the sea in entirety; "a partial miniature model of land and life surrounding the seas of the earth." (2 Chr. 4:2-5).[7]

The entirety of cosmos is portrayed in the miniatures of the tabernacle and temple. Inside of God's universal temple-creation, we find safety and kingship within and under God's glory. And as we discussed earlier in the book, God's glory can reference a home or dwelling.

God's desire to *tabernacle*, dwell, and live amongst his people in glory is a common thread throughout the whole narrative of Scripture. Toward the middle of the Bible, John uses the Greek word for tabernacle when he says that Jesus came and "dwelt ["tabernacled"] among us."[8] In the end, in Revelation 21:3, God again communicates that his plan, which was once a faint shadow held in the miniatures of the temple and in the suffering flesh of Jesus, comes to successful completion in the fully exalted, fully man, fully God, Jesus. In the New Testament, Jesus tabernacles with mankind via his Spirit in our hearts. He dwells with us, and we are his.

Moses intentionally portrays God's total creation (symbolized by the tabernacle's outer court), the garden itself—which is a sacred space separate from the outer world (the tabernacle's holy place), and Eden where God dwells (the holy of holies), as a universal temple home. We are to think of creation in this way. God fills *all* things. Universal. Cosmic. And yet God is still outside of our time scale. Though God lives amongst us and his presence is with us, his presence is also above us. All things are housed in him.

Moses alludes to God being above us in his use of the location of Eden. He says that the garden is *in* Eden. The prophet Ezekiel portrays Eden as being on a mountain (Ez. 28:14, 16) in the same way, the temple is portrayed as being on Mount Zion (Ex. 15:17). A river flowed out of Eden's mountain to water the garden, just as Ezekiel 47:1 says that water flowed from the holy of holies. Jesus is portrayed as a mountain in the New Testament. He describes himself as the wellspring of life that actualizes the temple of God in his church. To call Christ the temple cornerstone is another way of saying that he's the summit of the new creation, since the temple is a symbol of the entirety of the created world. As we discussed earlier, Christ is in us (water imagery) and we are in him.

The sky also symbolizes something of the reality of God being over us. The temple's vast ceiling references God's creation of the sky. The priest would walk into an atrium filled with engravings of the forest, jewels, and precious stones on the walls and seven lampstands lighting the room. The lampstands reflect the seven light-sources visible to the human eye (five planets, sun, and moon). We know this because the author of Genesis uses the curious word "lights" instead of "sun" and "moon." The term lights is used ten more times throughout the Pentateuch only to refer to the tabernacle lampstands.[9] Revelation 1 also uses the symbol of the lampstands for the seven churches, each of which have as its representative an angel, which is symbolized as a star.

The cosmos was conceived of as a huge temple. Not only is the temple a miniature representation of the whole universe that God made, but the New Testament also transfers this imagery to the church. We are the lampstands. The presence of God sits no longer in Eden or behind the veil of the temple, but it rests hidden behind and within the safety of our hearts. Within God's hearty-cosmos-temple, humans are to eat (via the shewbread) and serve (via the image of incense and loving sacrifice) the living God.

Adam, therefore, was not merely a keeper of the garden. Adam was not just flesh and bone. He was intended from the beginning to be a priest. All humanity from the beginning was intended to be priestly kings.

Even the Old Testament priesthood points to the reality of our status in the kingdom. The temple priests in Israel dressed in garb that also alluded to the cosmos. The outermost part of the priest's garments was blue and purple and ornamented with flowers to represent the fertile earth. The main body of the robe was bluish for the inner courts and was set with jewels that looked like the stars set in the sky. Lastly, the ephod was square and corresponded to the square shape (*tetragonos*) of the temple's holy place, the altar, and the mercy seat. Within the holiest place on the priest's chest was the Urim and Thumim, stones representing God's revelatory presence.[10] Today, the holiest place is in the chest of every man, woman, and child that professes Jesus as Lord.

THE GENESIS OF A CREATION-TEMPLE-CHURCH HOME

Moses' temple-creation imagery is picked up by Paul in his writings. He calls himself the wise master builder of the church in 1 Corinthians 3:10. In his letter to the Ephesians, he expands on this concept. The words he uses transport us back to that of the skilled workman of the tabernacle, as described in Exodus 35:31-32. Paul tells us what he's building. He calls believers a "temple of the living God." Listen to how he describes the human heart and the church in Ephesians 2:19-22; 3:17-18:

> ... but you are fellow citizens with the saints and members of the *household* of God, *built on the foundation* of the apostles and prophets, Christ Jesus himself being the *cornerstone*, in whom the *whole structure*, being joined together, grows *into a holy temple in the Lord*. In him you also are being *built together* into a *dwelling place for God by the Spirit* ... so that Christ *may dwell in your hearts* through faith—that you, being rooted and grounded in love, may have strength to comprehend with all the saints what is the *breadth* and *length* and *height* and *depth*, and to know the love of Christ that surpasses knowledge, that you may be *filled* with all the fullness of God (italics mine).

I'm absolutely aghast at how much of Paul's description of God's people is given in terms of building, measurement, and structure-type language. The people of God are now inhabited by God. We are his home. The people together (the church body) is where we experience the truest sense of home. We are no longer orphans and wanderers together. We are a people once dead and now made alive as a *kingdom of priests*. We carry our home with us. Home is the glory of God expressed in the totality of all he is and all he's made.

To understand the full weight of what life means in God's home, consider what was in the ark of the covenant in the Most Holy Place. Within the box were three things: the tablets with the ten commandments (representing God covenant with Moses—Ex. 20), the golden pot with manna (representing God's provision for Israel in the desert—Ex. 16), and the rod of Aaron that had budded (representing the authority of the priestly leadership—Nm. 17). These items tell the story of God protecting Israel through the law, providing for Israel with the manna, and empowering Israel through the Aaronic leadership. God's life saves us from the law, feeds us with the bread of heaven, and carries us into every situation with a worshipful and priestly heart.

This *homeland* reign we share with Christ is eternal. Timeless. Everywhere. Worship potential is a world reality. Walter Edward Brooks maintains that Jesus "is the eternal priest from the moment of his resurrection-exaltation because he possesses from that moment a life that does not end."[11] Christ's sacrifice was for all existence and beyond. Such life culminated in our

Messiah sitting down at the right hand of God. It involved one sacrifice, and it accomplished perfection for those whom the sacrifice was offered.[12]

The tabernacle is God's picture-book for babes in Christ.[13] God sent a picture before he sent the Person. The picture of the temple/tabernacle creation has only gotten fuller in the reality of Christ's coming. The message hasn't changed. Jesus has not only brought heaven to earth, but he's also brought earth to heaven. He's entered the true tabernacle above as fully God and fully man. He has done so in two ways: (1) as seated, and (2) as interceding.[14] He sits in rest because sin and death have been laid waste. He also sits as our High Priest poised in power; interceding for his saints as they come to fully realize the victory that he has already procured. He established a new covenant. Everything in heaven he has given to us for our benefit, and he has become our High Priest. He has called us priests and made available to us his resurrection power and grace through Jesus (Heb. 4:14-16).

Welcome *home*!

How Have We Changed the Definition of Home in our Way of Doing Things?

I hope we've done some worthwhile work in deconstructing the Bible's idea of home. The Bible points to home as being the very presence and glory of God which fills the believer as they walk everywhere throughout God's created world. Through God's people, he fills all things. Home invokes the idea of a cohesive human as a newly created temple that is presiding as a royal child of God over the welfare of the entire cosmos.

Why would God do it this way?

It's God's paradigm for ministry. We should think in terms of household. The idea of homes should be the center point of all centripetal motion—the thing toward which everything moves. Homes are external and visible reminders of what is invisibly internal to us.

Sadly the culture and even the church as an entity seem to wage war with the centrality of the idea of home. The church can all-too-unintentionally become a catalyst in actually propelling us away from becoming Christlike as a community focused on the home. The church bites the bait the world is casting by becoming absolutely strangled with programs. Programs angle to be the home that demands our time. Programming makes the church a slave to all and a servant to none. It fuels the desires of those making the demands. It is based on consumption. It ends up consuming people. Eating them. Burning them out. The church as an entity has become a machine that eats people. The church should not consume God's people, but rather equip them to do the work of ministry. God did not form us to be observers. He created us for production. To make. To feed others.

The church and culture's use of technology has become a huge barrier to building a productive and multiplying mentality of home. Technology, to a large degree, builds for us a life that is lived *apart together*. We're forever crooked-necked and staring down at our phones. We miss faces. We're so addicted to texting and responding that we barely know that our home suffers. I can't tell you how tired I am of people constantly snapping pictures and selfies to be enjoyed later, while the power of the moments we're in presently is completely lost. We've become absent in the moments that require us most. It's ironic that so many of today's inventions that claim to make us better at finding a home are robbing us of being *present* in the home which his *presence* provides.

A lack of presence has infiltrated the church. It's subtle, but it's profound. Consider how almost everything in the church has taken its cue from culture and is now aimed at a stage and screen. I'm not demonizing these things and saying there's not a place for them; I'm merely observing that they've taken over. They're central now. That's what idols do. They take over. When they sit in the driver's seat, they steal from us the things we're meant to experience. In the case of a home, we've lost aspects of being with each other as the Trinity is with themselves. Being with each other is what points truest toward God's glory. Home.

WE'VE COMPLICATED THE THEOLOGY OF HOME WITH THE METHODOLOGY OF CHURCH

As we've come up with bigger and shinier ways to reach the lost, we've developed methodologies that contradict any sense of a cosmos household. The Scripture is loaded with family language and imagery like home, son and daughter, father and mother, meals, marriage, and the like, and our spaces actually make these concepts hard to understand. Our environments are actually making the *right theology* and *understanding of biblical meaning* more difficult.

For example, the word *deacon* in Greek means "table servant." It's a family and household image. Deaconism as a theological concept is best understood when acted out in a household context. However, ask someone to tell you what a deacon is today and he will almost automatically picture a church political office or some high-level official in the congregation. Thinking of the church in terms of household imagery helps to best make sense of the biblical use of the word. Spaces should help explain the true meaning, not draw away from meaning.

I'm not a stickler about word definitions for church servants or ways or organizing churches, but I'm a stickler about theology. What we believe fundamentally is shown in the bedrock of our methods of doing church. Making what was intended to be an humble, household servant into a high office in the church apes the way of the world by structuring the church by the pattern of worldly organizations and utterly destroying the concept of the church as a family home. It is through what we show and do that people first are able to determine what the church is.

Let me give you another example of how the way we structure our churches can smother the gospel message. I have a friend who is an avowed atheist. I asked him over coffee one day to tell me why he's an atheist. He replied, "I could never worship a God that is so wasteful with money." Curious, I asked him to explain. He went on to describe a local megachurch, raving over the extravagance of one of its multi-million-dollar campuses. What he beheld in the model actually turned him away from the message. Granted, he'd never darkened the door of any church, and his judgments were hasty and ill-informed at best. But consider the "sermon" that the megachurch's building preached to him. The visual image of an elaborate and expensive structure was the only sermon he'd heard and may ever hear. It portrayed something to him that represents irresponsibility and lofty worldliness.

I use this example not to shame anyone, but merely to ask us to consider whether our methods are speaking louder than our message. The fact of the matter is, the gospel is nothing more than simple *show and tell*, and on many levels the show speaks louder than the tell. More is caught then taught. You have to see it to believe it. You know the catch phrases, so I'll stop.

My harping isn't simply over a church's building, but also the hardened street-corner approach to ministry that I mentioned in other chapters. In one sense the platform helps the preacher air the message—we even see this in the ministry of Paul—but in another sense complicates what's being said. As the preacher teaches about the family of God, the home of God, and all the family-shaped images that come with the gospel, the street corner and stage stand idly beneath our feet and scream an altogether different tune. People may hear the message, but they don't feel the embodiment of it. It hits them, but it doesn't hug them. We may even preach love and repentance in mercy, but the environment flavors the tone. Hearers experience a sense of judgment what is spoken comes *down at them* rather than *toward them* or *amongst them* as it would in a circle of friendship.

The scenario changes when someone is invited into a home. When one speaks the sweetness of the gospel and talks about brothers, sisters, mothers, fathers, husbands, and wives, not only can the person *hear* the kingdom, they can *see* the kingdom. The family talk is made alive in video format right in front of them.

We've Complicated the Idea of Worship in God's Home

We've shaped ourselves around methods of ministry that I would dare say the Trinity intentionally avoided. Our performances by preachers and talent engage the participant with all the romance of TV. Television is known to entertain, but the brain literally goes idly active, dormantly awake, and ultimately dies when the tube is on because it rests in its own death. Our ways of communicating shape worshippers to "play fetch" and "sit." We are trained as *consumers* as opposed to *producers*. It results in the church begging people to become active servants of the kingdom these days rather than passive consumers of the church's product. Why? Because mission and worship are not actively connected and correlated in how we do things. For one, the only vocation, trade, skill, or craft that is often shown as valuable from the stage and pulpit is video, oratory, and music. These are the only skills that the church shows, which leaves the impression that all other vocations are unrelated to ministry and service.

We've also succeeded in creating expectation in people that worship is only a gathered experience (which it absolutely is) and has little bearing on all of life (which it absolutely does). Worship is a world word, and we've made it much smaller.

We must re-remember that Jesus' style aims to engage people in active participation and producing in all of life, vocation, trade, and hobby. Making.

Something Better Change 'Cause this Ship we've made is Going Down

Think for just a second how easily breakable our models for Church have become. I'll give you a lens to look through to see how deep our problem goes. We live in a world where homosexuality, transgenderism, and all other kinds of immoral sexual expression is being pushed down our throats as the norm; even though only about 3 to 7 percent of the world actually claims any affiliation with these orientations. Consider the position this has put us in as God's family.

Only two scenarios can play out within the church in response to the current and future state we're in with gender wars. Scenario 1: A gay couple walks in and asks to be married, and we say yes. For reasons I'll explain later, this would compromise our biblical belief and identity. A yes, would spin us down into a torrent of compromise related to a host of other topics. Scenario 2: If we say no, we are labeled bigots and criminals, on par with racists and murderers. Both of these scenarios are currently developing into realities that are beginning to tarnish the church, and they will soon to grow to be debilitating. The rise of sexual revolution is fast becoming the catch-22 in Satan's arsenal of weapons to destroy the church—as if he could. Now that homosexual marriage has been legalized across the board, whether you agree with it or not, it will soon become a criminal offense not to support it. If a church doesn't fall in line, it will be treated as a criminal. Property will be stripped away. Rights will be shackled. People who support the 501(c3) entity will lose all tax exemptions for their contributors. If history tells us anything, in an increasingly violent society members of the church will eventually be carted off to coliseums and used in despicable entertainment and slaughter.

The NFL, NBA, and MLB, and churches have graciously erected for us the coliseums.

Some of these grim predictions may be consigned to the distant future, but my point remains. Do you see how easy it is for Satan to take down our contemporary model for "doing church?" Our methods simply can't withstand anything real in terms of opposition, and in the writings of Peter, suffering, rampant persecution, and a terrorizing of the church was normal. Peter councils us today in his letter to assume that the hostile climate is still what we should expect. In Peter's time churches weren't built around one personality or a central location, because both are far too easy to nail down and weed out. In fact, in 1 Corinthians, Paul actually condemns the cult of personality that was rising around himself and Apollos and others. Paul intentionally aimed at decreasing his personal appeal. Compare this to the media age where we're taught to inflate our brands and name.

At their core, personality- and location-driven models are too easy to take down. They are stationary and not mobile. They're heavy footed, and that's not a good thing when Jesus warned us that as Christians we would spend our existence as he did—being hunted. My logic, as frail as it is, concludes that if our all-wise and timeless God can see the beginning and the end all in one moment, it proves that he knew of all the adversity that God's household people would face in the whole of history. In his wisdom, he invented a paradigm in the dust of the Garden that carries that dust with him all the way through to the Supper of the Lamb in Revelation. God KISSed creation (kept it simple, stupid) with the beauty of home. All the messages and methods we can devise are humbled under the weight of his wisdom. Our ways simply don't last.

Home does!

16

A FAMILY OF FAMILIES

I t's the mantra that follows any successful Grammy speech. It's the refrain that resounds from the lips of every NFL Super Bowl champion, and it's the heart's cry of every graduate:

"I WANT TO THANK MY MOM..."

A desire for home and family is simply in us. Whether or not we were raised in a positive home environment, no one has an effect on us quite like our mothers and fathers. We live with the pang, the pleasure, and often even the burden of pain that is required to please them in all that we do. Whether we like it or not, our extended family and our immediate nuclear family is what most affects us. Even the most advanced and detached workaholic at some point acknowledges how his striving pulls him away from one thing most directly. Family. Workaholics inevitably reach a point where they wish they had invested more in those closest to them. Our need for family, and the importance of it, seems to be a realization that everyone eventually grapples with.

Inviteably we all ponder what we might like engraved on our tombstones. The inscriptions we consider are always family-shaped. We don't desire our stats, our awards, and our riches to accompany us by our bedside as we breathe our last breath. What we long for most is that those closest to us would be there to watch us slip into a forever sleep. While slipping us into the ground, our desire is that they proclaim us a "good friend," a "loving husband," their "loving sibling," or a "beloved mother."

The reason we cannot escape the importance of family is that God wired us this way. The Trinity is wired this way. Everything he is and everything that he does is family-formed. The Trinity's internal otherness is evidenced in us by our need to ascribe our successes and failures to the presence or absence of our families. We recognize that in every I there is always a we.

John Cotton, a Puritan, reflects on the rich familial imagery of God in God's common words about himself:

> "I will be your God." He asserts that what God claims is that he is "not only a good Father, a good Mother, a good King, a good Friend, but whatsoever is good in the creature, he promises to be to us. He will be a good Father, Ruler, and Friend, and Husband to us, partly in his own person, that if all those fails, he will be all these to us, or else he will dispense himself so in those instruments so that we shall see God's goodness in every creature."[1]

Before the Fall, we naturally took great confidence in Cotton's description of our family identity. If you take a quick read through Genesis 1–3, you'll find that before the Fall, humans spoke in collective terms like "we" and "us." After the Fall, one of the first shreds of evidence of sin comes in Adam and Eve pointing fingers at one another in blame. Notice that the language of Genesis quickly turns to "me, myself, and I," and the finger in blame turns toward someone else.

One of the tragic losses of the Fall is our acceptance of our family disconnection. We know we've lost it, and yet many glory in its shame. Some try to find it again in false notions of world peace or some concept of harmony of self, and yet it constantly alludes us. Our search to find tranquility within ourselves and this world only leads us to one conclusion: it's not there.

Until we utter something to the tune of "I want to thank my God for all that I am, all that I have, and all that we are together," we will never find any closure.

THE FAMILIAL THREAD OF THE BIBLE'S TIMELINE

The Bible's storyline is woven together with the thread of family. There's a reason why its story does not begin with the image of a business, a school, a government (in the way we think of it), or even a building. God's design, that allows for universal flourishing, peace, and expansion at any time, place, and circumstance, begins with a man and a woman in marriage.

Notice that marriage comes not only with insightful spiritual overtones but also with pleasurable physical benefits. God allowed man and woman to enter into his *perichoretic* dance of friendship with each other in the act of facing each other. They became one flesh. The act of sex, penetration, and the mutual entering of man into woman while both retain their uniqueness is an illustration that points to the reality of God.

We should ponder the images given to us in marriage and sex carefully and deeply. God intends for us to experience some semblance of the joy of his unending and unyielding oneness. Bruce Ware concludes that there's another intent to God's creation of the sex act between man and woman: "I believe joy is one of the many reasons why God has made the sexual experience in human life to be as pleasurable and wondrous as it is. Image-of-God procreation is designed to reveal the pleasure God has in creating people in his own image, and the joy of bringing yet more of these humans into existence."[2]

The way in which husband and wife relate to God and each other is designed to point to and draw inspiration from God. This was the plan from the beginning, and Satan hates it. War emerges surrounding this subject of marriage in Genesis 1–3. Adam and Eve weren't alone with God in the garden. The enemy prowled around in their midst waiting to attack. The context of marriage is set against the backdrop of war. God will forever uphold the truancy of marriage with equal and greater fervency to that of Satan's attempts to tearing it down. Evil will forever be waging battle on the family. Any attack on the institution of marriage—whether through skewed definitions, twisted versions springing from the sexual revolution, prenuptial nonsense, easy-way-out divorce, or feminist or chauvinistic campaigns—is an affront to God's design. God is in the business of building marriages that point to his glory, and Satan is forever in the business of trying to undo it.

Immediately after Satan succeeded in getting Adam and Eve to doubt God's plan in the Garden of Eden, he quickly turned to prevail over Adam and Eve's offspring in Genesis 4. He aimed his arrows not only at God's intent to reveal himself through a husband and wife but also through those that bring us the titles of father and mother. Adam and Eve's first children, Cain and Abel, entered the world, and Satan's attack takes on a whole new dimension. The first murder takes place. Brother against Brother. Competitive Cowardice. Satan passes on his wielded sword of arrogance toward God to humans, and Cain buys the lie hook, line, and sinker.

One might expect God to abandon his mission of family or take a different route altogether, yet the Scriptures tell us that Seth is born to Adam and Eve. Genesis 5 immediately gives us the genealogy of Adam's lineage through Seth. Though genealogies are things that we often love to hate when reading through Scripture, in the Near East, and in Jewish thought, genealogies are always written with an intended meaning. Genealogies tell about the faithfulness of God. In Genesis 5, the genealogy begins with Adam and Seth and ends with Noah and his sons, Shem, Ham, and Japtheth. What's the meaning here? Simple. God has not abandoned his commitment to fleshing out his image on earth through the family. He reinforces the original plan. God has sound reasoning and remains faithful to it.

I'm afraid the sad story repeats itself. Humans fail under evil attack again, and perversity rules the day in the time of Noah (Gn. 6). God again rescues his family (Gn. 7–8) from wickedness and judgment through the means of an ark and a flood. He reinstates his family promise to Noah after the waters recede (Gn. 9), and in Genesis 10 we're met with another genealogy. God orders Noah's children and their lineage into his family plan, and thus God keeps on keeping on.

Humanity keeps on keeping on as well. In Genesis 11, earthly children continue to reveal their growing arrogance against God in the building of the world's tallest tower. We all know what happened there.

When competitive cowardice supersedes the level of brotherhood (Cain and Abel) and grows to infect nations, wars and worse break out. Slavery happens. After the time of Noah, the human race grew increasingly at odds toward one another, and so did God's family (Gn. 12–36). While God was still at work revealing his plan to live amongst his people and be their God throughout the Old Testament progression, things on earth kept getting increasingly darker. In spurts, God breaks through the disaster. His purpose permeates the undercurrent of the story. God's plan for forgiveness amongst broken families emerges greatest in the life of Joseph and his brothers. They are named as the twelve tribes of Israel (Gn. 37-50).

You'd think a family that experiences complete forgiveness would change, but they again forgot. Their prejudices again reach a summit. Sin makes war and slaves, and the Egyptians rise to power over the Jews in the time of Moses. The book of Exodus tells us of the 400-years of exile.

Again God surfaces in the story to free his people from their own pursuit of sin. Following the 400 years in Egypt, the enslaved torment, the ten plagues of Moses, and God leading the people across the Red Sea into freedom on their way to the land God promised, we arrive at a particularly intriguing scene in Numbers. Before God's people enter the wilderness to walk toward God's intended home for them, note what God does first. In the first chapters of Numbers, God orders and counts his people very specifically:

> In ordering the multitude in Numbers chapter 1, God begins his account of the people by placing them into families (heads of the home). He moves to clans (extended family), he then forms tribes (clusters of families), and then in chapter 2, God orders the people into standards (networks of tribes) around the tent of the meeting. … In beginning with the heads of the households, the men, the God of heaven reestablishes the protection of the home. Israel had seen a legacy of permissive fathers go before them. The fathers had grown insecure and/or belligerent in their treatment of their families as a result of what was done to them each day at the hands of the Egyptian whip. God's plan was to structure the family again—to restore the hearts of the fathers back to their children and their spouses. Since the Garden of Eden, which began with a man protecting and expanding the garden and with the creation of a beautiful wife to help in the task, God's foundational image had always found its origin and best expression in the home. To reassemble a people that would bear his image, God first needed to restore the ethic of the garden by reforming the family.[3]

Despite accumulating human failures, God's R.easoning for reflecting his nature rests unchanged. Through the Fall, sin, murder, flood, famine, slavery, suffering, and sacrifice, God reiterates his intention again and again. In Numbers, he does so through yet another genealogy. God seeks to remedy the damage of evil division and bring the people back to the simplicity of family.

What I'm begging you to see is that family is God's intended and logical system for human flourishing on the earth. It works in every time, place, and circumstance. It is eternal. We must pay it greater attention! It continues on through the Old Testament trajectory into the man Jesus, the church, and even into the forever kingdom of heaven in Revelation.

In the Gospel of Matthew, we see that the early disciples understood this timeline, emphasis, and trajectory. Matthew begins his gospel with the phrase "book of generations," or *biblos geneseos*. *Geneseos* is a form of the word "Genesis" and infers that Matthew intends to write a "new Genesis." A new account of creation. Matthew alludes to the fact that he is going to frame his entire book around the life of Israel in order to demonstrate that where God's people (the Israelites) messed up the family plan of God, God made it right.[4] What begins Matthew's gospel is yet another genealogy. It traces Jesus' line all the way back to Abraham. Abraham was named the *father* of nations (Gn. 17:4). Matthew links Jesus with the continuation of the family and covenant promise made to God's people through Abraham.

Luke's account links Jesus' genealogy back to Seth and Adam. Luke does this to represent that Jesus is the new Adam, the new creation, and to confirm that the Trinity's family plan is still unchanged.

The gospel writer's go to great lengths to record that Jesus was born into a family lineage (Gn. 1:54-55) but also into a family proper—to Joseph and Mary (Mt. 1:18-25). John's gospel is brutally honest and does not side-step the fact that Jesus' family was continually skeptical of his God-status (Jn. 7:3-5), but in Acts 1:14, after the resurrection, we see that Jesus' family is among the first to believe that he's God.

It's here. In Acts chapter 1. We arrive at the inception of the church. Luke purposefully leaves bread crumbs linking us back to the Book of Numbers and the Tower of Babel. He documents the coming of the Holy Spirit with images that cause us to rewind for a full interpretation. In coming, the Spirit brings unity to language again—a unity that was lost in the fragmenting of languages at the Tower of Babel. People hear the gospel in their own tongue, even as Peter preaches in his own native language. God reverses Babel.

The state of Israel at this time would have been similar to that of the state of Egypt except now the Jews were the ones enslaving others to their rules, laws, regulations, and oppression. The Holy Spirit came at Pentecost and continues to come to release disciples from their prison of sin and the law into the freedom God meant for us to enjoy. Freedom means loving our God and our neighbor. Once released from the captivity of sin and the law, notice the first thing that God's people do in Acts 2:42-47:

> They devoted themselves to the apostles' teaching and to fellowship, to the
> breaking of bread and to prayer. Everyone was filled with awe at the many

wonders and signs performed by the apostles. All the believers were together and had everything in common. They sold property and possessions to give to anyone who had need. Every day they continued to meet together in the temple courts. They broke bread in their *homes and ate together* with glad and sincere hearts, praising God and enjoying the favor of all the people. And the Lord added to their number daily those who were being saved (italics mine).

Those released from slavery on Pentecost were again numbered. God took all 3,000 of them and put them into the lifeblood of the home, the meal, and the family. The way in which God accounts for and orders the life of Israel after slavery is very telling of his design for the church. We are not a building, a central location, and a crowd. We are a family. The front door into the membership of the church is baptism, and baptism brings people into a household-family kingdom.

The timeline presses forward through the New Testament into the paramount painting of Revelation. In the final chapters, Christ is portrayed as a husband to his bride. Those in his family are referred to as his temple and the holy city in which he dwells.

In further describing the holy people, John says in verse 2, "It was made ready as a bride adorned for her husband." Here John borrows magnificent wedding language. In Jewish customs, there were various parts to a wedding. First was the betrothal. It's like an engagement, only far more binding. Upon betrothal, families pledge the two young people to one another in a contract signed and settled. Next came the presentation. The bride was brought out and presented to the groom followed by a week of feasting. Finally, at the end of the week, there was the ceremony. After the ceremony came the consummation.

The environment God establishes in heaven is that of a consummated marriage supper of the Lamb. God's kingdom in heaven as it is on earth is one of marital unity with him. It is accompanied by eating and drinking. The storyline is the same throughout.

One theologian, whom I can't recall, sums up the unity of the story even more succinctly. He says the Bible is a story of the hero defeating the dragon and getting the girl. That description is quite Disney, but it is true. God conquers Satan's plans to sneak up and nab his family. God is a husband relentlessly pursuing and protecting his bride.

We are drawn to the simplicity of the meal, the home, the marriage, and the family, along with the redemptive nature of brokenness restored, because that's the storyline we're in. We're in God's story. We may see lesser shadows of God's grand plot emerge through the thank-you speeches of Grammy award winners, NFL MVPs, or college graduates thanking a parent for their success. But the greatest reminder of our desire for home is truly put on display and made a reality in the Trinity, in a kingdom people, and in us.

Let me say in closing, "I'd like to thank our Father for allowing me to be a part of Christ's bride—the church. A family. A family of families."

THE LORD'S SUPPER

I T IS A SMALL MOMENT IN A CHURCH SERVICE if it is observed at all. It's a spectacle marked by people walking in parallel lines and grids as they turn away from each other after grabbing at the elements. Some sit idly in impersonal pews as they are handed a plastic beaker tasting more of Dimetapp than of good wine, and a baked-dough chicklet pretending to be bread. The leadership asks those observing the moment to do so in individual reflection. Members are encouraged to sit in silence amidst their own private world to analyze Christ's death and resurrection. The desired effect is that all those in the room would meditate on their sin, see their Savior, and reflect on their current state in relationship to God. We call it the Lord's Supper.

My question is, how did we come to individualize, privatize, and over-spiritualize the Lord's Supper when it is supposed to be robustly about community, justice, family, and celebration?

We need a shot in the arm from the Bible's storyline concerning meals. We need open heart surgery from our surgeon Jesus. We need him to open us up and show us the beauty of his ministry—a ministry, as Luke 7:34 asserts, that is defined by, shaped by, and aimed at eating and drinking.

Even up to the time of Constantine in AD 325, the whole of the Christian gathering was referred to as the Lord's Supper. The Christian community and fellowship weren't defined by locations, buildings, staffs, and productions.

Christian life was simply meals. The supper wasn't a hidden moment inside of another event, it *was* the event.

In this section I will discuss the concept of meals from a biblical perspective and specifically expound upon what is and what isn't the Lord's Supper. In the process, I will present my own view of the meaning of the Lord's Supper.

CLARIFYING THE ISSUE

Let's begin by clarifying what we are and what we are not going to be talking about. I'm not going to be discussing in depth what happens to the bread or the wine. Such discussions tend to make us lose touch with core issues. Jesus is very clear, as are the gospel writers, that the emphasis in the meal is to be placed on the *message* and the *man* of the sacrament, not on the *elements*. We must think on what is symbolized in the meal and what is visually shown through its pregnant imagery. I believe it most profoundly shows the kingdom of God and what it is like if we'd take time to look and think. The Supper is a piece of art, and it should be digested as one.

I realize that some of you may not continue reading this section if I don't first address the historical debate over the elements. So I'm including here a section from my book *Reconsidering the Lord's Supper* to give a brief synopsis of my point of view. My hope is to quickly assert a moderate stance pertaining to the debate that's raged throughout history so we can shift our focus to what I deem to be more important matters.

One of the most ingrained and prevailing historical views of the Supper is the view of Roman Catholicism. Roman Catholics believe in what is known as *transubstantiation.* They believe that the presence of Christ moves *across, beyond, and/or through* the bread and wine. Though to the naked eye it looks as if the bread and wine retain their outer substance, the Roman Catholic believes that something is happening invisibly to the elements in their substance. A Roman Catholic believes that the bread and wine literally become the body and blood of Jesus. Roman Catholics believe that through the priestly consecration of the bread and wine, a change takes place wherein the whole substance of the bread turns into the substance of the body of Christ our Lord, and the whole substance of the wine turns into the substance of his blood.

Of course, there is a rebuttal to this outlook that normally stands in disagreement over the fact that Jesus' position and *location* is currently in heaven. He is not locally *here*, but he is Lord sitting on his throne now. In whereabouts, Jesus, as God-man, cannot be *in* the elements for he is now *in* heaven. The Scriptures also tell us that Jesus left us his Spirit to live *in* us. The reason for this is because his tangible physical human presence would be going away and would not return to earth until that event we call the Second Coming (Jhn. 16:7; Acts 3:20; Phil. 3:20-21; 1 Cor. 11:26).

The negation to the tran-substantive opinion also resides around the idea of *inhabitation*. Jesus is very clear about the fact that his Spirit was sent to inhabit the believer, but he never once says that his physical presence would inhabit anything else, including bread or wine.

Following, in what could be considered the contrary position to that of the Catholic view is that of the Lutheran view. Lutherans believe that the presence of Christ is *in, with, and under* the elements. This view is known as *consubstantiation*. This is the perspective that the glorified body of Christ is now omnipresent everywhere. Sometimes this viewpoint is referred to as the Sacramental Union of the bread and wine. In other words, Christ's body and blood are present "in, with, and under" the elements, but never does Christ fuse with created things. Martin Luther, though he never used the term consubstantiation, explained his view by using an analogy of an iron rod placed into a fire: both are united in the red-hot iron, yet both are also distinct. To preserve the idiosyncratic nature between Christ and Creation, Lutheranism rejects the view of the Eucharist as "making present" Christ's sacrifice on the Cross.

Often the denial is forged against a consubstantiation view over the fact that Jesus in reality has a localized *physical* body and *spiritual existence* seated at the right hand of God (Col. 3:1). In some manner through the cross and resurrection, Christ was able to restore physical existence and its harmony with spiritual continuation. The two can now dwell together on earth and in the kingdom. A hardline consubstantiation view would have a hard time with the creation and created somehow intertwining other than in salvation. Yet, Scripture is very clear that Christ fills all things. Paul is very clear that though our spirit is now restored through the indwelling Holy Spirit, our physical bodies in the sinful, known, universe will be cast off once we're dead. We will maintain our spiritual existence as it is now, yet without the torment of sin and satanic temptation that remains alluring to our fallen physical flesh. Christ will clothe us with new redeemed bodies that are also fully physical. This stance preserves distinction between matter and supernatural, but a closer connection is maintained between Creator and creation than may be comfortable for one holding to a typical Lutheran view.

A third viewpoint is that of the Reformed stance. Calvin believed in what could be later coined as the *Real Presence*. He believed in the combination of the physical and spiritual but believed that it happens not through Jesus' coming down to earth at this time, but through our mystically ascending to heaven. He emphasized our real communion with Christ in heaven and the nourishment of our faith in the Supper. Christ is therefore not present literally in the elements, but he is spiritually present. Conclusively, again, one could argue that this engages the mystery of faith in who we are *in Christ*, which seems to be the reality that Scripture emphasizes (phrase used over 270 times), but it limits the emphasis on another phrase used in the New Testament merely 70 times ... that of *Christ in us*. Again, it would appear that the struggle still comes down to the degree in which physical and spiritual can be united. Are they distinct completely, completely intertwined, or is there some variance of both/and? Also, what "things" can be combined; for example, people, or substances, such as bread and wine?

Here enters the final predominant viewpoint, the Evangelical *memorial* or Zwinglian view. Memorialists believe that *The Lord's Supper* remembers and honors Christ and his covenant toward us. Many also believe that in this Supper the Lord memorializes us, and that the Father remembers Christ's work and bestows grace again and again on the church as a result. Zwingli also believed that the elements didn't transubstantiate (change), but that the person transformed into the likeness of Christ in remembering Christ. It would seem that the emphasis in this view definitely places greater stress upon the person rather than the elements.

The problem with this memorial view is that it does not take 1 Corinthians 10:16 seriously when it says that the Lord's Supper is a real "participation" or communion (*koinonia*) in the body and blood of Christ through the Spirit, by faith. Paul's words to the Corinthians would suggest that there is more at work here than our imagination and memory.

All of these **views** to some varying degree preserve intrigue. All of them come with a host of problems. Trying to figure out a "mystery," is just that, a mystery. We're naturally going to have some trouble with this topic as humans when we try to quantify and theologize over the *exact*. It would be my suggestion and observation that we are asking the wrong questions, and thus dividing over the wrong things. We were never meant to divide and do a doctrine dance around and over the Supper, but rather we are meant to embrace the ambiguity. As a result of this conclusion, I'd like to boldly consider history, but also challenge the divide that has grown up between believers in an effort to unify over this issue at least in some degree. I believe we should consider the more unified approach from the more philosophical stance known as *transposition.*

The idea of transposition comes from the great Christian philosopher C. S. Lewis. This way of perceiving the world came to him one day when he came upon a toolshed in the woods. Listen as he describes the occurrence in *Meditation in a Toolshed*:

"I was standing today in the dark toolshed. The sun was shining outside and through the crack at the top of the door there came a sunbeam. From where I stood that beam of light, with the specks of dust floating in it, was the most striking thing in the place. Everything else was almost pitch-black. I was seeing the beam, not seeing things by it. Then I moved so that the beam fell on my eyes. Instantly the whole previous picture vanished. I saw no toolshed, and (above all) no beam. Instead I saw, framed in the irregular cranny at the top of the door, green leaves moving on the branches of a tree outside and beyond that, 90 odd million miles away, the sun. *Looking along* the beam, and *looking at* the beam are very different experiences."

Lewis realized that everything in all of creation is but a shadow. All created things can only offer to us a taste of the real thing toward which they point. In *The Weight of Glory* he says, "The suns and lamps in pictures seem to shine only because real suns or lamps shine on them; that is, they seem to shine a great deal because they really shine a little in reflecting their archetypes." What this implies is that everything in creation—trees, rivers, mountains, animals, and even human beings themselves—are reflections of something greater. The created world is not to be *looked at* in order to define and find reality, but it is to be *looked along*.

John Piper responds to this train of thought;

"So we can say that when we look along the heavens and not just 'at' the heavens, they succeed in their aim of 'declaring the glory of God.'

That is, we see the glory of God, not just the glory of the heavens. We don't just stand outside and analyze the natural world as a beam, but we let the beam fall on the eyes of our heart, so that we see the source of the beauty—the original Beauty, God himself. This is the essential key to unlocking the proper use of the physical world of sensation for spiritual purposes. All of God's creation becomes a beam to be looked along or a sound to be heard along or a fragrance to be smelled along or a flavor to be tasted along or a touch to be felt along."

The view of *transposition* invites us to a middle ground at a both/and angle, and I believe it to provide a more deeply engaging ground at that. Not only does the view of transposition bring some harmony between all the viewpoints of *The Lord's Supper*, it also engages us in a way of seeing the whole world as sacramental. Soon, every created thing becomes something to be looked along in order to envision the kingdom; which stands just within reach, and yet so far away.

First, ponder how transposition as an idea engages the Roman Catholic view of transubstantiation, and the Lutheran stance of consubstantiation. When engaging with physical elements—in C. S. Lewis' experience it was "light"—the effects of created things are so transcendent they can actually intersect the physical. In the case of light, the warmth and brightness of the sun intersects us physically and very literally. It moves *beyond, across, and through* us in the same moment that it is *in, with, and under* us. Its Vitamins enrich our physical bodies when the light itself eclipses what we can see. It moves within us beyond what we can explain in a manner more attune to chemistry. When we stare directly into the light, everything becomes light, and when we gaze upon it, it merely casts color and clarity, and shadow and symmetry upon all that is before us. For analogy's sake, it is not hard to see how *The Lord's Supper* can interact with the known world in much the same manner. *The Lord's Supper* can be diversified in nature and unified through the view of transposition.

The view of *transposition* can also be of service to the Reformed opinion of Real Presence and to those of a more Zwinglian or Memorialism stance. The nature of light, much like the smell of bread and wine, envelops us. We are in it and it is in us. Though there is distinction between smell and substance, there is an interaction of meaning. In much the same way as light illumines a dark room and causes us to remember what we've stored in the attic, our olfactory sense of smell ignites and connects us to memories; linking our present to ancient past. The light transforms our countenance; the bread and wine transform our bodies with nutrients.

All in all, *transposition* provides us with a both/and "table," if you will, around which we can all sit as God's family. We can bring our different recipes and varying ingredients, and they all harmonize to our palette to a degree when enjoyed around the same meal. Not only can we unify and appreciate the nuance and flavor in our different viewpoints, though we may disagree, we can engage now in a discussion. We can also speak of things much deeper than bread and wine as we can go further into discussing the main thrust of Christ's Supper.[1]

It is my belief that Jesus was not obsessed with the elements themselves but was concerned more with what the **event** demonstrates about his **nature**, and with the **paradigm** communicated in the actual event itself. He intended the Supper to shape how we see all of life and the kingdom. It is to be looked 'along' not looked 'at.'

BIBLICAL TIMELINE OF MEALS

Now I hope it's safe to lean away from the issue of *elements* and *method* and to move into a discussion of *meaning* and *paradigm*. I'd like us to think of the Lord's Supper as being more like a painting rather than a science. As we gaze upon the spectacle of it, it comes alive with intense imagery.

Let's begin by considering the timeline of meals in Scripture. I believe we'll be able to trace the thread of meals across the landscape in a way that's enlightening, deepening, and helpful.

We begin in the Garden of Eden. The same garden that lays for us the foundations for home, and family also lays the groundwork for meals. Adam and Eve are created in the image of God, and in Genesis 2:16 one of the first things God tells the two lovebirds is, "You may eat of every tree of the garden." God made Adam and Eve flesh and bone. Basic nourishment is a requirement for life. Humanities grandparents experienced hunger and thirst before ever sinning. It's timeless.

In fact, if we fast-forward to Jesus after his resurrection in Luke 24:42-43, we see Jesus eating in his newly resurrected, natural, and physical body, even though he also remains divine. His new body is more real than our reality because we learn in the text that he can walk through walls. The disciples think he's a ghost. To dispel their fright, he eats a broiled fish in their presence. The disciples are astonished when they see nothing falling to the ground, as it would if he were Casper the ghost. Their perfect Spirit Lord eats in his physical body.

The point is that a resurrected, holy, and pure flesh-and-bone body, dwelling together in perfect unity with the Spirit, was God's intention in the beginning. Eating is intended to aid us in experiencing the pleasure of the kingdom. Eating and drinking with God in our hearts somehow connect his presence and his power to earth.

Just as soon as beauty and sustenance is revealed to Adam and Eve, a sour note quickly blares. The conditional curse. In Genesis 2:16-17, God lays out a provisional clause to his blessing of nourishment. He states, "but of the tree of knowledge of good and evil you shall not eat, for in the day that you eat of it you shall surely die." Here we're given the symbolic nature of food. On the wheel of food, blessing and curses turn. Obedience or rebellion are offered in a meal.

So the story goes. Adam and Eve eat from the tree that's forbidden to them, and death comes. In Genesis 3:7 it says that after eating the fruit "their eyes were opened." Eating meals is the hinge point for blessing and cursing, and it's a swinging door that remains open throughout the whole of Scripture.

Consider what happens immediately after the Fall in Genesis 4. Murder. Cain kills Abel, and over what? Food! Cain brings in fruit as a sacrifice of worship before the Lord, and Abel brings the prime choice animal of his flock. God blesses Abel and curses Cain, not based on their offering, but on what their offering revealed about their heart. Cain brings in a minimal gift. God is an afterthought to Cain. Abel brings in the best he has.

To Abel, God is the only occupying love of his deepest affections. Hearts are revealed over food and through the vehicle of food. Through an offering of what is essential to a potential meal, Cain's jealousy is ignited and he slays Abel in competitive cowardice.

This isn't the last time that food is used to symbolize whether one is "in" or "out" in regard to blessing or curses. In Genesis 7:1-3, God provides for Noah on the ark via the survival of beast and provision (blessing); whereas the rest of the world's sustenance and life is washed away. After getting off the ark, we see Noah and his family make the first burnt offering (food). Also, it is here that the first designation in the Bible is made between "clean" and "unclean" food (Gn. 9:3-4).

Following the Noahic covenant of blessing, and a bit further down the road of biblical chronology, God visits Abraham in what we are told is the image of "three men" (Gn. 18:2). We're not sure if these are angels or a Trinitarian *theophany* (appearance), but the fact that Abraham bows to them and they don't refuse his honor and worship (as angels do elsewhere in Scripture) is a sign that this is God himself visiting Abraham. And the visit occurs over a meal (Gn. 18:6-8). The Abrahamic promise made by God to all humanity is conducted over eating and drinking.

Abraham's lineage leads to Isaac and Ishmael and then to Jacob and Esau, who are a pair of siblings always in rivalry. Esau is the oldest, and as the firstborn, he is destined to receive the father's blessing. Jacob is jealous of Esau's afforded privilege, and so one day Jacob cooks up a nice pot of food for Esau and offers it with one condition: "Give me your blessing."

A famished Esau hastily welcomes the offer and quickly parts with his blessing in order to quench the screaming pangs in his stomach. Once again, food shows up as a marker of what is filled and what is kept in lack.

In Genesis 37-52, we have the record of Joseph. He's thrown into captivity by his own family, tossed into an Egyptian prison, and is raised up later by a miracle as Pharaoh's right-hand man. Joseph's story is an epic tale of redemption and reversal, but we often miss what Joseph is raised up to do.

In that day, famine swept the land. Joseph was exalted by God just in time to take the reins, provide a brilliant plan for storing food, and see the people through the famine. For those of you who don't know the story, Joseph's whole family ends up having to come to Joseph's hand to beg for the bread in his storage. Joseph, rather than destroying them in bitterness over what they had done, forgives them. The forgiveness of the betrayal done to Joseph at the hands of his twelve brothers, and on a larger scale the twelve tribes of Israel, is couched in the imagery of food. Feast and famine. Provision and desolation. Lack and fulfillment.

Similar to the time of Joseph, the table of blessing and cursing turns up in the time of Moses. God's people find themselves again in dire straits under the authoritarian hand of Pharaoh. God leads Moses to free his people from Pharaoh's grasp. Nine times Pharaoh refuses to obey God. Nine horrific plagues result. Finally, on the tenth plague, Pharaoh relents. He lets God's people go. God kills the firstborn child of every family in the land not protected by the Lamb's blood smeared over their doorway, and Pharaoh's son dies. In one of the bloodiest nights in all human history, the people of Egypt cry in pain and curse the heavens as the Israelites rejoice in their freedom and blessing. As a result of God's judgments, something in every house died that fateful night. The only thing sparing anyone's firstborn child from experiencing death was the blood of the lamb smeared over the home's doorpost.

Here in Exodus 12 is the origin of Passover. Passover, even up until the time of Jesus, was celebrated and remembered through a ritual meal. Need I say it again? God's provision and curse are symbolized through a meal. In the Passover, however, a new element enters. One of sacrifice. A theme of salvation. The Passover contains imagery not only of sustenance but also suggests that how one eats points to who one worships. Passover paints a picture of those who are in, and those who are out; those who are free, and those who choose to willfully embrace rebellion. The only necessity required to be added into God's kingdom is simply to bow down to him as the Savior and Lord—the source and provision for all of life. Pharaoh refused, but many in Israel and in Egypt accepted. Meals capture the essence of life and death.

Despite God's goodness in providing a way into freedom, humanity is a desperate lot, and just like you and me, the Israelites were prone to wander away from God. They doubted God's provision soon after their conquest in Egypt. Though it seems crazy, they actually thought the grass would be greener if they went back to Egypt. Can you believe that? They wanted to go back into bondage. And why? Well, in Numbers we're told that God gives them manna (food) from heaven as they journey toward the promised land, and they shake their fists at the sky and demand steak. Suddenly, like a battering wind, God answers their prayer in Numbers 11:31-32. He brings in droves of quail from the sea, so much, in fact, that the people gather and feast until they're sick. The quail was so abundant that the people literally stood one and a half feet deep in dead birds. They couldn't possibly have consumed them all, and so the rotting flesh of dead sea fowl began to pierce their noses. The text tells us that the anger of the Lord burned against the people. He had provided manna, and his people had once again said, "not good enough." The manna was intended to be a blessing, and they shrugged it off. As a result, the people were handed a curse in the form of quail.

On and on through the Old Testament meals secure the central theme of covenant imagery. In the story of Boaz and Ruth, we see God's provision for Ruth (a non-Israelite) through Boaz as he leaves behind gleanings of food for her to gather as a poor sojourner. When we come to Daniel and Esther, we again see the dimension of food as a blessing and a curse. Daniel is offered the chance to eat at Nebuchadnezzar's feasts, and Daniel declines. Daniel's faithfulness to follow God and his refusal to bow and worship Nebuchadnezzar's way of life is measured in his willingness "to eat, or not to eat."

In like fashion, Esther confronts the wickedness of Haman over a meal with the King, and in a great turn of events, Haman is exposed for the devil he is. As they dine, Haman's plan to exterminate the Israelites is revealed, and God's people are spared from genocide. After Israel successfully defends themselves against Haman's armies, they celebrate in another feast. Purim (Est. 9:20-32).

Our biblical history of the meal is rich, and it has set the stage for Jesus. Is Jesus going to continue to associate meals with the theme of blessing and cursing? Does Jesus understand eating to be symbolic of one's obedience or disobedience to his kingdom supply?

Matthew and Luke seem to think so.

Take for example the moment Jesus first addresses evil in Luke 4. Satan comes on the scene in the wilderness, and as the serpent had done with Adam and Israel, Satan again raises his hand to try and dissatisfy Jesus with tricks. What does Satan first use as a tool for temptation? Bread.

Apparently Satan recognizes what is at stake over food. He used the fruit of the tree in the garden to cause humanity to slip, and he tries the same old worn out sleight-of-hand with Jesus. Fortunately, Jesus is privy to Satan's scheming and he defeats the attack. Jesus never sins. He never falls for the magic show. He comes up out of the desert victorious and enters his ministry in Luke 4:14 ready to reveal to the world the power of his kingdom through meals. In fact, both Luke and Matthew are the ones that refer to the entirety of Jesus' ministry as one of "eating and drinking."

Particularly in Luke, we see that his whole narrative is structured around meals. There is never a moment where Jesus is not going to a meal, at a meal, or coming from a meal. One scholar even called Luke's gospel "The Gospel Around the Meal." It is filled with symbol and parable likening the kingdom to a Banquet (Lk. 14:15-24). Jesus is shown feeding the thousands, attending meals at the house of despots and crooks (e.g. Zacchaeus, Lk. 19:1-10), and leading the Last Supper before his death (Lk. 22:7-23). The disciples are also known by their eating and drinking (Lk. 10), and Luke implies that all believers are to be characterized as a people waiting for their master to return from a wedding banquet, so that when he comes and knocks they can immediately open the door for him (Lk. 12:36). Luke also writes the Book of Acts, which many coin as *Luke Part 2*. Luke begins the account in Acts with a similar refrain to his gospel. What does he tell us that the early church is doing at their very birth? Breaking bread.

Food is predominant at the beginning of the church (Acts 2:42). It is the sustaining symbol of God's family and life in the Lord's Meal (1 Cor. 10). Food is carried into the New Testament by the apostles in the same manner as the Old Testament. It's used to differentiate between religion (a curse) and freedom (a blessing only found in Christ—Col. 2:20-23), thus becoming a metaphor for weak and strong faith (Rom. 14). In closing out the entire narrative of Scripture, John likens the image he sees of God's kingdom to a wedding feast hosted by the Lamb. The context of the victorious supper and reign of King Jesus in Revelation 20-22 is in a restored garden. A restored tree. A restored meal.

The imagery of blessing and cursing is a theme carried along on the coattails of the meal. Food symbolizes our willing submission to or rejection of our King's rule. Though God is gracious in providing food for the whole earth to enjoy each day because of the *common grace* streaming from his work on the cross, there is a *saving grace* that affords only those who believe a place at his forever wedding celebration feast. Currently, God invites all humankind to consider the bounty of his creation upon which they feast. All the created things that we consume, produce, grow, and make, serve as mile markers leading us to Jesus. All made things are hyperlinks. When we click on them, they point us to and open to us the reality of a new world. Kingdom.

The gospel shows up in the meal and beckons, saying, "Will you receive Jesus and gain his blessing and life, or will you reject his provision and find yourself sitting at the table of demons instead?"

PAUL, JESUS, AND THE JEWISH AND GREEK IMAGERY OF THE LAST SUPPER

We arrive at a question. What does all the former information have to do with the Lord's Supper, worship, and its place in making us like Jesus, our Trinitarian Savior? I think immediately we can concede that the Supper is much more than a wafer and some Welch's grape juice. In diluting the way we observe the celebration, we've watered down its formational significance. I think Paul undoubtedly agrees.

In 1 Corinthians 10, Paul discusses the Lord's Supper in correlation with the idol feasts that were taking place in Corinth. The feasts observed in the name of pagan gods in that culture were full-on meals. The fact that Paul associates the two strongly suggests that the Lord's meal was thought of as a feast. Paul likens the Lord's Supper to a "better" meal than the idol feasts, in that it is able to satisfy the whole of hunger—including spiritual hunger. Paul also mentions the Lord's Supper as it alludes to the body of Christ in the loaf of bread presented at the Supper (1 Cor. 10:14-16). Logically, a pre-made plastic chicklet posing as bread absolutely compromises what is preached through the symbol of a more robust loaf of bread and a full-on dinner.

For the Corinthians, the participation in the feast of idols was a community event. The Lord's Supper was not thought of as an individual activity, as it is presented in most churches today (i.e., when we turn down the lights, ask everyone to retreat into themselves, and solemnly ponder their sin). The feast was characterized by jovial feasting and the celebration of a King, all the while maintaining soberness toward one's own sin and one's commitment to the needs and brokenness of others that were also there. Plutarch summed up the character of the meal when he describes the "friend-making character of the table."[2] It was an outward event. It brought outliers together.

Consider Paul's logic as he builds his argument. In his discussion of the meal, he systematically turns our minds toward worship and community along with justice. Paul begins in likening the Corinthian idolatries to the communal way in which Israel turned to idols in the wilderness in Exodus (1 Cor. 10:1-13). He talks about the meal, associates it with a feast, and then moves into a discussion on proper practices for worship (1 Cor. 11:1-16). He speaks as if the predominant worshipping event in the life of the early church surrounded the Lord's Meal. In Paul's idea of church, the meal is a powerful experience. It preaches louder in symbol than in any word uttered and provides the context whereby the preached, prayed, and sung word makes the most sense. The message of the Trinity is one of worshipping embrace, and a meal at its core shouts loving "hugs and handshakes." Paul's train of thought then moves from the supper into worship, and finally into a discussion on the body of Christ and service to one another through the plethora of shared and unique gifting.

The famous spiritual gifts chapters in Corinthians are Paul's attempt to confront perverted worship that had snuck in and offer correct instructions about how the body should employ their gifts together in a different manner than the pagans at their feasts. He suggests that the unwarranted divisions in the church were robbing people of experiencing unity at the meal and that the proper use of gifts is not to individualize people but to unify them. Does the language here remind you of anyone's nature? That of the members of the Trinity, perhaps?

The disunity had grown so perverse in Corinth that Paul actually says the people were bringing enough food and wine on which to get drunk and bloated. They were depriving those in the group who were poor and less fortunate of the simple provisions of God's bounty. Because the gathering was overflowing with men, women, and children of all class and status, I'm inclined to say there were both saved and unsaved people at the feast of the Lord's Supper—just as Judas was present at Jesus' last meal. The meal was an act of justice that aimed to bring in those far off, as well as to house the perfect environment for the gospel to be understood by those within God's family.

Some may erroneously assume that the above infers that I think both believers and non-believers should participate in the Lord's Supper. Please attend carefully to my explanation so you won't attribute to me a heresy that I do not believe. Historically, there was a first part of the feast where everyone shared in the bounty together (properly known as the *Agape* or *Love Feast*). Everyone needs to eat. And God feeds everyone. God's justice presides over the event when he willingly feeds all classes, demographics, races, genders, and faith affiliations present. They all prepared food together, ate together, conversed, and enjoyed God's invitation to the larger embrace of not only feeding their bellies, but also of hearing clearly of God's desire that everyone be saved. The event would then proceed to the *Eucharist* portion—a more formal time of breaking and bleeding Jesus' body together in remembrance of Christ's cross for all those already believing. The second part of the meal was the altar call, so to speak. It was an invitation, a reminder, and a proclamation of the Lord's death to all made alive in Christ, but a "come to Jesus" call to those still dead in sin.

Take note, that Judas took flight to betray Jesus in the second part of the event at the Last Supper. The raised cup and broken bread was *for* believers, and a call *to* the realities of damnation for those not saved. When the saved ate of the elements, the unsaved would feel the exclusion. They would fail to taste of the elements, which would lead them to come to grips with their lostness through all their senses. They were cut off from a God who provides generously not only food but also eternal life. They would feel the distance and be beckoned to come close and believe.

Even in the Corinthian church, after the hunger of all was satisfied through the real meal, the table was then fenced off. Here a distinction is made between the *rites* offered to believers for their partaking, and that which is a mere invitation to unbelievers. The division is not a separation of peoples, but rather a separation between two ceremonies.[3] The separation of ceremonies made a statement to all people: God provides for saint and sinner alike, to a degree, out of his mercy (in withholding from us the doom we deserve), but beckons that all can be saved into his family by his grace (in giving us a blessing we don't deserve).

Sadly, what's grown commonplace over the historical timeline is that we now separate people out in ceremony, distinction, time, and place. The division started most profoundly with Constantine. He moved the meal for the believer to Sunday morning in the basilicas and atriums, and the meals for the poor into the evening. He divided the meal's meaning. The divide forever introduced a separation into the way we do ministry today. We minister _to_ the poor, as if we consider ourselves those of privilege, not _with_ the poor to show we consider ourselves their equals in God's economy. The meal has lost its embracive power as well as its ability to make a call to those outside God's Kingdom feast. We've missed the point and failed to connect the cross with consumption, community, and creation. As a result, we've changed the shape of how ministry is done.

The truth is that both a common meal _toward_ and _with_ all people was the norm in Christian feasts. The with-ness and embrace of the table is what made Christian feasts unique in relation to the everyday eating of those in the Greco-Roman society. In the Christian community, people ate together, and after that the ceremonies were separated by a connecting link. Paul doesn't connect the two by saying "please refrain from eating if you're a non-believer because this table is not for you" (which is how it's typically done in churches today). No! Paul says, "examine yourself." But how? Again, he's addressing the people as a collective, not as individuals, so the intention in his call doesn't aim at inviting people to turn inward and "think about one's sin." Paul says, you need to discern the body in your eating and drinking. This discernment is two-fold.

First, you must discern whether or not you're in Christ's body. The doorway into God's family is faith. As I have explained above, the call of the Supper is a call to believe. It asks those in attendance to consider whether they are inside the blessing God offers or willfully outside under the curse. People are challenged to consider whether they accept the embrace of God's family or willingly choose to exclude themselves from it.

The meal is the altar call. There's no pulpit, no stage, and no prayer team up front. The meal is a far greater image of the Trinity. It presents what one is being invited into. Belief. Christ. It's a family. It's a body.

Second, to "discern the body" not only implies something about our relationship to Christ but has "one another" implications as well. The Corinthians were completely favoring the wealthy over and above those in the family who had nothing. In addressing this abuse, Paul linked the meal of the Lord to the correction of injustice. Paul's logic headed upriver toward a giant idea. The inclusivity of the meal has ramifications that address all matters of social justice, human rights, or however one might articulate the need to fight for those wronged. Paul connects the Lord's Supper to the needs of the world —the fatherless, the widow, the orphan, the oppressed. the Lord's Supper is a salvation event focused on embracing those saved and inviting those unsaved while meeting the needs of the whole body—particularly the most physically and circumstantially needy.

What we can conclude about Paul's understanding of the Supper is that it's much more Trinitarian than we might have once thought. Many of us have been reared since birth to walk aisles, go to potlucks that focus on gluttony more than on gospel, and associate gospel to food only in saying grace or via taking the tab and trinket on Sunday morning to remember the Lord.

Does Jesus' idea of the Lord's Supper follow suit? Would he agree with how Paul has taken the event and pressed it out into church planting philosophy? Well, Jesus doesn't instruct us in words on this matter, but if we turn to Luke's gospel, I think that Jesus gives us an image of the Lord's Supper that is congruent with Paul's view.

JESUS AND THE LORD'S SUPPER

I mentioned before that Luke's gospel is known as a "Gospel of Meals." Not only does Luke form his outline around meal imagery, he also writes to a Greek audience. The Greeks very much understood the value of meals. Luke's account is strategically aimed at the Gentiles in order to clarify their rightful place in Christ as legitimate members in his kingdom.

To communicate to his audience, Luke includes a unique telling of the Lord Supper event in Luke 22:7-38. Unlike the other gospel writers, Luke records the raising of *two cups of wine*. The two cups couldn't possibly be aimed at the Jew and their understanding of Passover because at a typical Passover observance, which is historically Jewish, there are six or more cups of wine that are drunk. The cups are also surrounded by songs sung from the Psalter and couched in prayers and discussion based on the Torah (the first five books of the Bible).

Why does Luke record two cups?

In my research, most of which can be found in my book, *Reconsidering the Lord's Supper*, I've found that Luke's unique detail actually fulfills his intent to communicate the gospel specifically to the Gentiles in the Greco-Roman culture.

In that day, eating and feasting clubs were all the rage. To form a club was simple. All you needed was the *symposiarch* (or host), and those he invited. The format of clubs was equally laid back. The host would send out dinner invitations to a guest list filled with hootie hoo's, highfalutins, and other guests of considerable importance. When guests arrived, they would be greeted, served, satisfied, and picked up after by dogs and women. In that day, women were prized no more than slaves and vermin.

To begin the feast, the host would raise cup number one to welcome the guests in and signal the beginning of the feasting. After bursting belt buckles, meat sweats, and drunkenness began to set in, the host would stand and raise cup number two. Cup number two was the introduction to a political statement to honor and toast the king, or the lord of the supper. The host spilled a touch of the wine on the floor, hailed the Roman lord, Caesar as king, and the guests moved to the second part of the evening. The Symposium.

The Symposium was filled with lively entertainment and discussion of all kinds. Sexual favors, musical and artistic performance, as well as philosophical debate on a wide variety of subjects was offered by the host, all based on his interests and agenda. And of course, there was always more drinking.

Luke's use of the two cups made perfect sense to Gentile ears. In Roman culture, this also made sense to God's family. They were already viewed as an *ekklesia*—a church or an association. Romans knew them as another club. The meal-driven nature of the love feast of Christians would have been tolerated only because of its club status.

Notice in Luke 22:17 that little is said about the first cup's symbolism (we'll say more on this in a moment). He records Jesus giving thanks and passing out the food. The real detail in Luke's writing starts with the second cup. Jesus hails himself as the *Son of Man* as he raises the second cup. The imagery of a chalice in the air links us to the kingdom portrayal of the Messiah in the Old Testament. After the cup is raised, Jesus exposes Judas as his betrayer. The Symposium begins. Jesus initiates the topic. Disputes and debate break out amongst the disciples about who might betray Jesus before Judas gets up to leave.

In raising the second cup and hailing himself as King, Jesus makes a political and a spiritual statement—one that gets him killed. The message of the chalice is loud and clear: "I've come to dismantle the kingdoms of the world, and that includes Caesar." Jesus likewise throws water in the face of the club hosts and symposiarchs of that day. He references these leaders when he uses the word *benefactors* in Luke 22:25.[4] The benefactors were the influencers in society. The Greek language also links them to what we might now call *liturgists*, or *worship leaders*. The ancient world's understanding of leading worship was not so narrow as we have made it today. The idea of worship applied more to the cultural setting than the ceremonial.

The benefactors were those who influenced the loves and affections of people through their funding of the arts, athletics, business, government, education, media, and so on. They were the culture makers. Each benefactor had his or her place in the pecking order as prescribed by the host and by one's standing within the Roman hierarchy. Value and humanness were highly determined by one's eating partners.[5] Jesus' raising of cup number two screams politics, but with an altogether different view. It shouts a louder message of worship. Jesus was hailing himself as king, and he was commanding that all revere him. Jesus portrayed the ideal society, "a utopia in miniature."[6] To an onlooking Greek, the call to worship makes sense because their meal too was a worship service. It was held in worship to a different king. Caesar.

Though Jesus makes demands of allegiance and lordship, he shifts the way in which those demands are made. He informs the disciples that allegiance to him means a different way of living. In Luke 22:25-27 Jesus says, "The kings of the Gentiles lord it over them; and those who exercise authority over them call themselves Benefactors. But you are not to be like that. Instead, the greatest among you should be like the youngest, and the one who rules like the one who serves. For who is greater, the one who is at the table or the one who serves?" Jesus couches his kingship within a call to service. He elevates himself not as a dictator, but as a servant. He flips on its head the coin of what it means to be king, and he does far more than change the landscape of what king and lord mean.

Consider also who was made to serve as slaves at the Greco-Roman meals. In particular, the poor slave and the female were treated like dogs. This explains why in Matthew 15:27 when approaching Jesus—who was, of course, a man—a woman likens herself to a "dog eating crumbs that fall from a masters table." The woman's position was comparable to that of a slave. Contrary to the corrupt leaders of that day, Jesus' whole meal ministry was about elevating, eating with, and giving dignity to those who were assumed to have the lowest stature—namely women, the outcast, the poor, the sick, the lame, the slave, etc. Jesus was constantly affirming women. In Matthew 15, Jesus affirms the woman's value by hailing her as an example of faith. He even allowed women the counter-cultural honor of being the first to see him after his resurrection and announce his rise to the world.

Jesus' meals were a visual representation of the servant- and value-driven kingdom. When Greeks and Jews saw Jesus hailing himself as a king, all the while serving in the midst of and surrounded by woman, tax collectors, despots, lepers, poor, widows, orphans, and the like, it made an absolutely subversive statement about who and what he believed himself and his kingdom to be. Jesus revealed truth through the *meal*, the *man*, and the *message*. The meal is art. The sermon of the meal spoke loudest without words. It shouted justice, political upheaval, true family, and the reign of a good king.

I write in my book, *Reconsidering the Lord's Supper*:

> This is why whenever early Christians met for a communal meal they saw themselves as participating in a subversive non-violent act against the Roman Empire. They not only enjoyed a subversive meal in hail of a heavenly a King, they too shared in the ministry of the "Word." In 1 Cor. 14:26b-31, we see that a whole set of "contributions to a community conversation" existed at a banquet. Both "participation and spectacle" had their place. What this means is that the message that was spoken and what was seen were equally important in conveying the message of the gospel and the Trinity's image.

Not only was the meal itself confronting to pagan culture, but the symposium following the meal equally challenged the Jewish religion:

In contrast to the Essenes, and in parallel to the Romans, these Christian banquets were festive; 'every banquet included post-meal entertainment of some sort, which might include music, lectures, debates, philosophical discussions, lively discourse extolling emperor and empire, recitations, drama, the unraveling of riddles, dancing, party games, and the like.' Their belief was that art can be enjoyed on its own merit of beauty and pleasure—a sense of sheer aesthetics. Entertainment and performance were truly valuable for the truths they conveyed.

The very nature of the meal was one of worship and celebration. It was a kingdom community family that neither rebel nor religion could understand.

The Supper provides the context for proper interpretation of the meaning of Scripture, and the Symposium fits Paul's portrayal of the use of the gifts in 1 Corinthians. Paul pictured an aftermath to the meal that exploded with the priesthood of the believer under the right authority of Christ, his manner of life, and church overseers. Today, our churches leave little to no space for interacting with truth, let alone processing it creatively, expressively, uniquely, inventively, personally, and artistically together.

WHAT ABOUT THE JEWS IN ALL OF THIS?

We've made it clear that the second cup, in particular, would have spoken volumes to the Greeks, but what might the first cup at the beginning of the meal have implied to the Jewish understanding?

In Jewish heritage, feasting is not only linked with Passover symbolism, it also correlates with a Jews understanding of *betrothal* language. Marriage. When a Jewish husband desires to marry a bride in Jewish culture, the father of the daughter initiates the agreement over a meal. The husband's father accompanies his son and brings gifts with him, along with what is called a *bride price*, to be presented to the Father of the bride. If the Father accepts, a cup is raised, wine is spilled, and a *ketubah* covenant is written on shards of pottery as a covenant agreement between families. (As a side note, notice how marriage is a family affair, not merely one of individuals dating and finding their way to the altar on their own.) The Jews, as family units, believe they become one in a spiritual and mystical sense.

Following is the *mikveh*, or betrothal ceremony. This ritual is marked by groom and bride being washed nude in a pool (or *living water*) in a gender-separated ceremony. The Jews believed in the frailty, sin, and imperfectness of the human, and the bath symbolized the purity of entrance into marriage. To seal the covenant, the *erusin* followed. The erusin is a celebration that spares no expense. It confirms the betrothal as complete. One of the main events at the erusin is the filling of the *cup of joy*. The cup symbolizes that the two are now one.

After this, the groom prepares a place to take his bride. The bride is tasked to ready her things, light her lamps, and wait for the groom to come to retrieve her when their abode is ready. Often, the groom would come for her under the cover of night, so she must be always watching.

In recording two cups, Luke alludes not only to Greek symbolism but also to all things Jewish. Jesus' raising of the first cup undoubtedly makes sense to Jews from a bridal standpoint. This groom, Jesus, was about to bring his gifts and bridal price before the Father in heaven. Jesus' betrothal to his bride, the church, would cost him his life. The Father accepted Jesus promise and purchase agreement, and therefore, Jesus is able to spill wine, find joy in the cup offered, and also proclaim a new *ketubah*, or a new covenant with his people. To enter into salvation, as symbolized through marriage, a person needs only to be washed of their sins (as symbolized in Christian baptism and accomplished in Jesus' blood). Upon entering into the family of God through Jesus' blood, body, meal, and baptism, we now become the watchful bride. Jesus is preparing a place for us.

Light your lamps. He's coming.

By understanding these historical rituals, the bridal imagery, Jesus' banquet parables, and virgins and their lamps in waiting should make sense to us as believers. Luke's gospel is framed in a way that helps us understand the sermon in the sacraments. The message in the meal. Jesus' place within the meal is that he is both, as Revelation says, "one who walks among the lampstands [his church]" as king, and the one that has gone to prepare a place for us, as groom. He will retrieve us at a time quite unexpected and unpredictable. He will take us to the place where we will spend forever with him in oneness. Unity. Trinity.

Without further ado, to answer the question posed at the beginning of this long section, my answer is "Yes!" Yes, Jesus and Paul are simpatico in their view of the Lord's Supper. It's a forever, timeless, and eternal spectacle that visualizes the kingdom from all angles. The Supper is a painting that tells of God bringing Jew and Gentile alike into the kingdom. It best reflects the

Trinity's nature. It best shapes the human into "humanness." It forges wealth alongside of poor. It heals sickness amongst health. It obliterates injustice with justice. It unites division. It portrays unity. It helps the body use its gifts. It decentralizes personality and shapes a people who all bring to the table something to offer. And best of all, it glorifies Jesus' nature as the God-man— one who is truly flesh and blood (like bread and wine), but who is at the same time beyond time and space.

ONE MAN UNITING TWO

In the two cups, Jesus shows us the kingdom. In the message of the meal, we see his plan to bring Jew and Gentile together in a new Israel—Jesus himself being that new Israel. Jesus is not only the new Israel, but he's also Israel's God in the church, which is composed of Jesus' people. The Lord's Supper is absolutely bursting with symbolism and nuance, and we often miss it because our ways of doing church have sadly become quite trite.

What takes place in the gospel of Jesus' kingdom is a true miracle, and the event of God's people eating together in remembrance of him is a proclamation of his death and life until he comes. Not only do words speak, but the spectacle speaks. The meal is audio and video. We see the kingdom best portrayed when we look upon the meal. "Behold, the man," as John might say.

You may be reeling over what this might imply about our methods and modes as churches in the modern day. I hope it has called you into a conviction about how you are now to eat. Eating is a kingdom event. It's an evangelistic event. It's far more profound and yet more simplistic than any of our inventions, seminaries, buildings, operations, and fancy training.

My hope is that you will draw one simple conclusion and keep expounding, growing, and thinking from here. We must conclude that the above information changes everything about what we may think doing church means. My prayer is that you dig deep into God through prayer, study, and feasting with others so that we can understand the Trinity better.

Before you begin your sit at the tables of God's feasting, let's wrap up this chapter by bringing all our discussion to a conclusions in regard to home, family, and meals together. Let me leave you with one of the most beautiful verses in all of Scripture that puts into words what the Lord's Supper presents to us in visual form:

Therefore remember that at one time you Gentiles in the flesh, called "the uncircumcision" by what is called the circumcision, which is made in the flesh by hands—*remember that you were at that time separated from Christ*, alienated from the commonwealth of Israel and strangers to the covenants of promise, having no hope and without God in the world. *But now in Christ Jesus you who once were far off have been brought near* by the blood of Christ. For he himself is our peace, *who has made us both one and has broken down in his flesh the dividing wall of hostility* by abolishing the law of commandments expressed in ordinances, that he *might create in himself one new man in place of the two, so making peace*, and *might reconcile us both to God in one body through the cross,* thereby killing the hostility. And he came and preached peace to you who were far off and peace to those who were near. *For through him we both have access in one Spirit to the Father.* So then you are no longer strangers and aliens, but you are fellow citizens with the saints and members of the household of God, built on the foundation of the apostles and prophets, Christ Jesus himself being the cornerstone, in whom the whole structure, being joined together, grows into a holy temple in the Lord. In him you also are being built together into a dwelling place for God by the Spirit. (Eph. 2:11-22, italics mine)

The Lord's R.easoning, and way of doing things, is profoundly wrapped up in a home-bound, temple family that eats and shares life together. May our discussion pertaining to the matters at hand help us to drink deep of the meaning of the gospel.

LITURGY & RHYTHMS

C HRIST IS THE FILLER OF ALL COSMOS, CHURCH, AND CULTURE. If this is so, then every home, meal, family, and common rhythm of life is a container brimming with the potential for allegiance. Each and every moment in which we find ourselves is like a glass already filled with kingdom meaning. We need only the tools to see it. We can either fill our time, talent, and treasures with lyrics that sing of a kingdom we are building unto ourselves, or our daily routines can explode with the proclamation of our King.

How we conduct our *rhythms*, as some would call daily *liturgies*, is invaluable in our process of becoming like and R.easoning like Jesus.

Meals are the most essential of liturgies. Breakfast, lunch, and dinner. They are markers to us. Reminders. They stencil our day with eating and drinking so that we remain anchored to the gospel. Over and over we revisit the opportunity to bow our heads, pray, and feast together in remembering and talking lavishly of his glory and fame. Any recipe or cultured drink set before us, no matter how brilliant in flavor, is never intended to be a taste that is "to die for." Christ is the one we die for. Feasting brings to mind the only person and prize whose glory and beauty provides the fullest flavor. It's to remind us of the sweet death of our Jesus.

Feeding ourselves amongst the people we love most, and in the place we call most familiar—home—is the frame and canvas on which to hang and paint the rest of our life. Like a fashion designer putting clothes on a mannequin, we mold and form art with our daily schedules, habits, rituals, routines, etc. But the meal anchors our routine in relationship, not in mere rigor. By learning to connect heavenly ends to day-to-day liturgies, we enhance, define, and beautifully reveal the purpose of Jesus' filling of all things.

If it's true that all created things are packed full with meaning for our exploration, then presiding over all motion is the one conducting the symphony. Christ prays, sings, intercedes for, atones for, pleads for, and speaks a better word in and through his person as he waves his maestro's wand. He is undoubtedly our sole Worship Leader. In fact, Hebrews 8:2 names Jesus' actions as that of a maestro of the universe's musical performance. His work is that of the *leitourgos*. A Liturgist. A Shaper. A Former. It's the closest biblical word we have to the title of worship leader. Christ's leading calls planets to spin like percussive beats, stars to twinkle and orbit like the flute, oceans to crash like the cymbals, birds to sing like violins, humans to flourish for the good of all things like the sun, evil to flee like the dark of night as the sun rises, and mountains to sing majesty.

The true meaning of Jesus being our Worship Leader casts vibrant new light on our currently dim philosophies and reasoning for worship. Worship isn't as paper-thin as the stage, skinny jeans, and music albums. We must abandon such a small caricature. When the Scripture attaches the idea of worship leading to the planets, the angels, even pagan authorities (Rom. 13), and also to those practically meeting the needs of the orphan, the fatherless, the widow, and the marginalized (Rom. 15), we must learn to think and train ourselves in such ways.

In our obsession over singing and the central gathering of God's people—which is important—we go far beyond what is healthy and altogether miss what worship has to say about our life as the scattered church. We miss how worship connects and interacts with our cosmos and culture in function. We completely overlook that worship is a formational and structural word. Worship doesn't merely speak into our life as a singer. It's an "everything" word. Worship is a world word.

A new paradigm for categorizing worship in deeper ways needs to include the mundane. In our day-to-day rhythms, we mold everything around our texts, day planners, budgets, calendars, and beyond. These become our mannequins around which we hang all meaning. These forms begin to occupy our greatest allegiances. More aptly put, they *reveal* our greatest allegiances. Worship pastoring must take place in these places. The most practical, efficient, and spreadsheet-based things of our life orbit whom and what we follow.

Remember, worship points. If we worship a hobby, all our time, talent, and treasure will aim itself at gearing us up and readying us for said interest. If our central thing is a girl, an ideal, a goal, a business, an art form, or whatever else we might prize, we will aim everything in life at that supreme thing—to the exclusion of everything else. It's not really that hard to picture, really. Remember that time in high school when you discovered the opposite sex and became enamored with your first love. Almost immediately everything and everyone else disappeared. Nothing else mattered any more. The two of you were swallowed up into one another.

Any object of worship that is not Jesus will swallow us up, not build us up. When we worship something lesser than Jesus, we subject ourselves to its rhythms (literally, its liturgy), ethic, vision of the good life, marketing slogans, buying practices, and so on. By nature, we begin to embody what we attend to most closely. We are nothing more than a worshipping, bowing, prostrating, humbling, serving, arm-raising, dancing, shouting, praising people. We are created to devote ourselves to what most excites us. Our worship reveals what we make primary. What we honor we most allow into our lives. We soon begin to form ourselves into the image of what we worship.

The upside to our created nature is that we can become increasingly like God if he occupies our greatest seat of honor. The downside is that if we bend our knee to creation rather than the Creator, we begin looking like, acting like, and performing like the latest, greatest star in sport, cinema, and stage. We turn to every hobby, electronic gimmick, marketing pitch, or commercial to convince ourselves that we need _____ in order to be happy.

THE LEITOURGOS ... NO, IT'S NOT A CHARACTER IN STAR WARS.

To help us remedy our current cancerous state, and better understand the relationship of worship to life, I want to return to the previously mentioned Greek word *leitourgos*. It's the source of our English word, liturgy. The word refers to the rhythms of Christ's service in, to, through, and for us. Its reference is not to our work, but to his life and performance as it lives through us. Our work is nothing more than a response. In responding and aligning to his rhythmic liturgies in cosmos, church, and culture, we will find his best offering of health and wellbeing as servants under his Kingship.

Let's revisit more deeply three specific uses of the word *leitourgos*, as were previously mentioned. In Hebrews 8:2, Jesus is called our "minister." As our Worship Leader, he prays, sings over us, pleads his atoning work on our behalf before the Father, and works the gospel into the restoration of all things present, and all the "new heavens and new earth" future. He does all these things 24/7 and beyond time. Christ's leadership on our behalf presses into everything in the known cosmos. I note in my book *Reconsidering the Worship Leader and the Cosmos*:

> Even more amazing is that the same word used of Christ as "minister" in Hebrews 8:2 is used in the Hebrew form in Psalm 103:19-22 to refer to God's angelic and astronomical hosts; "The LORD has established his throne in the heavens, and his kingdom rules over all. Bless the LORD, O you his angels, you mighty ones who do his word, obeying the voice of his word! Bless the LORD, all his hosts, *his ministers*, who do his will! Bless the LORD, all his works, in all places of his dominion. Bless the LORD, O my soul!" God holds a cosmic "church-service" each and every day, over which presides his angels (Gk. *Angelos* meaning "messengers of grace"), his spheres, his oceans, and every fault line running through the earth's crust. They all sing, move, dance, and sway to the praise of his name. Like a giant conductor, our God fills all in all. He sings over all in all.[1]

Because the Trinity is actively working his supremacy into every aspect of time and created space, we can expect that all universal habits, astrology, patterns, and forms speak his great name. Which they do. God uses his created things to mark time. Both *kairos time* (circular or seasonal time), and *chronos time* (linear historical timeline). As fall, winter, spring, and summer come, and as the daily routine of sunrise and sunset happen, humanity and living things of earth, sky, and sea are all told when to sleep and when to rise. Our biochemistry tells us when to eat and when to drink. We automatically register heat and cold, stress and calm, logic and irrationality, truth and lie. Woven into the fabric of the universe are things that are absolutely true and necessary for the preservation of life.

Science is wonderful at teaching us about the health and wellness found in God's created order. Study after study confirms that lunar patterns, mathematical precision, climate, nutrition, emotional and psychological health, and spiritual connection is absolutely necessary for our flourishing. All discovery reveals to us is that "God was right." When we observe the rhythms of his creation, use everything given us in the manner intended, and produce creatively in a fashion that points back to our Creator and source, we experience what John 10:10 calls "abundant life."

Ironically and curiously, the same word used for Jesus in Hebrews (the *leitourgos*) is used in Romans 15 to refer to Paul's collection of alms for the poor within the global body of Christ. In Romans 13:4, Paul again uses the word to reference the secular and evil authorities of our world. Paul's use of the word demonstrates how God's natural liturgies and routines in the created world serve as vehicles for worship. They point! We either rightly assimilate God's resources unto the worship of him and the loving and caring for all of his people—particularly those less fortunate—or we succumb to a purely human way of interpreting God's rhythms. When one interprets the intricacies of God's creation without consulting the answer key of Jesus and the Bible, we invent ways of doing things that aim everything at a vision of the good life of our own making.

For the believer, empowering work in the realm of civil and ceremonial service is held to the same standard as that of our service directed specifically to God's family. It is our mandate as Christians to make meaning of the world via our worldview.

THICK AND THIN

Christ practically interacts with our everyday life in order to produce worship and Christlikeness in us. James K. A. Smith in his book *Desiring the Kingdom* talks briefly about what he calls *thick and thin* routines. He considers anything thick to be moments and matters of high significance or relational effect, like a bible study, a church gathering, or a prayer meeting. He associates thickness with anything that is inherently ceremonial. He might categorize a rhythm in our schedule as thin if at first glance it has little meaning (e.g., brushing our teeth, taking a bath, driving in our car). In one regard I agree with Smith. We treat hygiene regimens, commutes, cubicles, charts, texting, textbooks, hobbies and interests, line items, and finance, as second-tier commodity. What I might add to Smith's thinking is my analogy of a drinking glass. Every element of our day is simply a container. It can remain empty (thin) if we neglect its significance through our own anemic contemplation, or we can increase our sensitivity and recognize how everything is filled with meaning (thick).

If Christ is over cosmos, church, and culture, then everything is thick. We cannot consider certain things sacred and other things secular. Many have fallen into the error of making certain things holy and others off limits. A proof of the increasing divide is what I see in my McDonald's-loving youth pastor friend who stands up on stage at 350 lbs. Overweight as he is, he declares pornography the cardinal sin. What underlies his statement is a gross misinterpretation of worship. To him, your "eye life" is thicker than your "mouth life." He considers what we watch to be important to our worship life, but he considers what we eat to have no bearing on the kingdom.

We do the same with our hygiene. We think of our morning routine as being thin. We miss the truth of the matter—that our getting ready in the morning is the readying of a *priest*. If we are truly the priesthood of God, then we must take more seriously our grooming regimen.

Consider the principles of the ceremonial law found in Leviticus. Though those laws are no longer binding, they outline principles that still yield sound wisdom in terms of preparing one's self for work.

Dare I take my grooming and readiness rhythms any less seriously than God does?

As I shave and comb my hair, I'm readying myself for a day as a priest. I'm walking out before a people. They are to smell on me the incense of a well-groomed, well-maintained man. What they take in of me, my home, my work, and my trade, through their five senses will speak far louder about the Trinity than perhaps what I might say I believe.

In all actuality, all our rhythms are intended to be thick. Sadly, our natural bent is to go through life on cruise control and assume that common, mundane things have little significance.

How Worship Infuses Formation

True transformation in making thin rhythms into thick, when we disengage our internal cruise control—merely coasting through daily routine—and start to engage our deeper desires. For me, this change happened with the activity of driving.

My cruise control—my subconscious desire—used to be pre-programmed for me when getting into a car. I'd turn the key and reach for the radio. I didn't think. My rhythm had me set. My car rides were just thin times to tune out while the radio tuned in. About ten years ago, I engaged. I actively moved a subconscious desire to the forefront of my active and decision-making brain. I desired to actively pray more, and I was traveling a lot. So I decided to fill my driving routine with the thicker rhythms of prayer. For about thirty days I jumped in my car, turned the key, and had to stop my hand from turning on the radio. My brain naturally remembered my *liturgy* almost involuntarily. But after thirty days, I jumped in the vehicle, started the engine, and was surprised when my mouth instantly opened, and I began to pray. To this day, when I get in the car I begin the weird ritual of talking to my God.

It makes carpooling awkward.

Bad Joke.

The rhythm of driving is now forever thick to me. It's infused with the prayer ministry of heaven. I've also recently infused my hygiene regimen with meditations on my baptism, holiness, and cleanliness before God. I am often brought to tears every day in my shower as I remember the simple words hovering over Jesus as the first waters of baptism cascaded down his face and into my heart: "This is my son, in whom I'm well pleased." For me, showering has become a way to reaffirm and embrace my identity in Christ. Doing so sets up the rest of my day for success. I work *from* love, not *for* love.

I know a friend who has turned the task of managing mind-numbing budget woes into a heavenly interaction with God regarding his heart for the fatherless, the widow, and the orphan. For others, TV sitcoms and news clips have become a training ground. Watching has turned into a time for worldview formation and mission preparedness. As they view, they dissect the ideals, present idols, and cultural goods and evils that are loudest today. They use the weapons of the world against the adversary to better equip themselves to engage in conversation about the thin shows that capture the affections of so many. These entertainment nuggets are thin, but they are thickly consuming the thoughts of co-workers as they meet around water coolers and in break rooms. It would do us well to change our philosophy of worship and engage more deeply with our everyday coworkers about the vacuity of our current entertainment.

Slowly but surely, by shutting off cruise control we begin to attune ourselves to God's natural rhythms. We welcome the sleep patterns he sets as the sun rises. We eat foods that are nutritious and not genetically engineered. We refuse to let the glimmer of the iPad and lights of Ben Franklin alter our relationship to the earth. We engage in God's seasons of remembrance, contemplation, thankfulness, and harvest (fall); his advent and appearing amidst the darkness of the world (winter); his new life of resurrection and ascension (spring), and the wonders of his flourishing kingdom life (summer).

Becoming like Christ is no longer about scattered worship that awaits our time as a gathered people. It's about learning gathered rhythms when we are together so that those liturgies overtake our scattered lives.

The Gathering and the Scattering

Bringing worship into the rhythms of everyday life does not negate the critical importance Christians gathering to worship. It actually heightens our need to think more deeply about what we're doing in gathering as a Body.

In observing some of the key passages on worship in Scripture, one can see a distinct conversation of call and response emerge in Christian gathered worship. The conversation regarding how God gathers his people presses its way into us as a body and then explodes in and through us as we are sent out into all our daily schedules. We are the light of the world.

Many major sections of Scripture reveal a pattern in how God deals with his people and his creation. This pattern gives us good, biblical wisdom about how we are to worship when we assemble together. Here is a nutshell outline of that repetitive pattern that defines what occurs in assembled worship as it arises throughout God's Word:[2]

God's Character is Recognized
(We adore and praise God)

Human Character is Recognized
(Our sin's exposed & we confess)

God Initiates Grace
(God assures us of our forgiveness)

Human's Respond to Grace
(We respond to his gift in thankfulness)

God's Initiates Instruction

(God teaches us through his Word)

We respond in Obedience
(We obey him, living out his mission)

God's Promise
(We're dismissed from the assembly and promised God's presence)

Our Blessing
(We are blessed to go out and be a blessing)

The pattern of God's revelation, initiation, and our response to his pursuit, is clearly seen in Scripture. To a great degree, this regimen is to be hammered into our subconscious desire week-in and week-out as we gather. The repetition drives the meaning deeper and deeper, and as we are sent out from the assembly, the liturgy then begins to interact with the rest of our life. We form a way of worship that embeds itself in our cruise control and influences each moment as we enter into in a way that processes worship into godly action.

When God is revealed, we see our sin. When he forgives, we rejoice. When he teaches us how to live, we obey. When he promises to be with us, we are blessed. Worship is about all of life, and we should strive to maintain this conversation and storyline in our worship. God certainly took time in his Word to show us how regularly and normatively the same pattern of worship occurs:

CREATION: GENESIS 1

- God's pursues creation (v. 1)
- Creation's character revealed (v. 2)
- God's grace given in his presence over the waters (v. 2)
- God's instruction for the creation to obey (v. 3)
- Gods assurance that it is good (v. 4)
- God commands the light to separate (v. 4)
- Promise of blessing and assignment to roles (sending) (vv. 4-5)

THE FALL OF HUMANITY: GENESIS 3

- God's character recognized in initiating grace (v. 9)
- Human character recognized (v. 10)
- God's pronouncement of judgment (vv. 14-20)
- God's grace exhibited (v. 21)
- Promise of covenant blessing, sending and assurance (v. 15)

BURNING BUSH: EXODUS 3

- God's character recognized through pursuit (vv. 2-4)
- Frailty of man and creation recognized (v. 3)
- God's grace exhibited (v. 7)
- God's grace assured (v. 8)
- Instruction for obedience (vv. 7-9)
- Response of doubt (v. 11-12)
- Promise of covenant blessing and sending (v. 10)

SINAI WORSHIP: DEUTERONOMY. 5

- God's character recognized (vv. 4, 22-24)
- Human character confessed (v. 5, 22-27)
- God's grace exhibited (vv. 2-3, 6)
- God's grace assured (v. 2-3)
- Instruction for obedience (v. 6-21, 32-33a)
- Response of thankful devotion (v. 27)
- Promise of covenant blessing (v. 33b)

ISAIAH'S VISION: ISAIAH 6

- God's character recognized (vv.1-4)
- Human character recognized (v. 5)
- God's grace exhibited (vv. 6-7)
- God's grace assured (v. 7)
- Response of thankful devotion (v. 8)
- Instruction for obedience (vv. 9-12)
- Promise of covenant blessing (v. 13)

SOLOMON'S WORSHIP: 2 CHRONICLES 5-7

- God's character recognized (vv. 5:1-5)
- Human character confessed (vv. 5:6-10)
- God's grace assured (vv. 5:13-14)
- Petition (vv. 6:12-21)
- Instruction for obedience (vv. 6:22-42)
- Response of thankful devotion (vv. 7:4-9)
- Promise of covenant blessing (vv. 7:10)

THE GREAT COMMISSION: MATTHEW 28

- Jesus appears to the disciples and they worship (v.17)
- Human character recognized (v. 17)
- Instruction, assurance, and command (v. 18)
- Promise of blessing, covenant, sending (vv. 19-20)

ROMANS PART 1

- Instruction in God's nature (vv. 1-11)
- Explanation of grace through faith (vv. 2-11)
- God's character recognized (vv. 11:25-32)
- Human character confessed (v. 12:1)
- Response of thankful devotion (vv. 12:3-8, 9-12)
- Promise of covenant blessing (vv. 14:1-15:13)

ROMANS PART 2

- God's character recognized (vv. 11:33-36)
- Human need for mercy (v. 12:1)
- God's mercy assured (v. 12:1)
- Thankful response (v. 12:2)
- Instruction for obedience (vv. 12:3-13:14)
- Communal care for one another (vv. 14:1-15:12)
- Charge and blessing (v. 15:13)

EPHESIANS

- God's character recognized (Ch. 1)

- Human need (vv. 2:1-3)
- God's provision (vv. 2:4-10)
- Instruction in godliness (vv. 2:11-6:18)
- Communal care for one another (vv. 6:19-22)
- Benediction (vv. 6:23-24)

ESCHATOLOGICAL WORSHIP: REVELATION 4-21

- God's character recognized (vv. 4:1-11)
- Human need and sin (vv. 5:1-7)
- Prayer for assurance of provision (vv. 5:8-10)
- Thankful response (vv. 5:11-14)
- Cycles of God's Word opened with heavenly and earthly reactions (vv. 6:1-19:5)

* The Seven Seals (vv. 6:1-8:5)
* The Seven Trumpets (vv. 8:6-11:19)
* The Seven Signs (vv. 12:1-15:8)
* Babylon Announcements (vv. 17:1-19:5)

- Communion in Wedding and Royal Supper (vv. 19:6-10 and 11-21)
- Charge of Judgment and New Creation (Rv. 20–22)

The repetition of how God gathers his people to worship remarkably mirrors how Jesus taught us to pray. First, we are to focus on the character of God, not the actions of God ("Our Father, who art in heaven, hallowed be Your Name"), which leads us to see his character in what he's revealed ("Your kingdom come, your will be done, on earth as it is in heaven"). We then recognize our needy and sinful nature ("Give us this day our daily bread, forgive us"), we are assured of God's protection and salvation despite our fallen condition ("Lead us not into temptation, but deliver us from evil"). God then graciously sends us out to live for his glory. Amen.

The rhythm of gathering trains our scattering. When we encounter the character of the world, our limitations in countless areas, and our need for help, we drill down into our cruise-control desires to find a godly way of dealing with things that assault our conscious decisions. Rather than descending into the worship liturgies of the world (stress, worry, depression, condemnation, self-deprecation, false optimism), we are equipped with a liturgy to bring the world to Christ.

Ironically, Christ's rhythms are the exact opposite of our own. Our human liturgies tend to center on ourselves. They lead us to search for our own fame and fortune and leave us wallowing like the prodigal in our own slop. Our chase after our own glorified entitlement lines the pockets of every counselor and psychiatrist out there. Healthy wisdom, on the other hand, teaches us to make much of Christ, confess and welcome our limitations as a means through which he is glorified in grace while receiving his transformation in order to fight better next time.

Our fleshly liturgies only preach half the gospel. Satan whispers to us over and over the bad. He repeats in our ears that we've fallen short. We're inadequate. We don't have what it takes to be a Christian. The fact is, what Satan is telling us is true, as far as it goes. It's just not the complete story. The rest of the gospel is what puts the "Amen-cherry" atop the good and equally true news that undermines Satan's half-truth. Christ's liturgy completes the story. We rejoice in the fact that we can never measure up, and that Christ has stood tall for us. He did not fall short. When a rhythm of Christ-centered worship is enacted over and over within our seemingly thin rhythms, it forms into us the thick meaning of God-glorifying victory. One moment, one liturgy, one rhythm at a time.

THE TRINITY ANSWERS REASONING

I n our previous section on C.ommunity, I included Figure 3.1. which I am repeating here to provide a visual that helps us in our thinking on the Trinity.

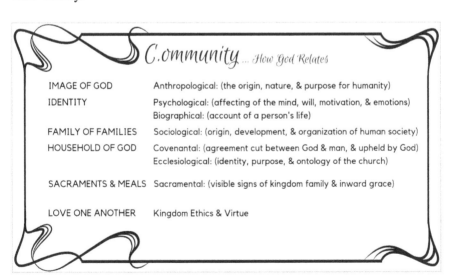

C.ommunity ... How God Relates

IMAGE OF GOD	Anthropological: (the origin, nature, & purpose for humanity)
IDENTITY	Psychological: (affecting of the mind, will, motivation, & emotions)
	Biographical: (account of a person's life)
FAMILY OF FAMILIES	Sociological: (origin, development, & organization of human society)
HOUSEHOLD OF GOD	Covenantal: (agreement cut between God & man, & upheld by God)
	Ecclesiological: (identity, purpose, & ontology of the church)
SACRAMENTS & MEALS	Sacramental: (visible signs of kingdom family & inward grace)
LOVE ONE ANOTHER	Kingdom Ethics & Virtue

Fig. 3.1

We will expand our look at community in this chapter on R.easoning (Fig. 3.2) by building a case for what I like to call, a philosophy for flourishing life in all time, places, and circumstances.

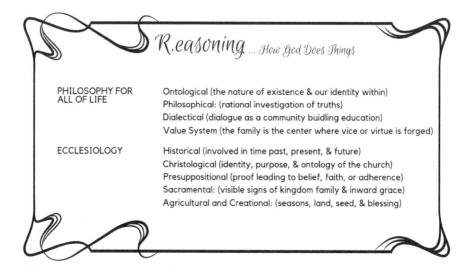

Fig. 3.2

Jesus, home, meals, family, and marriage are timeless symbols that are woven deep into the fabric of everything, and they show us the foundations we tend to overlook. They anchor us to rhythms of eternity.

We need to reevaluate through the lens of such repetitions the reasons why we do *anything* because much of our innovation, creativity, and ingenuity in culture, and in doing church over the millennia has actually pulled families away from the simplicity of life in the Trinity. Our foundation. We've allowed our adventures to convince us that there's "more beyond the horizon," when in reality, the more global our world has become, the more it's resulted in the brokenness of the home and the sickness of being alone together. We've forgotten that true philosophy, exploration, and advancement should bring us back to ageless and ancient principles that existed from the beginning.

The majority have bought into a life that hands us only a tissue box for our tears, as it continually opens sores via its liturgies that spawn aloneness. We may say we're individualists, feminists, environmentalists, pacifists, or any one of a million ways we strive to prove we're somehow better than God and others. But the fact remains, much of our language springs from closeted loneliness. We've created identities that try to make sense of our despair, and we've created environments and methods that actually show rather than cure our isolation.

We can hope that in becoming so utterly despairing in our own sickness, many are reaching the end of themselves and groping for answers. It is my suggestion once again that we need to think in paradigms, not in methods. If we anchor ourselves in the bedrock of what is timeless (Jesus, home, meals, and family/marriage) and we spin our thinking and daily rhythms toward these centers, it will affect and balance everything.

THE CURRENT MUDDLE OVER THE REASON FOR OUR BEING

The "ologys"—psychology, sociology, biology, and the like—build on a seriously flawed foundational philosophy. These disciplines seek to explain who we are and how we function based on an erroneous theory of origins. God gives us an accurate account of the beginnings of our being. We did not evolve into social creatures from cells that emerged randomly out of an impersonal, primordial goo. The second law of thermodynamics shows that undirected movement toward increasing complexity is impossible. Our being and who we are originates somewhere outside nature and by logical necessity sprang from a being greater than we are. Any "ology" that fails to take that foundational fact into account will paint a false picture of what and who we are.

Our inevitable origin in a source beyond nature also tells us that our capacity for reason lies beyond what thinkers like Aristotle and Descartes suggest. Aristotle suggests that knowing one's inner self is the beginning of wisdom. Descartes suggests that our mental capacity to think and know is what makes us human. The thinkers of the world have boiled our essential being down to only what we find inside our minds and hearts. They've divorced us from any meaning beyond what can be explained by the mechanics of the physical world. Even our thinking processes are considered to be nothing more than the movements of atoms within our brains. Thus it is beyond the capacity of our earthbound sciences and human philosophies to find metaphysical or spiritual meaning in our everyday realities.

As a result of wearing such blinders, the world's philosophies provide no satisfying answers to our deepest questions. Indeed, they only raise more questions that lead to a dark, dead-end. Despite their claims that we are ever evolving toward a utopian existence, suicide rates keep climbing.

People become dissatisfied with life because they feel a persistent sense of guilt and alienation that no philosophy or psychology can explain. Hedonism tells us to fulfill all desires. Eastern religions tell us to deny all desires. But a yoga-ish retreat into our inner "om" of consciousness only brings us to the conclusion that a journey either toward or away from earthly desires is really a road to damnation. We're damned if we do, and we're damned if we don't. We're imperfect apart from any action or as a result of any action. Nor is psychology of any help. It denies the guilt that underlies our problem of sin and pride. Behavior modification, will power, and self-restraint fail to ride herd on our persistent, self-destructive tendencies.

All probing into the true nature of our existence will be futile unless it becomes an outward search instead of an inward probing. A search for our true source. Jesus claims to be our source, and until we conform our worship and our everyday lives to him, we will never understand the true nature of our being.

A PHILOSOPHY FOR EDUCATING THE WHOLE COMMUNAL-IDENTITY OF A PERSON

God is not confused or muddled. He has clear reasoning behind his drive to form human-*beings*. He invented the family and marriage to shape us as complete people. True humans. We are to know who and whose we are and to know from whom we come. Teaching us how to embrace God's simplistic reasoning requires a different educational system for building God's values into a fully embodied humanity.

I'd like to have some fun thinking about what God's opinion might be on the matter of educating and developing true humanness. My hunch is that it differs entirely from our popular approaches.

Let's imagine what parenting, training, education, and the holistic "human-building" process might have looked like with Adam and Eve had the Fall never happened. I know it's a bit hypothetical, but I think there's some warrant to imagining what should be as we ponder what actually is.

The Proverbs are very helpful in telling us what utopia might look like. For example, a child becomes most human in learning to honor his or her father and mother. The family is structured around honor and authority, and it paints a picture of how God relates within himself. Before sin corrupted everything, Adam and Eve would have been viewed as real authorities to their children, and their children would have joyfully resolved to love their parents. They would have easily understood the safety found in submitting to their parents' superior knowledge and resting beneath their protective wings. Therefore, to educate the youth and young adult into maturity should be to assess how well they hear and heed the voice of the older and wiser. It's hard to accomplish generational respect today with the family becoming so disconnected—living countries apart and connected only by media, and us carting elderly people off to nursing homes for annual visits. Add to these facts the notion that we live a world that worships and elevates the folly of youth in both the culture and church, and we have a recipe for lost authority.

The Scriptures also tell us that human parents are called to "train up children in the way they should go." Training would have been the norm in the garden economy. It's normative still in God's economy. What does this training look like?

Children are to be oriented toward home. They are to be oriented toward what glorifies God. They are to be steered toward the blessing in the meal and the health of marriage. Parental training should reflect the parents' values and image, just as the Trinity designed humanity to reflect God's image.

The Proverb's portrayal of training delves much deeper into human education than what we find in the good but partial models employed in public school, catechism, doctrine, or even physical training (such as spanking or physical discipline). In Proverbs, training reaches far deeper than mere blind obedience. Sound discipline multiplies the image and love of God. Loving disciples require a loving environment. Love implies that all those involved are allowed to be who and whose they truly are. Only a family can provide a multi-angled camera view of love in all its beauty and through any adversity. To forge a fully loving human, the center must be family.

The word translated as training in Proverbs is the Hebrew word *paideia*. This word is understood in the Jewish mind as indicating the "whole" of a person. A child is made up of emotional, social, physical, spiritual, and mental attributes, and parents are required to teach, instruct, provide balance, give ideas, nurture, and craft each of these. Parents are not given free rein, however. They do not shape the child in the manner they see fit, as if to equip the child for building a car without providing the chassis. Without a car's foundation, the pieces are just meaningless chaos. To fit and function rightly, every piece has to anchor, weld, and pin to the central core of a car's frame. The frame for shaping humans is the nature of God and his liturgies we previously mentioned. If we try as parents to pin, weld, or tack onto our children any human inventions of genetics, sexual preference, life choices, or sexual identity, they will plummet into chaos.

The purpose in forming all rhythms of humanness to the mold of the Trinity is not merely to produce good families, but to raise children that grow up following the same desires as their parents and of their Inventor. The goal is to raise children that hold to the desire to resemble the glory and image of God.

The Hebrew word paideia also brings to mind a person's palette. It's an eating word. Literally, the Hebrew suggests that we learn our tastes from what is parented into us. We learn what sounds good to the ears, tastes good to the tongue, feels good to the touch, looks good to the eyes, and smells good to the nose from what is taught us. We learn not just by receiving instruction or by testing, but by immersion of the whole person into the experience. It's an education that orbits meals and a home. The family presides over and best facilitates an environment where proper tastes can flourish in all areas of life— the arts, leadership, politics, governance, and entertainment. The world suggests an opposite trajectory.

Today, a child is thought to be socialized by those outside the family. We are trained to look to the government and to culture to define our values, ethics, virtues, rituals, and conclusions to major issues. We are taught to look to Apple and Amazon to shape our tastes for what is good art and music.

In forging a taste for the philosophy of how things are done in God's economy, we uncover very quickly how far our world has fallen short.

The world is always pushing to parent us. It's always pushing to put on our tongue what is most "reasonable" and "right" to them. To resist this constant pressure to conform, we've got to allow our paradigm to anchor us. A meal of ethics, virtues, leadership, and politics is best ingested face-to-face across a table in an environment sheltered by authority and guarded with aging wisdom. Brothers and sisters learn manners face-to-face. Conversation and openness are learned face-to-face. Respect for another's opinions and logic are learned eye-to-eye, and at the same time, everyone is called to compare their ways and wills to Jesus, not to each other. Around this table, a servant is born and fashioned. The broom becomes the training ground for industry; the barfing child is the perfect textbook for patience; and the sometimes annoying, albeit endearing teenager becomes the teacher of listening and shepherding skills.

Hospitality to both sinner and saint alike is an invitation to learn equality and friendship rather than hierarchy and the formation of god-complexes. When two opposing people sit across from one another, they're lovingly forced to consider another. The poor learn from the rich, and the rich from the poor. The unsaved learns of their need from the saved, and the saved remembers their humble need in the eyes of the lost. The old trains the young in insight, and the young inspires the old in zeal. The humanness of each person in a family is laid bare around the meal and its training process.

Because the world—and the church, frankly—has weaseled out from under the umbrella of the *paideia* process, we've begun compartmentalizing people. We train people in boxes, not as wholes. We teach at schools. We socialize at parks. We spiritualize at church. We lead at clubs. We serve at shelters. And what has been the result? Many of the inventions that our reasoning has produced has led to what I call *passive participation*. Because we're so concerned with isolating people into defining themselves as individuals, our whole system teaches people to follow one way, one person, one interpretation, and our own definition of truth. It's postmodern. The essence of the game is to fight for glory, to stand out, to be noticed.

The mentality of the world screams, "My individuality trumps yours." We're okay with someone else as long as he also clings to "agree-with-me" type of thinking. Schools teach students what to think, not how to think. Testing today aims only to measure how well a student memorized what was expressed, not to assess how well he can develop thinking of his own. At church, people are trained to sit in a pew, listen to one person's interpretation, and are only named as members, servants, or allowed access to use their gifts as leaders if their thinking reflects that of the majority. The posture we're forced to take, and the way our methods are mandated to work, is to shape everything toward a "center." The center of everything may come in the form of a stage, a personality, a model, a denomination, or some other distinctive. Regardless of what that center is, people are encouraged to consume what is handed them. If they don't, they're merely tolerated and given small say in the system, but never allowed full integration, much less, embrace.

BEING THE CHURCH, NOT DOING CHURCH

The result of our individualized paradigm for forming true humanness is that it is now attempting to close the eyelids of family, marriage, Jesus, and the home. The outside structures of culture now dominate the conversation. Rather than heart and home influencing societal structures, the process is now reversed.

The results are slavery and control. For example, today big government is put in the place of mandating morality. The government is great at making moral issues political, and political issues moral. Government now believes itself to exist to control people—to herd them into cattle stalls, all facing the same direction. The thinking is utterly backward, and it doesn't work. Governance, leadership, sociality, identity, and all matters of taste are to be forged and trained within the family. Training true humans requires a reallocation of resources.

My driving questions that loom in response are, Why aren't all our resources aimed at developing families to disciple other families within their homes? Why isn't our worship together taking place in an environment where the people of God being the church makes most sense? Around the meal. Why isn't the body of Christ hurrying people back to the very real life spaces in which they most deeply encounter the words of discipleship (i.e., husband, wife, siblings, parent, and child)? The conversation bears incredible weight in our *ecclesiology* (how we do church).

Church has largely grown into a concert venue based around a personality-centric model. The infinite wisdom we've dreamed up is that we need to pull families away from their homes to train them to be a family in their homes. We've created a home away from home, and I'm not sure it looks like home at all.

The institutional church, rather than being a "residence for God's presence," has grown into a monster that eats people. People are put into the machine in the manner best determined by a few leaders at the top, and over time 80 percent of the work is done by 20 percent of the people, with about 2 percent actually utilizing what they feel to be their passions. The results? Burnout. Pastors are falling left and right into the trappings and pride that comes from unhealthy praise, and congregations are fueling their rise and fall. The church has settled for addition, church hopping, and church transfers, and has lost any semblance of multiplication. And it's because we've killed the priesthood of the believer by dividing members into categories of clergy and laity. Ministry has become a job for which one is hired. Ministry is done by professionals before an audience. The rest are expected to watch the show.

Meanwhile, Adam's most human attribute dies on the vine. God mandated Adam to go and make, produce, and multiply. That charge has been replaced by a methodology that says come and get fed. Pews are filled with fat sheep who know what to think but are not taught how to interpret the Bible for themselves, or even to create and innovate out of the principles they find. What's left is a co-dependence. The audience is dependent on those with Bible-learning because they themselves don't know how to interpret Scripture, and those in influence are desperately tethered to the pleasure and power they find in the approval of man.

All the budget heft is shifted toward sustaining the central location of the church and its programs. Everyone recites the same mantra in waking up Sunday morning: "Let's *go to* church." The connection to a more theologically appropriate understanding that *we are the church* has all but been lost. Meanwhile, the needs of the orphan, the widow, and the oppressed are pawned off on parachurch organizations who operate as adjuncts to God's family. Parachurches often wind up doing what the church should be doing via the building but cannot because brick and mortar consumes most of the church's budget. Seminaries get stuck with the task of educating people in the Bible and away from the context where they actually live. The education format actually sets up people for failure. Psychology departments take over the role of training the next generation in how to pastor people's hearts. They're doing a treacherous job because counseling is no longer understood as a community event. People have all but lost what the counsel of the Holy Spirit looks like in the nature of God's family—the church. We together have the mind of Christ. We've isolated psych and wellness, and we've made them into draft pools for narcissism. Big production and publication companies have more sway over the minds and hearts than community thinkers, voices, and proven wisdom. Business, governance, and vocational curation is no longer seen as a spiritual duty of those calling themselves the church.

All of the aforementioned doesn't even consider how our current systems for building humanness have actually caused many of our most glaring modern-day problems. Rather than the church uniting God's diverse people, our paradigms lead us to divide people, splitting them apart into classrooms based on age, interest, ethnicity, saved, and unsaved. The totality of our humanness is lost.

TOP DOWN RATHER THAN ACROSS … THE COMPROMISE OF THE GOSPEL

A by-product of anchoring to timely methods rather than timeless ones has compromised our ability to think in terms originating in the garden. Our *philosophies* for *how we do things* have reshaped how we define what it means to be human. For example, Adam and Eve knew a perfect authority and submission structure of friendship that exists between parent and child. We have trouble with this concept in lieu of the things taught to us in our day. We've reinterpreted true authority and submission as a *top-down* structure. We've introduced it into everything human. It has all but silenced the *across* structure of friendship and family power.

Let me allude to two examples of additions we've made to the church that explain this change further—one from historical meal rituals and another from historical architecture.

Before the time of Constantine, we have still extant many artistically painted portrayals of Christian gatherings. Most often they show Christians facing each other, eating together. Trinity. Ministry was thought of as towards, amongst, and with each other. Friendship. Everyone was there—the rich, the poor, the unsaved, and the saved. Post Constantine, we have a visible separation appearing most vividly in the artistic expression of architecture. A growing divorce between the professional and the layperson shows up in new architectural buildings. The church started building atriums. People no longer prioritized circles. Buildings were constructed with vaulted ceilings and with long and rectangular shapes. People began facing an upfront platform and no longer faced each other. The meal for the believers (Eucharist) went to Sunday morning, and the meals for the poor (Agape Feast) shifted to the evenings. The splitting of mealtimes and the architectural changes brought a growing distinction between those qualified and those not. Professional ministry and vocational ministry split. Sacred and secular. Trained and untrained.

Over time, performance and stages began to rise, and huge, vaulted canopies at the front of meeting spaces were enlarged. The leadership was raised higher and higher on platforms ever growing, and everything amplified the reality of setting the congregation below and apart from the clergy. Leadership ministered *down* to the people, and the people followed suit. People learned from the shape of ministry they feasted on. Following the example of their leaders, the new laity class of people began to find ways to elevate themselves above their peers. Christians began ministering *to* the poor in the evenings in a one-way relationship. The fortunate served *down* to the needy. Through it all, they attempt to escape their neediness within.

This change in worship altered our view of theology and of Christ himself. Christ's very incarnation reveals to us that he abandon his throne in heaven in order to live amongst men. He ate with them and called them his friends. The historical reasoning behind ministry is found in Christ himself. It's defined by hospitality. Today, one is hard pressed to find even the nuclear family living together cordially, let alone the extended family. It's even rarer to find hospitable families following the friend-making nature of Christ's model in the home. And it's virtually impossible to find people willing to invite into their homes the wider cultural family outside the comfort zone of their own class— the homeless, widow, orphan, the underpaid and over-starved college kid or artist.

We've reached a point where hospitality doesn't even make sense to us biblically anymore. We've reframed the meaning of it. Ask any Christian what hospitality means, and they will equate it with fellowship. We dine with those like us. However, hospitality in Scripture means dining with those most unlike us. We are commanded to invite in the scum of the earth and to remember that we are all scum together without the bleaching purity of God.

It's hard to develop a passion for such a counter-cultural brand of hospitality when we're busy erecting enormous buildings that could be just as well used for soup kitchens. We shift our responsibility as family onto the corporate entity. Meanwhile, we have very graciously blessed and wealthy people in the church who already have houses enormous enough for significant gatherings, and they lie virtually empty to accommodate the growing-old process of two people. Because our trajectory of ministry has shifted, we can't even compute that we don't need any more buildings to meet and grow in. We fail to see that we only need to turn our focus toward the plethora already given to us. Our homes. The centers for growing in hospitality and true fellowship.

Clearly, our models in the new era are just that: "new." We've fallen into what C. S. Lewis has called "chronological snobbery." We think that just because we're further down the road of history that we're also further along in knowledge and wisdom. Nonetheless, take a look at the New Testament church. The early Christians were fraught with problems, but in large part, they continued the historical traditions of Scripture in keeping the church a meal, a household, and a family. The problems they had to deal with, as a result involved people *getting too close to one another*. The people of Corinthians got way too close! So close, in fact, that sons-in-law were sleeping with step-mothers. It's grotesque sin at its worst, but the closeness exposes the lack of depth in us. Personally, I'd rather deal with a hundred problems that result from us getting too close over the myriad of problems we normally face today that grow from being too far from one another.

Our modern models force us to deal with an altogether different set of problems. All our issues seem to surround the topic of why we're so far apart. Both sides of the communal coin have problems. It's really just a matter of which problems best point the way to solutions. What problems ultimately reveal the deepest parts of our brokenness and can allow for the greatest confrontations of holiness and purity?

Because we've lost the historical emphasis of Scripture in our R.easoning and ways of doing things, I believe we have moved more into methods we invent than paradigms and principles that were handed down to us. We force ourselves into the place of having to dream something up afresh over and over instead of resting in the fact that Christ has already laid out a clear plan. As a result, rather than our creativity moving us toward remembrance and embrace of the ancient path of biblical tradition, we've detrimentally invented a way of life that I really feel neither Paul nor Jesus would recognize.

It's affected everything.

Another example of how our model-centric methods have shaped our theology is *dispensational theology*. The Left Behind book series presents a view of when Christ returns that is divorced from traditional legacy and sound biblical interpretation. It's a recent theological innovation that is only about 150 years old. Making a literal rebuilding of the physical temple a necessity and requiring a literal ethnic Israel to be restored before Christ can return is not a respected theology in other parts of the world or in most theological or biblical and scholarly circles. It reinterprets the meaning of classic biblical terms through the models we've created. Our models today are very building-centric, so of course, we think that a new temple is coming. We fall prey to the same lie that the Jews did—that we're waiting for an earthly Messiah to set up an earthly reign in a physical structure here on earth. Jesus, on the other hand, seems to imply that he's preparing a place "not made by humans hands." A kingdom built and ruled in the human heart. The heart is not made by hands. He's also not coming back in a manner we can predict. He doesn't live in buildings or in locations, but in people. The temple language of the New

Testament always refers to a people who are the church, and never to a building. Our methods have revised our theology.

Our corrupted methodology is also revealed in the anemic portrayal of the gospel today in the sacraments and message. Let's consider how our "pop-theology" view of the Lord's Supper has shaped our view of the gospel. The gospel message is that "Jesus saves sinners." And to this belief I respond with a hearty "Amen." However, the Bible and the meal teaches us something about agriculture and creation as well.

At mealtime, individually un-tasty and disunited ingredients are flung on the counter and assembled through recipe into a sumptuous meal. Visually, in this process we see that the gospel is not just about Jesus saving sinners, but also putting creation back into order. Christ came to fill all things. His filling extends to all vocations, all created life, and the entire cosmos. He fills his people so he can drive his presence around in us and press out his wisdom into every realm of home, work, and play.

In sitting around the meal, we're taught a posture in how to view all things. The meal trains us in speech and in the spectacle. In it we hear, see, taste, feel, and smell the gospel. Our *paideia* is formed. Our whole self. The sacraments are signs of inward grace to us, and they teach us to see all of creation as sacramental. By looking at anything made, either by God, or by the work of our hands in any form and fashion, including our careers, endeavors, and vocations, we connect redemption and the gospel to all things.

With a proper view of the meal in place, we are now free to think sacramentally about the entirety of the rhythms of our day. Worship explodes beyond the doors of the building and into a people. A feasting people. A celebrating people. A contented people. No longer are we chasing the hierarchy of money and fame that we've invented, but we willingly descend down into peace as we hold hands and thank God for our bowl of soup.

WHAT ABOUT HOW WE SHAPE WORLDVIEW?

There are many ways to go about proving God or proving existence, but the Trinity also offers a better word in shaping how humans view life.

The classical apologists attacks the problem of "god" and "existence" by believing that one is only convinced of the gospel if he admits theism first. Others believe that the evidence of fact, science, and discovery is what most convinces us of God. These are the evidential apologists. Cumulative apologists believe that the mind is most convinced of the gospel by piecing together the whole of things as everything relates together. Then there are the epistemological apologists who attribute our inner sense of the divine to be the sole evidence that God exists.

The Trinity drills down into deeper reasoning. He's revealed what is called *presuppositional apologetics*. This mode of apologetics reaches the greatest depths of discernment because to believe that theism, evidence, or unity in all cumulative things teaches us anything first means that we must presuppose that these concepts are necessary to our conclusion. To even think that there's a conclusion to anything, we must presuppose that there's a place of *origin*—a place where questions resolve. The Trinity is the only being that provides such answers to every area of study and to our unique search for beginnings. Presuppositions also assume that a sense of the divine is actually evidence of something divine. Therefore, presuppositions are the gateway to admitting that all the other apologetics bear weight. And they do.

The reason I mention presuppositions is that our human reasoning is driven by our basest and lowest level. Every act of righteousness is in its simplest form an act driven at knowing God, and every act of evil is an active revealing of rebellion against God. All reasoning and philosophical thought spin on the axis of good and evil, and this is where the gospel operates in a stratospheric category far above all philosophies. People spend time either speculating upon and describing the bad news—what makes us imperfect—or they engage in the good news, which is the fact that the perfect can be known. The entity that actually drives the argument for both the believer and the unbeliever is the Trinity. Without God, apologetics serves no purpose. If we only believed in isolated individuality or intellect, we'd seek only within ourselves to find answers. However, what we do in fact is seek answers outside ourselves. We try to find meaning for existence that reaches far beyond our own isolated identity. Even unbelievers do this because a Trinity image is flying under the radar to drive their quest. Despite their professed belief in a godless universe, their hunt inevitably reaches outward, probing for facts, evidence, and proofs that when found will show their worldview to be inadequate to support their sense of being. They do this because the fact of God is embedded in our very nature. It's our fabric. Our greatest apologetic for a communal and logical God is found in the very reason that we exist at all. Without God making a reason for "another," our existence and universe wouldn't have even been necessary. Quite honestly, the Big Bang and evolution don't even make sense unless there's an innately recognized image that one is trying to break out from or evolve into.

We must begin to discuss the nature of the Trinity in all our philosophy and reasoning when it comes to apologetics and the logic for believing in all things divine. It's because we're all presupposing "another" and an "image" that we keep moving along as if there is one. We don't have to reason or make sense of our origins to make it real. We don't have to find evidence to make it real. Simply look at the trajectory. Before considering anything physical and tangible to humanity as the existence to God, pondering the Trinity himself actually puts everything else into proper perspective.

O.RGANIZATION

It would stand to reason, that if God is all about C.ommunity in how he relates, and if he has a reason for how he does things (i.e. meals, marriage, family, home, and liturgy), he must also draw up some plans for how to specifically move that vision forward. To make sure that paradigms are preserved, overseen, shepherded, and protected from the million other competing voices and methods out there, God institutes organization, policy, and a mission statement. In the following four sections we are going to turn to how God O.rganizes life.

PART V
O: HOW GOD ORDERS LIFE

ORGANIZATION

PPK HOUSEHOLD

Marriage, Gender, Sex, Gratitude, & Glory.

M arriage is fundamental to God's organization. It's the starting place for how God orders life.

Today, there's a war surrounding marriage! When people attempt to speak of it, they are often quickly dragged into a debate over gender equality, LGBTQI agendas, and political affiliations. Ultimately, the attack on gender and male and female roles has little to do with us and our preferences. It's an attack against the nature and O.rganization of God.

Though the Trinity most certainly is Spirit, and not a gender, both genders originate from him. Both genders are housed in him. He projects all unity within himself into two complete people that embody his love with and toward one another.

As we've noted in previous chapters, God's nature is the very substance of love, and for the *hypostasis* of God to be love, there has to be a Lover (the pursuing Father), a Beloved (the object of affection), and the Spirit of love that springs from them like a cloud of incense—a sweet prayer that tickles the nose. Because the nature of our God is very familial, so must be humanity. If humanity is to reflect the very image of God, the form it takes must also be one of lover, beloved, and that which springs from their love.

To deviate from the image of a family in any way is to put the Trinity's nature on trial. Ordering life like the Trinity is far more the central issue in the male and female debate than any attempt at logic, complimentary biblical allusion, or egalitarian stab. All our responses will continue to be short-sided and attack only the symptom not the germ if we don't first talk about the Godhead.

Before I launch too heavily into the nature of gender and family in light of our Triune God, let me reveal my stance on the hot cultural subject of equality first. If I don't define equality first, I fear many will misunderstand my intentions in the latter part of this chapter.

It is my absolute conviction, and the Bible's teaching, that relating to the topic of marriage, masculinity, and femininity, the genders are equal, as is each person in the Trinity. However, the Bible also preserves distinction. Unlike our world, which wants to boil down equality in a way that makes the sexes exactly alike in every way, God's sense of equality is different.

All members of the Trinity are unique and yet distinct. They are equal in dignity, value, and worth,[1] and yet they maintain different roles. Males and females are likewise in nature. Both genders are equal in their status and standing before God[2] and are equal in inclusion amongst God's people,[3] but like the Father, Son, and Spirit, equality has nothing to do with their *roles*. The Godhead is distinct in the functions the three members perform even while exhibiting tremendous unity despite their diversity. Males and females are likewise different in the roles they serve. To think that we have to make equality about both sexes doing the same jobs is missing the point.

For those that may protest too quickly, think back to the countless times in our scriptural investigation how the Trinity embodies hierarchy through a Father-Son-Spirit ranking while at the same time each of the three dwells is in mutual submission to the other. Clearly, the Trinity preserves distinction in roles, not in worth or value.

God similarly differentiates humans according to the purpose they'll serve. In 1 Corinthians, Paul uses the language of function, administration, and roles to speak of all Christians and their spiritual gifts. Paul gives us a word picture to show how diversity works in unity within God's family. He likens all believing humanity to a whole body. He distinguishes each body part, not on the basis of value, but on function.

If one were to attempt to separate body parts by value, he or she would undoubtedly fall into error. He or she might discard the pinky toe because it seems small, useless, and is always hidden behind a shoe. But the pinky toe is essential to balance, and if lopped off, the whole center of gravity for the body goes waxing and waning. The pinkie toe may be small or unnoticed in function, but it is assuredly equal in value.

Deep down we all recognize the value and difference that exists in every created thing, particularly humans.

Having clarified equality and its relationship to role and function I will now move forward with my primary argument. From here on, we're assuming that every man, woman, and child is a priceless treasure.

God first knit human treasures into marriage. He began with man and woman. Scripture tells us that man was created to be the head,[4] and woman the helper.[5]

Scripture references headship in a way that literally means source and summit. The idea of headship is applied to two entities in Scripture—man, and Christ. Christ is the head of the church,[6] and man is the head of the woman.[7]

For those who immediately scowl in disgust at the idea of headship, the Scripture throws in a helpfully clarifying statement. Ephesians 5:23 says that man is to be the head of the woman in the same way Christ is head of the Church. When we think of headship we are first to think about how Christ has loved. Christ gave up his kingdom in heaven, took on human form, welcomed temptation and pain of all types, remained steadfast without sinning, and gave himself up on a cross to be bludgeoned, beaten, run through with nail and sword, and sacrificed, all so you and I could have life. The picture of the headship of Christ displays that kind of love.

What person when offered the chance to be served, loved, adored, cherished, enriched, equipped, and fought for in the same manner Christ fought for us, would say, "No, I don't want headship over me." When Headship is properly framed within its intended meaning, we get a picture of how Adam should have used his role as head of the woman. He was to be a lover in the most profound sense—a sacrificial lover as Christ is.

Adam was intended to be what theologians call *the federal head*, meaning, Adam was created first, and therefore he serves as the summit and source of all human loving. God's closeness of love began in Adam. He was put in the Garden to portray all of God's intention in headship. Adam was constructed literally for the purpose of loving, taking care of, naming, and nurturing the animals, the plants, the landscape, and all that would emerge from within the Garden's ethos (e.g., family, commerce, invention, and the like). Adam was created to be a servant. He was created to lay down his life for all that was entrusted to him. He was absolutely fashioned and tight-knit for responsibility, work, worship, and companionship.

In Genesis 2:20-22, God observes only one incomplete aspect of Adam. Adam didn't have a helper. We are told that God puts Adam to sleep and removes one of his ribs. He fashions from it the beauty of Eve. The rib symbolizes Eve's role as a *helping friend*—one who is literally "called alongside."

According to Timothy Keller, "the word 'helper' is not the best translation for the Hebrew word *'ezer*. 'Helper' connotes merely assisting someone who could do the task almost as well without help. But *'ezer* is almost always used in the Bible to describe God himself. Other times it is used to describe military help, such as reinforcements, without which a battle would be lost. To 'help' someone is to make up what is lacking in him with your strength. Women are made to be 'strong helpers.'"[8] This quote from Keller goes a long way toward framing how we are to think of a helper. There's a strength in Eve that is absolutely lacking in Adam. God knows it. Adam knew it. The correct use of Eve's strength is what we need to discuss.

Wielding strength is like swinging a sword. It is only useful if it is done correctly. One wrong swipe and it can be deadly; both intentionally and unintentionally. In 1 Peter 3:22-23, Peter describes the proper use of strength within gender and marriage. He links his discussion of strength to Christ's use of his own power and deity. Christ, being all-powerful—able to lift the universe upon a fingernail, and blow away mountains with a breath—is portrayed this way; "When he was reviled, he did not revile in return; when he suffered, he did not threaten, but continued *entrusting himself to him who judges justly*" (italics mine). On the cross, Jesus demonstrates both sides of true strength. At the moment he defeats sin and every satanic warlord that might seek to harm his family, Christ also maintains all composure and does so as a gentleman. His strength is found in *trusting in the one who judges justly*. Trusting God is the source of Jesus' strength, and it is the true source for all feminine and masculine power. Confidence resides only in trusting in deity. Being all-powerful means that Christ possesses all exhaustive and perfect authority to reveal all power and conceal or restrain power.

Peter follows up his argument and says that husbands and wives are to love and serve each other "likewise." He says that wives are to likewise submit to their husbands, as Christ submitted even unto death as an honor toward his Father in heaven. Husbands are to likewise love and consider their wives in a self-forgetful, sacrificial manner, and with the same all-out abandon that Christ demonstrated in dying for us. When it comes down to brass tacks, who wouldn't want to be loved like this? Who wouldn't want to know the valor in service like this?

C. S. Lewis offers some helpful words here:

> Headship, then, is most fully embodied not in the husband we should all wish to be but in him *whose marriage is most like a crucifixion*; whose wife receives most and gives least, is most unworthy of him, is–in her own mere nature–least lovable. For the Church has no beauty but what the Bridegroom gives her; he does not find, but makes her lovely. The chrism of this terrible coronation is to be seen not in the joys of any man's marriage but in its sorrows, in the sickness and sufferings of a good wife or the faults of a bad one, in his unwearying (never paraded) care or his inexhaustible forgiveness: forgiveness, not acquiescence. As Christ sees in the flawed, proud, fanatical or lukewarm Church on earth that Bride who will one day be without spot or wrinkle, and labors to produce the latter, so the husband whose headship is Christ-like (and he is allowed no other) never despairs. (italics mine)[9]

To help us understand the power of the helper, we must ponder the way in which strength was ripped from Adam. Eve was literally snatched from, and crafted, using his rib. She was not grafted from his spine, that she should walk behind him as his slave (as chauvinists would think of power), nor was she ripped from his sternum that she should rule over him as his authority (as feminists would think of power), nor would she be tasked with the duty of guarding or governing his heart. All humans are called to guard their own hearts (Prv. 4:23), and only God is capable of making a back straight (Eccl. 7:13). God's use of the rib artfully pictures how life between genders is supposed to operate. The painting prevents us from perverting the male and female relationship into one of the following categories: Domineering (Eve being taken from Adam's spine) or Passive (Eve being taken from Adam's sternum). The intended relationship between Adam and Eve was to be one of Friendship (Eve taken from Adam's side). In literally being ripped from Adam's side, she was called from a place that rests under his arm. Herein lies her strongest strength.

She's portrayed as one who walks leg to leg with the man in an equality of value, and if anything, her strength steadies him. To say then that's she's somehow exactly the same as the man would be to undervalue her. It would also cast a shadow on the strength of God because the imagery here is intentional Trinitarian.

In the New Testament, the Holy Spirit is referenced as the *paraklete*, a Greek word that means advocate, or more precisely, "one called alongside." The etymology of *paraklete* paints a picture of companions. The woman's role best mimics the duty of the Holy Spirit in the Trinity. In being the helper—the "paracletic-called-alongside" one—and servant of all, she images God. More specifically, she portrays the Holy Spirit. The Bible calls her the glory of man, and that's a beautiful role indeed because man is called the glory of Christ (1 Cor. 11:7).

God doesn't need another sternum or spine in the world. Adam was specifically lacking because he had not the appropriate rib. The woman, as a helper, is not to use her strength to pull or push. A woman, when she is strongest, wields her sword of iron to help. Her strength to help is only found when she trusts in God's design for gender and relationship.

Today the trouble that surrounds the topic of gender, marriage, and the family-fabric of society centers on the idea of trust in God's nature. People are lashing out in gender wars because we don't listen to God's intention in creating the sexes from within his being. The Trinity is the core issue. What we say about gender has everything to do with our theology and trust of God.

Don't believe me?

Turn quickly to Romans 1:18-32. Paul, under the inspiration of the Holy Spirit, lays an ax at the root issue of the tree that grows up within the gender debate:

> The wrath of God is being revealed from heaven against all the godlessness and wickedness of people, who *suppress the truth* by their wickedness, since *what may be known about God is plain to them, because God has made it plain to them*. For since the creation of the world God's invisible qualities—his eternal power and divine nature—have been clearly seen, being understood from what has been made, so that people are without excuse.
>
> *For although they knew God, they neither glorified him as God nor gave thanks to him*, but their thinking became futile and their foolish hearts were darkened. Although they claimed to be wise, they became fools and *exchanged the glory of the immortal God for images made to look like a mortal human being* and birds and animals and reptiles.

Therefore *God gave them over* in the sinful desires of their hearts to sexual impurity for the degrading of their bodies with one another. They exchanged the truth about God for a lie, and worshiped and served created things rather than the Creator—who is forever praised. Amen.

Because of this, God gave them over to shameful lusts. *Even their women exchanged natural sexual relations for unnatural ones. In the same way the men also abandoned natural relations with women and were inflamed with lust for one another. Men committed shameful acts with other men, and received in themselves the due penalty for their error.*

Furthermore, just as they did not think it worthwhile to retain the knowledge of God, so God gave them over to a depraved mind, so that they do what ought not to be done. They have become filled with every kind of wickedness, evil, greed and depravity. They are full of envy, murder, strife, deceit and malice. They are gossips, slanderers, God-haters, insolent, arrogant and boastful; they invent ways of doing evil; they disobey their parents; they have no understanding, no fidelity, no love, no mercy. Although they know God's righteous decree that those who do such things deserve death, they not only continue to do these very things but also approve of those who practice them. (italics mine)

In the first chapter of Romans, Paul discusses all of creation as an aid to revealing the gospel. At the core of his argument, he tells the Romans that the attributes of our triune God are evident through all God has made. Paul concludes that all wickedness, particularly when we begin to doubt God's plan for male and female humanity, is rooted in a denial of that truth. It's a failure to trust. In the instance above, humanity fell into a distrusting relationship toward God so perverse that it affected their very own understanding of the sexes. Paul reiterates that God clearly makes the truth plain to them regarding all of his creation, but the people of that time were willfully overlooking what is right for two reasons—ingratitude and the rebellious seeking for one's own glory.

In the day of the Romans, men were defiling other men, and woman other women, and not just out of homosexual desire, preference, proclivity, orientation, or nature. They were doing so out of an ungrateful heart and a refusal to glorify God. The bottom line was that they didn't want it God's way. God's way wasn't good enough.

All fights over marriage and sex are, at their core, an issue over giving God glory and gratitude. When we aren't thankful for the honesty of our Creator in telling us about the truthful origins of good, we break away from his words and ways and pay more attention to other ways of defining reality. We look to created things. We look, as Romans 1 says above, to the beast, bird, and barnacle. Our search for *summit* and *source*—headship—leads us to the only logical conclusion we can devise. Humanity itself.

Without God, we logically conclude that humans are the pinnacle. We turn our worship, our allegiance, and our honor over to what the creation says about itself. Of course, leaving our definition of life and humankind up to the three pounds of brain matter between our ears—of which we only use about 3 percent—is a recipe for disaster.

Our chaotic hurricane of thought reaches its worst in the topic of sex. Logically, if we conclude that humans are the highest created beings, then worship itself is at its best in sexuality.

Sex is an act of worship. It's conducted on the altar of the bed, and it affirms our highest allegiances. We want to find love in the highest glory we can experience without God, and therefore we define sex as "making love." It's our attempt at fashioning our own lover, beloved, and spirit of love. It's our attempt to fashion a Trinity. "God is Love," after all. Just as the Bible tells us.

But we flip the coin.

"Love is God."

Idol worship.

The act of sex in our culture has led to anything but "making love." Statistically, we have grown more sexually perverse. One in three girls is molested and/or raped before eighteen along with one in six boys. Making love has resulted in breeding hate between two star-crossed lovers turned broken. Children are thwarted by robbers. Our youth are growing up to buy into the disconnected promises of love made by Tinder, Pornhub, LGBTQI, and the like. One-night stands and loose sexual experimentation brings only shackles of shame, guilt, regret, rape, drug-induced coping, alcohol-entrenched denial, murderous abortion, cheating, homosexual dysfunction, loss of identity, broken homes, and broken marriages. Romans tells us of the conclusion to all this madness of forsaking gratitude and glory—God gives us over to our error and its due penalty. The due wages we bring upon ourselves by doubting the Trinity is death and all forms of division.

What we worship has come to define our identity. Today we have people walking around making *identity* statements like "I am gay," or "I am bisexual," or even obvious males saying, "I am female." The defining marker of who we are is now our sexual identity. And what has this god of sex given us in return? Only a broken mess of molestation, false promises, porn addiction, psychological chaos, incurable diseases, and orientation confusion. What we've discovered, in all irony, is that God was right. He told us that sin makes everything confusing, and my, oh my, how confusing have things become! Almost every day another letter is added to the LGBTQI string. I've lost count of how many genders psychologists say now exist. People can't find themselves in the confusion. Even the queerest little creature when asked, "What are you," will say, "Well ... kinda ... not really ... maybe ... this ..." Them. Us. They. It's confusing.

We live in a day where everything is cloudy, ambiguous, and obsessed with sex and death, and sin is driving it all.

God wants more for us. He wants clarity.

WHAT ABOUT SEX, CHILDREN AND THE TRINITY?

Let's talk about children in relationship to headship, help, and gender. God ordered life around the headship and helpership of the man and woman to preserve life, not to bring death. Let's face it, whichever way you slice it, male and female are needed in order to make love. Heterosexual sex, within the bond of marriage, is the only thing that has the ability to make anything lastingly healthy. Sex brings children. God's organization plan for the household prioritizes the health and wholeness of children. Statistically speaking, the simplicity found in the together family bodes well for the wellbeing of the human body, child development, identity formation, closeness, education and intellect, protection, provision, and a slew of other things. The wholeness of a person involves his or her mental, emotional, social, spiritual, and physical capacities, and these are absolutely forged within the home. What is most loving to a human, and what brings life is God's way in the family.

Even when people supporting the homosexual lifestyle disagree and claim their way of life to be the most loving (all the while blatantly flying in the face of every statistic out there) they still arrive at two logical fallacies. First, claiming that gayness is essential for life and love is at its core nonsensical. Everyone at the end of the day still has to admit that man mating with man, and woman mating with woman can't *make*. Homosexuality is a formula for extinction. Second, saying that someone is born gay is also nonsensical. Even if there was a supposed gay gene, we learn from the world's invented theory of evolution that our ability to evolve from such a gene would be impossible. A gay gene can't reproduce without something *other*. Gayness would have been extinct a long time ago in such a scenario. Gayness does not reflect a process of humanity *getting better* in our logic; it demonstrates that we are *devolving* in our ability to see reality clearly. We're reverting back to our base animal instincts. Sex becomes merely an animal function of humping and self-pleasure and has nothing to do with making life. It's more simian than human. We're getting closer to apes in our appetites rather than actually growing up into maturity.

God, on the other hand, created sex and sexuality in order that we might mature, make, multiply, and grow. God's plan in maleness and femaleness is not to condemn us or isolate us, it's to embrace us in a powerful, fervent, and strong life-giving love. To accept a view that offers anything less is to miss out on one of God's greatest gifts.

The gospel, or "good news" in all this discussion, is that God created a weightier and more dignified existence that speaks life into broken homes, broken identities, and bruised sexualities. God doesn't stamp "No" on the LGBTQI card with aggression and judgmental hate. He simply whispers in our ear. Faintly his voice echoes through the canyon of confusion and speaks a better word of clarity. God calls us back to the Garden to rediscover our origins in his image. He wants us to see that making Adam and Eve male and female is not just about gender; it's about ensuring that flourishing life multiplies throughout all time and created space.

If God had created both Adam and Eve asexually—both with the potential to make children on their own—he would have deprived the world of oneness that comes from unity with another. Similarly, he didn't create them both with the same gender because they would have died off. God made it impossible for any one individual or one sex to lay claim to the process of multiplying the human race. Love was going to be together work. Children were to complete the Trinitarian shape. They were to completely express the love between both man and woman. Procreation, sex, the entangled dance of skin, and the penetration of one entity into the other—in a way that absorbs them into oneness, while still preserving their personality, dignity, worth, and uniqueness—gives us a profound picture of the very nature of God. The family completes the image. Man, woman, and child.

The multiplying nature of our God is not only captured in marriage but extends to parental ability and love. The Triune shape of the family speaks in the spectacle of a three-in-one God. God has very specific ways in which he understands child-rearing.

In Ephesians 6:1-4, following his discussion on the design for males and females in marriage, Paul talks directly to kids. He doesn't break stride in his understanding of headship, helpership, and the structure of love and submission when speaking to children. He connects the same expectation of submission to them as well:

> Children, obey your parents in the Lord, for this is right. 'Honor your father and mother'—which is the first commandment with a promise—so that it may go well with you and that you may enjoy long life on the earth.' Fathers, do not exasperate your children; instead, bring them up in the training and instruction of the Lord.

Linked to the household nature of our God are children. We will discuss this topic, along with sex, in greater detail in our S.ignature Mission section. But for now, let's conclude that sex and children are part of the Trinitarian life. Any system that perverts sex or makes children impossible falls short of the flourishing life that God has promised.

SIN HAS FRUSTRATED EVERYTHING IN GOD'S ORGANIZATION, BUT IT DIDN'T UNDO IT ...

At the halfway point of this chapter we've built a case for how humans are equal in value, dignity, and worth, but are different in uniqueness through function and role within the family. We are to celebrate these roles out of trust in our Savior's design. Only in thinking rightly upon the Trinity can we correctly know how to best glorify, be satisfied in, and express thankfulness toward our God via our gender. Thinking rightly about the Trinity does not just inform the state of family, the home, and gender, but it affects all of life outside of family into the whole of the Garden—the world around us.

Our lost sense of identity and harmony in the home is now reflected all over the earth. The Fall has frustrated our ability to follow God's original intention for humanity. It begs us to ask, "Does the Fall mean that God's original intent is no longer applicable? Is gender differentiation, headship, family, and following the model of the Trinity still a viable option in this sin-damaged world?"

My answer is yes.

To explain the extent to which God's intent has or has not been thwarted, let's read what Wayne Grudem says on this topic of frustration:

> In the punishments God gave to Adam and Eve *as a result of their sin*, he did not introduce new roles or functions, but simply introduced pain and distortion into the functions they previously had. Thus, Adam would still have primary responsibility for tilling the ground and raising crops, but the ground would bring forth "thorns and thistles" and in the sweat of his face he would eat bread (Gen. 3:18, 19). Similarly, Eve would still have the responsibility of bearing children but to do so would become painful: "In pain you shall bring forth children" (Gen. 3:16). Then God also introduced conflict and pain into the previously harmonious relationship between Adam and Eve. God said to Eve, "your desire shall be for your husband, and he shall rule our you" (Gen. 3:16). … the word *rule* (Heb. *mashal*) is a strong term usually used of monarchical governments, not generally of authority within a family. The word certainly does not imply any "participatory" government by those who are ruled, but rather has nuances of dictatorial of absolute, uncaring use of authority, rather than considerate, thoughtful rule. It suggests harshness rather than kindness. The sense here is that Adam will misuse his authority *by ruling harshly* over his wife, again introducing pain and conflict … the curse brought a *distortion* of Adam's humble, considerate leadership and Eve's intelligent, willing submission to that leadership which existed before the fall (italics mine).[10]

The trick of sin today is the same as it was in the Garden. Satan knows the hoax very well. In the Garden, he spoke to Eve first to bypass headship.[11] Adam chose to relinquish his responsibility as head to care for, protect, and love rightly his wife, and instead pointed in blame toward Eve for the sin. Eve pointed to the Serpent to blame him for her going against the authority invested by God in her husband. "He made me do it," she screamed.

With all the blame-shifting going around, God had to step in and reaffirm his plan amidst the turmoil of humanity's first family. He came to Adam first,[12] not to Eve because in God's mind Adam represented the human race. In 1 Corinthians 15:22 we are told that "in Adam, all die," because of this man's "one trespass."[13] God links the responsibility for all creation and humankind to the male. Adam's passivity brought about a mess, and God attributes the giving up of responsibility first to Adam. God affirms headship not only in blessing it, but also in assigning to men the consequences due to our failure.

For all the woman out there who want to be equal in function to men, I would draw them to God's reaction in Genesis, along with 1 Corinthians 15:22 and simply plead, "Why would you want such a thing?" The treacheries of man reach deep. So much so, that Jesus calls himself the second man, and the "last Adam." He does so to help us understand how far Adam fell. Adam dragged all humanity into perversion. The perversion reached all the way into the Patriarchs (Adam, Abraham, Noah, Moses, & David). Notice they too were all male. The dissension polluted the leaders of all the tribes in Israel who are also identified with all male ancestors (i.e., Reuben, Simeon, Levi Judah, Dan, Naphtali, Gad, Asher, Issachar, Zebulun, Joseph Ephraim, Manasseh, and Benjamin). The twisting grew so entwined that Jesus himself had to come as a male to raise up the twelve male disciples[14] in order to establish a new headship—a new creation. A new source.

Jesus entered into our sin-filled world not to obliterate his original design of headship, helpership, and family, but to reinstate and reaffirm what was being lost in the wake of sin's destruction. In living and loving perfectly, and by dying and rising unblemished for our sake, Scripture names him "the last Adam." Jesus did things right; unlike our first Adam. Jesus loved us as intended. In becoming a literal man, and in choosing male Headship to be over his new creation the church—built on the apostles and prophets—Jesus confirms and affirms what was patterned from the beginning. He redeemed headship and reiterates that it is still to exist in the male leaders of the church[15] and in the husbands of the family.[16] He made right the distortion. He corrected the course of the ship, and we must hear his original intentions afresh.

Jesus also confirms that helpership is still necessary for human flourishing. As he ascends to heaven in Acts 1, he sends the Spirit into the hearts of all mankind—men and women included. As men remain the embodiment of what cherishing love and headship is to look like (in Christ's headship), women remain the embodiment of nurture, respect, and service (in the Holy Spirit's power).

Further, consider what is implied in 1 Timothy 3:8-13 and elsewhere as it adds significant weight to both the strength of men and women. In Paul's words to Timothy, he mentions the role of elders and stresses that they are to be "husbands of one wife" (implying that Jesus' model for male headship in his family still remains). In the following verses, however, both the husbands *and* wives are mentioned in conjunction with what it means to be a deacon.

In case you've forgotten, the root of deacon means *table servant*, and seeing that family and meals are central markers in God's paradigm for discipleship, we must assume that women are powerful in the servant structure of how God orders life. In fact, in Romans 16:1-15, Paul greets all those prominent and serving in the churches in the area surrounding Rome, and over half the list is filled with feminine names. In God's church, the women were and are crucial within the fabric of God's family. They exude the beautiful smell of Christ's service to us as the men bring to the nostrils flavors of Christ's sacrifice.

Together we are called to reflect the same Triune God.

Within our unique servant placements, God holds us to the same expectations of oneness, character, and Christlikeness. Paul in Colossians 3:12-17 says these words *to all believers* right before reiterating that a man's role is fulfilled best in loving his wife, and a wife's role in submitting to her husband:

> Put on then, as God's chosen ones, holy and beloved, compassionate hearts, kindness, humility, meekness, and patience, bearing with one another and, if one has a complaint against another, forgiving each other; as the Lord has forgiven you, so you also must forgive. And above all these put on love, which binds everything together in perfect harmony. And let the peace of Christ rule in your hearts, to which indeed you were called in one body. And be thankful. Let the word of Christ dwell in you richly, teaching and admonishing one another in all wisdom, singing psalms and hymns and spiritual songs, with thankfulness in your hearts to God. And whatever you do, in word or deed, do everything in the name of the Lord Jesus, giving thanks to God the Father through him.

The expectations of both man and woman are the same. Equal. We are both chosen, holy, beloved, and loved by God. And in Colossians 3:12-17 we find that God expects us to model the Trinity wherever we go in the same manner. Paul also encourages us in the passages immediately following, Colossians 3:18-20, that both roles are still necessary.

Husbands and wives portraying the unity of God together is what Paul has in mind when he uses the phrase "mutual submission" in Ephesians 5. The word for submission, or "be subject to" is the Greek word *hypotasso*, which always implies a relationship of authority.[17] In the context, Paul is talking about the responsibility of both men and women to act out in their marriages as a unit underneath a willing and mutual surrender to God's oversight via his church Body.

The church in Scripture represents the authority of God on the earth. All Christians are called to mutually submit their role to Christ and the church as a unit, in order that we can best become who we are intended to be as individuals. Our mutual submission is the absolute key because it allows us to flourish in our designed roles.

Let it be clarified, that mutual submission together as a marital unit within God's Body still preserves the household structure. Wives are still to submit to husbands, but Paul tells wives to be subject "to *your own* husbands," not to everyone in the church or to all husbands![18] Scripture provides ample guidelines to preserve the balance between home organization and the collective church.

The bottom line is that male headship and all female helpership serves to complete one picture. The picture is of authority. Structure is in place to ensure that we live out the authority of God together for the good of all. Without the dance of authority/submission, we can't become strong or humble. Humility is the truest strength that is forged in those that know authority.

In 1 Peter 5:6, Peter implores all believers to "humble themselves under the mighty right hand of God so that at the proper time he may exalt you." This passage comes within a context that speaks about God's shepherds, pastors, overseers, and elders in his church (all these titles are used synonymously throughout Scripture). God's formational hand of authority is pressed into the structure, servants, families, and governance of his church, and in submitting to it we become humble as our Savior is humble. We learn to trust again. We become strong again.

Prophets, Priests, Kings, and the Trinity … Oh My!

Let's backtrack now into the Old Testament to build a bit more foundation as to how authority and submission develop as it reaches beyond gender, marriage, and family, and begins to express itself in society and amongst God's people.

All throughout the Torah, the Trinity remains the constant authority over his people, even in the larger society. He himself comes to Adam, Noah, Abraham, and Moses, in order to govern, instruct, command, and lead his people, even though time and time again God's people reject his authority. Israel, in particular, spends a long time throughout the Old Testament with one foot out and one foot in when it comes to following the "I Am." The Trinity relentlessly attempts to lead Israel, provide for Israel, and protect Israel, but the people rebel constantly. They reject actively the organization, order, and governance of God. Their outcry rings with a simmering whine against the spirit-realm. They scream for physical leadership.

Ultimately God's people's dissatisfaction with God as their leader over them in the simple things like marriage and family, reached an all-time high in the days when God ruled them through judges. Ironically, the people got fed up with the human leaders that they spent so much time whining to acquire, and then blamed God for them once they got what they wanted. To add insult to injury, they turned right around and asked for another human to lead them. In Samuel 8:6 the people came to Samuel, the judge, prophet, and priest at that time, and screamed "give us a king to lead us."

This was not a positive request. In fact, we're told that their desire was motivated by a refusal to obey Samuel's voice as God's spokesman.[19] We're also told that God was grieved, and he commanded Samuel to obey their tantrum, but with a very interesting word. God said, "Obey their voice and *make* them a king." This word "make" hints of made idols. The people wanted to fashion for themselves an idol in the very image of a man. They had forgone trust in God and wanted to trust something they could see.

Though many have loosely tried to argue that the people's desire for a king in 1 Samuel 8:5 was a noble desire inspired by Deuteronomy 17:14, it simply isn't true. Though Samuel presents Saul as "him whom the Lord has chosen,"[20] the context plainly conveys their misunderstanding of the promise made in Deuteronomy. God gives them over to their idolatry, and the rest is history.

Throughout the remainder of the Old Testament, God allows the people what they want. He gives them up to drink from the shadow of what real governance is. Kindly, he never relinquishes his claim to Trinitarian leadership, particularly his commitment to the family. He continues moving behind the scenes to prevent humanity's utter destruction as it chases its tail.

God smuggles his very nature into the midst of his rebellious people in an effort to prepare them for the Messiah to come. He did it through the Triune offices of prophets, priests, and kings.

If you'll remember, Samuel is the first and only person to be called a king (a judge in that time), a priest (adopted into the priestly training system by his mother Hannah, under the tutelage of Eli), and a prophet, and he's the particular one God uses to set off the system in anointing King Saul. Samuel is the only one in the Old Testament to hold these three offices simultaneously, and rather than starting over with the people's horrid request, God plays a bit of holy trickery. He gives them a king, but it's only through Samuel his anointed. Samuel is the foreshadowing of Triune-ONE to come, and also a messenger pointing back to the Triune-truth that always was.

What results from the short-sighted tantrum of the Israelites is a fragmented society. Kings are relegated to matters of governance. Priests are relegated to all things sacred. Prophets served as a bit of a go-between in bringing both together. Kings predominantly assumed matters of *policy*, priests dealt mostly with matters of *people*, and prophets operated in *precepts*. Division of personhood grew more substantial. A false allusion between sacred and secular realms inflated.

Joyously for us, our loving, unified, and redemptive God still grants his people our often-disgusting requests in hopes that we may taste the bitter fruit of rebellion and be reawakened in thankful satisfaction to God's loving headship. God never surrenders his labor to purposefully love his people from behind the curtain. He refuses to abandon the Trinitarian imagery of his story. He does so in an effort to remind us that he never changes.

A KING

Let's consider the curtain call of God in the Old Testament as he smuggles his image into those tasked as kings, priests, and prophets. His work in these three offices demonstrates for us that his Trinitarian plan for order reaches into gender and marriage, of course, but also into his people collectively, and into the world as a whole.

First of all, God grants the people their wish. He gives them a king.

A king in Scripture was seen as the anointed representative and a mediator of the judicial and executive power of God among his people. The king was a judge.[21] He initiated war in response to wickedness and/or on behalf of righteousness.[22] A king of righteousness would fight for the poor, the fatherless, and the widow. He would initiate and carry out decrees, policy, religious practices, or actions in an effort to lead his Kingdom.[23] As a leader in administration of sorts, he would organize his kingdom. He did this through letter writing,[24] oversight, and personal visits,[25] as well as by drawing specific people together around a common purpose to serve at his side.[26] A noble king had great influence and would even take responsibility for the blessings or consequences of actions made by himself or on behalf of others.[27]

The king was also involved in spiritual or covenantal matters. The prophet Nathan announced a special covenant relationship between the Lord and the dynasty of David.[28] Many times the King exercised personal leadership in favor of worship to the Lord.[29] David even combined the heart of king with his administration abilities in the priestly sector. He did this in greatest fashion when he organized the Levitical and prophetic worship movement. He also enabled his son Solomon to carry out the actual construction of God's temple,[30] the center for worship.

Solomon lived righteously for a time as well, and he dedicated the sanctuary to God, offered extended prayers, and participated in sacrifices.[31] Because the king played a pivotal role in the governance of God's world, kings used their authority to raise up true or false gods, and either to lead people into rebellion and destruction, or toward becoming God's blessed people.[32]

Ultimately, God was and is the King of Israel all along, and we know that the role the Trinity enables in 1 Samuel points to the Messiah. Jesus enters the scene in the New Testament and proclaims himself as a king when he fulfills the prophecy in Zechariah 9:9. He declares himself as king in cleansing the temple,[33] in healings,[34] through his response to children,[35] and through his victory over death and Satan. Though the storyline of earthly kings is a mere shadow of the true reign of God, God's plan advances seamlessly and is unwavering. Jesus's entrance into human history as a man and the King of Kings and Lord of Lords[36] brings redemption and truth to all our false conceptions of leadership.

Jesus' kingly role in the kingdom-family, in the workplace, the community, and in the work of ministry and church, is one of great importance. A king protects freedom, protects people, protects God's mission, protects God's commands, protects God's truth, and protects how people do things through organization. By policies, administration, systems, vision, and good legislation, Jesus aids people in taking hold of all that God has planned. Today, God's Kingly role still works in and through his people toward the same end—building up the Body of Christ into a household family.

A PROPHET

The Jewish prophets were individuals considered to have been chosen to deliver God's divine message to the people and leaders of Israel. They were the spokesman in the Triune "spokes" of God's bicycle. According to Abraham Joshua Heschel, the prophet is not a mouthpiece, but a person; not an instrument, but a partner, an associate of God.[37] The early prophets were classified in the following groups:

PROPHET TYPE
Pre Classical
NAMES
Moses, Samuel, Nathan, Elijah, Elisha
DESCRIPTION
They were prominently involved in politics and communal affairs, and were consulted by
Israel's leaders for advice.

PROPHET TYPE
Classical
NAMES
Amos, Isaiah, Jeremiah, and Hosea
DESCRIPTION
They were men who, through inspired and articulate admonitions, preached to the people of Israel and Judah, warning of harsh divine punishment should the people not reform their behavior and obey God's commandments.

PROPHET TYPE
Exilic

NAMES
Daniel and Ezekiel

DESCRIPTION
During the destruction and desolation of Israel at the hands of kingdoms such as Babylon, these prophets dramatized God's judgment, made future predictions about the temple, and foresaw the future coming of the worldwide reign of the Messiah.

PROPHET TYPE
Post-Exilic

NAMES
Haggai, Zechariah, and Malachi.

DESCRIPTION
They spoke into the rebuilding of the temple and into a crushed people of Israel, bringing
to them messages of hope of an end-time restoration.

In the earlier times, prophets were ordained by the Spirit of the Lord as they spoke on God's behalf (e.g., 1 Sm. 10:10; 1 Kgs. 22:24). Their authentication is often accompanied by words such as these: "The word of the Lord came to" the person (e.g., Jer. 1:2, 4; Ez. 1:3). The prophet was one who proclaimed the truth of God to the people. The prophets acted as God's guiding and rebuking voice to his people.

The prophet was a mediator between God and men, and he would speak to men on behalf of God.[38] He spoke only via inspiration as heard from God[39] or from what God had shown him.[40] The prophets directed Israel and spoke warnings against Israel.[41] They directed, rebuked, consulted and encouraged kings.[42] They were used by God to uncover the secrets of men's hearts.[43]

The New Testament helps us understand the intended function of the prophets in the Old Testament. In almost every use of the words prophets, prophecy, or forthteller in the New Testament, the text refers us back to the prophets of the Old Testament and their ministry. New Testament writers understood prophecy and the work of the prophets as compasses pointing toward the Messiah. That's the function of the prophet still. John in the book of Revelation says that "Jesus Christ is the spirit of prophecy."

The writers of the Bible realized that the correct interpretation of prophecy points *back* to all that was said about *the man*, rather than trying to look forward and predict some other kind of vision of the good life that only pales in comparison to Jesus. The New Testament knows nothing of how we've learned to portray "prophets" today—namely as shamans, psychics, and predictors of the future. The apostles, on the other hand, call us to *look back* rather than *forward*. Their understanding is that the work of Jesus is built on the "foundations of the apostles and the prophets,"[44] and they stay true to their word.

As I traced prophecy, prophesy, and 'to prophesy' throughout the whole Bible, only about 17 percent of the prophecies uttered were related to prediction and future, and over 333 prophecies that were preached to the people in their historical context, were ultimately fulfilled in Christ. The root of the word prophesy in Hebrew is therefore rightly referring not to "forth-telling" as a psychic visionary practice, but rather means to "stand before" and speak the truth of God. Jesus is ultimately that truth.

The prophets played an active role in being God's spokesman, preachers, and communicators as they stood before the people and gave God's word to them predominantly in and for the time and space they were living. Prophets were to carry the message of God and proclaim Jesus, though he was still thinly veiled in mystery. The mystery, which was once hidden, is now plain to us—the mystery is Christ.[45] The mystery of all that God was doing in the Old Testament is now seen in the church and salvation.[46]

The voice of the prophet that once rang out against sin, false religions (Babylon), and the lostness of man now proclaims the same truth in essence in our day. Every time a person "stands before" a people of any creed, race, or size and preaches the man Jesus as Savior and Lord, true prophecy is heralded.

Today, the Spirit of God serves as God's strong arm of prophetic unveiling on earth. Though Jesus is also called a prophet in Scripture, his role on earth as a man was brief. Jesus now sits at the right hand of the Father, prays for us, and directs the church. The Holy Spirit is now the presence of the Father and Son on earth, and he lives in people's hearts. He heeds Jesus' voice and direction. The Holy Spirit now carries out the prophetic function of God as his mouthpiece—a person—glorifying God in Jesus. As Jesus said in John, "It is for your benefit that I go away, because if I don't go away the Counselor will not come to you" (Jn. 16:7 HCSB).

God's work through the prophets served only as physical representation and shadow of the complete work of our Holy Spirit's personality and function.

The Holy Spirit comforts us, convicts us, and counsels us.[47] He exceeds the ministry of the Old Testament prophetic office because he is everywhere at all times.[48] He is all-powerful,[49] has all knowledge,[50] and has no beginning and no end.[51] The Holy Spirit is thus with us and in us as a person and equips us with the power of heaven to continue to proclaim the good news of the Kingdom.

Isaiah 61:1 captures the Holy Spirit's role as a prophet in the life of Jesus. Christ himself testifies; "The Spirit of the Lord God is upon me because the Lord has anointed me to bring good news to the poor; he has sent me to bind up the brokenhearted, to proclaim liberty to the captives, and the opening of the prison to those who are bound." The Holy Spirit's message makes central the revealing of Jesus. In the Godhead we have a prophet, and we should get to know the Spirit so that we can best proclaim truth, comfort, counsel, rebuke, teaching, and admonition.

A Priest

During the Passover in Egypt, God spared the firstborn men of Israel and set them apart for his own purpose. The tribe of the Levites was set apart for service in the temple as priests. A priest would stand before the altar each day and make offerings to God and sacrifice animals for the sins of the people. His primary message was to instruct people to bathe in the purity or the laver and sacrifice for the forgiveness of their sins.

The priest also served as the only one allowed to enter the inner courts. There in the temple was the shewbread, the lampstand, and the incense. Each symbol represented to the priest and the people the Word of God, the illumination of God's light, and gifts, prayers, and the worship that is acceptable and pleasing to God. Once a year the high priest on Yom Kippur would enter into the holy of holies and pour the blood of the sin offerings over the mercy seat of the ark of the covenant. In the ark was the budded rod of Aaron (symbolizing priestly leadership), the Ten Commandments (symbolizing the perfection of God), and a jar with manna (symbolizing God's provision). Though the (p)riests served a role and function, these items in the ark were a symbol of how God's perfect (P)riesthood, in Jesus, could only be filled by God, and that only God could truly supply and satisfy his people. Hebrews 10:11-14; 19-25 says;

> Every priest stands daily at his service, offering repeatedly the same sacrifices, which can never take away sins. But when Christ had offered for all time a single sacrifice for sins, he sat down at the right hand of God, waiting from that time until his enemies should be made a footstool for his feet. For by a single offering he has perfected for all time those who are being sanctified.... Therefore, brothers, since we have confidence to enter the holy places by the blood of Jesus, by the new and living way that he opened for us through the curtain, that is, through his flesh, and since we have a great priest over the house of God, let us draw near with a true heart in full assurance of faith, with our hearts sprinkled clean from an evil conscience and our bodies washed with pure water. Let us hold fast the confession of our hope without wavering, for he who promised is faithful. And let us consider how to stir up one another to love and good works, not neglecting to meet together, as is the habit of some, but encouraging one another, and all the more as you see the Day drawing near.

Our high priest intercedes on our behalf. He is the spotless Lamb who made atonement for our sins, and he stands in the gap for humanity—and in perfect human/deity form. His is payment for our sin and the purchase of our holiness. Jesus' role as high priest within the Godhead is foreshadowed in the priestly work of the Old Testament, and it serves the same purpose today. Jesus' priestly role keeps his family tied to the Father in intercession and his atoning work pleads our innocence before the Father.

TYPES, TITLES, AND TENDENCIES: A LOOK INTO THE NEXT CHAPTER

God snatches out of the dust our flimsy requests for visible kings, priests, and prophets, and says, in effect, "Let me teach you about myself through the broken lens of your fallen understanding." These three titles carry much more meaning than meets our eyes. Within them are the types and tendencies of the kingdom image. Humanity was intended to be royalty; kingly, prophetic-natured priests tending to God's garden. The Trinity's society of prophet, priest, and king has always been a reality.

As the family of God grew beyond fathers, mothers, and children, these types of the Trinity were pressed down not only into the simplicity of gender, marriage, and children, but also into the larger ordered fabric of the world. As the timeline of humankind developed and sin entered the picture and fragmented God's glory, God preserves his likeness and kindness. He doesn't obliterate or abandon his prophetic, priestly, and kingly nature, but he hides these tendencies within Old Testament officials known as prophets, priests, and kings and within the titles for overseers of the New Testament.

As we press into the next chapter on church polity, we'll demonstrate that even though the titles have changed in designating how God orders his family, the Trinitarian tendencies and types remain consistent and necessary to proper order.

CHURCH POLITY

THE ORIGINS OF CHURCH POLITY IN TITLE AND TYPE ...

A t his ascension, Jesus reveals to us a continuance in his Trinitarian organization. In Acts, God organizes and governs his people as he always has. He reaffirms male headship in dispensing twelve male apostles to inaugurate the church much like he did in ordering the twelve tribes and patriarchs of Israel. As the believing community of God grew beyond the nuclear family structure, the single homes grew into a combination household. A family of families. The church.

With the coming of the Spirit, the homeless, orphaned, and seemingly abandoned followers of Jesus were given his glory. His *kabod*. His home. Much like in the Exodus, they are led by a pillar of fire by night and a cloud by day within their very chests. They received freedom, but they needed a structure in place, not only to ensure the right use of God's kingdom-power, but also to guarantee that the provision, protection, and purity of heaven would be properly pastored and assimilated into God's people.

The preservation of God's image through formational structures is known as *church polity*. Polity literally refers to a civil government or constitution. Jesus thinks of the Body of Christ as a kingdom. It's a city. It's temple-people. Jesus himself makes reference to this *new people* and *new creation* under his authority and lordship in Matthew 5:14 when he calls the people who follow him a "city on a hill." The apostle John later refers to the people of God as God's holy city and his temple throughout the book of Revelation.

The holy people/city of God are a together-nation who in unison tell of the glorious image of the Trinity. As 2 Corinthians 3:18 says, "We all, with unveiled faces, beholding the glory of the Lord's, are being transformed into the same image from one degree of glory to another. For this comes from the Lord who is the Spirit." Throughout the first century, in particular, the city and kingdom of God, and his unveiled glory, grew rapidly. As it grew, the apostles adopted and instituted a very consistent pattern for proper governance and oversight. It is no accident that their chosen structure for those serving, equipping, and edifying the family of God takes on a similarly tri-partite, or Trinitarian form like that of the Old Testament. Take a look at figure 5:1. Note how the Trinity's titles are pressed out into the types referenced in the Old and New Testament:

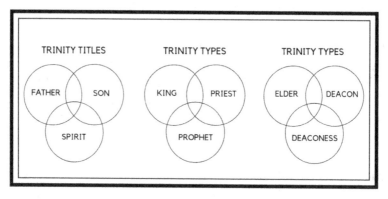

Fig. 5.1

The apostles instituted offices that reflect the Trinity's names in their types. First, they appointed elders (also called pastors, bishops, overseers, or presbyters) in each church,[1] and Paul later directs other churches to follow this process in every town.[2] The appointing of an *episkopos* was essential when combining more than one household into a single household.[3]

Paul makes it clear that the qualifications of said elders must center around the image of God—Christ's character. In 1 Timothy 3, Paul instructs his protege Timothy to find men that are above reproach, a husband of one wife, sober-minded, self-controlled, respectable, hospitable, able to teach, not a drunkard, not violent but gentle, not quarrelsome, not a lover of money. These men must manage their own household well, with all dignity, keeping their children submissive. They must not be a recent convert, and they must be thought of well by those outside the church.[4] In 1 Peter 5:2-5, the apostle Peter also describes the role and posture of those pastoring God's people:

> Shepherd the flock of God that is among you, exercising oversight, not under compulsion, but willingly, as God would have you; not for shameful gain, but eagerly; not domineering over those in your charge, but being examples to the flock. And when the chief Shepherd appears, you will receive the unfading crown of glory. Likewise, you who are younger, be subject to the elders. Clothe yourselves, all of you, with humility toward one another, for "God opposes the proud but gives grace to the humble."

These overseers were and are tasked to *teach aptly* the Word of God.[5] Their primary role is to give themselves over to the passion of rightly understanding, passing on, and living out God's Word before the people. Notice my emphasis on living out the Word of God *before the people*. Being before the people implies that the maturity of overseers be primarily assessed in the environments of the home where people mainly lived life. Shepherding grew in maturity in the family, not in some other entity! They were to be, above all else, men similar to Paul. Imitable examples of moral uprightness[6] and models of good deeds.[7]

Paul clearly institutes male leadership, not as a slight to woman, but in order to carry the thread of Genesis forward as it weaves its way through God's storied tapestry. For those that may still sneer at the idea of male headship within the church, I would ask you again to keep in mind two things. First, remember how the Bible frames headship in the manner of how Christ loves his church. To dwell safely under the brand of love that Christ demonstrates is both a privilege and a blessing. Only within and beneath Christlike love can both men and women truly become wholly human. Second, for those that say women should be elders, overlaying a differing view upon these passages despite the textual evidence to the contrary, I would ask you to tread lightly when suggesting that we institute something that is found nowhere in Scripture, whereas male headship is everywhere in Scripture.

Furthermore, Jesus himself came as a man, not as a woman, and this should inform how we see headship going forward in the family of God.

Pastor/elders are gifts to the church. So too are deacons. Deacons are first referenced in Acts 6:1-6 by the Greek verb *diakoneo*. The *diakonoi* were to seek out the distressed and to relieve them. They are assistants to the pastor/elder (*episkopos*) in their charitable work. The deacons' primary role is that of helper. Servanthood. They attune themselves to the *leitourgia*, or the economic life of the Christian community.

Likewise, deacons were required by Paul to be of the highest character and moral excellence. In 1 Timothy 3:8-13, he even likens deaconship to pastors and elders, but with one notable difference. In his explanation of the deacon he includes the husbands *and* their wives:

> Deacons likewise must be dignified, not double-tongued, not addicted to much wine, not greedy for dishonest gain. They must hold the mystery of the faith with a clear conscience. And let them also be tested first; then let them serve as deacons if they prove themselves blameless. *Their wives likewise* must be dignified, not slanderers, but sober-minded, faithful in all things. Let deacons each be the husband of one wife, managing their children and their own households well. For those who serve well as deacons gain a good standing for themselves and also great confidence in the faith that is in Christ Jesus. (italics mine)

Though the language used in the Greek in these verses is still predominantly masculine, the implications of the deacon's role extends to the man and his wife. The deacon and his *deaconess*. The name of deacon really describes best what the man and woman do together. It is not so much a description of title as it is the assumptions of function. The word describes their actions. Their type. The deacon tendency is to serve their table. Their home. They position themselves in the same manner as Jesus at the Last Supper, who as the text tells us in John 13:3 "Knowing that the Father had given *all* things into His hands... he got up from the supper, laid aside his garments, and taking a towel, he girded himself... *to serve*" (italics mine)

Did you catch that?

When given all authority over heaven and earth, Jesus used his first acclaimed moment as the all-sovereign King to bend his knee and wipe the literal crap off his disciples' manure-infested, calloused, and aromatic feet.

Deacons and their beautiful wives (the deaconesses) deploy their power in Christ in the same manner. They lay aside all that they would want, and they display the kind of moral fortitude that completely forgets oneself and spend their energies on others.

Paul affirms that the deacon has a role of authority, and is as the elder, a husband to one wife. Headship in the home and church are to be preserved, but the woman is a powerful accompanying factor. She bears the weight of the helper. She is that Holy Spirit-like presence of comfort, counsel, and conviction in the dwelling and in God's household—the church. And if you think about it, she's called to mother the sons and daughters within her care. Therefore, she has a profound influence on the formation of male headship within the family and the church. She mothers boys and young men in how they are to grow up and love and cherish women. She also has a dynamic influence upon the female. She's to train into them the strength of service.

OUR INTERPRETATIONS OF POLITY

As the centuries have passed, we've done a lot to the titles and tendencies of pastor/elders and deacon/deaconess. We've theologically dissected these words and come to our own conclusions about how life should be ordered.

Let me give you a birds-eye view into the predominant ways that the church over the centuries has seen fit to order the life of God's people. The Episcopalian System puts in place an archbishop that has authority over many bishops. These bishops, in turn, rule over a *diocese*, which is a network of churches under their oversight. The individual churches themselves are led by rectors.

The Presbyterian System is more locally infused. Local churches elect their elders (collectively known as presbyters). Each church and their elders belong to a larger presbytery. It includes a portion or all of the elders that are local to a nation or region. These leaders meet together occasionally in what Scripture refers to as the *presbyteroi*, which denotes a meeting between Christian leaders who are known individually within their respective communities (i.e., *episkopoi*). This is why often *episkopos* is used to refer to individuals within a group, and presbyteries are collectives.

The Congregational System has a variety of uniting similarities and distinct differences. The most common uniting principle is that a senior pastor or elder is designated the leader and is elected by an immediate board of deacons or eldership. The differences in the congregational and non-denominational system usually revolve around who votes and how is the leadership and those doing the electing put in place. Out of a voting system comes the logic of a Church Board System where an entity outside the local church or from within its midst, helps the local body determine what's best for that particular congregation. Usually, specific orders are delegated into and under the particular oversight of the council. If the church-board system is rejected, then a church might accept a purely democratic system where everyone votes equally.

All of the systems noted above have their merits and their pitfalls, just like any human invention. And that is their primary problem. All the systems we've devised are to a great degree humanistic rather than theological, and they result in the ordering of life based on definitions to biblical words that hold meanings altogether different from their usage in the Bible. Through these redefinitions, we've largely lost the original biblical meanings of kingdom oversight and service. As a result, these terms bear less and less Trinitarian likeness.

Alistair C. Stewart notes in his book *The Original Bishops: Office and Order in the First Christian Communities* that though we've redefined the words of pastor/elder and deacon/deaconness into offices, the "elders are not offices but rather persons of esteem within the church ... Ignatius observes that *episkopos* is a type of the Father."[8] In fact, history shows that the family word "dad" was synonymous with the word "elder." It describes the nature of someone within the family. His tendency. It describes the person's "actioneering," if you'll let me invent a word. The action of fathering. Aristotle makes clear that the *episkopos* held status as a householder and exercised a single rule (*monarchia*) over the members of his household.[9] His role was not merely one of managing or administrating the family, but the word means that he had pastoral functions.[10]

The raising up and electing of elders to an office, rather than affirming their natural character and manner of serving in their home, has led us to some profound misuses of authority. The greatest misuse is our concoction called the senior leader. We've invented the CEO, the frontman, the face of the organization, and the top dog. We've invented the personality-driven model of leadership because we assume that the church functions more like an entity than a family. Our invention of seniority is unhealthy and has led leaders to fall again and again.

Continual moral failures accompany church leaders today because the hierarchal ordering in so many churches creates distance. In the early church, it's clear that leaders were so well known and personal within the community that they merely emerged out of a relationship. Today, however, ministries grow so far away from the central leadership that relationship with the primary leader is non-existent. Organizing as a corporate entity silences any sense of family.

Having been an integral part of six church plants over the last twenty five years, I have rarely actually "known" my staffed-pastors even though I knew a slew of other men that frequented my home that pastored their families in many ways far superseding that of the hired leaders.

I'm utterly convinced that the reality of the senior leaders not being intimately known by those they serve wreaks havoc on their soul and on those that attempt to follow their brand. Everyone in the scenario, particularly those at the top, are either swallowed up in loneliness and reach out for affection in all the wrong places, or they fall prey to the pride of being at the top. Their fall is always inevitable.

The senior leader is also formed by their expectation regarding their position. As a result, they learn to relate in a particular way. Their title exudes authority of a top-down nature, and it forms a vast gap that is immediately perceived and felt between leader and laity. The gap remains intact no matter how one might intend to close it or despite one's best efforts to admit how much they hate its reality. The senior leader thus is always put in an "over" stance above everyone else, and let's face it, when people feel looked down upon by those supposedly leading them, they will never expose who they really are. The relationship that's created encourages performance and people-pleasing rather than the embrace we see modeled in the Trinity.

Our invention of senior leadership appears nowhere healthily in Scripture. In fact, a quick word search for the word leader in Scripture will reveal that almost 99 percent of its uses reference false teachers leading God's people astray. It's fascinating to consider how Scripture negatively frames leadership when we live in a day obsessed with it. No one writes about the obvious. Jesus asked us to *follow*.

Consider also the idea of the singular leader as compared to the more plural nature of leadership in the Bible. Don't you find it odd that when John in the book of Revelation gives us a glimpse of what's behind the curtain of heaven, he sees that surrounding the throne are twenty-four elders? Heaven itself is represented by a plurality. That means when we pray for "God's will to be done on earth, *as it is in heaven*," we by very definition are praying for a plurality of guides. Multiple. A mutual submission of governance that reflects the very nature of the Trinity.

Plural oversight is not just hierarchy or relationship. It's a dance. It's much less defined than we'd like, and I think that's why humans are reticent to get out on the dance floor. Of course, the dance itself can also be distorted. I've been around plural oversight structures where it seems they are always dancing and deferring to the other. As a result, they rarely move anywhere. They fail to see within the Trinity that there's a "first among equals." Though the members of the Trinity are completely equal in value, dignity, and worth, there are many moments where the work of one or the other is highlighted or hailed as going before the others. On the contrary, I've also been in plural guided environments, where the first among equals overseer will not spend any time deferring at all, and it leads to reducing the others to the position of yes-men.

The fact remains that we will never be Trinitarian without a hierarchy, without egalitarian equality, or without complimentary function. As Christians all worshipping the same God, we must humbly admit that plurality is absolutely the essential to the way God orders life, and from here we can discuss in unity all the practical ways to best flesh this out as his people. One thing is for sure: The topic needs to be discussed far more between us than it currently has been. We stay in our corners. We need to come to the center ring. My hope here is to light the match to a forest fire of dialogue. I encourage all those reading to take the flame and go light the fire where you are. See what healthier forests can grow after the soot settles.

For some reason, something within us fallen humans rejects the rightness of kingdom organization. We gravitate toward human-centric models. But we must ask ourselves, Where is a case of successful single senior leadership ever found in Scripture? From where does our idea of the single sent missionary develop? Even Jesus came to earth under the will of his Father and in the power of the Holy Spirit. He came individually but immediately accumulated friends. Jesus' ministry was family shaped. Paul, Luke, Peter, Mark, Barnabas, and all the globally dispersed church-planting teams in the book of Acts were just that: *teams*.

Therefore, I must pose to all those that hold to the invention of church offices and the individual missionary the same question I asked previously in regard to headship: Why should we accept a church structure found nowhere in the New Testament, and reject a pattern that is everywhere in the whole of Scripture?"

What Oversight Should Look Like

The apostle Paul would be amazed at the way the modern church has implemented God's oversight over its people. When Paul pictures a church, he sees a meal, and all the functions are framed in that context. We, on the other hand, imagine a building filled with glitz and programs. Whether we admit or not, our culturally devised way of meeting influences how we understand Scripture.

Paul envisions the family imagery when speaking of the "actioneering" of the elder. It's at the family level that most pastoring function is deployed, and in the home is where the elder best comes alive. Herein lies another problem with our current models for raising up leaders. If we never observe our leaders in the environments where they're most at ease in their gifting (at home in their marriage and amongst their children), how are we to meet the biblical paradigm for finding and assessing Godly overseers? Better investment needs to be made into the practical aspects of how we develop, discover, and deploy the best male heads and male and female servants from within the makeup of the hospitable home. If our litmus test for oversight is the home, it absolutely changes everything.

Consider the hospitable family in light of the proper way to assess a deacon. They are ones that clean up—the ones that put the home back in order after the chaos of hospitality is over. A deacon is one that organizes the whole affair so that every moment within the event points to our allegiance to Jesus. The deacon is a powerful preacher and teacher far more through what is seen than heard. They are masters of home decor and *feng shui*. Bad joke!

Alistair Stewart notes that hospitality in the home was the defining character of the early church, and thus the role of deacon was crucial: "Fundamental to the ritual of Christianity was the gathering to eat. This meal is the focus for the church's activity in worship, but also in socialization, as patronage and leadership may be exercised and charity offered through the provision of food. It is by virtue of this liturgical context, therefore, that economic officers and patrons come to exercise leadership in worship and leadership in Christian communities overall."[11] The early church shaped and formed Christians through the methodology of a meal. It was the environment for education. Content and courses (pun intended) were consumed together.

Deacons are no longer servants; they now hold political offices. They have to go through trainings, seminars, and have required reading. I'm not necessarily opposed to reading (small joke), but all their training aims at teaching them how to best hold an office, not how to best serve within the home by exercising exemplary hospitality. It's seems that we can't even recognize the original meaning and intent of the biblical term "deacon" because the word is so sieved through our cultural filter.

Note how Paul helps us return to equilibrium by reinforcing the family-elder-deacon logic in Titus 1–2. He begins by characterizing an elder as "the husband of one wife." In 2:1 elders are commanded to teach what accords with sound doctrine. In 2:2-10 watch the flow of thought. Rather than explaining sound doctrine as an academic precept, he links it to the proper actioneering of older men, older women, all those younger, and all servants in a place of submission of any kind. When Paul talks about doctrine, he talks about the community. He talks about the nature and demeanor of how Christians are to be *with and act toward* one another. He ends the section with the phrase, "in everything adorn the doctrine of God our Savior." The adorning of the truth of God is like ornaments on a Christmas tree. The tree provides the framework (doctrine), and the lights, tinsel, and beauty enhance and draw attention to the truths believed. We must think critically about what our organizational adornment conveys about how people are to relate to and believe truth.

THE FRONT AND BACK DOOR MUST REVERSE

I've mentioned in brief the analogy of the church being like a house. Currently, our front door into the house of the church is through the gathering at a central location—usually marked by a building filled with all the charm of programs and entertainment galore. Most of the heft in talent, time, and treasure is spent maintaining this proverbial front door. Budgets, staff, maintenance, volunteers, parking lot attendants, greeters, and even the elder/pastors, and deacons spend the majority of their time maintaining, meeting over, and administrating this central location and all that happens at the gathering within it. Meanwhile, the back door to the house of ministry, the small groups, really serve as an afterthought. What goes on in the homes merely supplements the actual church central, but we don't consider these homes to be churches themselves. The homes are like moons orbiting the sun. They are the satellites. They take orders from and are subject in everything to the central gathered entity. Ironically, all the priority is dumped into maintaining a central entity that only meets a few hours out of a week. The activities of the members are largely subject to and controlled by a single, distant office-holder. A senior leader.

The orbiting structures of God's organization reverse everything. The front door of God's family is the home. Home means far more than a house, by the way. It's a way of thinking. It's far more organic than we make it. All the heft, and rhythms of God press themselves out into the everyday life of God's people where they live most of their lives. A family of families (the church central) may have gathered but a few hours within a week back then. Or like in the time of Pa in the classic TV series *Little House on the Prairie*, a family may only have made it into town a mere once per season because of distance, elements, and less-than-ideal modes of transport. People throughout history have needed a more timeless way of doing life together that enables God's community to flourish no matter the circumstance. A structure that is built to equip even Pa and his household has to make use of a different "front door" than the one we currently have made.

The church's front door should be at the meal. Within the home.

Making the jump in our thinking is not really that hard. Even at the Passover supper there would have been songs sung, worship led, liturgy and prayers performed, gifts used, leaders trained, and messages taught and discussed. The family was the home base of all things pertaining to discipleship because the emphasis was placed upon the father—the head of the home—in training up and equipping the *paideia* of his children and marriage.

If the front door of ministry is the home, it makes sense why all the pastoral letters use family language in the same manner as all the writings of the Old Testament. In fact, in the Old Testament, gatherings together took place in larger festivals a few times throughout the year—the feasts of Passover, Unleavened Bread, First Fruits, Weeks (our Pentecost), Trumpets, and the Day of Atonement. The day-to-day sacrifices of animals, gleanings, fruits, grains, and the like ensured that the majority of worship took place in the home-filled-rhythms of the moment-by-moment work of God's people. God's primary investment was placed in the hours lived among people who were scattered throughout the land.

Likewise, the primary investment of Jesus' ministry was made by going into the homes and lives of those he served. He observed the feasts and larger gatherings, but they were not his primary focus. He didn't show up at the office each day; he showed up at the kitchen tables of lives within his care.

A profound example of the paradigm shift that our front-door and back-door analogy can bring is encapsulated in the man Richard Baxter. He did the bulk of his living and serving in the town of Kidderminster, a town in Worcestershire, England. Considering himself to be a bit of a non-conformist to typical church polity, Richard began entering homes. Revival swept the land through the simplicity of a man reclining at tables with mothers, fathers, and children while discussing with them their biblical nature as a family. He did nothing more than train them in how to live out Scripture as a family unit. Upon leaving each home, he simply challenged each household to go about mission doing the very same thing he'd done for them—going into family units and training them to train others. His paradigm was not individual discipleship, but family disciples. It was about family image.

Compare Baxter's approach to the discipleship of families today. We disciple individuals. If we do attempt to take on the whole family, we have invented a model where the family actually expects to be separated on a Sunday morning, not brought together. Men with men. Women with women. Children and elderly go on into their own respective hymn-sings and children's programs. We train the unit of the family by dividing them; which makes no sense to me if we look at the flow of logic in Paul's letters and training material. Consider Ephesians 5-6. Paul goes straight from speaking directly to husbands and wives to speaking directly to children. He doesn't talk *about* children as if they're not there in the room, nor does he talk *about* parents. He speaks *to* all. He assumes in his writing that the family is together, not apart.

ORDER BEYOND THE HOME

Please don't hear me wrong and think that my position is that the only place an elder-pastor or deacon-deaconess role is revealed is in the home. I have an equally sharp ax to grind about how our current church models have undervalued the role God's gathered worship plays in shaping culture.

Hans Liebmann notes that the head of the Ephesian mint is known as *episkopos*.[12] There is no question that the term *episkopos* was widely used in Hellenistic associations and in civic government.[13] This seems odd. But should it? Today, our titles, architecture, methods, and many other things involved in doing church have contributed to the growing divide between what we call culture and church. We've actually pastored ourselves into a problem of separating faith from everyday life and culture. We've created a gap between those in ministry and those not. We can talk and talk until we're blue in the gills about ministry being about the people, not the leaders; worship being about a life lived, not a song strummed from a stage; all of life being filled with Christ; or the equality of vocations between the church staff and those of attending members...

But ...

... talk is cheap when the show speaks louder than the tell.

We have hemmed ourselves in when speaking of leadership, pastoring, and deacons, because we have made intentionally cultural and familial words into church words. When thinking of the roles of elders, deacons, and their wives, Christians today tend to picture committees and buildings because we've conditioned them to think in these terms. We've also invented a whole other office in the church and called it the worship leader.

We've discussed the worship leader previously, but let's bring it back for a short, added insight. The *leitourgia*, or the "form of worship" as referenced in Scripture and applied in the Greco-Roman culture, was used to reference the work of wealthy citizens. The provision for food to the poor was considered a *leitourgia*.[14] Funding the loves and desires of the culture in the arts, government, media, entertainment, education, family, and beyond was understood to be the job of the *liturgist*. God's people within these realms of culture were understood to be affecting people's worship on a direct level through their work. To put it another way, their everyday vocations were considered avenues through which they rendered worship to God by performing his will within the context of broader society. We don't readily make this connection much today.

Worship leadership has been poisonously reframed. In changing the vantage point on this and other titles from society to church performance stages, we reinforce our modern theologies. By changing the language of Scripture, we have emptied virtually all societal vocations of any connection to worship and isolated worship within the walls of a church building.

When we thus change meaning and methods, we create an unbiblical division between sacred and secular and in the process devalue the vocations we've walled out because they seem to lack an overt religious component. For example, oratory, teaching, music, and maybe a few other skills, are elevated in importance because they have value to ministry. Those who practice other vocations are not encouraged to see their work as connected to the service of the Trinity. The value statements we make in these practices come across very strongly to our church members. For example, when I spoke in a church about this very topic and invited people from other vocations within the congregation to come up and pray for the church through their particular lens of work, I was met with tears by one man who said, "I never knew the gospel was for my job."

It is imperative that we recover the meaning of the *episcopate* because we've all but lost what it means to the cultivation of home and culture. When I speak of recovering the *episcopate*, I am referring to the role of the *episkopos* in ensuring that the poor are recognized within the eucharistic community (around meals) and also to a recognition of the meal as a means of bringing about economic and social justice (the Lord's Supper). Our distribution and redistribution of goods within the Christian society is a light unto the world and focuses the church's caritative ministry.[15]

Because we no longer characterize worship ministry as meeting people's needs, worship and justice have become two different topics. Never blended. People no longer see themselves *as* being the church wherever they go—the infused sanctuary-house of the Holy Spirit. People no longer link vocation to the gospel and the imparting of spiritual impact. We need to recover vocation and church, and it starts with how we order life and our meeting together.

Our ordering is crucial, not only for our own families' wellbeing, but also to our ability to carry out and fulfill the Great Commission. What's at stake here is the fullness of the gospel. What's at stake is the fullness of Trinity oversight. True pastoring should infiltrate, infuse, and overtake the home, the marketplace, and the trades of all men, women, and children.

TITLE, TYPES, AND NOW TENDENCIES

Allow me to revert back to figure 5.1. You may be wondering what I intended to indicate in comparing the prophet, priest, and kingly types used in the Old Testament to the types used in the New Testament—pastor/elder and deacon. What does any of that have to do with church polity today? Easy.

My conclusion is this:

The Trinity is the One Senior leader of all cosmos, church, and culture, and over time, humanity has rejected and lost that oneness at the hands of sinful rebellions and rebel dynasties; but God preserved his commitment to our betterment by continuing to operate behind the scenes through the office *types* of the Prophet, Priest, and King. In the man of Jesus, the Trinity comes out from behind the curtain, and Jesus fulfills in perfect all *types*. The Apostles remained consistent to the structure of the Old Testament order as they carried the Prophet, Priest, King *types* into the Pastor/Elder and Deacon, and Deaconess. In doing so they also continued to uphold a unified perspective of what Jesus' work accomplished for all believers. Through Jesus, every believer who is **in Christ**—not just overseers, are referred to in the New Testament as a "lower case" (p)riest, (k)ing, and (p)rophet *(from here on referenced as PPK)*. Every overseer, leader, and follower of Jesus now carries the office of prophet, priest, king internally in *type*. Through the indwelling of the Holy Spirit, we've now been infused. These *types* of the Trinity's nature come out of us through acts of service and ministries. I call it *tendency*.

As we go about our work and our play, we all tend to see life through a colored PPK lens. We lean toward a proclivity. We tend toward a flavor of how we approach everything. We all have the tendency to carry out our roles, functions, or types of ministry and service in either a more priestly, prophetic, or kingly way. Whether you're a parent, an elder, a sibling, an employee, an artist, a sports figure, or fill any one of a million other professional, ministerial, or family roles, you are just like each member of the Godhead in that you carry out your work with a particular bent.

You may be more priestly (concerned more with the empathic—the hands and *life* of Jesus). Or you may be more prophetic (concerned more with right truth—the mouth and *truth* of Jesus. Or you may be kingly (concerned more with order—the *way* of Jesus).

Tendency, function, administration, and role get us very close to how the New Testament writers speak of spiritual ministries (some call them gifts). A Trinity-shape exists in the gifting of Christ's body. People overlook the Trinitarian mandate in the spiritual gifts because we individualize them into superpowers. As a result, we misunderstand them, misuse them, and mar them. Many view the gifts through man-centered and efficient lenses and fail to see how the spiritual gifts lists in Scripture are intended to be anything but exhaustive or individual. The gifts lists are communal. They are meant to point us to the image of our Creator. They are types and tendencies enabling us to go about serving as a whole.

The lists for spiritual gifts (we're going to call them ministries because that's closer to the Greek implication here) in Romans 12:6-8, 1 Corinthians 12:8-10, 1 Corinthians 12:28, Ephesians 4:11, and 1 Peter 4:11 are not complete lists. Each ministry listed (a total of about twenty-eight) is a type or representation of all the ministries collectively. We know this because in the New Testament alone we have over 270 other ministries/gifts listed (see Appendix 7 for the complete list). Paul does not intend us to read the spiritual ministries lists as efficient inventories that can quickly categorize our personality, purpose, or potential, but he tells us how to read his lists by the opening words he includes before he starts the list.

Paul is fairly unified in introducing all of his roughly 143 lists in Scripture, and if he had intended the ministry lists to be read as individual abilities, he would have said as much. Instead, prior to listing the gifts, he introduces them as functions, administrations, and roles, not abilities. He also lists the majority of them in the context of speaking of the church as a body. He speaks to us as "we" not "I." He's very Trinitarian in how he thinks in one-another terms. Ministries result from the Trinity living amongst as we journey together.[16]

In addition to introducing us to a plethora of types of ministry, Paul links these to the Trinity-types of PPK and the ministries of elder/pastor, deacon, and deaconess. In 1 Corinthians Paul lists the gifts in a Trinitarian form to help us interpret them:

- A Word of Wisdom
- A Word of Knowledge
- Discerning of Spirit

- The Gift of Special Faith
- The Gift of Healings
- The Working of Miracles

- The Gift of Prophecy
- The Gift of Tongues
- The Interpretation of Tongues

Notice there are three gifts that shepherd, three that act, and three that speak. Even in the list of types, Paul structures them in a way that alludes to the priestly (shepherding), kingly (action), and prophetic (speaking) tendencies. Note figure 5:2 below:

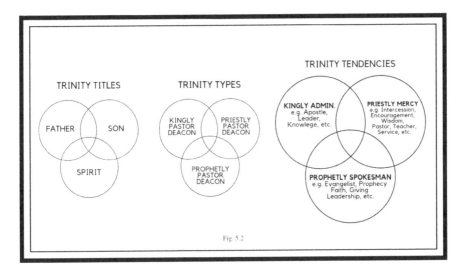

Fig. 5.2

Paul's comparison highlights the power of Jesus as he carries out his leadership on earth through his gifted "we." His Body. We are a combination of his overseers and his gifted bride. Jesus enables us to be a collective community. Some of us carry a proclivity toward action and administration; some a tendency toward using words as spokesmen, and others carry an extra sense of merciful compassion and attentiveness to other people. A more kingly individual might be natural at "working on" the family of God, whereas the priestly type person is more prone to "work in" the family amongst the people. The prophetically geared person may find peace in speaking to the people. Kings attend to policy, prophets to precept, and priests to people. The Way (policy), the Truth (precept), and the Life (people) of Jesus are needed in fashioning God's family into Triune likeness.

The logic above might also prove helpful in confronting, reforming, and equipping all current approaches to church polity from a place of unity. I think it's biblically clear that a plurality of overseers is absolutely essential. And most churches would do well for the health and wellbeing of the congregants and their continually failing leaders to reconsider their position of senior leader and/or their democratic structures for doing church.

But beyond plurality, what about other practical specifics? How are the overseers and the priesthood of believers to lead in unity while still getting things done without falling into the pride that comes from being lone rangers?

PPK thinking is very helpful. If multiple leaders are intentionally trained within their tendencies to act out a spiritual ministry within the community through the lens of PPK, then a balanced whole will result. People are committed to the way of God through kingly leaders who equip them. They are committed to the truth of God via the prophetic people that speak to them, and to the life of God via the priestly people who are examples to all of how to love and nurture God's family. Trinitarian teams are deployed. Trinitarian churches result. Trinity-shaped people are balanced. The life of the Trinity speaks through the paradigms of our show and tell.

If Paul traveled throughout his ministry and church planting endeavors in Triune-pods, why can't we? He often took Luke and Barnabas with him. I believe he did so intentionally, and with an eye on balancing his Trinitarian approach. Paul's writings have all the flavors of prophet, priest, and kingly emphases, but he most assuredly leans toward being a spokesman. He needed others to balance him out. Luke was very ordered and kingly in his account of Jesus' life and the early church, and we must assume his administration, order, and efficiency aided Paul on his journeys. Likewise, Barnabas was an encourager. He was the agent of priestly mercy and ministry. Together, these men worked in a "Triune-pod," if you will.

In fact, Ralph Winter makes distinct the two Triune-pod structures of the church as seen in Acts. He notices that there is an integrated local and global way through which the church replicates itself. He calls these two spheres the *sodal* and *modal*. Modal leadership structures are geared to pastor the local people, whereas sodal, or global teams, are sent around to various local churches to encourage them, equip them, and edify them. Today, modal (local churches) and sodal systems (namely parachurch Christian ministries) separate because they think differently about how to press out the image of God within a local and global climate. However, if we think about church planting more in terms of home-based Triune pods that release church planting teams, we might better reflect the Trinity as we go. We might find that our local and global service as Christ's church is awakened in how to best walk and work in tandem. I believe we'd find a more unified, family-centric, whole-person-forming, and God-glorifying way forward in planting churches.

Not only would these sodal and modal systems produce a greater unity of paradigm across the board, but they would also flow into all vocations. Consider the example I used of Trinity-tendencies as you think about the craft of Paul's writing. In the very pens of New and Old Testament writers, one can see variants of the PPK outlook. Peter and Paul definitely lean toward being truth-oriented spokesmen, whereas John is very pastoral in his aim and flavor, even as he brings truth along almost secondarily. James, Mark, and Luke are very ordered and kingly in their emphasis on logical progression, timeline, accuracy, and the action of faith. Matthew's gospel is very priestly, not so much in the fact that he writes to Jews, but that he structures his whole book around Jewish history. On and on it goes.

What if a PPK thought process were to permeate churches and our discussions not only about building kingdom community but also about engaging culture? Much like the Trinity smuggles his nature into Old Testament structures through the offices of PPK, he does so still today, and we must take notice. We could experience something similar in smuggling the truth of the Trinity into where we live, work, and play. Connecting the dots for people in how the gospel works itself out in their application of policy, customer service, or research would be eye-opening. What about how a king's protection, a priest's compassion, and a prophet's exactness might revolutionize healthcare, government, education, and so on? The whole of society would begin to look like our King. Image.

Our ministries, together with our service, are to be like the Trinity. Order begins with and presses out from gender, through marriage and family, and out into society via a PPK framework that models the truth, way, and life of our God. We are one and another. One another. God unites how we see ministry by naming us equally as prophets, priests, and kings in Christ. Title. He allows our tendencies to flourish and flow out of us in unique ways. God requires the same image to be experienced by all and through all regardless of one's trade or station in life. On the other hand, God also preserves hierarchy and variation within the sameness as he lifts up those within his family to help govern toward the right aims. The right aims namely being his glory, home, and meals. They pay tribute to our Trinitarian-Jesus.

A BRIEF ON GOVERNANCE

BIG GOVERNMENT & PROVIDENCE

The spiritual ministries in title, type, and tendency, work toward the one aim of helping humanity to focus on the essentials of God's glory, home, meals, and Jesus' kingdom. It's toward the fullness of the gospel that we are mandated to govern, take dominion over, and properly rule the earth. The command given to Adam extends to us in the hands of the perfect Christ. Jesus rules and reigns and "puts everything under his feet" for us and through us.

Most people have a real problem with what the above mandate to govern looks like. Many think dominion means dominance. Christians go around *praying at* sickness, demons, evil, and circumstance rather than *praying to* God. Some walk around trying to tell the rain and clouds what to do, or to stop the sun in some kind of Joshua experiment. Some hurl God's Word to people in a condemning manner and expect that everyone will dance with joy under the chastisement. Still others will avoid the topic of dominion altogether and figure that the kingdom is merely one of passive silence and maintaining untarnished ideals. They'll assume that God's kingdom is only about saving us individually from sin. They will comply with the message of a get-out-of-hell-free card but will fail to submit to the Lordship of Christ. Many passive Christians may admit that God can rule victoriously over their heavenly destiny, but they'll buy into the lie that God's reign has little to do with this life, creation, and the fulfilling of all things here and now.

To balance the passive perspective of dominion with the active, let's look at governance as a whole. As previously discussed, marriage, gender, family, and organizational structures not only imply order, but also authority. Dominion. Rule. God calls himself King and Lord, and learning what his rule and reign over his kingdom looks like is imperative to our living rightly.

God's kingdom is not ruled like a dictatorship. Command. God's kingdom is not passive-aggressive. Tolerance. Which is it? Active or Passive? Desire or Decree? Empire or Embrace?

To understand how God goes about the oversight and the governing of his holy-city people, we must speak of two things: providence, and the heart. Big and little government.

First, providence.

Christopher A. Hall asserts that "the manner in which we approach the problem of providence will ultimately determine whether we reach the goal of comprehending how God is at work in history."[1] I'm inclined to agree. If we don't first deal with God's providential government as it reigns, rules, and directs us toward his plans, promises, and purpose through the whole of history, then we'll fail to understand government and order. Let's consider the **extent** of God's rule, his authority's defining features, and his relationship to governing amidst our sinful world. The extent of God's dominion leaves no stone unturned.

God controls nature,[2] the animal kingdom,[3] human histories, and destiny.[4] He is sovereign over life circumstances (e.g., Hannah, Mary, Paul, David), accidents,[5] sinful acts,[6] Satan,[7] and yes, even evil.[8] In Luke 4, Jesus asserts that he is Satan's Lord. Satan has no right or power to offer false provision, power, or protection. Satan may be too proud to believe that he has no real control, but nonetheless everything allowed him is by God.

God's rule is universal. God is big government. God is big brother. He's the hope out of reach when people attempt to achieve democratic and communistic utopia. In angling for control, we desire something of the divine, but the trouble with human desire is that it gets twisted. We demonstrate our unfitness for absolute power by placing our own human thinking above that of God. Our attempts to make things right through our own benign dictatorship always end in disaster. Always.

God, however, is perfect in his rule. He rightly and fully favors the just and unjust alike,[9] is good to all,[10] reflects perfect concern over his children's wellbeing in all matters,[11] and is completely free, unbiased, untarnished, full of understanding, and utterly complete in all aspects of order. His perfection is the extent and defining feature of his reign.

How are we to understand how God's perfect government rules within a sinful world? God claims to be good, and yet our world is so horrifically horrible. Many shake fists at God or discount him altogether solely because they can't reconcile the presence of evil with a good and gracious God.

We ask, Why bad things happen to good people? But the question springs from the wrong footing. The more God-centered, biblically sound, and theologically correct question is, Why do good things happen to bad people? The Bible asserts that our base conclusion about humanity should be that we are all bad. To understand this shocking judgment, we must apply the right standard for defining bad. God made us to be like him. He is perfect, and we are far from it. We are bad in comparison to God, who is the only legitimate standard by which goodness can be defined.

Most people see the apparent dichotomy that exists between God's goodness and our badness through the lens of narcissistic humanism. We want to believe we are entitled, infused with inherent goodness, and deserving of the best. God's view is very different. Our self-induced fall from perfection brought about the greatest historical atrocity ever known. The killing of our Savior, Jesus. His death is the ultimate grotesque evil. Pondering his sacrifice might give us a better perspective from which to answer our questions about why we experience evil. The apostle Peter describes, in words more poignant than my own, the lengths to which God's sovereignty will go to bring about good for us despite our willful plunge into evil:

> For Christ also suffered once for sins, the righteous for the unrighteous, that he might bring us to God, being put to death in the flesh but made alive in the spirit.... Baptism... now saves you, not as a removal of dirt from the body but as an appeal to God for a good conscience, through the resurrection of Jesus Christ, who has gone into heaven and is at the right hand of God, with angels, authorities, and powers having been subjected to him. (1 Pe. 3:18-22).

The greatest injustice ever committed—the crucifying of the all-perfect and good satisfier of every soul—was willfully ordained by God. His desire in choosing such a tragedy to take place was and is to "bring us to God." At the same time the Father willed the horror to occur, Jesus also willingly "laid down his life"[12] out of his own authority. Humanity's act of willing seemingly brought about a bad doom. God's act of willing led to a good and glorious resurrection.

When man sinned, God could very well have written him off as a failed project and abandoned us to the death we brought on ourselves. Jesus could very well have called down legions of angels out of his own will to bludgeon and slay his wardens of death. But he chose to refrain. Why? He decreed a fate he most certainly didn't desire in order to gain something he ultimately deemed most good. Because he chose to *willfully move* in a manner that makes no sense to the narcissist or idolater of entitlement and comfort, we got salvation over abandonment. So we need not talk about why bad things happen to good people. There are no good people. Because of Jesus' willful and loving sacrifice, good things happen to bad people.

DESIRE AND DECREE AND THE MAGNET

Throughout Scripture, and most clearly in the death and resurrection of Jesus, God is revealed to us as maintaining two sides to his will. A will of *desire* and of *decree*. The two sides mean that nothing is outside of God's perfectly *permitted* or *allowed* will, nor is there anything outside of his *active* and *affirmed* will. When we speak of the will of God, we must know precisely what we're talking about on both sides of God's tandem of action and permission, or we're going to skew the conversation in anti-theological directions, especially in matters involving evil and human suffering.

God's governing volition operates in ways entirely different than ours, and yet it is similar. We will things by doing them (commission) or by choosing not to act (omission). God wills his action or inaction similarly. However, he sees the righteous manner by which to govern all things with an all-knowing sense of the past, present, and future. He has perfect wisdom concerning all things yesterday, today, and tomorrow. His motives are unified and unflawed in all matters. When he acts or chooses to refrain, he does so with the whole picture laid out before him.

Our view is limited. When we're wronged, we cry out for justice. When we wrong others, we cry out for mercy. We reveal our self-centered motives and measurement of what we perceive right or wrong to be. Our core motive is really just preservation of self. We overlook or even exalt our brokenness and imperfections while telling ourselves the lie that at heart we're good and deserving. God's sole desire and motive is different. He aims to exalt his glory, his fame, and his name, because he is the sole fountain of holiness, rightness, and goodness.

God exalts his own name most perfectly in bringing us to himself. And why? It's because he knows that if left up to us, we would never lay down our lives for those we consider our greatest enemies. When God wills to hand his love to those that hate him most, he separates himself from the masses. He shows us that in him operates a power far more other-worldly than our own. He operates within and from a different kingdom. He shows us a whole different way of existing. In his uniqueness we see the road that leads to a satisfaction far beyond what we can grasp for ourselves. God's motives for actively willing something positive through desire or allowing something negative to occur for the good it will ultimately bring, are always based on his unwavering commitment to a better kingdom.

The way in which he conducts himself is captured in 1 Peter 3:18-22, which is quoted above. God governs in a power that exhibits balance. He perfectly executes power and perfectly restrains power.

God can surely prevent our sin and all the evil we do,[13] but he does not always prevent it.[14] He can also direct any evils toward his aims, so that their results ultimately bring about good.[15] And he can limit sin and its diseased effects, both spiritually and physically, to any degree he wishes.[16] Or he can refrain from limiting it.[17] In one respect, God enables human volition, and in another he intercepts volition and superimposes his will over it. Unlike us, God is completely unbound in his will. He is also not obligated to us. He lovingly chooses to pursue us despite his freedom to walk away from our mess with no strings attached.

We, on the other hand, are landlocked in a prison of sin. We can will this or that throughout the day, but one thing is beyond our grasp—life beyond our stranded island and prison bars. Our willing is done within the framework of what is bound. Scripture tells us that there's only one way off the island, and that is that God "would first love us." Only when his Spirit is present in us is there freedom. His choice to utilize all his legions and fleets of resources in order to organize our rescue mission off this island is made in complete and unhindered freedom. God is unacted-upon by any imprisoning realities, and his choice to love us, to come to get us, and to loose our chains of living on this island of sin awakens our *choice*, not merely our *will*. Our will still remains bound, but now God in his sovereign way offers a choice.

The choice of man is therefore not determined by God as some form of cruel fate, but choice is most assuredly ruled by God in every possible way. It is this absolute rule and reign of God's lordship, kingship, and governance that causes the nations to rage. The world hates submitting to any authority but self. Therefore, it hates the truth of God's sovereignty over our choice. Psalms 2 says it more eloquently than I can:

> Why do the nations rage and the peoples plot in vain?
> The kings of the earth set themselves,
> and the rulers take counsel together,
> against the Lord and against his Anointed, saying,
> "Let us burst their bonds apart
> and cast away their cords from us."
>
> He who sits in the heavens laughs;
> the Lord holds them in derision.
> Then he will speak to them in his wrath,
> and terrify them in his fury, saying,
> "As for me, I have set my King on Zion, my holy hill."
>
> I will tell of the decree:
> The Lord said to me, "You are my Son;
> today I have begotten you.
> Ask of me, and I will make the nations your heritage,
> and the ends of the earth your possession.
> You shall break them with a rod of iron and dash them in pieces like a potter's vessel."
>
> Now therefore, O kings, be wise be warned,
> O rulers of the earth.
> Serve the Lord with fear, and rejoice with trembling.
> Kiss the Son, lest he be angry, and you perish in the way,
> for his wrath is quickly kindled.
> Blessed are all who take refuge in him.

God portrays the dance between his willing and our human volition as a giant magnet that skitters about when positioned adjacent to its polar opposite. If two magnets are faced in the correct direction toward one another, they quickly pull harder toward each other the closer they get. If the magnets are placed in polar opposition to one another, as you move one magnet toward the other, the chased magnet scurries away in all-out fury. If the human heart can be likened to a magnet filled with sin, we can say that humanity stands in polar opposition to God. Any man, woman, or child bent on rebellion will rebel when confronted by his or her opposite. Love. It's actually the very rescue mission of God in pursuit of us that brings about the greatest fury of rebellion, causing us to resist him like scurrying magnets.

We can understand through the magnet analogy why Isaiah 45:7 quotes God saying, "I form light and create darkness; I make well-being and create calamity; I am the Lord, who does all these things." Our analogy helps us resolve how God's good and holy pursuit causes so much evil.

As far as magnets go, God is always the positive. He's always the pursuing magnet. His effort of forever-pursuit is always one of good intention, love, and a desire to bring many sons and daughters to glory. When God's loving pursuit is met by a heart that he's caused to be reborn and remade, his initiation of salvation is welcomed. The one who has been made alive by the Spirit of God can't help but run into the arms of the approaching lover.

The human that rages and the king that wages an all-out assault on God posture themselves quite differently than one who is redeemed. Their hearts are unborn. Dead. Polar opposite to life in God. When God pursues the rebel out of his internal loving and desirous will to know them, he carries only one willed outcome—that *all* might be saved.

In fact, it's God's unwavering agenda to seek out every lost person that keeps the universe intact. Peter writes about it in 2 Peter 3:9: "The Lord is not slow in keeping his promise, as some understand slowness. Instead, he is patient with you, not wanting anyone to perish, but everyone to come to repentance." Many of us might think it just fine for our enemies to be put to death immediately if it meant justice for us. Not God. He willingly withholds justice on the wicked so that he can do what is most seemingly unjust—give love to people that don't deserve it. God's justice is far deeper and more profound than ours. It almost seems backward. We must thank God every day that his love is backward and remains committed to pursuing the undeserving.

It's the very patience of God in holding on just one day longer that keeps us alive and affords evildoers one more chance to repent.

God continues to move toward dead human hearts with life. His magnet moves with the base intention to pull men and women close to his bosom, and yet a dead heart wants nothing to do with anything alive. As God presses toward us in righteousness, he also allows for the occurrence of the evil things that come in response to his righteousness. As he pursues kings, malcontents, sinners, and Satan's legions of physical and spiritual armies, they run as fast as they can from his waiting arms. In carelessly dashing over the river and through the woods (to grandmother's house they go), they fail to care about who they destroy, run over, devour, or bleed out along the way. So, we can rightly say that in a sense, God does cause evil. He does not *will* the evil to occur; it occurs because humanity and demonic beings rebel when approached by his goodness. This is how we're to make sense of how a good God causes evil and calamity.

When reading passages like Isaiah 45:7, we must neither minimize the words and explain them away as a misspoken speech, nor overemphasize them and come up with some outlandish determinist philosophy of God that makes him into a non-relational monster.

Isaiah is very intentional to link God's sovereignty to things most evil in order to ensure the preservation of our trust in him. He's got our back in all matters. Even in the greatest of evils. Jesus ran even through the finish line of a wooden cross. He embraced the greatest evil the world has ever known. He ordained it. He decided that the greatest injustice would be taken out on the purest, most innocent, holy, and undefiled being ever to walk on earthly soil.

SMALL GOVERNMENT: A HUMAN HEART, THE CHURCH, AND GOVERNMENT

God is providentially reigning over all things, and the greatest portrayal of the beauty of his reign and dominion is seen in the way he deals with the human heart. Small government. The greatest dominion to be had is not over demons, storms, sickness, etc.—even though this is a part of it. Going after evil things is not the priority. If we make it so, we will end up so obsessed with evil that we become like it (loud, angry, fearful, depressed, impatient, short-lived, short-sighted, and out of control). Jesus gave us a bigger power. In filling us with the Spirit, he brings out in us the following fruit: love, joy, peace, patience, kindness, goodness, gentleness, faithfulness, and self-control. The greatest throne upon which true rest sits is found in human chests.

The fruit of the Spirit, God's governing legislation and ethics, are pressed out, into, and through human hearts. The fruit of the Spirit best describes the demeanor and manner of Jesus, and it should describe our demeanor as well. His authority is far less vocal, demonstrative, attention-seeking, loud, disruptive, performance-based, personality-driven, and nagging than we might think. His authority is seen in the common moments of a heart ruled by him. It's seen in a heart that maintains the best authority over one's self.

I'm not implying control. Controlling oneself and circumstances is far from what authority implies. Control is a game of arduous work, and it yields horrible results (stress, fear, burnout, etc.). Control puts the executor's cleaver to our back. Yielding to God's authority, on the other hand, is a rhythm of rest.

Picture the Israelites walking through the desert. When God's cloud moved, they moved, when his fire rested, they rested. The ones that got loud and obnoxious under Moses were the ones resisting God's authority. The ones resting in God were quiet, humble, and willing to go where he led them. Authority transforms a person and motivates him to love others. Connect the idea of authority to the display of the fruit of the Spirit. Every fruit is necessary to achieve loving relationships with others and requires that we rest under God's control for proper action. The strongest arm of love is seen only when faced with one opposing in hate. Joy can only ring true when all other circumstances turn unhappy. Joy rides above the current of circumstance, whereas happiness is based on happenings. Peace is only visible in tempests and torrents—perhaps similar to the picture of Christ sleeping in the hull of the storm-tossed boat as the disciples ran around in fury. Patience shines brightest when things don't go our way; kindness shouts loudest when met with a vulgar enemy; goodness comforts most when it embraces the hardest of people; and gentleness, faithfulness, and self-control conquer all when a person bears all things, hopes all things, and endures all things.[18]

For the Spirit's fruit to be seen in vivid color, God's works must absolutely be laid against a contrasting background of horror. The backdrop of evil and sin amplifies the display of God's glory as seen through his people's fruit. Just as in the beginning when the Spirit hovered over the formless waters that were devoid of any ability to sustain life, the power of God's governance shows its face in whatever chaos might come.

Maintaining authority over the human heart is small government. It is a profound government. It is the most essential form of control, and it is no small matter indeed. Chrysostom understood the "wrestling of the human heart" to be a lost and useless battle without the Spirit of God's intervention:

> It is not possible to be a master of one's self, being in a passion. Like a sea rolling mountains high, it is all hurly-burly: or even as a pure fountain, where mire is cast into it, becomes muddied, and is in turmoil ... It is your own soul that you have cut open; it is there that you have inflicted a wound: you have flung your own charioteer from the horses, you have got him dragged along the ground upon his back.[19]

So far gone is the human heart that Romans 3:10 tells us that "no one is good, there is none that seeks God, no not one." In fact, so hopeless is the cause of the human heart that when Paul speaks of the spiritual ministry of miracles he uses a word that literally alludes to "the amassing of resources." What Paul deems a miracle is far more commonplace than we might assume. He connects its meaning to discipleship purposes. Miracles are not miracles just when resources are amassed for any reason, but they become miracles specifically when brought together in a way that rejuvenates the human heart. Salvation. The saving of a human heart is a literal miracle. God describes it as being born again.

Rebirth of a human heart is a resource we do not have outside of God's Spirit. It's his miracle and his decision. What say does a child have in the miracle of his own birth? Earthly parents, like our heavenly parents, decide on our birth. It's a heavenly decision.

Because the human heart is the throne of all self-governance, it is also the throne upon which our king sits. A call to salvation is political because whoever, whatever, and whoever occupies the allegiance of the human heart will control who a person worships and how a person goes about ordering and controlling life. If we believe in Christ, our reality is that the society, city, and government of the kingdom reside in us; not just individually but as a family. The fullest display of God's power comes not in a shout but in a whisper. It comes through a people who work quietly with their hands, and yet loudly proclaim in word and deed that only one government is capable of bringing about the reform we desire in climate, order, morality, policy, taxes, and politics alike.

The governmental nature of the human heart and the believing church is conveyed many times in Scripture. In 1 Corinthians 5, Paul instructs the church on how to handle matters of injustice surrounding issues like sexual immorality, greed, idolatry, drunkenness, and swindlers. Paul speaks of the gathering of a church family with believing hearts as being its own governing and judgmental body.

Hear me right when I speak of judging! We are not to judge those outside the church, but to judge those inside. We are not to do so by our own devices, but by Scripture. Authority. For all those that place themselves under the Scripture as their authority, the family of God is to act rightly toward one another in keeping each other accountable to its truth. Judgment is not a practice to be rejected within the church but embraced. It reveals to us where we're out of line with God's best for us. Becoming aware of the ways in which our flesh continues to trick and tempt us into sin helps us cut the enemy off at the pass. In being corrected and rebuked by fellow friends, we see where we're walking away from the Trinity's embrace rather than toward it.

Paul tells us that to be outside of the family of God and unaffected by other Spirit-filled hearts is to be under the government of Satan. In 1 Corinthians 5:5 he says that all those unwelcome in God's household because of willful sin have made themselves willing citizens of Satan's governance. Paul says to give these people over to their choice of picking Satan's ways over God's, not to judge them but to bring them around. God's purpose in having us allow the unrepentant person to freely go is so that his or her "spirit may be saved in the day of the Lord." Jesus ordains for those unrepentant a season under the slave-mastery of Satan. He does this so that they might taste how awful judgment is and turn toward Jesus for deliverance.

Jesus affirms, along with Paul, that the world already stands condemned in sin. Those who turn to worldly ways do not need any more judgment, nor do they understand sound advice. Right judgements offered to a dead heart fall on deaf ears, and calls to repentance are like casting of pearls before swine. The only message that can awaken a heart is the gospel.

Our job in the world outside the church is to preach and live the gospel in a manner of embrace. Once people are embraced into God's family, they will sense the difference in being under God's reign as opposed to Satan's. Paul sees the church and the world as two kingdoms with two different ethics. To embrace the church family is to embrace the authority of God, and to reject it, is to give Satan's worldly rule a giant hug.

Jesus actually called this duty of church governance or church discipline "binding and loosing." In the context of Matthew 18:15-19, Jesus speaks of disciplining a brother that sins against another. He tells us to first approach our brother when an offense is committed. If the brother refuses to listen, we are to seek an intermediary person from within the church for help in arriving at a just outcome. If a brother's heart still hardens toward reconciliation, the matter is to be brought before the entire community of a local assembly (the home church of the family of families). If no repentance or resolve is effected, Jesus refers to the family's decision-making process as one of binding and loosing. The local family is then to assume the authority of God in allowing the unrepentant person to leave the household. A decision of such magnitude must never be made hastily. It must be done prayerfully.

Jesus also speaks about prayer in the context of the above words about discipline: "where two or three are gathered, I am in their midst" (Mt. 18:20). This verse specifically pertains to matters of justice within the body. It is often misapplied to marriage and to simple matters of prayer, whereas it's a very specific promise of God's presence amidst times of discipline. God promises his attendance so that believers will accept their duty to love, judge, and rebuke each other by utilizing proper authority.

Peter adds another layer to how God's authority, lordship, and rule are pressed out within and through God's people. In 1 Peter 5:1-11 he discusses the role of overseer and elder, and he calls all believers in response to those in oversight to "clothe yourselves, all of you, with humility toward one another." In the context of oversight and governance, Peter continues: "Humble yourselves, therefore, under the mighty hand of God so that at the proper time he may exalt you." Peter correlates the "mighty hand of God" to the oversight of eldership. Learning humility under God's rule and reign has much to do with our response and demeanor toward those in positions of oversight.

A strong understanding of God's rule in the heart and through church polity results from a strong theology of God's providence. A weak understanding of God's sovereignty leads to an anemic view of the church, its reign, and its role on earth. Without a strong theology of both, our submission and humility as believers hang in the balance. Limited, finite, and worldly wisdom has a hard time comprehending submission structures and humility due to only one factor. Trust. To benefit from the kingdom city of God, we must trust his plan through his family of families, the church.

WHAT ABOUT THE LAWYER?

Governance involves laws. Our culture is full of regulated laws that both honor and dishonor the manner of Christ. How are the people of God to relate to and understand the civil law of today? What are we to make of the many confusing laws in the Old Testament?

In the Old Testament, we have three types of laws through which God presses out his reign among mankind: moral, ceremonial, and civil. Moral law is founded in the character of God and is thus eternal. The basis of moral law is summed up in Leviticus 19:2: "You shall be holy, for I the Lord your God am holy." The moral law can be broken down into subcategories as follows:

1. Reject idolatry (Lv. 26:1-13)
2. Love God (Dt. 6:4)
3. Love your neighbor as yourself (Lv. 19:18)
4. Do not oppress your neighbor (Lv. 19:13)
5. Do not steal or lie (Lv. 19:11)
6. Do not sacrifice children to Molech (Lv. 20:1-5)
7. Shun all Sexual sins: adultery, incest, bestiality, homosexuality, etc. (Lv. 18:20; 20:9-21; Nm. 5:12-15)

Moral law is what James refers to as "royal law" and Jesus summed up as "the law of loving God and others." The Ten Commandments are unavoidable for humans, regardless of race, religion, or creed. We all acknowledge they are universal. For example, murder is not prized in any culture. Its prohibition is universal. People groups across the board understand that the unjust taking of life violates something inside our deepest parts. The reason murder offends us so deeply is because it crushes how we were morally created to function. We were created to value life. If we were not created to value life, and we were in essence just evolving, then murder would be logical to us, not abhorrent. In fact, many of those who have taken evolution to its logical conclusion—such as dictators like Hitler—have made murder into a moral solution in exterminating those who are weak. Such faulty thinking brought about the Holocaust.

Ceremonial laws, many of which are found in the book of Leviticus, deal with the Old Testament priesthood. They include the initiation of priests and procedures to uphold their office, sacrifice, and service. Ephesians 2:14-18 speaks of the abolishment of these once-timely ceremonial laws:

For he [Jesus] himself is our peace, who has made us both one and has broken down in his flesh the dividing wall of hostility *by abolishing the law of commandments expressed in ordinances*, that he might create in himself one new man in place of the two, so making peace, and might reconcile us both to God in one body through the cross, thereby killing the hostility. And he came and preached peace to you who were far off and peace to those who were near. For through him we both have access in one Spirit to the Father. (italics mine)

Implied in this passage is the abolition of the ceremonial law, which expired with the fulfillment of the priestly work of Christ (Mt. 3:15). God made a distinction between what was required of priests and the rest of the Israelite people and does away with the outdated version by no longer separating Jew from Gentile. Here is a sampling of what types of things the ceremonial law addressed:

1. Cleaning the house of a leper (Lv. 14:33-57; Nm. 5:2)
2. Festivals (Lv. 23:1-25; Nm. 29:39)
3. Laws on animals for food (Lv. 11:1-47)
4. Law of Atonement (Lv. 16:1-28; 17:1-16)
5. Offerings (Nm. 29:39)
6. The consecration of priests (Ex. 29:1-46)
7. Priestly duties (Lv. 7:1-37)
8. Regulations for priests (Lev. 21,22)
9. Various sacrificial offerings for sin (Lv. 1–6)

Now we will address the civil laws handed down in the Old Testament. Many matters of civil law were given in particular to the Israelites for the Israelites. Their purpose was to help settle individual disputes and describe proper behavior amongst God's people. These laws, along with the ceremonial laws, expired with the demise of the Jewish civil government. They have been fulfilled in the person of Jesus in *specifics* to culture and ceremony. This abbreviated list gives examples of what these laws addressed:

1. Justice to the poor, (Lv. 19:15)
2. Cattle of neighbors (Dt. 22:1-4)
3. Rebellious children (Dt. 21:18-21)
4. Debt (Lev. 23:34-43; Dt. 31:10)

5. Divorce (Dt. 22:19)
6. Dress, attire (Dt. 22:5)
7. Hate in the heart (Lv. 19:17)
8. Inheritance (Nm. 18:26; 26:53-56; 36:8-12)
9. Justice practices (Lv. 24:17-23)
10. Kidnapping (Ex. 21:16)
11. Landmarks (Dt. 19:14)
12. Property redemption (Lv. 25)
13. Murder and killing (Dt. 21:1-4)
14. Ethics in commerce (Lv. 19:35f)
15. Robbery, extortion, false witness, and restitution (Lv. 6:1-7)
16. Sabbath-breaking punishment (Nm. 15:32-36)
17. Theft (Dt. 5:19; Lv. 19:11)
18. Warfare (Dt. 20:1-20)

Though the above laws are fulfilled in the person of Christ, as is the moral law of love, the civil and ceremonial laws in specific still hold within them principles that are wise. For example, though we no longer have mandates for festivals, restrictions on food, priestly regulations, sacrifices, and cleanliness issues, all of these items still affect us. There is much wisdom to be gained in how God ordered the life of Israel in recurring feasts and celebrations. We can acknowledge that purity in eating, sex, and other issues are also helpful. In addition, we are all called "priests" and "living sacrifices" in the New Testament. The priestly language of the apostles draws our minds back to some of the ceremonial laws of the Old Testament with this implied advice: "Though you no longer have to live directly by these laws, still consider their wisdom and the principles they teach us for living a holy life today." Upon the principles of the Old Testament civil law we can derive great wisdom in how we are to rightly govern our own cultures in matters of justice.

The only thing that the New Testament seems to change about our understanding of moral, civil, and ceremonial laws, is our posture toward them. The laws in the Old Testament ultimately foreshadow a reality that has come to pass. All perfect obedience to the law is now a reality in the man of Jesus. Our law is no longer a script written on parchment; it's written on the man Jesus. Through his Spirit, Jesus infuses his law-abiding nature into our hearts in a more complete way. He observed the law in a way we never could. Perfectly.

In 2 Corinthians 3:3, Paul says that we reveal that we "are a letter from Christ... written not with ink but with the Spirit of the living God, not on tablets of stone but on tablets of human hearts." Because the law of Christ is now in our hearts, the big government of the kingdom and the local government of the nature of the Trinity reigns in the same place. The heart.

JESUS ISN'T AVERSE TO POLITICS

Just because I'm saying that proper governance is intended to be found in the providence of God, the family, the family of families (the church), and the human heart should not imply that the Godhead is indifferent to our civil government's laws, restrictions, and mandates. I'm saying that we must place the marker of emphasis in the same place God does. His kingdom maintains sovereignty.

We live within a world where governments are trying to side-step family, the church, and the human heart in governing individuals. Entities filled with politicians consider themselves to be the best model for controlling human moral issues. Instead of fulfilling their mandate to point toward and uphold what already is absolute truth, they take the throne and define what they think to be true. Big government falls into the trap of thinking it can rule over the universe better than the providence of God. This explains why government today takes on moral issues and makes them political (i.e., abortion, marriage, human sexuality), and takes on political issues and wrongly makes them moral.

Jesus trains us in how to relate to pagan and godless dynasties across all time and space. On one hand, he says to honor them. Compliance. Romans 13 says to honor our leaders. The original language implies a posture toward all those in governing positions. We are to honor them in a way that is so loving that it demands an answer as to why we're different. We must not confuse respectful submission with blind and willful disobedience to God's ways. We are told specifically that there is "no authority except from God, and those that exist have been instituted by God." Submission in Romans 13 requires that we show honor when laws and leaders affirm Godly ends, but it also requires that we live lovingly in opposition to all authority structures that would ask us to disobey God's law. When we live in opposition, we can still carry ourselves with a posture of respect.

Jesus modeled defiant compliance. Revisit in your mind all that was said in the visual display of *The Lord's Supper* model. The meal was a subversive meal of political proportions. It was such an effective silent protest that it led both Greeks and Jews alike to grow angry in hostility at Jesus' claims and way of life. Jesus' political adversaries were so offended they were willing to murder a man that had done nothing lawfully wrong, all because of the way in which he dwelt among us.

Consider also Jesus' teaching about turning the other cheek. Many interpret this as a Scripture of compliance. The historical context teaches the exact opposite. It indicates *defiance*. In that day, the governing authorities would assault anyone they considered to be lesser than they with the back of their hand. To hit someone with the back of the hand was to communicate to them that they were a dog and a slave of no value. Jesus instructed the person slapped to turn the other cheek. The victim offered the other cheek to challenge the authority to swing again. This time the assailant would have to strike using the front of their hand. To strike with the front of the hand would be to affirm that the assailant and victim were equals. Jesus is not encouraging compliance to social norms that are blatantly wrong, but rather commanding gentle defiance that upholds the ethics and manner of the kingdom.

Jesus didn't shy away from artfully expressing his kingdom rule and reign over the political rulers of that day either. Take for example Matthew 8:28-34 and Mark 5:1-13, when Jesus sends a mass of demons named *legion* into a herd of pigs. He sends them plummeting over a cliff to their death. The occupying forces of the Roman Empire in that area sported the name *Legion* and had as their mascot the pig. Jesus' actions in the demonic deliverance are more akin to a painting than a script. Jesus doesn't lambast the authorities in a way that is loud, defiant, or even apparent at first glance, and yet through the demonic exorcism, he attaches meaning to the pigs and to the legion. The Roman authorities would have certainly understood. Through his spectacle of protest, Jesus publicly states that he is a king far greater than anyone in Rome. His kingdom is greater than any empire. He carries the power to conquer and control both earthly and spiritual realms.

The God-man Jesus and the people that he rules are to be *compliantly defiant*. We are to trust so wholeheartedly in the universal reign of God's sovereign lordship that we can carry ourselves as a gentle, humble people. We so fully entrust ourselves to God that we commit to the foundational things of life: church and family. As we mature and grow up into a temple-building of

God—literally becoming a city of people within our cities—we model governance that is a beacon of light to those in power around us.

The world is supposed to take notice of our life together. Our love amongst each other should, and will, ruffle feathers if we're living in public displays similar to Jesus. We're not to go looking for spectacle and attention, but if we live like no one's looking, eventually someone will. If we're living and believing in Jesus rightly, our hearts, our family, and our way of life will undoubtedly be put on trial.

My question to you is, has the order of your life, household, and church ruffled any feathers lately? It should.

Take up your cross, my dear friend, and follow him!

THE TRINITY ANSWERS
ORGANIZATION

A s seen in figure 5.3, considering the O.rganization of the Trinity and how he orders life can help us to better consider how we multiply across the world both in church and culture.

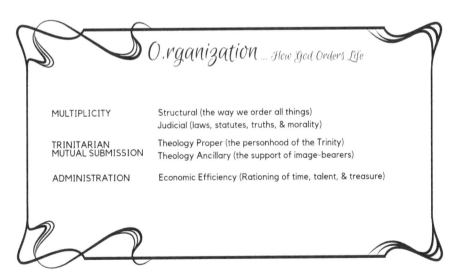

Fig. 5.3

The Trinity's structure of unified plurality must influence leadership structures. Let me first remind you of how to view the topic of leadership. At best, we can describe some of the Scripture's best leaders by calling them guides. For example, Moses didn't set agendas, vision points, and mission like some expect leaders to do. He merely guided. He kept righting the sheep as they would wander from the center and reminded them to keep looking up at the cloud of fire which was leading them. Moses also was not defending the people from, nor even aware of competing communities that lay in their path. Balak's empire of Moab and its armies were out of sight for Moses. He couldn't lead something he knew nothing of. His guidance was trust. Trust is possibly why the book of Numbers speaks of prayer over eighty-eight times—far more than most other Old Testament books.

The people of God have never known the future, and thus they can never lead. All we know is the man. Jesus. Trust. Our only tool is to guide people toward his hand, his mission, and his vision, for he knows where the Moab's lie.

In the spirit of challenging the nature of leadership, I offer the PPK assessment (Appendices 1–5). It can aid us in better training and affirming guides. Most assessments today want to nickel and dime us down into a set of skills that others can use. After mastering these skills, we are then called leaders. However, our greatest asset is image. It's what we are, not what we bring that makes the difference. The PPK's aim is to assess and ponder the Trinity as a means of understanding ourselves. Most other tests and assessments for governance look solely to the individual using imperfectly designed tools that were fashioned by imperfect people. The PPK paradigm is designed to help us better assess personality, purpose, and gifts within the whole of companies and churches. We can assess the whole of a human. Whereas Myer's Briggs and other personality tests tend to pigeonhole human personality into boxed and fixed categories, a consideration of PPK tendencies allows humans to be defined, but to remain imaginatively unique in their expression.

We must examine the Trinity to uncover some of the disgusting patterns that have taken hold in how we organize life and authority in our home, church, and culture. In most cases, our bent is to reject mutual submission, not because we don't see the merit and value in it, but in our inability to do it. It's hard. Nay, it's impossible without the Trinity. There's something most beautiful and other-worldly about it. Meanwhile, the world attempts to prize as virtues the qualities of mutual submission, service, and sacrifice, though they are unattainable without the work of Jesus. We see the good, but we just can't pull it off. Our nature imprisons us. But within our intended and untarnished image of God, virtue is most natural to us. Here's how one author expresses the nature of our love for one another as it is played out in marriage:

> It's against nature for a man to love a woman as a wife that is rugged, daring, and presumptuous, and trusts to herself, and thinks she is able to protect herself and needs none of her husbands' defense or guidance. And it is impossible that a woman should love a man as a husband, except she can confide in him, and sweetly rest in him as a safeguard ... Wherefore, the dispositions of soul which Christ looks at in his spouse are a sweet reliance and confidence in him, a humble trust in him as her only rock of defense, whither she may flee.[1]

The Trinity also bears significant weight upon how laws and the governance of morality can be universally absolute and yet remain culturally relativistic. Many in the world today are suggesting that we either lean toward absolutes in trying to govern everyone globally through one lens, or that we should lean toward relativism or postmodern thought by allowing everyone to dream up what's "best for them." Neither model works, but a Trinitarian paradigm might help us achieve balance. God is both simultaneously. God is absolute, and in creating the universe he based all we know on absolutes. There are natural laws such as gravity, thermodynamics, and boundaries to logic. Universally, we recognize that things like murder, lying, stealing, coveting, adultery, and the like produce vice; whereas protecting, truth-telling, giving, celebration, and fidelity, statistically produces human flourishing in all aspects. God's Trinitarian absoluteness can help us discuss relativism with helpful boundaries. To discuss preferences with the assumption that there are also absolutes can give more meaningful conclusions about how the game of life is played.

Consider how the Trinitarian O.rganization can also help us better discuss *theology proper* and *theology ancillary*. Don't get scared off by the big terms. Theology proper is the study of the attributes, works, and inter-relationship of God. Often theology proper includes pneumatology (the study of the Holy Spirit), the study of the Father, and Christology (the study of Jesus Christ).

Understanding God's personhood and identity can help us make better sense of God, but it can also help us better makes sense of ourselves.

Making sense of self in relationship to God leads us to more complete conclusions about how we relate to all that is other. This is ancillary theology. Ancillary refers to any support system outside ourselves. It can be the study of government, industry, operation, management, production, commerce, systems theory, etc. Believe it or not, all of these areas of study have theological implications. Remember, everything is worship. All these supportive elements either help us to thrive or become the culprits who are left deprived.

For example, consider the distribution of food. Statistics reveal that we produce enough food in the world to feed every man, woman, and child four full meals a day. In one hand the world addresses the problem of world hunger but is having the wrong conversation about how to solve it. It doesn't take more rallies and banquets. These do more to make us feel important when in all reality, the banquet takes another meal away from someone in the world. Our problem is our own greed. It's our own devices of distribution. We pull more resources into and under our own control, rather than giving it away.

On the subject of food, a friend shared with me a quite a different but helpful perspective. She works in the weight-loss industry and attends a church filled with many members who are overweight. One Sunday the church had raised $2,000 at a bake sale to help the country of Haiti. Sounds good right? Wrong. She knows something deeper. She knows that eating baked goods and sugar causes people to spend, on average, $10,000 a year on losing those calories. She did the math. In that megachurch, they could have raised $900,000 for Haiti had everyone just given their yearly allotment for weight-loss instead of adding more to their thighs and hips through bake sale treats. Again, we devise wrong solutions to the right problems because we fail to follow Scripture. The cure in Haiti is not more infrastructure to poverty and natural disaster, but rather control over our own gluttony.

Consider another example in how we address problems with the wrong solutions. I worked in the government for about five years. My job was to be a support to anything involving family. I know, government and family seem like an oxymoron. Nonetheless, one thing I did was to assess unemployed persons, help them craft a resume, build experience, and then land a job in the community. I'll never forget one day when a man told me he wasn't going to come to class anymore. I asked him why. He told me that he made more on welfare checks every month than he would if he actually got a job.

Do you see the problem? On the one hand, the government offers jobs, and on the other it gives incentives not to work. This is chaos. It's ludicrous. What's worse, this man had settled into believing that his dignity and value only went so far. He had cashed in and given up on attempting to make anything of himself or experience the honor that comes with providing for oneself and family. The gravest tragedy in the scenario is that the man had been taught that to give up is to get a reward. These incentives are bad. It's bad economics, bad government, and bad "parenting" of the whole individual.

Plymouth Colony Governor Bradford summed up a better way to achieve a positive economic impact on human life, dignity, and health of the family. He notes in his journal a particular time of crisis where food was not readily available, and how the situation was handled in a manner that better addresses the human needs of both nourishment and dignity:

> Every family was assigned a parcel of land to work for their own provision, according to the proportion of their number, for that end, only for present use and ranged all boys and youth under some family. This had very good success, for it made all hands very industrious, so as much more corn was planted than otherwise would have been by any means the Governor or any other could use, and saved him a great deal of trouble, and gave far better content. The women now went willingly into the field, and took their little ones with them to set corn; which before would allege weakness and inability; whom to have compelled would have been thought great tyranny and oppression. Not only were all hands more industrious—the incentive to harvest communal corn before it was fully ripe, a problem equivalent to poaching in the case of wildlife, was also eliminated.[2]

The problem in our systems of provision, economics, and vocational life today lies not in what's missing in supply, but rather what's missing in our view of what constitutes support to humans. We assume that what best supports humans boils down to simple economic concepts like supply and demand,[3] costs and benefits,[4] opportunity costs,[5] diamond-water paradox,[6] incentives,[7] money supply,[8] interest rates,[9] inflation,[10] unemployment rate,[11] and the idea of a "free lunch."[12] Humans are much more than consumers, data points, and targets for marketing campaigns. What every sales pitch, ad, product, and facet of economic rise and fall is doing is exposing two things: to whom we are giving our allegiance, and what kingdom we are building.

Economics is very telling about the state of the human worldview and worship.

Economics reveals to us that when left to ourselves, humans naturally come equipped with four things for self-support and preservation: **a pedestal** on which to stand—made of our work, hobby, beliefs, schedules, race, and class; **an intention** to set ourselves above all the rest by declaring our supremacy in some form; **a dollar** to prove our worthy entitlement, and **a sword** to self-protect and fend off anyone who might seek to take our worth or knock us off our self-made throne. The world's economy is filled with worshipping, self-protecting, entitled, and autonomous demigods ready to knock anyone around should they pose a threat.

Economics is very instructive. It reveals to us where we as self-acclaimed demigods tend to allocate our time, our talents, and our treasures. Economics reveals to us the imbalance of value, the way in which we assess human life, and the way we interpret what is most satisfying.

When we contemplate the Trinity in light of economics, we can shed light on some of the apparent negative aspects and reinforce the positives. The Trinity is timeless and can teach us to organize for the eternal, not the temporal.

Though much of what I've mentioned may sound idealistic, it's not meant to appear out of reach. If believers across the globe simply began thinking in Trinitarian ways on small levels, incremental changes would appear in every facet of culture. We all have jobs, don't we? Think of how simple shifts in paradigms could infiltrate where you have influence. The aim of contemplating, emulating, and applying the unity we find in the Trinity's organization allows us a goldmine of inspiration that never runs dry. Even within a fallen reality where sin has complicated everything, the Trinity can appear in even the smallest of ways to show how beautiful simplicity can be.

PART VI
S: HOW GOD TEACHES AND EXPECTS US TO LEARN

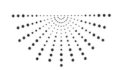

SCRIPTURE

24

HERMENUETICS

WHAT IS HERMENEUTICS?

W e have now considered how the Trinity is united in how he relates, how he does things, and in how he orders life. We now turn to consider how the Trinity teaches us, and how he desires us to learn. The way the Lord instructs us and speaks to us is through Savior, symbol, and script. At the center of all three is what is known as the Typology of Christ and the Gospel of the Kingdom.

Before unpacking these five items, it is important that we first discuss a concept known as hermeneutics. This enormous word refers to the correct way of interpreting something. In collegiate circles, this science is usually restricted to the methodology of studying the Bible. Tragically, we overlook how God speaks through a variety of other ways, and in turn, we often fail to apply proper interpretive methods to how we hear him shouting through the man Jesus and the whole of creation.

INTERPRETING THE SCRIPT

We must begin with what is most familiar. Let's start talking about how to rightly interpret the Word of God. Believe it or not, there is a correct way and an incorrect way to approach Scripture, and many have been taught incorrectly or not taught at all. To get us started, let me include a brief look at a hermeneutical approach to Scripture that is simple:

> I heard a Professor in college once say that most Christians are struggling deeply with their faith because they believe in a "(c)anon within a Canon." He made this statement while teaching the history behind how we received the 66-books in our Canon (or standard) of the Bible. What he meant in this statement is that most Christians are like flower pickers when it comes to biblical interpretation. Most people cherry pick verses from the Scriptures in whatever manner they like and assemble the truths (apart from their context) into beautiful worldview bouquets that fit their taste. Unfortunately, this causes major parts of the Bible to be completely ignored.

> There is a proper way to approach the Bible. When I was in college I took whole classes in major systems and approaches to Biblical Study. The main areas of study that are generally explored are Biblical Theology, Systematics, and Christian Theology. Rather than try and rehash what all of these mean in detail for you, let's keep our look simple. Let's boil these huge areas of study down to this simple process: The LOOK, The HOOK, and The TOOK. **Biblical Theology LOOKS into and across Scripture.** Our posture toward any text should be to first ground the text in the context of the author's intentions and then to square the central meaning in relationship to the whole Covenant thread of Scripture. If we do our due diligence of understanding an author's intended *one meaning*, we can then do our Systematics. **Systematics assesses the "Big Ideas" or the HOOKs that a text highlights or emphasizes**. If we don't first LOOK into the original setting and context of the author, we'll arrive at the wrong BIG IDEA, or we'll inadvertently insert or devise our own, and we will fail to apply Scripture correctly.

> If we look into Scripture first, we can then look across Scripture and out into culture with the correct meaning and principle from the Bible. This is Systematics. In our approach, not only do we now have the ability to identify the hinge points and main ideas that the Scripture sets for itself, we can then assess the pressure points of the culture that are similar to that of the Bible's writings and apply truth in a variety of ways effectively.

> **Lastly, the TOOK is our Christian apologetic**. We must seek to apply the truth, answer current objections, and redeem certain societal norms with the correct interpretation of Scripture. This step attempts to apply the living and active word of God in timeless ways to countless situations. This results in

God's word working redemption in and through people no matter what their circumstance or culture.

These catch words are borrowed loosely from Andy Stanley's view of preaching and teaching, but Pastor Stanley would order these things in a different way than I. His suggested order in proper study is to first find the HOOK, then the LOOK, then the TOOK. He and many others can tend to put the systematic, or "Big Ideas" in front of the Biblical study. This is a typical topical approach. This approach is popular because it allows us to first assess our time and culture based on what we think are the priorities and needed points of discussion. This can give all of us a sense of certainty and control. However, all of us have a tendency to come to Scripture with our own presuppositions about what the needs and "Big Ideas" should be, and if we're not careful to study first, we can create a system of major emphasis points that totally misses Scripture's strongest aims. We run the risk if we mess up our Biblical hermeneutics, of identifying points in which we relate to most and completely overlooking others.[1]

We must not be cherry pickers. We must not make the mistake of reading the Bible unlike we read any other book by divorcing individual passages from the logic of the author or from the overall point the writer or passage makes within the whole of the book. Most Christians have been taught to read the Bible and pick out verses to their liking and divorcing them from the whole storyline of Scripture. Cherry picking theology leads to the formation of a "hole-filled" worldview, not a holy one.

We also must not put our story at the center of God's story. We must not make the assumption that every passage has multiple meanings, thus freeing us to make any application we want. Assuming a passage has multiple meanings is an enormous no-no. Yet I see Christians doing it all the time, especially in my work as a Professor. People confuse meaning with principle. The two terms are quite different. The author always has one intended meaning within the words he is writing, and we must find out what he meant, and how the audience would have originally understood it. Once the meaning is found, limitless principles begin to billow forth.

To illustrate this, let's take a very commonly misused passage which we highlighted previously: "Where two or three are gathered, I am there in their midst" (Mt. 18:20). Many people completely overlook the context of this verse, which pictures Jesus talking about dealing with conflict in the church.

Jesus is emphasizing the Spirit's concentrated presence as our mediator in situations of conflict, sin, rebuke, and church discipline. Many have applied this verse to worship and a variety of other things, but we've missed something crucial. This verse encourages us to press into conflict and confrontation, not shy away from it. It encourages us not to sit back and be comfortable in God's presence but to embrace discomfort, suffering, struggle, and moments of extreme conflict, because we know that the Spirit will bring comfort in the midst of it. In misinterpreting this verse, we've become a shallow and insecure church that shies away from calling each other into question, and we've retreated in cowardly tolerance.

The author's intended meaning now gives us a context. It's for the church. It's for discipline. It's a promise for divine help during conflict and dealing faithfully with those caught in dark and disobedient sin. We shrink back from conflict because we fear. Into this fear God says, "fear not, I am with you."

The principles residing in the passage now can bubble to the surface and extend far beyond what we might originally have thought. We can now think through all the areas of conflict in our marriage, our jobs, our churches, our world, and beyond, and we have assurance of help when we press forward. Prayer equips us to go to war. It's our bazooka. Because we are spirit-filled believers, we carry the church wherever we go, and we are linked to the church as the people of God. We're not alone in any suffering, and the church together has an intense privilege of bringing justice and freedom into situations that lack any sense of them.

We must strive for the correct interpretation so that we can apply God's truth with all the power intended. Unfortunately, I see many being robbed of interpretive power. I see students coming in all the time filled up with what their pastor says and what they have concluded in their private devotionals. And yet as I dig into their theology, I find that Jesus doesn't even fit into many of their ideas.

Worse yet, I have some friends in underground China in the persecuted church who told me that they have experienced remarkable unity in their country when all they had was the Bible. But when Americans began sending them books, disunity ran rampant. Why did unity grow complicated when all the different perspectives entered? It's because most writings today are trying to teach you and me *what* to think. People pick their verses and their pet peeves and build whole worlds around them that are incomplete; whereas

God's manner of education lies more along the lines of teaching us *how* to think.

We don't need more books about one person's pet perspective on self-help, twelve steps to success, or even a book about your "best self." If blessing and suffering are viewed through a self-help, prosperity, and void-of-suffering viewpoint, the life and death of Christ absolutely make no sense; nor does the ministry of Paul and all the early followers of Jesus. Proper interpretation doesn't drill down into your own original idea, which results in complicating who Jesus was and is. Sound hermeneutics teaches you and me to harvest from Scripture the intended thoughts and the actual character of the Trinity.

God transmitted his one message through every passage of Scripture via a real author, to a real audience, in an actual context, and through a real genre. In fact, the whole storyline of Scripture was written by over forty authors, hailing from a host of vocations and professions (i.e., farmers, kings, shepherds, tax collectors, lawyers, historians, scribes, political officials, fisherman, etc.) over a period of 1600 years. It is filled with historical narrative/epic,[2] law,[3] wisdom,[4] psalms,[5] prophecy,[6] apocalyptic literature,[7] epistles,[8] and various literary forms and figures of speech.[9] Amidst all its variety, the whole of the storyline tells one unified story, and each text maintains one intended meaning. Yes, you heard me say it again—one intended meaning. I must emphasize it. We have the joy of taking any text of Scripture, dissecting it, and discovering all its intent in order to arrive at its one, big idea. We can then take the one timeless meaning and blow it up into a million timely principles that can transform people, places, and things, in any space.

The Bible is a book like no other. It's filled with every facet one would expect of the bestselling piece of literature of all time. Not only is it *Time Magazine's* all-time best seller, it's also proven to be the most factual and historically accurate document in existence. We now have almost 30,000 historical manuscript copies of the Bible, which dwarfs the closest runner up in the race for preserved relics, which is Homer's *Iliad* with 650 copies. We can accurately document the time periods of these manuscript copies, placing some of them only a few decades from the time of the original writings—giving the Bible manuscript copies far closer to the originals than any other ancient writing. With thousands of manuscript copies to compare, scholars have determined that only about forty words in the entire Bible are in question. These words are mostly mere connective tissue like "and," "the," and words that have no effect on the author's intended meaning.

Add in the fact that in the early years of the Bible's compiling process, so many atheists quoted the Scriptures trying to disprove them that we can reconstruct the Bible, in total, and word for word from the works of those who didn't even believe it.

Thank you, atheists, for preserving the Christian faith with such accuracy!

To top it off, the Bible itself makes audacious claims about itself. It claims to be the verbally inspired Word of God, the final authority for faith and life, inerrant in the original writings, infallible, and God-breathed.[10]

My, oh my. That's a mouthful!

Suffice it to say, it is absolutely the duty of every believer, every literary and historical scholar, every atheist, and every person of any worldview to learn to read Scripture. We must uncover its timeless meaning and come up with answers as to why this book claims to be divine. We can and should plumb the Bible's depths by digging into its context and the author's purpose —utilizing literary devices, textual criticism, and literary and historical analysis while coming away with the proper hook within the text for proper application to our current audience, congregation, or culture. Yet despite taking such care, we can still miss point. Critique and proper interpretation of Scripture are not enough. Stopping at the point of interpretation leaves something bigger on the table. We have to read Scripture through the lens of worship. Who does Scripture exalt? Who does Scripture make much of? Who does Scripture minimize? To whom does Scripture point? To whom does Scripture point away from? To read Scripture rightly requires one last step that can only be learned at the feet and under the precision of a master. And no one teaches us to read the Bible correctly quite like Jesus.

INTERPRETING SAVIOR & TYPOLOGY

In Luke 24:27 we are given an interesting glimpse into Jesus' perspective on how to correctly and hermeneutically interpret the Holy Scriptures. Before giving you a bite of a seriously juicy meal of truth, let me paint a picture of the upcoming scene in Luke so you can understand the state of mind of the disciples.

Jesus had just been crucified. His horrific death had left all of his disciples and friends sick to their stomachs, disillusioned, and afraid for their lives. Before they got Jesus' body off the cross, wrapped in linens, scented with burial preparations, and lain in a tomb, all those who had been associated with him ran into hiding. Every believer shrunk in cowardice after his death because they thought they'd believed a lie. Worse yet, they thought they too would be crucified if people found out that they bought into the audacious hoax that Jesus was the Messiah.

Not only did they believe Jesus to be the Messiah, but they believed him to be the wrong kind of Messiah. They thought that he would be a ruling political king. His death absolutely made no sense to them. Their perverted take on Christ being an earthly king was actually a quite commonly held view amongst Jesus' followers. We see it in the response of Peter in Matthew 16. When Jesus asked Peter, "Who do you say that I am?" Peter replied, "You are the Christ." Jesus affirms Peter's response and says, "You couldn't know that unless the Holy Spirit told you." What a joyful moment! Peter got the answer right. Or did he?

In the very next set of verses Jesus launches into a speech about his coming death and crucifixion. He begins describing what kind of suffering King and Messiah he is to be. Peter gets feisty with Jesus. His face turns red with rage, and he rebukes Jesus. He rebukes Jesus! The gall!! Peter says to him, "There's no way you're going to suffer and die." Peter's misinterpretation of the nature of Jesus' kingship comes literally face-to-face with truth, and he's found wanting. Because Peter expected a ruling and reigning king, he could not comprehend a king that would be humiliatingly crucified and murdered. Jesus' response to Peter is equally abrupt. He says to Peter, "Get behind me, Satan!"

The underlying current is that Peter had filled the words Christ and Messiah with a caricature of a ruling and reigning earthly king. A wrong interpretation. And where did he develop his viewpoint? The Scriptures. He developed a Satanic view from the very Word of God. Jesus clearly points out to Peter that his interpretation of Scripture is one of Satanic origin. Peter had developed a way of seeing God from God's very own Word that was not only incorrect but was filled with the intentions of evil. He wanted the Messiah to be a political king that would give Peter the right-hand seat to the west of his throne. Peter couldn't fathom a suffering servant nailed to a cross.

With the above backdrop in place, let's fast-forward to the moments after Jesus' resurrection. A similar scene to that of Peter's encounter involves two other disciples. Here is how it unfolds in Luke 24:

That very day two of them were going to a village named Emmaus, about seven miles from Jerusalem, and they were talking with each other about all these things that had happened. While they were talking and discussing together, Jesus himself drew near and went with them. But their eyes were kept from recognizing him. And he said to them, "What is this conversation that you are holding with each other as you walk?" And they stood still, looking sad. Then one of them, named Cleopas, answered him, "Are you the only visitor to Jerusalem who does not know the things that have happened there in these days?" And he said to them, "What things?" And they said to him, "Concerning Jesus of Nazareth, a man who was a prophet mighty in deed and word before God and all the people, and how our chief priests and rulers delivered him up to be condemned to death, and crucified him. But we had hoped that he was the one to redeem Israel. Yes, and besides all this, it is now the third day since these things happened. Moreover, some women of our company amazed us. They were at the tomb early in the morning, and when they did not find his body, they came back saying that they had even seen a vision of angels, who said that he was alive. Some of those who were with us went to the tomb and found it just as the women had said, but him they did not see." And he said to them, "O foolish ones, and slow of heart to believe all that the prophets have spoken! Was it not necessary that the Christ should suffer these things and enter into his glory?" *And beginning with Moses and all the Prophets, he interpreted to them in all the Scriptures the things concerning himself.* (italics mine)

This passage serves as a crowning exclamation point in the tragic comedy of wrongful interpretation. The disciples had so expected Jesus to be a political king that when he was killed, they absolutely thought it was the end. When Jesus appears to two of them on the road to Emmaus after he's resurrected, not only do they not recognize him, but they still don't understand. In fact, they are so blind to who Jesus is, that the text goes on to say that it's only when they return home for dinner, and Jesus breaks bread to give to them that their "eyes open, and they recognize him" (Lk. 24:31).

Lost in continual disillusionment resulting from their inappropriate reading of Scripture, Jesus addresses their faulty handling of God's Word in Luke 24:27. The text says, "And beginning with Moses and all the Prophets, he interpreted to them in all the Scriptures the things concerning himself." The thing that the disciples had missed in all their study is that every verse, character, story, and symbol in Scripture was and is ultimately about Jesus.

The God-man. The suffering servant. The crowned King of heaven. Theologians call it *typology*.

What typology means is that when we read the story of how Joseph's family sells him into slavery for twenty pieces of silver, resulting in his descent into prison, which is then followed by his miraculous rise to the right hand of Pharaoh, through which he saves the land from famine and ends up feeding and forgiving his very brothers that betrayed him in the first place, we are supposed to picture Judas' hand full of money after betraying Jesus. We're supposed to understand Jesus descent into the belly of hell, his preaching victory over the realm of the demons,[11] and his miraculous resurrection and ascension back into the right hand of his Father in heaven, whereby he now stands as the Bread of Life and High Priestly Lamb who was slain—feeding and forgiving all of us whose sin killed him.

When we read the story of Jonah, we're supposed to understand Jonah's three-day trial in the belly of the whale as a type or shadow of Jesus' three days in the dark slime of hell.[12] When we read John's gospel and see how he structures his book around seven specific miracles and seven "I Am" sayings that allude specifically to the ministry of Elisha, we're supposed to understand that John is intentionally connecting John the Baptist's ministry with Elijah and Jesus' ministry with the works of Elisha.

When we read Paul's account calling Jesus the "last Adam" and the "second man," we're supposed to understand the full account in Genesis as being about Jesus' redemption story. When the promise is made to Eve that a seed would come from her that would crush the serpent's head,[13] it helps us make sense of other types that comes later, such as in Judges 4:21 where Jael plunges a stake through the evil Sisera's skull. Ultimately, both of these stories provide types of a reality that is to come, helping us make sense of why the good news of Jesus' victory is spoken of in Luke 10:19 as "treading on the serpent's head."

Jesus might applaud the great Charles Haddon Spurgeon who said about proper teaching, "Deal with the text and then make a beeline for the cross." Jesus' approach to Scripture is identical to Spurgeon's. Jesus views every story of Scripture and every nuance of prophecy as pointing to himself. Every character, place, thing, storyline, and symbol from all the Old Testament serves as but a shadow of the real thing. This is Jesus' thinking. Each type, or what some have called the *hyperlinks* in Scripture, when clicked on, opens up to one webpage. Jesus.

The New Testament presents prophecy in a Christological manner. The majority of references in the New Testament concerning prophecy point back to what's been fulfilled, not forward to what still is to come. New Testament authors view prophecy and the whole of the Old Testament as one giant hyperlink that when clicked, displays their ultimate fulfillment in Christ the man. The rock on which the apostles and prophets stand is Jesus himself—the cornerstone.

Listen to Paul's response to the early church congregations as they were swirling around in incorrect interpretations, false teaching, personality worship, and an oblivion of miracle seeking, sin validating, prideful knowledge, power hunger, cultural syncretizing, and demonically misguided perversions of God's pure intentions:

> When I came to you, I did not come with eloquence or human wisdom as I proclaimed to you the testimony about God. *For I resolved to know nothing while I was with you except Jesus Christ and him crucified.* I came to you in weakness with great fear and trembling. My message and my preaching were not with wise and persuasive words, *but with a demonstration of the Spirit's power so that your faith might not rest on human wisdom, but on God's power.* (italics mine)

Amidst the spinning hurricane of perspectives—an almost postmodern frenzy—Paul identifies the source of confusion. He tells the people that all their invented logic, reasoning, and philosophy had fallen short of the goal of correct theology. Paul brings it all back to Jesus. He equates the simplicity of Jesus's death with the source of power. He implies that any message or interpretation, particularly concerning the Word of God, that doesn't come back to the glory of Christ in his death and resurrection, is void of any power.

INTERPRETING SYMBOL WITH SCRIPT

Not only does Jesus assert that the **Script** of Scripture is about him, our **Savior**, John also makes a correlation between the word spoken (*logos*), and the word embodied in Jesus and his creation. **Symbol.** John 1:1-3 says, "In the beginning was the Word, and the Word was with God, and the Word was God. He was in the beginning with God. All things were made through him, and without him was not anything made that was made." John says that truth is a person. He asserts that Jesus' person and his spoken Word are the source from which all created things originate. If we take John's reasoning to its logical conclusion, we must now assert two things: One, Jesus' being becomes the foundation for all correct biblical interpretation. Two, Jesus' truth, way, and life is written somehow on every facet of all that he's created. In essence, the whole of the created universe reveals to us what is in the mind of God. It's God's thoughts on display.

Let's first address number one. If Jesus is the perfect representation of the Father and is the embodiment of what the Christian experience is to be like, then all our thoughts about God must form in a way that can include Jesus. For example, the prosperity gospel no longer includes Jesus. Jesus was poor, homeless, and persecuted most of his life, and so those that promise only health and wealth exclude Jesus. He simply doesn't fit.

Others with a perverted sense of truth try to heal, deliver, bind, and command the demonic influences that plague people to be gone. Sadder still, other Christians avoid praying for healing and deliverance altogether and overlook where the supernatural nature of God's kingdom is now intersecting with our earthly realm. Either view excludes Jesus. There are moments where Jesus affirms his sovereignty in willing human suffering and sickness to continue unto his glory, and there are moments where Jesus heals and delivers people immediately. Also unto his glory. There are moments where Jesus commands spirits to leave, and they obey, and there are moments—like on the cross, for example—where Jesus, in complete control, allows the full weight of the demonic to wash over him, crush him, and kill him, all for the joy set before him. Again, that he may be glorified.

Think of all the glory that Jesus would have lost and all the satisfaction we would have forfeited if Jesus had willingly fit nicely into our tight little black-and-white theologies on suffering. We must consider Scripture's description of Christ the man and Christ's use of the Scripture as we seek to theologize on and live out God's truth and character rightly.

None of our black-and-white thinking includes Jesus. If he's God, and his nature is the perfect mold for what we are to be molded into, our most important question should be not "What would Jesus do," but "What is Jesus like?"

Two, God's creation is his mind on display. This means that every hill, ocean, star, and critter say something about him. Maybe it's in how the lion speaks of God's kingship as the Lion of Judah, or how the lamb tells of his gentle sacrifice as the Lamb who was slain. Maybe it's how the mountain tells of the heights of his righteousness in the Psalms, the ocean tide tells of his justice, or the unreachable watery depths allude to the extent of his love. Not only do inanimate things and animals point to Jesus, but so do circumstances, visions, dreams, and ultimately his church body. Everything is like a hyperlink. It all points to the truth and life of Jesus the man. The bigness and awe we sense in all of creation are rightly understood not through a naturalist's invention, a Buddhist's mantra, or even through a scientific text. God's Word tells us exactly how to interpret all we see correctly.

God's Word is like the Supreme Court. It stands above all the other courts and interprets correctly. All points to him. It exalts him. It's intended to be used to worship him.

Scripture also uses signs and symbols that are interpreted correctly through the lens of Jesus and his Word. For sake of brevity, let's consider two examples: the tree and the dove.

I'll admit, I'm guilty! Guilty of walking by one of the most meaningful objects in all of creation and missing its beauty and artistic significance each and every day. The tree! Have you ever really stopped to ponder the tree? Every tree, branch, leaf, and twist of bark is unique in color, pattern, function, and intrigue. Every tree is a masterpiece—packed with awe. Trees are themselves art, but they also turn pollution into clean air, rubbish into paper for writing and expression, and its most prized rings are turned into things like guitars—which make music beautiful to our ears. We should take a long look at trees and consider just what their art says about the artist!

At the dawn of the universe, God said, "Let the earth sprout vegetation, plants yielding seed, and fruit trees on the earth bearing fruit after their kind with seed in them"; and it was so" (Gn. 1:11 nasb). All the food of the garden was given for the enjoyment of Adam and Eve, but in particular, two figures of God's garden were made to stand out. Genesis 2:9 tells us that, "In the middle of the garden God placed the tree of life and the tree of the knowledge of good and evil." Forever these two trees serve as images of blessing and judgment. If, like a tree, a man or women are to plant their roots in God, eat from him, and sow seeds of righteousness,[14] they will harvest the fruit and nourishment of the Spirit. Sadly, if a man and women are to plant their roots and pull their provision from the world's ways, their fruit will reflect their polluted water source, and they will die in sin, bearing all of death's curses.

In sowing seed in the Garden, God grew for himself trees of beauty.

However, the seed of rebellion that Adam planted in his disobedience led to isolation from God, and a pending outgrowth of destruction in the world followed. Still remaining, as portrayed in God's artful trees of promise, is a contrast between blessing and judgment. Though mankind forgot its identity in the land of God, God still remembers the land and has planned accordingly to bring man back into it once again. The word for seed used in Genesis 3:15 contains God's promise to bring humanity back into a land containing the Tree of Life;[15] "And I [God] will put enmity between you and the woman, and between your seed and her seed; it shall bruise your head, and you shall bruise his heel." A promised seed (Jesus) is divulged to Adam and Eve—a seed from the woman, which would save man and will crush the head of evil.

Because of humanity's rebellion, cities, civilizations, and nations of evil were birthed. The Old Testament often uses trees as symbols for powerful and evil kingdoms.[16] Trees symbolize power, strength, growth, and protection, and a person is supposed to experience this only in the shadow of God's wings—not in a nation of any kind. As these powers arose, they trampled God's people in the same way sin had done even in the Garden. In Ezekiel 17, God pronounces judgment on the nation of Judah for seeking protection of foreign nations when Babylon marched against Jerusalem. Babylon conquered and deported most of the Judeans, leaving only the poor and weak in the land, unable to do anything but droop and rustle like a willow tree. Ezekiel uses the tree to symbolize this judgment, as later Isaiah uses a stump to illustrate how evil can rise to such a degree that it topples God's people.

Nonetheless, Judah still occupied the Promised Land, though weak and under the foot of a foreign power. God remained faithful. He would again raise his people up, producing boughs of a vine that would sprout and flourish. In Jeremiah, the Lord likens his promise to perform to a quick, timely, and efficient sprouting almond tree.[17]

The image of the tree serves to tell of God's kingdom coming. His kingdom rises quickly, timely, and efficiently, and a new King, like David, would sit enthroned over the world's evil powers. Bob Utley says, "Whereas David's reign was incomplete, Jesus' would be complete in that it would be a present kingdom, where 'with righteousness he shall judge the poor, and decide with equity for the meek of the earth' (Is. 11:4) and a future kingdom where the 'wolf shall dwell with the lamb.' (vs.6). The concept of a 'shoot,' 'stem,' or 'branch' (cf. Is. 11:1) becomes a Messianic symbol of the restoration of the Davidic seed (cf. 1 Sm. 9; Ps. 89). The Branch (cf. Is. 4:2; 11:1;

53:2; Jer. 23:5; 33:15; Zec. 3:8; 6:12; Acts 13:23; Rom. 15:12) becomes the hope of all mankind for God to fulfill His promises to Israel and to the nations!"[18]

If you'll remember, Jesus is portrayed as "the Branch" in Isaiah. In the gospels, Jesus was baptized in the river Jordan before entering his ministry. The heaven's open up and the Spirit like a dove descends upon him. Remind you of anything? Remember the dove in the days of Noah? The dove returned after the flood of God's wrath upon the earth holding an olive branch in its beak, the hope of a new, emerging Promised Land. Similarly, here at Jesus' baptism the Spirit like a dove descends on Jesus. He is the new Promised Land, and this time, the dove does not hold a branch but holds *the* olive Branch that was foretold.

Jesus' ministry began as the Branch and ends with him hanging on a what? A tree![19] Like Noah's ark was made of trees, God built another rescue vessel out of trees—the cross; a tree upon which would bear our King. On a tree, he bore the wrath which we deserved for our rebellion. Trusting in Jesus' payment now grants people access to the kingdom and back into the Garden once again. Revelation 22:14 says, "Blessed are those who wash their robes, so that they may have the right to the tree of life, and may enter ..."

In 2 Samuel 5:22-25, as David prepared to route the Philistines, God asked him to hide behind the balsam trees and go up and fight only upon hearing the sound of the balsam trees rustling. The Lord shared that this sign would be an affirmation to David that God would go before him. The Spirit's rustling also blew like the wind on the disciples at Pentecost to tell them that their wait was over and that the new Kingdom of the Son of David had routed in victory every evil and is now putting it all to death. Every time we see the trees waving their branches in the wind, as worshippers wave their arms in worship, we can find peace in knowing that God is ever-present through his Spirit. He went before us in the past, he walks among us presently, and he is coming in the future.

In the in-between-time of living in the kingdom now and waiting for the kingdom not yet, God likens our journey to that of growth. A man who walks in the counsel of the Lord is like "a tree firmly planted by streams of water, which yields its fruit in its season And its leaf does not wither; And in whatever he does, he prospers."[20] A tree of health and blessing is planted in God and his kingdom, and it is a picture of health and trust.[21] Proverbs 11:30 says the fruit of the righteous is a tree of life, and we are to be rooted and grounded in love.[22] Every good tree bears good fruit and every bad tree bad fruit.[23]

Enough said about the tree. Let's rewind a bit. Go back to my mention of the dove at Jesus' baptism. This is image two.

John baptized this man Jesus, and as he laid his body and head under the water and then raised him up to the light of day, the Spirit of God descended on Jesus like a dove, followed by a voice from Jesus' Father in heaven: "This is my beloved Son, with whom I am well pleased" (Mt. 17:5). This is the epiphany (revealing) of Jesus' ministry.

The image of a dove elicits all kinds of meanings. The "like-a-dove" image of the Spirit descending on Jesus gives us one of the first clear appearances of the revealed Trinity. The dove is used to conjure up all kinds of additive imagery. During the flood of Noah, the dove indicated that it had found exposed land when it from its journey holding an olive branch in its beak. Not only does the branch allude to tree-like imagery, as noted before, but the dove in the Old Testament was the prescribed animal of sacrifice for the poor. The dove foretells the nature of Jesus' ministry; it is defined by his suffering with and for the least of these. He quotes Isaiah 61:1 at the beginning of his ministry: "The Spirit of the Sovereign Lord is on me because the Lord has anointed me to proclaim good news to the poor. He has sent me to bind up the brokenhearted, to proclaim freedom for the captives and release from darkness for the prisoners."

The epiphany of Jesus and his intentions are revealed through the symbols of the dove and the tree. The manner of symbolism can be linked to any of the images in Scripture, not just the dove or the tree. Those who wrote the Scriptures associate rocks and seeds to spiritual images and interpret big symbols in Christ-centric ways as well. For example, John structures the whole of his gospel around the symbol of the temple to emphasize the fact that Jesus is the one that takes away the sins of the world and brings us into the presence of God. Consider this description from Peter J. Leithart:

The entire book (John's Gospel) can be understood as a stroll through the tabernacle. The opening chapter, which introduces the "lamb of God" who comes to take away the sins of the world, brings us to the bronze altar for sacrifice. Chapters 2–4, with their focus on water, are at the laver. Chapters 4–7 center on the feeding of the five thousand, in which Jesus distributes the bread of the presence from the golden table. In chapters 8–13, John lingers at the lampstand, musing on Jesus as the light, and the Upper Room Discourse, especially chapter 17, displays Jesus as the intercessory priest, raising his hands before the golden altar. John is at pains to show us that the empty tomb is the new Holy of Holies. The slab on which Jesus body no longer lays is flanked by angels, like the ark, and Peter, like a high priest, is the first to enter. On this scheme, the theme of light in John 9, already associated with creation and the Feast of Tabernacles, is given a fresh dimension, linked with the golden light, the lamp on the lampstand that is the disciple (cf. Mt. 5).

THE CONFUSING QUESTION

Thinking upon how God speaks through the Savior, script, symbol and type bring us to an obvious question. How do we "hear" God's voice? It would seem that we've opened Pandora's box by claiming that everything has some form of speaking power. If we're not careful we could wind up seeking God's voice much like a psychic does, listening only to fleshly impulses and intuition; or like a spiritist philosopher following only vision; or a pantheist or panentheist listening only to the voice of creation; or an atheist or agnostic chalking Jesus up to be just another liar, legend, or lunatic, or even like a dried-up theologian using the Bible as some parched study tool. There are so many people out there looking for God's will and trying to "hear" him, and their claims can be confusing when everything we see, smell, hear, touch or taste can speak of God's glory. How are we to take action or believe rightly in the midst of multiple circumstances, doors opening and closing, feelings of peace accompanied by hesitancy, dry and wet fleeces, and a number of the other standards that people often use to measure whether they're "in the center of God's will."

I won't claim to have all the answers, but I believe there are three crucial principles we must utilize in making decisions and hearing God's voice: **order, emphasis, and body**.

The Scripture is very clear that order is important. Jesus models for us that his personhood as Savior comes first in our interpretation. That's what we mean by order: Jesus first. His revealed character is first in the order of standards for interpretation. If Jesus and his teachings don't fit our decision, dream, or incantation, then it's probably not the right voice or the right direction. Mormons and Jehovah's Witnesses pride themselves on how their incantations and visions supersede Scripture in their order, and they have fallen into false teaching as a result. Many in highly mystical streams of Catholicism and charismatic traditions follow the same manner of believing. Order is important in hearing God's voice, and the man Jesus, and his scripted Word supersede and precede all our devices.

Not only have cults formed and fallen in forgetting Jesus' way of interpreting Scripture, I know many people in my Christian sphere who believe they hear God's voice solely through word picture, vision, and impulse. When making a decision they don't seek God in his Word; they seek him in meditation, mindfulness, philosophy, logic, impressions, feelings, and systems of thought. Without realizing it, they search for truth within themselves. They undervalue what Scripture says about the corruptness of our desires, our flesh, and our sin, and they follow what they see, feel, and intuit. They forget the truth that what we find at the end of our rope is more hopeless imperfection. The road toward "one's best self" leads to a mirage. Our best self is a sinful traitor at best. A traitor in need of a Savior.

Where my Christian brothers and sisters fall, is that they make the mistake of prioritizing their vision's voice even over Jesus and the Scripture. They will call it the voice of the Spirit, but it is really their own voice, and it inevitably overrides their reading of Scripture. They become "overstanders" rather than understanders. An overstander interprets Jesus and Scripture through the authority of their own biases, experiences, and held beliefs, whereas one seeking true understanding submits their biases and preconceived ideas of reality to Jesus for correct interpretation. If left to follow our impressions long enough, people begin to reshape the Bible around the truths they feel are correct—to the exclusion of what they may not like. They can call what they're following the Holy Spirit, but when it voids the Word of God, it's a different spirit.

If we're not careful, we stand over Scripture as an authority and interpret everything in it through our faulty judgments. This mentality has spawned most of what we now know as modern philosophy. Philosophy thrives on speculating beyond the bounds. What results from an imagination unbridled is some pretty wonky thinking that is void of any truth. It's simply not helpful.

To stand under Scripture as an authority is altogether different. It brings understanding because it provides properly helpful boundaries. Boundaries define limits and provide meaning. The boundary lines on a soccer field actually preserve the freedom of the game. If the lines are removed, the game descends into anarchy. It's the same with Bible interpretation. When we allow

God to set the boundaries of reality, he does so rightly and theologically. The boundaries are defined by his nature, and within that wide field, enormous philosophical freedom is possible. It's not that God disallows philosophy; it's that theology must come first. Theology leads and instructs our dreaming, not vice versa.

When our visions, predilections, feelings, intuitions, and devices, contradict Scripture, we are to change. The Bible calls it transformation. I've met a lot of people who've read the Bible for years and have never transformed, and what this tells me is that somewhere in their theology they are still assuming authority over Scripture rather than allowing Scripture to take the lead over them.

Let me give a quick example of the horrendous mess that a wrong order of hearing can cause before I offer two more helpful cautions. There was one point in my life where I was experiencing a tremendous amount of trial, suffering, and persecution as a pastor of a church. Still being very young in my faith, I gathered friends together to pray with me for a way out. I received what I thought to be a vision. The vision seemed to imply that God was wanting me to move on from the situation. Of course, in the circumstances, I also failed to pay any attention to what Scripture says about faithfulness, steadfastness, and the place of suffering and trial in my growth and maturing process as a believer. I just wanted the pain to stop.

My theology determined my biography. I viewed trial and suffering as something to be avoided, whereas Scripture and Jesus clearly model otherwise. So I fled. My life followed suit from there with a string of incorrect decisions, and an anemic way of hearing God's voice followed. To this day I look back on that moment as a very instructive mistake. It brought about almost ten years of what I would call wandering in my life. I believe wholeheartedly that I should have remained steadfast and waited to see God work in me and the situation for his glory. I believe it would have resulted in me hearing God's voice in deeper and more transformative ways.

God was gracious during that time and used my failings to bring about fruit. I stand here today with a broader picture of how God speaks as a result.

Let's now talk about emphasis. When we speak of hearing God's voice and following his will, there's not only a correct order of hearing that's helpful, but Scripture also has a way of accenting what God's will actually is.

If you do an exhaustive study of God's will, purposes, plans, and promises in Scripture, you'll arrive at two conclusions. First, Scripture is remarkably consistent in how it speaks of the Father's will, plans, and purposes as having already been realized in Jesus. The Bible speaks of God's will and final say in things as a matter resolved, not one that lies still in uncertainty. Many of us treat God's will as something that is out there in the never-sphere waiting to be discovered like the object of a giant treasure hunt. This way of thinking may seem mystical and fun to us, but it's still wrong.

Most of the Scriptures on God's will refer to what we're becoming, not where we're going. Most people seeking God's will in their decisions are waiting for an answer to the proverbial "What do I do next?" when the Scripture makes it very clear that determining what comes next is God's job. God simply says to seek his kingdom and righteousness first and he will add everything else. God's kingdom is defined by who we are to be. When we start playing around in the future or past of things, God says, "That's not your job." By taking on that job, we take our eyes off what is our job. Our character. Jesus tells us to leave the future up to him, and Paul tells us to count the things of the past as lost and rubbish for the sake of knowing Christ. Christian transformation happens in the present and in the presence of Christ.

In your situation, God is going to speak, and when he does, he's going to speak less about the 'something new' and more in terms of reminding you of what you already know to be true. God is not going to rescue you **out of things** so much as he's going to help you **through things**. Yes, admittedly, there's a place in Scripture for both, but we must remember that Scripture's priority is on making us into the image of Christ presently. Being in the present requires trust that God has sealed up the past and future in Christ.

Order and emphasis are important to biblical interpretation, but the Body of Christ plays a final role. There's a curious passage that lies between the time that Jesus ascends to heaven and the Holy Spirit comes to earth. In Acts 2:12-26 we're told that the believers are together in prayer seeking God's will as they find a replacement apostle for Judas. Judas had committed suicide, and therefore a twelfth apostle who was an eye-witness to Jesus' life, death, resurrection, and ascension was needed to integrally preserve the message as it spread throughout Jerusalem, Judea, Samaria, and to the ends of the earth. As the community met, they sought the Lord as to whether Joseph called Barsabbas or Matthias was to be the elect. To make the final decision, they performed a curious mystical practice. They threw dice. The dice landed on Matthias.

God spoke through dice. He spoke in chance. He speaks in all things created, but notice how the mystical was kept accountable to truth. The people met together. God guides and instructs us most wisely in the presence of his Body.

I must speculate that most of you reading this book right now do not consider the family of God to be important in your individual or family decisions. God's body is crucial to you hearing the voice of God amidst all the messages that are flooding your ears through Savior, script, symbol, and circumstance. You must remember that Jesus is portrayed as walking amongst the lampstands in Revelation, which symbolizes his people as they gather together. Amongst his people is where Jesus is. It's where his spirit is (the mind of Christ). It makes sense that with his people is where we hear, see, and sense him most vividly.

It would be crazy for us not to consider order, emphasis, and community as we hear, interpret, and follow God's will rightly.

It All Speaks of Kingdom

One thing remains in learning to hear how God teaches us. Not only does God reveal himself to us in the God-man Jesus, or even as his shadow infuses every person, place, and thing of biblical history and creation. God weaves together the entire storyline through the lens of the kingdom. Jesus refers to the whole plot of his life and ministry as the gospel of the kingdom.[24]

What is the kingdom of God? Is it what Mcknight calls the "skinny jeans" kingdom—meaning that kingdom is any good deed done by good people (Christian or not) in the public sector for the common good?[25] Or is it the "pleated pants" folks who reduce the kingdom to redemptive moments, which are sometimes seen in the inner heart, in healings of all sorts, and also in the public sector? Is the kingdom like that of Essenes (one of withdrawal), the Zealots (anarchy), the Sadducees (moral and political), or the Pharisees (religious law)? Is God's kingdom restricted to the purely sacred or secular realm, or does it saturate any realm where Christ's lordship is governing and ruling?

On one hand, Jesus says his kingdom is not of this world,[26] and on the other he tells a story in which it fills all things. John seemed to think that the kingdom was at hand when Jesus was "made flesh and dwelt among us."

So what is the answer?

Maybe we should begin tackling this enormous subject for our brief purposes here by looking at how Scripture references the kingdom:

KINGDOM VERSES: Ex. 19:1-6
DESCRIPTION: God promises Moses and Israel that they are going to be a holy nation of priests. He makes a covenant with them.
KINGDOM PRINCIPLE: *GOD'S KINGDOM IS A BELIEVING PEOPLE, NOT A PLACE.*

KINGDOM VERSES: I Sm. 15:28; 28:17; Ps. 103:19; Dn. 4:17
DESCRIPTION: God allows kingdoms to form amidst mankind in the world, and he also takes them away. His throne and rule are sovereign within, over, and through evil constructs.
KINGDOM PRINCIPLE: *GOD'S KINGDOM ADVANCES SOVEREIGNLY THROUGH KINGDOMS SET UP ON EARTH.*

KINGDOM VERSES: Ps. 145:13; Is. 37:16
DESCRIPTION: The kingdom is spoken about as an everlasting kingdom and a dominion that Christ holds through all generations. He's faithful to all he's made.
KINGDOM PRINCIPLE: *GOD'S KINGDOM IS BEFORE US AND AFTER US. IT'S BOTH NOW AND IN CONTINUANCE.*

KINGDOM VERSES: Is. 9:7; 60; Dn. 2:44
DESCRIPTION: These verses speak of Christ physically reigning from David's throne.
KINGDOM PRINCIPLE: *GOD'S KINGDOM IS FULFILLED IN JESUS RULING ON HIS THRONE—ONE WHO IS DESCENDED FROM DAVID AND WHO IS FULLY GOD AND FULLY MAN.*

KINGDOM VERSES: Jer. 18:7, 9
DESCRIPTION: God's kingdom builds, plants, uproots, and destroys.
KINGDOM PRINCIPLE: *EVERY ACT ON EARTH HAS SOMETHING TO DO WITH A KINGDOM. GOD'S KINGDOM OR OURS.*

KINGDOM VERSES: Dn. 7:18, 27
DESCRIPTION: Saints possess the kingdom forever and receive it from God.
KINGDOM PRINCIPLE: *GOD'S KINGDOM IS A GIFT TO US, AND IT BEGINS THE MOMENT OF SALVATION.*

KINGDOM VERSE: Mt. 3:2
DESCRIPTION: The kingdom's call is to repentance.
KINGDOM PRINCIPLE: *GOD'S KINGDOM REQUIRES A CHANGE OF MIND AND A TURNING FROM SIN. SIN IS THE HALLMARK OF SATAN'S KINGDOM. SPIRIT IS THE HALLMARK OF CHRIST'S KINGDOM.*

KINGDOM VERSES: Mt. 4:23; 12:28
DESCRIPTION: Jesus brought the kingdom with him, and healings and deliverances resulted—both physically and spiritually.
KINGDOM PRINCIPLE: *GOD'S KINGDOM IS ADVANCING IN OUR LIFE IN ANY HEALING, DELIVERANCE, PROVISION, AND REALIZATION OF HIS PROMISES, PROVISION, AND PROTECTION.*

KINGDOM VERSES: Mt. 5:3-10, 19; 11:11
DESCRIPTION: Beatitudes teach us that there's a different form of greatness in the kingdom of God.
KINGDOM PRINCIPLE: *GOD'S KINGDOM IS EVIDENT IN DIFFERENT CHARACTER AND PRIORITIES IN THIS LIFE. KINGDOM IS EVIDENCED IN*

HAVING A HEART THAT BREAKS, CARES FOR, AND LOVES THE THINGS GOD DOES IN THE WAYS GOD LOVES THEM.

KINGDOM VERSES: Mt. 6:10, 33; 7:21
DESCRIPTION: His kingdom is to come on earth as it is in heaven. We are to actively seek it first in the here and now, and no one enters except those who do the Father's will.
KINGDOM PRINCIPLE: *GOD'S KINGDOM IS ENACTED ON EARTH AS IT IS IN HEAVEN—NOT THROUGH THE OLD TESTAMENT INTERSECT OF THE TEMPLE, BUT THROUGH THE NEW TEMPLE OF THE HUMAN HEART.*

KINGDOM VERSE: Mt. 8:11
DESCRIPTION: God's kingdom continues to honor the covenant to the patriarchs.
KINGDOM PRINCIPLE: *GOD'S KINGDOM IS STILL A CONTINUANCE AND FULFILLMENT TO THE COVENANT MADE TO ABRAHAM.*

KINGDOM VERSE: Mt. 11:12
DESCRIPTION: Since John the Baptist, the kingdom has been advancing.
KINGDOM PRINCIPLE: *GOD'S KINGDOM APPEARS TO INTENSIFY IN THE MAN JESUS.*

KINGDOM VERSE: Mt. 12:25
DESCRIPTION: The kingdom is unified.
KINGDOM PRINCIPLE: *GOD'S KINGDOM MANIFESTS WHEN WE SEEK UNITY IN THE TRINITY.*

KINGDOM VERSES: Mt. 13:31, 24, 33, 38, 44; 18:3-4
DESCRIPTION: Jesus likens the kingdom to yeast, a mustard seed, a seed sown, a treasure hidden in a field of priceless value, and little children.
KINGDOM PRINCIPLE: *GOD'S KINGDOM IS SIMILAR TO SOMETHING BURIED AND DISCOVERED. IT IS CONNECTED TO THE WORK OF CHRIST, AND THE REBIRTH OF PEOPLE INTO GOD'S FAMILY.*

KINGDOM VERSE: Mt. 13:43
DESCRIPTION: God's kingdom shines like the sun.
KINGDOM PRINCIPLE: *GOD'S KINGDOM IS CHARACTERIZED BY ANYTHING THAT REVEALS TRUTH RATHER THAN CONCEALS IT.*

KINGDOM VERSE: Mt. 16:19
DESCRIPTION: God's kingdom binds and looses.
KINGDOM PRINCIPLE: *THIS VERSE IS SO MISUSED. IT IS GIVEN IN THE CONTEXT OF HOW THE PEOPLE OF GOD ARE TO GOVERN AND DISCIPLINE.*
KINGDOM PRINCIPLE: *GOD'S KINGDOM MANIFESTS IN THE WAY THE FAMILY OF GOD MAKES RIGHT JUDGMENTS AND TRAINS PEOPLE THROUGH REBUKE, ENCOURAGEMENT, AND EXHORTATION.*

KINGDOM VERSE: Mt. 16:28
DESCRIPTION: Jesus is coming in his kingdom.
KINGDOM PRINCIPLE: *GOD'S KINGDOM IS IN PART FULFILLED AT THE RESURRECTION AND ASCENSION, BUT FULLY AT THE SECOND COMING.*

KINGDOM VERSE: Mt. 18:23
DESCRIPTION: The parable of a servant who owed the king.

KINGDOM PRINCIPLE: *GOD'S KINGDOM IS BUILT ON FORGIVENESS AND GRACE, NOT ON THE UNJUST HOLDING OF DEBTS.*

KINGDOM VERSES: Mt. 19:23, 24
DESCRIPTION: The door into the kingdom is narrow. It's hard for a rich man to enter. It's like a camel going through the eye of a needle.
KINGDOM PRINCIPLE: *GOD'S KINGDOM IS BUILT IN AND THROUGH THOSE WHO RECOGNIZE THEIR NEED AND PLACE THEIR TRUST IN HIM.*

KINGDOM VERSE: Mt. 21:43
DESCRIPTION: The fruit of the kingdom.
KINGDOM PRINCIPLE: *GOD'S KINGDOM CAN BE SEEN IN OUR DIFFERENT MANNER OF LIVING.*

KINGDOM VERSES: Mt. 22:1-16; I Cor. 6:9
DESCRIPTION: The kingdom is likened to a wedding banquet thrown for a son.
KINGDOM PRINCIPLE: *GOD'S KINGDOM IS A MEAL TO WHICH ALL ARE INVITED, BUT TO WHICH MANY REFUSE TO COME.*

KINGDOM VERSE: Mt. 25:34
DESCRIPTION: The kingdom is prepared for us.
KINGDOM PRINCIPLE: *GOD'S KINGDOM IS A TEMPLE-PEOPLE IN WHICH WE DWELL TOGETHER "IN CHRIST."*

KINGDOM VERSES: Acts 1:3, 6
DESCRIPTION: Israel thought the kingdom was for them on earth.

KINGDOM PRINCIPLE: *GOD'S KINGDOM RULES ON EARTH BUT NEVER IN THE MANNER THAT WE MIGHT THINK.*

KINGDOM VERSES: Acts 14:22; 28:23
DESCRIPTION: The kingdom comes through hardship and has to be preached.
KINGDOM PRINCIPLE: *ENTRY INTO GOD'S KINGDOM IS GAINED THROUGH TEACHING AND SUFFERING.*

KINGDOM VERSES: Rom. 14:17; 1 Cor. 4:20
DESCRIPTION: The kingdom is not talk. It's power. It's not eating and drinking, but righteousness peace and joy.
KINGDOM PRINCIPLE: *GOD'S KINGDOM IS NOT REACHED IN ADDITION OR SUBTRACTION, BUT IN UNDERSTANDING HOW TO RIGHTLY ENJOY ALL THING FOR HIS PURPOSES.*

KINGDOM VERSES: 1 Cor. 15:20-28; Rv. 16:10
DESCRIPTION: Christ puts all dominion under his feet.
KINGDOM PRINCIPLE: *GOD'S KINGDOM IS RULING AND REIGNING EVEN OVER EVIL.*

KINGDOM VERSE: 1 Cor. 15:50
DESCRIPTION: The kingdom is imperishable.
KINGDOM PRINCIPLE: *GOD'S KINGDOM REQUIRES A NEW BIRTH.*

KINGDOM VERSE: Eph. 2:2

DESCRIPTION: There's a counter-kingdom that pretends to be real but is "of the air."

KINGDOM PRINCIPLE: *GOD'S KINGDOM IS BUILT ON PROMISES, PROVISION, AND PURPOSES THAT ARE TANGIBLE, SATAN'S KINGDOM IS SMOKE AND MIRRORS.*

KINGDOM VERSES: Col. 1:13; 1 Thes. 2:12; 2 Tm. 4:8

DESCRIPTION: God brought us into his kingdom.

KINGDOM PRINCIPLE: *GOD'S KINGDOM IS HIS WORK THROUGH US.*

KINGDOM VERSES: 2 Thes. 1:1-5

DESCRIPTION: The Kingdom is evidenced in persevering and enduring troubles.

KINGDOM PRINCIPLE: *GOD'S KINGDOM IS AN IMPERISHABLE INHERITANCE THAT CAN'T BE LOST. IT'S SECURE.*

KINGDOM VERSE(S): Heb. 1:8; 12:28; 2 Pt. 1:11; Rv. 11:15

DESCRIPTION: The kingdom is eternal, forever, and it lasts.

KINGDOM PRINCIPLE: *GOD'S KINGDOM IS BUILT IN TIMELY WAYS THROUGH TIMELESS PARADIGMS.*

KINGDOM VERSE: Rv. 5:10

DESCRIPTION: A nation of priests fulfills the prophecy.

KINGDOM PRINCIPLE: *GOD'S KINGDOM IS A REDEEMED TEMPLE-PEOPLE-CITY.*

I believe the above verses bring a lot of clarity to how we view the kingdom of God. Many today are falling prey to the belief that the kingdom is the same as the Jews believed it to be—of this world and concentrated in and during an earthly kingdom reign of an earthly Jesus (the Millennium). Scripture seems to emphasize that God's kingdom has always been advancing eternally through believing people that are being built up into a temple kingdom. Furthermore, Jesus is portrayed currently to be seated on a throne in the Holy of Holies, heaven, ruling and reigning as our intermediary sacrificial Lamb.

Today God is living amongst his people as King as he lives inside them. God's trajectory of kingdom from the beginning has been to be a holy God dwelling amidst and within a holy people. Kingdom language in the Scripture seems to spin toward the centerpiece of the human heart. God's kingdom is not built with human hands, but it's fashioned within the very hearts of men whom he awakened with his very breath. Though his reign is ultimately pushing toward days of perfection when he will return to obliterate every evil, wipe every tear, and stop every sickness, his kingdom is on the move in the now and the yet to come. It's on the move in *you*.

The whole storyline of Scripture always seems to hover around what life looks like when lived in allegiance to the King and Kingdom of heaven, as opposed to what existence looks like when lived in allegiance to the kingdoms of this world. The Scripture does not describe a spirituality that is confined to individual quiet times, but it is explosively cultural, political, educational, familial, and overarchingly shaping to every facet of life. God's Lordship is everywhere. He is governing all things even amidst an evil-infested and satanically bound world, and he is doing it through servants who revere him as King.

To bring our discussion on the kingdom to a head, I think there is no better summary than that of Mcknight:

> The kingdom is the people who are redeemed and ruled by King Jesus in such a way that they live as a fellowship under King Jesus. That is, there is a king (Jesus), a rule (by Jesus as Lord), a people (the church), a land (wherever Jesus' kingdom people are present), and a law (following Jesus through the power of the Spirit).[27]

THE BASIC PRINCIPLES FOR LIFE IN THIS KINGDOM

Paul speaks about life within this kingdom of God. He uses the phrase "basic principles" many times in his writings, affirming that the Scriptures are unified in their teachings of the way of the Christian, regardless of time, space, or experience. Like a basketball coach whose fundamentals always include dribble, pass, and shoot, Paul's fundamentals of God's way of life and kingdom are consistent. Any time he mentions division, denomination, personality, biases, false teaching, particular slants on theological issues, and the like, he does so in order to reiterate fruit that comes from conforming to God's timeless truth, and the complications that result from adding or subtracting from them.

I could write a whole book on what these simple matters are, and how the church globally has widely forgotten them and invented a slew of add-ons and subtractions to complicate Jesus. But my purpose here is to make a simple point that I feel brings a mass of teaching together under one, unified principle. The world has failed to follow God's basic principles, and in essence developed one huge one of their own. As with many things before, Martin Luther makes my point better than I could about what basic principles motivate us if we are not living in Christ:

Martin Luther said that "Religion is the default of the human heart." Religion actually means to "bind back." What this means is that we feel like we all hold within ourselves this nagging feeling that we have lost something. We feel we have lost some sense of value, esteem, worth, fame, or piece of ourselves, and because of this, we have to forever try various avenues to try and bind back or work back to where we feel most whole. So we humans begin striving, stressing, worrying, and wandering, trying to scrape about in the darkness. Some of us find our identity in success, others in sex. Some find identity in family or even in ministry. The bottom line is that we are trying to desperately prove to ourselves that we are good people and worthy of something, although there's a nagging feeling in us that tells us somehow that we've lost it, and that we just cannot be good![28]

Our tendency as sinful humans is to divide from each other through religious addition and subtraction. We don't like the simplicity of Jesus being the Way, the Truth, and the Life, and so we exert our differences in ways that makes us feel validated, elevated, or better than others. Competitive assessment, coveting, one-upmanship, mandating preferences, eating habits, dress, and anything manifest outwardly is all mere religion. Striving to "get back to our best self" via the Enneagram, self-help, and countless other tools is religion. Achieving wealth for money's sake is religion. God's way is to build unity in diversity—a unity that goes much beyond what we usually dream up in uniformity. God's way is not to have us bind back to something we've lost, but rather to admit we've lost it. He allows his work to reach down and pull us up. That's the gospel.

God's basic principles root themselves in the gospel. The gospel is the good news telling us that we can't live the perfect Christian life, and so Jesus lived it for us and now lives it out in us. The basic principles of faith are altogether different from those of religion. Whereas the world is bound in stress, worry, anxiety, fear, confusion, misplaced identity, addiction, etc., Jesus' followers are to be defined by rest, peace, love, joy, and patience. All who don't know the truth of Jesus' perfect work are living under what Paul calls "elemental spirits" in Colossians 2:8: "See to it that no one takes you captive by philosophy and empty deceit, according to human tradition, according to the elemental spirits of the world, and not according to Christ."

The kingdom of the world has its basic principles and rhythms. Follow along too long, and burnout, compromise, workaholism, addiction, and escape of all flavors will follow. The elemental spirits of this world will involve us in any kind of binding-back practice or routine it can, as long as we are kept from the gospel:

> The word used in Greek concerning the word "elemental" in the Colossians 2:8 is the word *stoikhā'on*—it literally is the music term "rudiment." The writer is telling us that there are elemental rules that govern the way people think in this world, and they are as basic as the fundamentals are to music and the ABC's are to the alphabet. They are primary, simple, effortless, primal, and natural to how we live and think as sinful humans. The world carries with it doctrines and theologies just like any other system. Burger King says, "Have it your way;" Coke sounds its mantra, "Everything goes better with Coke;" and Nike resounds, "Just do it." If taken literally, these marketing slogans preach the primal and most basic principles of the world.[29]

When it comes down to brass tacks, the world, our flesh, sin, and the demonic all speak with the same language. Religion. They yell only half the story—"that we've fallen short." The tragedy is that their message conceals the other half of the gospel. The good news. The gospel gives us the bad news that we've fallen short, but Jesus also heralds the saving message that he's delivered us and made all things new.

As you continue on in your journey of learning how the Lord teaches us to listen to him, keep in mind the order and emphasis of Savior in typology, script, and symbol. But remember God's overarching theme of kingdom as you hear and make decisions in a world that is building another type of kingdom altogether. Learning a proper manner of education from God will help us interpret Scripture in the specifics of its correct meaning (the look, the hook, and the took), and will also form us into a holistically hearing family different than those in the kingdom of the world.

25

CREATIVE TRANSFORMATION

THE INFORMATION AGE AND HOW IT'S RUINED EDUCATION!

Every day we are bombarded with messages, worldview, and slogans that bring us to the brink of exhaustion. Bernard Marr explains just how deep the rabbit hole of information saturation goes:

The amount of data we produce every day is truly mind-boggling. There are 2.5 quintillion bytes of data created each day at our current pace, but that pace is only accelerating with the growth of the Internet of Things (IoT). Over the last two years alone 90 percent of the data in the world was generated. This is worth re-reading …

With so much information at our fingertips, we're adding to the data stockpile every time we turn to our search engines for answers. We conduct more than half of our web searches from a mobile phone now. More than 3.7 billion humans use the Internet (that's a growth rate of 7.5 percent over 2016). On average, Google now processes more than 40,000 searches EVERY second (3.5 billion searches per day)! While 77 percent of searches are conducted on Google, it would be remiss not to remember other search engines are also contributing to our daily data generation. Worldwide there are 5 billion searches a day.

Our current love affair with social media certainly fuels data creation. According to Domo's Data Never Sleeps 5.0 report, these are numbers generated every minute of the day:

- Snapchat users share 527,760 photos
- More than 120 professionals join LinkedIn
- 456,000 tweets are sent on Twitter
- Instagram users post 46,740 photos[1]

The modern-day explosion of fact and fiction has reshaped the way we view intelligence. In the modern-day education system, and in churches as well, intelligence has become one dimensional. Smartness is boiled down to one's ability to simply study dry textbooks and spill out facts in answering test questions correctly. Educators are now taught to train for testing. Pastors are taught to preach in lecture format with the assumption that Christian maturity lies solely in one's ability to retain and articulate theological or practical concepts. The information age has conformed students and educator's in church and culture to a pattern of learning and teaching that parrots people into what to think. What we've lost in this process is the importance of true intelligence and transformation. Learning how to think.

In our journey toward some better conclusions in how to learn and how to teach people to move toward transformation, let's begin by making some crucial points about intelligence. First, it's diverse. We think visually, we think in sound, we think kinesthetically. We think in abstract terms, we think in movement. Second, intelligence is dynamic. If you look at the interactions of a human brain, intelligence is wonderfully interactive. The brain isn't divided into compartments. In fact, creativity—which I define as the process of having original ideas that have value—more often than not comes about through the interaction of different disciplinary ways of seeing things. The third thing about intelligence is that it's unique to each individual. It's distinct.[2] We also know that the mind has three aspects: the intellectual, which gives us truth; the ethical, which gives us nobility; and the aesthetic, which gives us beauty. It is really impossible to separate any one of these things entirely from the other.[3]

Our process of learning and teaching has been completely corrupted through a one-dimensional information-capacity viewpoint of human intelligence. The most crucial aspect of intelligence that's been at best ignored and at worst demonized is imagination. I feel the word imagination encapsulates all the other aspects of learning into one definable word. The word imagination is used over seventy-nine times in Hebrew Scriptures. God makes it clear that it is the definitive and encompassing part of our thinking process, and yet many won't even discuss it out of fear that we might dive into waters that we can't control. All fears aside, we must take the plunge because the image of *God* is at stake if we don't.

The Bible makes it very clear that the distinct part of the mind of God is one of deep imagination. Isaiah 45:18 uses four different Hebrew words for the imaginative mind-play of God in creating: *bara'* (God creating the earth), *kuwn* (God establishing what he's made), *yatzar* (God imagining his creation in his mind before putting it into time and space), and *'asah* (his imaginative work in manufacturing all we know as the universe). Read Isaiah 45:18 for yourself:

> For this is what the Lord says—he who created [*bara*] the heavens, he is God; he who fashioned [*yatzar*] and made [*'asah*] the earth, he founded [*kuwn*] it; he did not create it to be empty, but formed it to be inhabited—he says: "I am the Lord, and there is no other."

Here God makes a definitive statement about his own uniqueness. He says, "I am the Lord, and there is no other." He builds a case for his one-of-a-kind stature on his ability to imagine, create, and make. Humans are made in the image of God, and therefore our ability to create, imagine, and dream is what is distinct to us. Sadly, the information age has implemented a model for education in church and culture that attempts to kill creativity.

Ken Robinson, a former University Professor and advocate for education stated the following in one of his popular TED talks:

> Something strikes you when you move to America and travel around the world: Every education system on Earth has the same hierarchy of subjects. Every one. Doesn't matter where you go. You'd think it would be otherwise, but it isn't. At the top are mathematics and languages, then the humanities, and at the bottom are the arts.
>
> Everywhere on Earth. And in pretty much every system too, there's a hierarchy within the arts. Art and music are normally given a higher status in

schools than drama and dance. There isn't an education system on the planet that teaches dance every day to children the way we teach them mathematics. Why? Why not? I think this is rather important. I think math is very important, but so is dance. Children dance all the time if they're allowed to, we all do. We all have bodies, don't we? Did I miss a meeting? Truthfully, what happens is, as children grow up, we start to educate them progressively from the waist up. And then we focus on their heads. And slightly to one side.

If you were to visit education, as an alien, and say "What's it for, public education?" I think you'd have to conclude, if you look at the output, who really succeeds by this, who does everything that they should, who gets all the brownie points, who are the winners—I think you'd have to conclude the whole purpose of public education throughout the world is to produce university professors. Isn't it?

They're the people who come out the top. And I used to be one, so there. And I like university professors, but you know, we shouldn't hold them up as the high-water mark of all human achievement. They're just a form of life, another form of life. But they're rather curious, and I say this out of affection for them.

There's something curious about professors in my experience—not all of them, but typically, they live in their heads. They live up there, and slightly to one side. They're disembodied, you know, in a kind of literal way. They look upon their body as a form of transport for their heads. (Laughter) Don't they? It's a way of getting their head to meetings. (Laughter)

Our education system is predicated on the idea of academic ability. And there's a reason. Around the world, there were no public systems of education, really, before the nineteenth century. They all came into being to meet the needs of industrialism.

So the hierarchy is rooted in two ideas. Number one, that the most useful subjects for work are at the top. So you were probably steered benignly away from things at school when you were a kid, things you liked, on the grounds that you would never get a job doing that. Is that right? Don't do music, you're not going to be a musician; don't do art, you won't be an artist. Benign advice —now, profoundly mistaken. The whole world is engulfed in a revolution. And the second is academic ability, which has really come to dominate our view of intelligence because the universities designed the system in their image.[4]

Ken makes many profound statements that I would encourage you to meditate and dwell on for deeper understanding. For now, consider how he equates the universities' system to a designed image. The information age has redefined the way we define the image of mankind as well as the image of God. As we've learned throughout this book, one of the primary facets of becoming like the Triune God is in our expression of creativity and in our ability to be relational. Today we are educating people out of their creative and relational capacities. I believe wholeheartedly that we don't grow into the ability to relate and create, but we grow out of it. Or rather, we get educated out of it.

This is what world renowned revolutionary educator Charlotte Mason has to say about how our modern inventions have not only pitted right brain against left brain and divided those that are imaginatively creative from those that aren't, but have also handicapped us in becoming relational beings with imaginative intellectual capacity:

> The idea that vivifies teaching ... is that "Education is a Science of Relations"; by which phrase we mean that children come into the world with a natural [appetite] for, and affinity with, all the material of knowledge; for interest in the heroic past and in the age of myths; for desire to know about everything that moves and lives, about strange places and strange peoples; for a wish to handle and to make; a desire to run and ride and row and do what the law of gravitation permits. Therefore ... we endeavor that he shall have relations of pleasure and intimacy established with as many as possible of the interests proper to him ... In this conception, we get that "touch of emotion" which vivifies knowledge, for it is probably that we *feel* only as we are brought into our proper vital relations.[5]

Charlotte hits the nail on the head as she basically describes the childlike faith that Jesus remarkably referred to. As children, we enter the world moving, making, imagining, inventing, narrating, and interacting with what Charlotte calls the "living books" of our Creator in creation. But as we grow up, we are funneled into chairs and pews and positioned behind screens. Invention is educated out of us. We are told to relate to textbooks and concepts as if this is true education. Forced to spend our time in text, testing, and data infusion, we fail to really work and play around with and in living books. We start associating learning *about* things with *knowing* them personally. It all creates great distance in relations. It cripples imagination.

Maybe it explains why we think we're evolving when we come up with the idea of AI (artificial intelligence). In all reality, AI is the logical end to our robotic way of training humans. We grow further and further away from concepts, the Maker of concepts, and the people teaching them to us. Our sense of distance is forming. It seeps into how we relate to our Savior, the script of the Bible, the symbols written all over creation, and the kingdom of God.

This passive funneling of pre-digested information into our brains has largely consigned creativity to exile, where it tends either to languish or reemerge in hobbies and pastimes. This tendency has formed a divide between vocation and identity. We plod along in our vocational cubicles to advance a career while doing what we really want after hours at home, whether it's painting, gardening, strumming a guitar, or writing a novel. Or, even sadder, in some cases we let our creativity atrophy, either from neglect or because we've swallowed the poisonous pill that says every person is either right-brained or left-brained but never a happy balance of both.

In God's mind, however, the foundational aspect of every human being's image is to make a connection between the heart of our worship of God, the head of our identity as his creatively imaginative and beloved family member, and the hands of the culture we make as a result of that image exploding out of us. This means that to retain our likeness to our Maker, we must exercise our creativity.

The information age has also reshaped the way we view education—the way we learn and the way we teach. Our view of distance in education and distance in relationship has certainly impacted the environments in which to teach people. Churches are set up in linear pews, and chairs and classrooms are pointed at video screens. Schools are identical. Living rooms are identical. Whether we admit it or not, our way of receiving information dominates all our living and working spaces.

The environment is important when we think of learning. And this fact brings me back to one of the primary points of this book—the ideal of the home as the best setting for teaching. To reinforce that point, I'm going to quote a philosopher who is not even a Christian. Mahatma Gandhi said, "There is no school equal to a decent home and no teacher equal to a virtuous parent."

What Gandhi observes is that education is more than information. The development of a whole-hearted child has more to do with the development of virtue. Love. Wisdom over data. Whereas cold code merely drives the human being internal, wisdom helps the whole-hearted person to interact with God's will, his avenue, and his timing in a physically, emotionally, spiritually, mentally, and socially imaginative outward posture of love. When concepts and content are connected to the family context, wisdom is learned in tandem with knowledge. Paired with study, is the fruit of the Spirit (joy, love, peace, patience, kindness, gentleness, goodness, faithfulness, self-control), and the human person automatically begins to connect ideas with how humans are supposed to be and with what humans are supposed to do to be most like Jesus.

Don't assume that I'm demonizing public education in any form and only advocating homeschooling. I'm absolutely not! However, my theology teaches me that Scripture absolutely makes central the table, the family, and the home in the education of wholistic human beings, and all that modern-day church entities, the restaurant boom, social media, and outsourced educational models have done is complicate the simplicity of God's original design.

You'd be hard pressed to meet an individual in today's world who when asked to describe his life will not say "Busy, full, and stressful." All of our add-ons have not made us better; they've just made us busier. We've settled for information, not transformation. Even the well-intentioned but over-programmed nature of the church tends to churn out person after person that may believe differently from the world but doesn't act or live differently. The church entity has also succeeded wildly in separating families as they're being educated by pulling them away from home, meals, and togetherness.

The family of God should succeed in prioritizing better ways to push families back toward what God makes central rather than distracting from it.

A PARADIGM FOR HOW GOD INFORMS AND TRANSFORMS HIS PEOPLE.

Because I'm an author and songwriter, a business owner, a professor, and have been a pastor, I'm surrounded by a wide swath of people. I've grown to love what every sector of human society has to offer in terms of how God can use it to shape people, educate people, and grow people. My experience has led me to spend a lot of time contemplating how humans are holistically informed, and also how they are worshipfully transformed into the image of God. My journey in processing God's way of teaching us and the desire he has for how we learn has led me over the last twenty years to create the graphic below in figure 6.1:

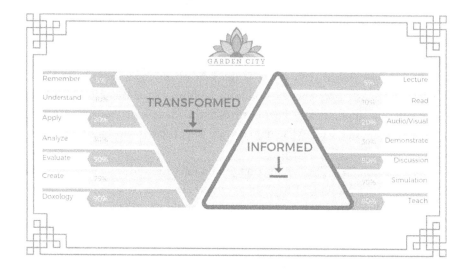

Fig. 6.1

On the right, you will see what is most commonly known within academic circles as "the way we learn." Typically students will be told at some point that listening to lectures is not learning, and if they want to really internalize the information given they're going to have to move to a place of teaching it themselves. The typical progression usually goes something like this: We only learn 5 percent of what we hear in a lecture, 10 percent of what we read, 20 percent of what we see and hear, 30 percent of what's demonstrated, 50 percent of what we're allowed to discuss, 75 percent of what we simulate, and finally 80 percent of what we attempt to teach others. I've shown this progression of how we're informed on the right of the image.

Before I go into the left side of the figure, please notice how the triangle of information moves from smaller to larger. The triangle demonstrates how we begin with a small amount of knowledge. As we broaden, we get closer to teaching what we know to someone else. The triangle implies an outward motion of information, meaning that the student is given the data with the end goal being to give it away. Giving anything away should be a loving pursuit if done in truth.

As a professor, I'm inclined to agree with the right side of figure 6.1. It implies that our sheer intellectual knowledge is not best formed in texts and lectures, but has to lean on greater relational and creative components of education to become true learning. As the triangle moves deeper, the amount of creativity and relationship with other people, places, and things must also grow in order to really teach anything. Nevertheless, in all my years as an educator, I've never once encountered anyone who has put much thought into the left side of figure 6.1. Transformation. I had to create this side myself.

Transformation is a worship word. It's what Romans 12:1 uses to compare the world's process of conforming to its image, to God's process of remaking us. Transformation assumes an image or desired vision of the good life that we are seeking to emulate or be like. Transformation is represented by a reversed triangle because I believe it works altogether different than how we learn information. The transformative triangle moves from bigger to smaller even as the percentages get higher and higher. It indicates how the information attained begins to make its way from outside of us to inside of us. My triangle represents the most difficult work of how information begins to become character. If you'll permit a metaphor: I'm trying to demonstrate the impossible miracle of how a caterpillar of data begins to metamorphosize into an altogether different species—a butterfly. The metaphoric butterfly is knowledge turned into wisdom.

We have a culturally coined word to describe the disconnect between what one knows in data, and what one acts out in true transformative practice. The word is hypocrite. The hypocrite is someone whose information and message contradicts how he lives. The hypocrite has a canyon between what he practices and what he preaches. In some area, we are all hypocrites. The Bible calls it sin. Even the believer, who is never once called a sinner in the Bible, but rather a saint, struggles with the tension between our inner rebellious child and the new creation that God has now given us. On one hand, we want to obey and we know the right things, but on the other, we can't seem to do the right things.

If you're having trouble identifying the disconnect between what you know and do in your own life, simply picture in your mind someone else. Picture the pastor who yells all the right theology but is impossible to be around. Picture the youth pastor that condemns lust as a sin, and completely ignores gluttony as he sports a physique fifty pounds overweight. Picture the husband or wife that speaks highly of purely committed love and yet slips around into porn or other people's beds. Picture the virtue-signaling politician who gets caught with his hand in sin's cookie jar.

There's a hypocritical disconnect in all of us. The hypocrite lies between what we know in information, and what we allow to transform us. We are in dire need to connect the two. Let's outline that process.

WE MUST REMEMBER IN ORDER TO UNDERSTAND

Too many people who are informed today, even to the fullest point of teaching others, lean too heavily on their techniques, quotes from others, Power Point presentations, and a variety of external ways of conveying information. We live in the computer age, and we're accustomed to storing our brains on Google and thumb drives. What we're deprived of when we make technology our crutch is any sense of truly remembering anything. We ignore the primary aspect of learning. It's that we first learn. When we don't retain the information within the flesh-and-blood brains inside our skulls, we lose any ability to internalize the information. We lose the ability to meditate.

Meditation was a crucial concept to those living in biblical times. Jews, in particular, have always been known for their amazing retention capacity and brilliance. Much of it stems from the fact that most are traditionally required to memorize the entire Torah by the age of seven to nine. That's right, all of Genesis, Exodus, Leviticus, Numbers, and Deuteronomy. Memorized. It makes me tired just thinking about it.

Memorization allows a person to do what Deuteronomy 6:7 says. It allows the truth to stay with us as "we sit at home, when we walk along the road, when we lie down and when we get up." When remembering takes place, what we learn begins to become part of us. The more we remember, the more what we learn begins to make connections to understanding.

Memory is the basis for understanding. Here's how a Jew might describe how memory makes its way into our understanding through meditation:

> The Jewish idea of meditation is similar to preparing a field for planting. When a farmer approaches a field for planting, it is filled with huge dirt clods that are too big and too infertile to create a healthy environment for seeds. To prepare the land to reap a great harvest, the farmer tills it over and over again. Finally, all the dirt clods would be broken down into their smallest form, and seeds could grow and flourish.

In the Jewish mind, theologies like God's oneness, his mercy, glory, law, redemption, etc., are like giant dirt clods of truth. They present huge concepts that need to be broken down before they can be swallowed, or they'll cause someone to choke. For a seed of belief to truly implant itself in someone's life, in order to begin to grow, it needs to be broken down into its simplest form. Then it will reap a harvest. The meditation of the Jews is not an "emptying of the mind" but a filling of the mind with God's truth. They break it down, think upon it, and carry it even upon their actual foreheads until the truth of it undoes all their false reasoning and assumptions.[6]

One of the primary reasons that Jesus spoke in parables is because they are easy to retain and they promote memory and meditation. Parables stay with you. We carry not only ideas around, but the ideas are embodied in familiar realities. As we've said before, God speaks in his creation. We carry around with us pieces of his mind that point us back to him. We interact with them creatively, imaginatively, and relationally. We find ourselves identifying with characters in the story and the God of that story. Meditation leads us to deeper concepts. Slowly but surely, the divide between relational imagination and creativity finds a bridge.

Memory and mediation allow us to do one thing of great importance. Rest. They allow us to recline with the information so it can seep into us from all angles. We must remember that the term "school" literally is derived from the word "leisure." Leisure means rest. Jesus invites us to bring to him our burdens and find his rest. At the feet of our Rabbi is rest. Flowers grow in fields of leisurely work for kingdom purposes. Posturing ourselves in a place of slow, but intensely laborious, meditative, worshipful, and imaginative play is the best place for school to take place. It's the best environment for spiritual formation. Unfortunately, in this day of frenetic and incessant busyness, leisure is a concept we no longer even associate with learning, or with God. The environments of today provide absolutely no rhythm for creative engagement because they're too concerned with drilling into us textbook after textbook loaded with what other people think. It takes too much time and it's too messy to let the reality of how the human brain works to unfold.

WE APPLY, ANALYZE, EVALUATE

Once a piece of information is unpacked and broken down into soil that's fertile for planting, transformation puts down roots. The learner can then apply, analyze, and evaluate concepts in ways that are digestible, but with one very notable difference from how we interact with data. Because the concepts are now pressed down relationally into the imagination of the individual with a God-centered orbit, the person no longer is simply sifting through ideas, but rather contemplating one's self in relation to what he's learning about God through the information. He's now bringing God into interaction with his own identity. Information, when deepened in us through the transformation triangle, puts us in face-to-face contact with ourselves and our Maker. We're forced to grapple with our inner hypocrite as we compare our imperfections to the intricate beauty of God as seen in all the logic and lions that he's made. We're forced to deal with our own sin. We're forced to sit down on the chairs we've made for the idols in our hearts and ask ourselves if what we're paying honor to in thought, word, and deed is actually Christlike.

At the foot of our very own internal idols, biases, and display cases for our own crowns, we can now posture ourselves for an education. We're humbled. Our realization of our own need before God and all he's installed in his creation turns us not to continue to look inward—for we've already uncovered the reality that we're broken—but turns us outward and heavenward to look for evidences of God's grace in his beautiful character, creation, and people. John Ruskin says that this is where the hard work of being a disciple (which means *learner*) is really forged:

> You will find it less easy to unroot faults than to choke them by gaining virtues. Do not think of your faults, still less of others faults; in every person who comes near you look for what is good and strong; honor that; rejoice in it and as you can, try to imitate it; and your faults will drop off like dead leaves when their time comes.

As we look to become "good" and imitate what is most excellent and tasty to the palette of our five senses, we can undertake what is essentially a scientific experiment. We assess how well we've learned the information we're now living out. We analyze and evaluate our lives in order to uncover where the disconnect still lies between our information and our transformation. We analyze differently from laboratory scientists, however. We dissect character and becoming, not conceptual knowing. Like the famous quote says, "You may not always live what you profess, but you will always live what you believe." Our goal in making this assessment is to learn where we are merely professing faith in God's beautiful truths, and where we are actually believing them.

WE CREATE

No disconnect in education is quite so expansive as the ravine that exists between knowledge and creativity. On one side of the chasm, educators dismiss the value of the fine arts entirely as being of no value. On the other side are the artsy types who claim art to be the highest expression of the inner self. They promote creativity to the level of a god and insist that works of art need convey no message to validate their value. The fact that the piece of art exists is its own justification. Both sides ignore the fact that the proper role of art is to convey truth and beauty—two values that are absolutely interchangeable. They are entwined in an eternal marriage that cannot succumb to divorce. One cannot exist without the other.

Message and medium cohabit. Right thinking and right making cannot be separated in man because they cannot be separated in God. Rewind back to our discussion on why God created "in the beginning." His only motivation to create came from the knowledge of his own love. Love is not just something God shows; love is something God is. He so enjoys his very own loving nature that he wanted to extend it and multiply so that joy could increase. Everything he cast onto the canvas of the universe with his divine paintbrush springs from the message of his love. Everything made that he calls good testifies to everything he is as a good Maker.

Interacting with all fields of study is important to learning every facet of God's love. By learning every facet of God's love, we begin to imitate him and transform into children of the Father. Beloved lovers. Many, like the great reformer Martin Luther, connected the dots between how meditation and evaluation naturally lead to creative and loving outflow.

Martin Luther paired the idea of meditation to creative expression in music. He understood how music helps a person to relate to, break down, and, in a fun, musical way, repeat the same idea over and over again until the truths of it reach deeper levels of understanding. This is why he combined theology with music. He wanted people to be able to remember the messages and truths of precise theology (left brain), so he put them into right-brain creativity, which allowed the melody to hook the believer onto the ideas—singing them round and round, deeper and deeper until their meaning produced a fertilized soul.[7]

I have a friend who simplifies how meditation explodes into outward expression. He calls it *see, savor,* and *sing.* His hypothesis is that we first see God's glory as Isaiah did. We behold the Lamb of God in the person of Christ and in all he's made and in all he's said in his word, and we savor it. Our response to seeing God's art is to respond in art ourselves. To sing! Every man, woman, and child is commanded to sing. Every song is a response that is written about the one a person's heart worships. If a person savors perversity, violence, volatile emotion, etc., they'll dwell on it and then smack it onto the page in lyric, blueprint, paint, or business plan. If a person savors the good of God in every element of culture and human character, he will respond by weaving the goodness of God into every thread of society's fabric.

Creating not only engages us in worship; it best values how God has made us to be. It's humanness. We are people, not parrots. Our way of learning and education must not reinforce that we are merely mimics who recall information, but rather we absorb into ourselves the beauty that's seen and savored in God's living book. Making it our own, we then must give it forth again with just that little touch that comes from our own mind.[8] Famous educators like Charlotte Mason call this *narration.* We regurgitate what we know through our own way of "storying" it.

The foundation of all human existence and human worship is one of response to what God has already made. In a 1925 *Parents Review* article on Chaucer, Essex Cholmondeley wrote:

If the works of the great poets teach anything, it is to hold mere invention somewhat cheap. It is not the finding of a thing, but the making something out of it after it is found, that is of consequence.

We make sense of the world by making something of the world. In fact, Andy Crouch in his book *Culture Making: Recovering Our Creative Calling* suggests that the truest form of poverty is not a lack of food, shelter, or the like, but the loss of resources, capacity, desire, and dignity that's found in our ability to make sense of the world.[9] Poverty is being cut off from cultural power.

If Crouch is correct, we're living in a dismally impoverished society, particularly among the most educated. I would suggest that the church also as a whole is brutally impoverished in our modern age because our models are built around ideologies of consumption, not production. We've continued to spoon feed people what to think rather than teaching them how to think, and we've not allowed them the space in church life to think and create deeply and at leisure.

In fact, this is where the Greek culture, Jesus, and Paul might again speak loudly to remind us about the Lord's Supper. All three make connections between the leisurely nature of eating and drinking and the spontaneity of learning and creating that springs from our celebration together.

If you'll remember, the Greeks logically connected the pleasure of eating together in leisure with the pleasure of creating together. Jesus linked the Last Supper to the Greek manner of supping followed by the symposium. He affirmed that discussing and making live together. Paul follows suit in 1 Corinthians. Let's follow his logic. He begins speaking to the Corinthians in chapters 6–7 about the church as a body, a society of lawful governance, and finally a marriage. In chapters 8–10 he immediately progresses into linking the community's experience with each other to that of food and eating together. In Chapter 11 he progresses into discussing worship and the Lord's Supper. In doing so, he clearly demonstrates his contextual understanding. It was second nature for him to assume that communities were meeting for worship within a covenantal, eating-and-drinking feast that displayed a free and celebrating society. Then finally in Chapters 12–14, he connects the meal to the symposium. He starts talking about everyone in the community bringing gifts, teaching, and offering up creative expression of all kinds under the shepherded oversight of fathers in the community. He cautions that the use of all gifts should be for the building up of everyone in love, and finally, in 1 Corinthians 15, he goes right into talking about Christ's resurrection at his first coming and ours at his second coming. It's as if Paul is indicating that the manner of discipleship—family, home, and meals—remains intact from the present when the kingdom is inaugurated as well as in the future when it is finally consummated as an eternal reality.

Creating implies a together act. It brings us to 75 percent in our transformative journey because it's not about self; it's about bringing what is other together. Whether its connecting separate ingredients into a savory meal; or isolated lyrics, rhythms, and harmony into a together song; or canvas and diverse oil pigments into a unified painting, the work of creativity does what

God intends. It brings elements together in ways that bring them to life. Just as God hovered over the uninhabited cosmos in Genesis 1 and in seven days shaped all the various ingredients together to make a habitable space for human life to flourish, we become most like our creator when we do the same.

THE FINAL DOXOLOGY

Now we arrive at an 80 percent transformation. I'm hesitant to go to 90 percent or even 100 percent because we are, after all, imperfect humans. I'll leave these higher marks to all those who have already died, gone onto glory, and are standing in the cloud of witnesses in their new pain-free bodies.

For us earth dwellers that still live in the presence of sin, we are still in the transformative process. We're still emerging from our cocoon. We've made great strides in considering how an ugly hypocritical caterpillar—who boasts and teaches about flight—can now actually fly like a butterfly. The final stop on our journey is not self-reflection, expression, or even creative community and togetherness. Our final stop is to return to where we came from. Glory. Doxology. Let me include these words from my *Reconsider* book series to quickly explain to you where I'm headed with all of this:

The word Doxology is a lesser-known word in church culture today, particularly when compared to our use of words like theology or philosophy. Doxology is a biblical term and concept that is crucial to understanding how belief is pushed into practice. The word doxology comes from the Greek word δοξολογία—a combination of δόξα, "doxa," or "glory" and λογία, meaning "logic," or saying. Essentially a good definition for the word is this; "the logical end to knowing God (theological input) is to glorify and praise Him (in doxological output)."

Many people are most familiar with the formal Doxologies often used in gathered worship services around the world after hymns, canticles, readings, or as benedictions both in liturgical settings and in Scriptural texts. They are widely known to intentionally function as expressions that respond to the truths of the Word of God. However, Doxologies, though they can be functional in Scripture, are also used in ways that are formational.

For example, take the treatise in Romans 9–11, arguably one of the most fought over and misunderstood portions in all of Scripture. The writer, Paul, goes into a lengthy argument concerning the nature of the true Israel, and his discussion causes him to plummet to the very ocean floor of deep thinking regarding election, the justice and mercy of God, the sovereignty of God to do as he pleases, the place for the Gentile in the kingdom, and the true nature of mankind. These are profoundly difficult concepts to understand. We would venture, to a degree in these passages that even Paul himself is left in stupefying awe at these great theological truths streaming from his own quill. He seems to ponder God's words in faith-filled speculation even as he's writing.

Paul lays out a legally defended account of sound doctrine not only in these three chapters but also in the whole of Romans 1–11, and he ends the section, the whole argument, and the deeply thoughtful apologetic with this doxology: "Oh, the depth of the riches and wisdom and knowledge of God! How unsearchable are his judgments and how inscrutable his ways! "For who has known the mind of the Lord, or who has been his counselor?" "Or who has given a gift to him that he might be repaid?" For from him and through him and to him are all things. To him be glory forever. Amen." (Rom. 11:33-36 esv)

It seems that the thrust of Paul's truthful words is not to leave the reader in a place of logic and measurement but to exhort those hearing to come to a place of expression and awe, exalting the mystery of God's supremacy as it reaches beyond our measuring. This is profoundly forming. Paul appeals to the intellect to awaken our worship. In seeing the depths of God's love and sovereign transcendence over all things, Paul, being overwhelmed, worships! This is his aim! This is theologies' aim. Sound truth should drive us upward and outward, not inward.

Not only does he sing a song of praise in doxology, but also this brief prayer hinges the first 11 chapters in Romans to chapters 12–16. Paul goes on to exhort the people not only to worship in word but also to go forth as a collective of living sacrifices who love one another. The ensuing chapters of Romans deal with spiritual gifts, how to serve under Godly and worldly authority, how to handle controversy, and how to develop wisdom and competence at living out the truths of Scripture in mission, one to another. Paul seems to imply that all theological reflection should flow out into comprehensive, expressive and mystifying worship unto God, and in loving, honoring, and edifying mission towards all people.

The final note played in our transformational song occurs when the believer becomes more like Christ. True education is realized when information becomes virtue. When content turns into character and contextual change. When words become living worship.

Living worship is not simple, mind you. It permeates everything. When a doxology takes hold, a believer views everything through one lens: "How can I use this or that, do this or that, say this or that, make this or that, or enjoy this or that in a way that glorifies God?" Suddenly everything explodes with beauty and meaning. Everything transforms into a container filled with good. The perverse twisting of the world falls off of our ideas, drink, food, culture, and every element of the home, work, and play, and we can see deep down to the good intentions of God in all things. We're armed with a sword for battle. We're armed with a viewpoint of redemption. Everywhere we go becomes a place living and teeming with the possibility to worship.

CREATIVE TRANSFORMATION CHANGES THE HOME AND ALL SECTORS OF HUMAN EXPERIENCE

At this point, I'm almost guaranteeing that someone reading this just can't seem to visualize their vocation, talent, trade, or area of expertise from within a creative, worship-forming framework. You may be confused about how the various ingredients of your life can come together in a manner that makes flourishing most enjoyable in all creative endeavors. To help tie up loose ends and show you how the Bible includes every testimony and talent that spans mankind's imaginative work, I want to leave you to consider one of the most creative and exhaustively inclusive works in all of Scripture: the rebuilding of the wall around Jerusalem after the Babylonian exile.

Picture the scene. The Jews, having been exiled into Babylon, are freed to go back to their home. The only problem is that their home had been decimated. The wall around their city was in rubble, their temple gone, and they were left to return to an unprotected landfill. On the throne at the time, ruling and reigning, was the King of Persia, Cyrus. One of his political officials was Nehemiah. Nehemiah's heart broke for the Jewish people as they were released to travel home to nothing. His compassion quickened him to travel to Jerusalem to survey the rebuilding project. He took his findings, his plan, and his proposed budget back to King Cyrus. Cyrus gave Nehemiah all he requested.

Nehemiah's role in this incident is more of a *kingly* one.

Nehemiah begins the restorative process of the Jewish home, first by giving each family a sword and a shovel. He tasks them to rebuild the portion of the wall that is directly in front of where their home will be. He gives people back their ability to make meaning out of chaos and to protect and fight for what they love most. As the people build, they quickly realize that it's not just their city or their home life that's been cast into disarray by their exile in slavery. Ezra, a preacher, enters the scene and begins to remind them of God's law, theology, thinking, and manner of life.

The people had been living under pagan and godless rulers for so long that they forgot God's commands. They had fallen into sin. One of the most grievous of all was tarnishing the marriage bed. The men had intermarried with women who did not claim to believe in the one, true God. The home had been compromised, and in one of the most tragic, sad, and horrific scenes in all of Scripture the men and woman hear God's law and repent to such a degree that they send their willfully unbelieving wives and families back to Babylon. Not only did potential enemies from within their hearts and homes seek to devour their faith and faithfulness to God, but discouragement and the threat of surrounding enemy attacks began to tickle the swords hanging from their sides. To encourage them, rebuke them, and instruct them in the hope that was on the horizon if they remained steadfast, God sent in prophets such as Zachariah, Haggai, and later even Malachi, to not only reinforce reintroduction to God's law, but also to point to what was coming if they chose to obey or disobey.

Notice the work of the *prophet* and *priest* in the above.

My point in telling this story is simply this: to bring to your notice how one of the most creative, transformative, and rehabilitative works in all of history needed the collaborative-community creativity that comes when the home sector, the vocational sector, the theological sector, and the artistic sector, work together. The work on the wall brought the world of politics, administration, banking, marketing, media, and business together in a worshipful way to provide for the flourishing of God's people (in Nehemiah). The work on the wall brought the world of the family, the home, the tradesman, craftsman, artisan, sculptor, and blue-collar worker together in a worshipful way (in the people working around and defending their homes). The work on the wall brought the world of the theological—the pastor, the prophet, and the shepherd —together in a worshipful way to counsel, convict, and comfort the people as they sought to move forward in a way that would best honor the Lord.

Creative transformation works very much like the work on the wall. Wholistic education should consider the work on the wall. The commissioning of God's people for gospel service and worshipful work amongst the church and culture should consider the work on the wall. We must think deeper about how all imagination, invention, creativity, personality, and innovative capacity can be forged and positioned toward helping God's people to flourish in all manners of life.

For his glory …

26

THE TRINITY ANSWERS SCRIPTURE

W hat we've learned about how God educates us significantly impacts everything. God's manner of education should influence how we move forward in considering our formation of people via story, belief, curriculum, community, and what it means to live life in the here and now before the end comes (see Fig. 6.2).

S.cripture ... How God Teaches & We Learn

STORY	Grammatical & Performance Bibliological (nature & function of Scripture)
BELIEF	Confessional & Creedal (historical acknowledgment of truth) Apologetical (a defense of one's beliefs)
KERYGMA & DIDACHE	Proclamational & Embodied Community (forthtelling & sharing) Doctrinal & Doxological (foundational beliefs that are correct) Educational (how we learn & teach)
COMPLETE	Eschatological (beginning & end to the consummation of creation)

Fig. 6.2

In my final challenge, I want to identify things that have bubbled to the surface in our chapter on S.cripture that may not yet have entered your mind. Going forward, I encourage you to consider how the Trinity alters our paradigm in the following areas:

- Questions & Monologues
- Performance vs. Criticism
- Production vs. Consumption
- Equipping vs. Eclipsing
- Expression *of*, or Expression *for* the Community

First, consider that Jesus taught more by asking questions than by monologues. As I've noted before, if you add up all the "red letter" words spoken directly by Jesus, you'll see that for every one statement he makes, he asks four questions. A 4:1 ratio. Even when Jesus speaks in monologues or lengthy discourse, he uses parables, stories, and proverbs. Story and proverb require that the listener engage and actively enter via imagination into the world that the words are forming in order to gain any insightful transformation. Jesus' teaching style is intentionally both clear and unclear. He both reveals the truth and conceals it in order to require the learner to become part of the telling process to gain any benefit. Jesus' communication style is almost devoid of the practical steps, bullet points, and clearly outlined takeaways by which modern lecture-pulpit style modes of teaching are often defined. Matthew 11:25 records Jesus in the wake of sharing a parable saying, "I praise you, Father, Lord of heaven and earth because you have hidden these things from the wise and learned, and revealed them to little children." Can you imagine what would happen if a modern-day pulpit preacher actually prayed this prayer after he spoke? It would definitely offend most people?

You may be asking why the above is the reality of Jesus' teaching. It should cause us to ponder Jesus' teaching method, but more importantly, it should cause us to question our own. Why are our methods for discipleship and learning in the church and universities today designed specifically around disconnected pulpit-monologues, and worse yet, online education models devoid of a flesh-and-blood teacher? I'm not demonizing Internet teaching, for I myself teach in online education environments. It's become a necessary evil that we need to work out of. I'm asking if we've overlooked something in the proper educative process. Learning involves far more than just assimilating concepts. Concepts must be imagined. Concepts must transfer into our context to become tangible character and Christlikeness. When we disconnect the content we're teaching from application to the real-life context of our lives, transformation becomes almost impossible.

My next point has more to do with interpretation and transformation than with directly learning data. Consider criticism as opposed to performance. When students in the modern day classroom learn to study Scripture, they'll learn all kinds of criticism methodology: textual,[1] philosophical,[2] literary,[3] compositional, historical,[4] tradition,[5] form,[6] apologetical,[7] archaeological, exegetical,[8] and redaction.[9] The process of digging deep into every nuance of Scripture is vital and important. Criticism is about testing the validity of God's truth from every angle. In doing so we get the full width of his beauty, apologetic, meaning, and application.

All critique is helpful, but we must remember that the context in which the Bible was written centered mainly on oral ways of learning. The literacy rate in Bible times ranged from 3 percent to 25 percent. Most likely only about 2 percent of the people Jesus associated with most were literate. Reading was relegated to the work of the Scribe. Therefore, most of the Bible is written in a way that the common person would understand. It's written in Greek. Greek is a verb-based language. It's action-oriented. It's dependent on gesture, dialogue, inflection, posture, tone of voice, facial expression, and other communication devices in order to arrive at proper understanding. In an oral culture that understood language much more through the visual, audial, and tactile experience of story, the performance of storytelling was much more widespread. Texts were interpreted best through performing them.

Performance fosters memorization. It's only when one memorizes a text that one best internalizes it. Internalization enables one to develop his own flavor of storytelling. His unique personality and gestures make the text come to life, with the characters in the plot taking on the flesh of the storyteller. When the interpreter digs more deeply into Scripture, he will begin to see between the lines of the text and uncover the social norms and nuances of personality subtly revealed within it. He will become able to visualize implied details such as the gestures, facial expressions, tone of voice, and sarcasm of the character he reads about. This will have the double advantage of acquainting him more deeply with what the text actually means and enabling him to convey it vividly to others.

Performance, acting, and creative expression of all shapes and sizes is normative to the transmission of truth. Before the printing press was invented, scrolls were not widely circulated. People had to be circulated. Performers who memorized texts had to be deployed. More common than dictating a letter was the acting out of the author's full intentions. For example, Paul dictates his message into the performance memory of Epaphroditus. Epaphroditus is then commissioned to carry the letter out to God's people in scroll and performance. Paul would likely have instructed him not only in the epistle's message, but also its tone of voice, it's demeanor, it's posture, and all the rise and fall of good communicative storytelling. Epaphroditus would become to the people a "living letter" by acting out Paul's intentions to those hearing.

Today many scholars have noted that performing Scripture, acting it out, and putting it into all kinds of creative audio, visual, tactile, enacted, and fragrant forms actually help us ask questions of the text that we normally would overlook. It's one thing to read a parable, but another to see it come to life in dramatic form.

Much of Scripture is written like a drama. A script. Dialogue. Characters. Plot. The all-too-common dry monologues of sermonizing and bullet-point preachers, and isolated devotionals and quiet times of today have really robbed us of elements that are communally experiential. Performance is needed to actually learn Scripture rightly.

I've taught churches the simplicity of acting out the Scripture rather than reading it. I've taught them to engage with the text on a visceral level. I've asked them to retell it in their own way. Something as easy as this opens us up to a world most Bible studies have never even touched. Putting Scripture into transformative environments—which means creating with it, dialoguing and questioning it, and making it malleable as we tell and retell it with each other —brings us closer to accurate interpretation. We arrive much closer to the truth because we use methods than modern seminaries often fail to attempt.

The above brings me to my next point. Most church environments today are set up for consumption rather than production. Many cannot even fathom performance because they are so geared toward intake over output. I've noted before how our pews and chairs facing a stage and screen form us into consumers. The stage reinforces certain types of learning—mainly through monologues and concerts put on by professionals telling us what to think, not teaching us how to think for ourselves as a community. What's lost is any intentional connection between belief in the gospel and our mandate to multiply and produce.

Adam was tasked to multiply. So are we. We are to make. Produce. Become. Not consume only. Yes, we must be fed on the Word of God, but the primary work of the church is to equip people to go and feed themselves and others.

The church must return to its orally-creative paradigm of teaching others. We must equip rather than eclipse the unique DNA of local people. Let me give you a story that illustrates what I mean:

> When I was in Uganda over two-decades ago, touring with a band and sharing the gospel, we often would travel deep into the jungles. I remember walking into one of the deep back-woods churches and hearing them singing nothing but Hillsong songs. Something in this scenario lacked the true cultivation of both the heart and culture of Africa. When I asked them to sing songs that reflected the heritage and lineage of Jesus in their culture—songs that were familiar to the African voice and heritage—the spirit of that local church changed significantly. I began to hear God's kingdom creativity in and through Africa.
>
> This phenomenon of eclipsing a local community's creative voice is not limited only to our singing. With current big production models curating market invention today, we often tend to **eclipse** the local church's "creative voice" rather than **equip** it. A growing need exists, whereby we need to walk alongside churches and help equip them to produce their own culturally enriching products for the good of those uniquely around them, rather than merely turning into passive consumers of our mass produced and globally Christian SWAG.

Training unique persons to voice their individuality together unto the glory of God in one synchronous voice is an art, not a science. It takes time. It's messy. It's not a model, it is a paradigm. A way of thinking. It's not static; it's timeless and flexible. It's something that Nashville and L.A. can't package on a CD. It's something Hillsong hasn't learned to teach others. We must deeply consider how we can use the modern devices of production and publication, not to silence local uniqueness, but rather to capture it.

Lastly, let's consider the eschatological implications of the shift in the educational paradigm. For those whom I've just sent spinning with my use of an extra-big word, eschatology refers to the study of end things. Or, for those who believe as Paul that we are currently living in the last days before Christ returns, eschatology is the study of *now*.

Eschatology is the study of God's work in bringing time and space to a close in the future presently. As an end-time community, the people of God are empowered by the Spirit to show forth his nature in various ways through the use of all they've been afforded. Because we are an empowered body of priests uniquely equipped to have Jesus do his ministry work through, in, and on us, our paradigms must unleash the power of this body.

Unfortunately, many models of ministry today unleash people only within the bounds and for the purposes that a select few decide, rather than opening up the floodgates and allowing the work of ministry to truly become a liturgy (Christ's work in, on, and through the people in every avenue of their home, work, and play).

If the church body is a unique, spontaneously expanding, gifted explosion of personality, creativity, and the end-time eruption of our coming King, we must focus less effort corralling people around the pet vision of a central pastoral personna, and rather curate the expression *of* God's people instead of attempting to have a select few stand on stage and produce an expression *for* God's people. Let me give you some practical scenarios for how these approaches differ:

> **Scenario 1:** I once served at a church as a hired pastoral staff member. I spent the mass majority of my time and resources designing the weekend Sunday event. As a staff member, the people paid me to "do ministry" for them. While they were busy in their vocations during the week, they left me to attend to the weekend, and they showed up to participate in what I and a select few designed. Sure, there were participants from the church body, and yes, we as pastors oversaw the liturgy to make sure the logic of God's R.easoning spoke loudly through the story of the service. But it didn't negate the fact that the people all fit themselves into the mold that I created. It reflected the views of a select few who were in full-time ministry, and those attending could perceive the ever-growing disconnect between our space for "worshipping God" and the rest of life that is their "job."
>
> The distinction between laity and leader and sacred and secular solidified, and people allowed the disconnect to take hold.

Scenario 2: In another church I also served to help God's people worship, but in a different capacity. I served more as a curator than a staff member. My role involved less planning of items that others would execute. Instead, it was to identify what people were already doing, step alongside it, equip it, and resource it to help people exalt and worship the Lord through their unique perspective, cultural role, and personality.

The focus of my worship leading shifted from the central gathering to training households in how to worship God. I took on a cultural role. One closer to how Jesus and Paul would have used the idiom of "worship leading." I trained families and groups of families to look like Jesus biblically, creatively, and as a together community. C.R.O.S.S.! Around the table, the people began to find their own "sound" as they found each other in expressing God together. Out of this environment sprung an explosively unique personality in each home. Businesses emerged to serve the community, bands ranging in all styles and genres began circulating in the community and amongst all our churches. Artists put pen to paper, hand to rock, and brush to canvas. Community leaders and regular employees of all shapes and sizes began to connect the gospel to their vocational and recreational work.

In all this I saw something happen that I never experienced before. Truth, talent, and testimony came together. Many churches try and plan for these assets and balance them in separate. Doing what I described above brought them out in unity.

When people showed up bringing what they had made, they had to simultaneously explain truth in a very deep way. They had chewed on truth in such a manner to make it digestible enough to put into words and creation. To do so, their life had to interact. Transform. To share the truth of the Scripture, it was necessary that they also teach facets about what they had made with their talent so we could understand their process and their artistic choices. Everything had to be expressed personally and often ended in their sharing through tears, vibrant emotion, and unique perspective. Truth, talent, and testimony were seen in one beautiful moment.

Because each home reflected the time and space of the people it was serving, our Sunday's became rambunctiously colorful. Altogether different from Scenario 1. As a curator of worship, I was no longer tasked to come up with and invent the contents of our liturgy; I was merely there to channel them into one glorious gospel storytelling event. The gathering literally became an expression of the people. I served merely as a conduit to funnel every item of contribution into the timeless liturgies of gathered worship that God has laid out for us in Scripture. Gospel groups sang in praise, Cameroonian drum circles chanted prayers, spoken word poets reframed creeds and responses, folk groups brought grassroots melody to our communion, whereas a multiplicity of people from all walks of life and vocations prayed through the lens of their passion, perspective, personality, and purpose within our local town.

In light of the two scenarios above, I would have to suggest that the job descriptions of pastors and those in worship settings need to alter drastically. Too much of the lingo of churches centers around controlling language that aims at preference, personality, and the vision of each church, rather than on paradigms of the combustively creative nature of curating.

Rather than us asking the most prominently modern question, "How can we use you to accomplish our vision?" the question can change. God's spiritual gifts are no longer viewed only as a means to an end. They become ways of revealing the Trinity to the world as our King is on the move, rather than workhorses for the vision of the staff under a one-dimensional thumb. It's about revealing God's image amongst his people over and above revealing the church's image. When we simply admit that God's vision is the same for all of us—to make him known—we stop wasting so much time personalizing everything to fit our mold. Our sole creative question to the body, as pastors of his people, will be "How is God already using you to accomplish his vision, and how can we resource, equip, and help it flourish for the good of all?"

Bottom line: Jesus is the Worship Leader of this whole thing we call life. He's conducting the orchestra of the end times as it hurtles toward the finish. As F.F. Bruce so aptly states in his commentary on Hebrews, "Only an appreciation of what is involved in Christ's priesthood will cure our state."[10] I would have to second that motion and say that the only cure to our sin-bent and currently anemic, incomplete, and interpretively silenced creative community is to rediscover the centrality of Christ's priesthood and mission as he fills his whole world with the potential for Trinity Worship.

PART VII
S: HOW GOD LEADS

SIGNATURE MISSION

27

EVERYONE IS A CHURCH PLANTER

Worship and mission are inextricably linked. What we love, we serve. What we admire, we become like. What we aim at is what we cling to. Whom we serve determines everything about who we are and what we do with this life and the next. Though many believe that eternity will put an end to mission, it will only create a reality where we can finally live in the proper response to mission. The pursuit of God and our pursuit of him is a forever reality. God will forever be on mission. His salvation will be the centerpiece to our eternity. Mission and worship are forever.

Our lives and styles of existence are never neutral. Robb Redman in his book *The Great Worship Awakening* says, "The nature and character of the God we worship shapes what we think is the best way to worship him."[1] He is saying that our worship of the true God will generate a lifestyle of love, benevolence, mercy, and forgiveness. If our lives reflect the opposite—hatred, selfishness, bitterness, and pride—then we're worshipping something other than God. It is thus worship that drives mission. Mission reveals worship.

In our following section on *Trinity Worship*, we are now able to discuss the last letter of our acronym—"S". S.ignature Mission.

WHAT IS HIS S.IGNATURE MISSION?

The first thing that still might pop into our minds when we think of mission is the sending of people out to foreign countries to plant the gospel. However, is this God's picture of mission? I dare say, no! It's a much broader subject.

Everyone is on a mission, not just the selected few.

Our God is forever on mission.

It's impossible for deity and humanity not to be pointed outward. His mission and ours proceed from our being. In God's infinite wisdom, he knew that no entity would best embody his sense of community, reasoning, organization, scriptural curriculum, and mission quite like the marriage, family, meal, and home. As God's mission has grown, we now know that there's no more holistic place for character, craft, community, and Christlikeness to form than amongst his family of families: the church.

On that note, let me state my thesis up front for the following section so I can build on it. If you are a follower of Christ, I believe that you are called to one mission—church planting—because at the core of church planting lies the only eternal logic for what it means to make Christ known to the ends of the earth. I admit this may seem like a pretty narrow hypothesis. I assure you it isn't. To unpack my thesis, let's first define "church" so we're speaking on the same wavelength.

Take a look at how Grudem summarizes how the word church is used in Scripture:

> A "house church" is called a "church" in Romans 16:5 ("greet also the church in their house"), 1 Corinthians 16:19 ("Aquilla and Prisca, together with the church in their house, send you hearty greetings in the Lord"). The church in an entire city is also called "a church" (1 Cor. 1:2; 2 Cor. 1:1; and 1 Thes. 1:1). The church in a region is referred to as a "church" in Acts 9:31: "so the church throughout all Judea and Galilee and Samaria had peace and was built up. Finally, the church throughout the entire world can be referred to as 'the church." Paul says, "Christ loved the church and gave himself up for her" (Eph. 5:25) and says, "God has appointed in the church first apostles, second prophets, third teachers..." (1 Cor. 12:28) ... We may conclude that the group of God's people considered at any level from local to universal may rightly be called "a church."[2]

When we speak of "church" from here forward, it's very important that we hear "a people," not a place or a building.

Now that we understand what a church is, we need to consider the ministry and mission of Jesus and the early disciples. Doing so will help us make connections between the continuity of their mission past and our mission presently.

It is clear in Luke's gospel that Luke intends to link Jesus' ministry and mission on earth with ours. Luke does this by writing the gospel of Luke and the book of Acts almost in parallel. Take a look at my crude copy of Peter Leithart's outline (next page) of the Lukan account of the ministry of Jesus and the mission of the people in Acts. They are mirrored:[3]

Luke	Content	Acts
1:1-4	Preface, with dedication to Theophilus	1:1-5
1:5-3:21	Time of preparation	1:6-26
3:22	Baptism of the Spirit	2:1-4
4:16-30	Inaugural sermon	2:14-40
Local Ministry		
4:31-8:56	Galilee / Jerusalem	2:41-8:3
5:17-25	Lame man healed	3:1-10
5:29-6:11	Conflicts with leaders	4:1-8:3
9:9	Martyr: John & Stephen	7:54-8:1
7:1-10	Centurion sends for Jesus / Apostle	10:1-48
7:11-17	Widow's son and resurrection	9:36-43
Journey		
9:51-53	Resolve to journey to Jerusalem	19:21
9:51-19:27	Missionary journey	13:1
9:31, 51; 12:50	Passion journey	20:3, 22-24
9:45; 18:34	Friends and disciples	21:4, 12-13
13:22	Ready to die in Jerusalem	21:13
Jerusalem, Arrest, Trial		
19:37	Joyously received in Jerusalem	21:17-21
19:45-48	Visit to the temple	21:26
20:27-39	Dispute about resurrection	23:6-9
22:14-38	Farewell address	20:17-38
22:15-20	Last meal	27:33-38
22:47-54	Seizure by a mob	21:30
22:63-64	Slapped before high priest	23:2
22-23	Four trials before three courts	24-26
23:4, 14, 22	Declarations of innocence	23:9; 25:25; 26:31
23:6-12	Sent to Herod for questioning	25:13; 26:32
23:16, 22	Opportunity for release	26:32
23:18	"Away with this Man"	21:36
23:47	Centurion with a favorable opinion	27:3, 43
24	Fulfillment of Scripture	28
24:46-49	Sent to nations / Gentiles	28:28

Not only is it obvious that the early disciples made an automatic connection between Jesus' mission and the conduct of their own, they assumed that the church (a family of families) was the agent to fulfill the promise of Jesus made in the Great Commission. Jesus left the disciples with the command to take the gospel to Judea, Samaria, and to the ends of the earth. Luke's outline of Acts shows the commission in action as the gospel spreads.

Note also (below) my outline for the book of Acts, and how Luke purposefully writes in segments. Each sub-section specifically documents what happens as a result of the gospel spreading in each region. He then bookends each account with a phrase to the tune of "the word of God increased and spread."

THE GOSPEL SPREADS THROUGHOUT JERUSALEM

Acts 1:1 - 6:7
Bookend 6:7: "So the word of God spread. The number of disciples in Jerusalem increased rapidly, and a large number of priests became obedient to the faith."

THE GOSPEL SPREADS TO JUDEA & SAMARIA

Acts 6:8 - 7:60
Bookend 9:31: "Then the church throughout Judea, Galilee, and Samaria enjoyed a time of peace and was strengthened. Living in the fear of the Lord and encouraged by the Holy Spirit, it increased in numbers."

TO THE ENDS OF THE EARTH | GENTILES & ANTIOCH

Acts 9:32 - 12:24
Bookend 12:24: "But the word of God continued to spread and flourish."

TO THE ENDS OF THE EARTH | ASIA MINOR

Acts 12:25 - 16:5
Bookend 16:4-5: "As they traveled from town to town, they delivered the decisions reached by the apostles and elders in Jerusalem for the people to obey. So the churches were strengthened in the faith and grew daily in numbers."

To the Ends of the Earth | Europe

Acts 16:6 - 19:23
Bookend 19:20-23: "In this way, the word of the Lord spread widely and grew in power. After all this had happened, Paul decided to go to Jerusalem, passing through Macedonia and Achaia. 'After I have been there,' he said, 'I must visit Rome also.' He sent two of his helpers, Timothy and Erastus, to Macedonia, while he stayed in the province of Asia a little longer."

The Ends of the Earth | Macedonia, Greece, Etc.

Acts 19:20 - 28
Bookend 28:30: "For two whole years Paul stayed there in his own rented house and welcomed all who came to see him. He proclaimed the kingdom of God and taught about the Lord Jesus Christ—with all boldness and without hindrance!"

Luke makes synonymous the fact that as "people" increased, "the word" increased. Luke helps us think not so much in regard to how a simple message of the gospel was expanding and growing, but how the visually-communal image of the Trinity was expanding in homes. The dance of the Trinity was erupting. People were becoming like him. They were learning to express their unique existence in a communal way, which is the hallmark of the church. True existence is what was spreading. God's heavenly nature was intersecting with the earth through the human family.

The church is the only place where the whole human can form in total. The church—a family of families gathered in homes while eating and drinking in remembrance to the Lord as a spectacle to saint and sinner of Christ's rule and reign—is the only thing that can capture the greatest image of God in our current existence.

Why?

Well first, the people of God are in and of themselves a relational unity. The church is the only place where through a people of many creeds, races, tongues, gifting, proclivities, biases, sins and sanctities, vices and virtues, and every extent of personality, the image of Christ can be fully put on display and made famous from every angle. It's the only place where true identity can form to the greatest extent; as our purest identity relies on others to give us titles (i.e., father, son, mother, daughter, brother, sister).

Second, the church is the only place where Christlike character can be encouraged, rebuked, edified, and holistically chiseled out. Sure, character can in some manner be forged in work environments where one is required to endure difficult circumstances, love difficult people, and serve and sacrifice on all levels, but in these arenas we can put on a face. We can pretend. Perform. We can to varying degrees put up the **Fake**book profile of who we want people to think us to be.

The family environment is the place where the depth of who you and I are come out. There is no other place where we are fully who we really are than when we are at home. It's in the family that we see behind the curtain. We see the lowest lows and the highest highs. We see the greatest valor and strongest vice. Only in an environment of such close extremes can encouragement climb its Everest, can patience and steadfastness run the full marathon, and can rebuke and correction hit the bullseye with the truest arrow. Embrace squeezes out the very best in us and the very worst.

It's under the protection of those that are most loving that our craft can be shaped holistically as well. The church today has lost its grip on our responsibility to be the shaper of trade and culture. The family and the church used to be the center of curating and making of all kinds. Gone are the days where we expect Bachs, Van Goghs, Handels, Michaelangelos, etc. to come from within the family of God. But in the past, the greatest minds and most talented people have emerged from amidst Christ's family. The church is now perceived to be on the periphery of life and is only concerned with offering sermons, sacraments, and programs. We've lost any connection to our role in how truth makes us into a city within the city where we live—a family from which the world around us should take its cues to achieve true flourishing.

Being the center of all that causes human flourishing is the intended reality for God's people. Christ indeed fills all things, and we indeed have the Holy Spirit. The mind of Christ. Therefore, it's together that the mind of Christ works in us, and it should be logical that from us naturally comes the best inventions. Not only the best ideas, but the most helpful ideas. Not just money-making ideas, but ideas that turn profit toward the least of these—the orphan, the widow, the fatherless, and the oppressed. When businessmen, politicians, artists, educators, media professionals, and every vocational person in the in-betweens begin thinking up ideas that are community-birthed, pastorally formed, and orbit around society's true needs and address all matters of injustice, the gospel goes forth. Not only do talents speak a louder word in packs rather than individuals, but when needs are met within communities there's a force reaching out toward people that goes far past just the immediate crisis. There's also a returning energy that spins toward family for long-term sustaining. It's like a never-ending tennis match. One player lofts the ball into the air and the other drives it back.

Here's how it works. If a widow is reached with the gospel and then left to herself, she still has a plethora of real needs that must be met. There's a hole in the home where dad and husband are gone. The whole of the home will never be the same. Many may meet the one need in giving them food or money, but only when they're ushered into the family of God are their needs met in full. In the family, they find a plethora of dads and husbands from the other family units to rally around them and provide leverage in the raising of the children. Both the adult and child find the wisdom of the older and more mature family members, not only to walk them through their time of turmoil, but also to cope with future events.

The church redeems the counseling of people in their psychological, sociological, and spiritual health. Modern counseling aims to restore people but cannot. Yet despite this fact, counseling is a major item of outsourcing in the life of God's people today. Because the church community has outsourced its role in counseling people mind, body, and spirit back into a healthy relationship with each other and God, the devices for psychological practice have multiplied. Because counseling sessions are done apart from the church body, and mostly in isolation with a considered "professional," psychological framework ends up breeding narcissists and forever-victims who talk about nothing but themselves and the others that they blame. Counseling done in and with the community helps the person heal and process their level of hurt in a restorative way. It heals the distance felt within friendship in real time. Believe it or not, most psychological problems are caused by the disconnect of isolation and can be remedied by re-integrating that person into the community. Where else would be better to do such a thing than in a gospel-centered home.

Whatever role in society you or I might play can never escape its tie to the family of God. Our responsibility is linked to people because so is our Creator's. We can pretend the call is not there, or try and run away like Jonah, but in the end, God will hold us accountable to two things: how we loved him, and how we loved each other. Within the family of God—the church—is where we carry out our command to love in the fullest sense. They will know us by our love (Jn. 13:35).

Your role in church planting is most likely not what you might envision as typical. Most roles are not confined to those in "full-time" ministry. The Scripture confirms our role in church planting as a basic element to who we are in Christ. Jesus actually speaks of it at the Last Supper. He refers to the *benefactors* of society in talking to the disciples. These were people serving in the spheres of culture and work. The worshipping *leiturgia*. Those working in, funding, or seeking to influence the loves of the culture toward Christ. He instructed the disciples not to be like the selfish benefactors of that day—powerful leaders who channeled all time, talent, and treasure toward worldly ends—but to be servants.

Remember, we've learned in speaking of worship leading that in Christ's and Paul's minds, a person who leads is best characterized as a community leader who actively funnels all the time, energy, and resources of cultural endeavors toward the aid of helping people flourish.

Consider how a biblical view of such a role would completely shift how we think of worship today.

Jesus and Paul actually spend significant time talking directly to those with the greatest cultural influence—even when talking to disciples of low standing in the world system. When Jesus speaks to the disciples, he envisions that they'll begin influencing people's loves on the most exhaustive level. They need to be ready to channel the power they gain from the presence of the Spirit within them toward right ends. This means not merely helping God's people gather; it neabs getting out on the highways and by-ways of real experience to pastor people in worship right where they are.

Jesus desires us all to use our worshipping power to move culture toward what God loves, desires, and embraces. We literally create a Jesus culture wherever we go by shaping forms and functions around what is most loving, peaceful, patient, and kind. Where the shift happens most practically is in the thick of where worship runs rampant. On the streets. In the marketplace.

Don't think Jesus and Paul's focus regarding those of influence are contrary to Jesus' heart for the poor. The top-tier structures of society and the low-tier structures are linked. What the rich and powerful do either gives to or steals from the less fortunate, and the decisions of the less fortunate become either an addition to or a drain on the life of a society. Remember, true poverty is the loss of our ability or desire to make meaning. Poverty can exist in even the richest of places if people are spending their lives chasing lesser lovers.

To make something of value of the world is the true journey of worship and mission. In encasing the idea of honor in cultural realms rather than restricting worship to the gathered body, Jesus and Paul preserve the connection between worship and justice. They link everyday vocation and the whole realm of work to the idea of our formation as followers of Christ.

Worship is about family formation. People Formation. Church formation. It's about resourcing and equipping all to function within the worship ministry of Jesus by connecting his work in, on, and through us to everything on which we lay our hands.

THE PAULINE CYCLE AND JESUS' MINISTRY CONTINUED

Not only does Luke's gospel and its sequel, the book of Acts, convey the unity of mission between Jesus and his people, but it's also seamless with the logic of Paul. The majority of Acts outlines the life and ministry of the apostle.

Paul had spent much of his unbelieving life as a Pharisee. Before meeting Christ, he spent most of his days seeking out Christians in order to murder them. You might say that the pre-saved Paul had a way of viewing the manner whereby faith interacts with people and the world, and Jesus' way was not cutting it.

But we all know the story. Jesus met Paul. Paul transformed. From the moment Paul met Jesus and forward, Paul's mission became remarkably unified. He used his gifts as an apologist and debater, businessmen (tentmaker), marketeer, writer, journeyman, politician, historian, theologian, and so on. He channeled all of his energies into one remarkably repetitive cycle. See figure 7.1.

Fig. 7.1[4]

THE MINISTRY and mission of disciples were intentionally identical, even though they served through their own uniqueness and personality. They were actively linking the message of Jesus to every facet of life in a way that brought about the formation and spontaneous expansion of God's family. In other words, everything connected to church planting.

The goal of discipleship is the multiplying of God's family.

I would assume that the cycle of church planting appears foreign to many reading this book. You may still be reacting to my dogmatic assertion that we all have a call to plant churches. You may have a good reason for your "huh?" reaction. Most modern churches replicate or multiply maybe once in their lifetime, if that. Churches today focus on building the huge entity that is the mega-church. In my travels to dozens of countries and thousands of churches, I've rarely witnessed much discussion about church planting as a topic that concerns everyone, let alone as a specific church's passion. We simply don't recognize the explosiveness, replicating, resourcing, and expanding synergy that was normal in the early church. We've been trained through the very systems we've created to react to that normal as if it's an oddity.

Our disconnect reaches further than just church-proper. Businesses led by Christians, though they might multiply their influence and finance, rarely aim their works of philanthropy directly toward the effort of planting churches. I would venture to say that most entrepreneurs, when seeking to step out in a venture of any consequence, consult the Harvard Business Review and TED talks and never think of seeking the counsel of the believing community.

Creative types may multiply their craft, but rarely is their primary vision focused on how they will use their talent as a primary tool to multiply God's people. Seminaries are also disconnected from church life. They preserve a gap between content and context, precept and person, and script and society. The chasm is forever growing, and we're seeing it impact everyone. People are paying larger tuitions and going into debt, then graduating four years later with the same phrase on their tongue: "I don't know what I'm gonna do when I grow up." Clearly, the education process is not adding up. It's building bank accounts, debts, and campuses, but not purposeful people. The divide makes it difficult for people to connect learning to the multiplying of a family when they are online, living away from home, and being gouged by debt collectors.

Counselors open clinics rather than turning inward to equip the body to holistically comfort, counsel, and bring the conviction of the Holy Spirit to the body. Artists, celebrities, and sports icons of all flavors spin away from close community and family to tour, play, and work. The need to tour and work on location in the music and film industry has convinced us that separation is actually necessary to vocation.

The ever-growing cycle of the world has certainly permeated our church life. It's spinning us away from multiplication. To confront and inform our church-planting short circuit, let's learn from Paul. His ways are remarkably consistent. He thinks in descriptive paradigms, not prescriptive models.

In Acts 13:1-4 we learn that missionaries are commissioned. Barnabas and Paul were prayed for, fasted over, and received the commissioning of the Holy Spirit through the laying on of hands. Notice how their missional mindset did not begin in individuality, but as a team looking to be sent out. Like Jesus, whose mission was conducted in a team—being sent from heaven to earth in the power of the Holy Spirit and via the will of the Father—so must ours be. As those being sent, Paul and Barnabas sought more than a support check, they sought the counsel and affirmation of calling above anything else. They began the work of mission in the family of God. The people together weighed the motives, ambitions, and desires of the men to determine the sincerity of their call and belief.

Paul and Barnabas demonstrate for us a starting place. These men tell us centuries later of the essential characteristics of leadership.[5] I believe their manner to be a normative point of entrance for all missions. It provides a model for guidance and decision-making. Trinity-shaped ministry must emerge within environments of friendship and multiples rather than in mission houses or sending agencies. I've seen what happens to missionaries that are individually deployed. They are isolated. Their isolation leads to one of three things: compromise, burnout, or ineffectiveness. Over time, their individuality-based model for mission ends up becoming the poison their soul drinks.

The men in Acts were sent from their local family to contact new audiences and share the gospel with anyone who would hear. Not only was the gospel something they wanted to share with others as a message, it was also a way of life to them. They embodied the gospel in living with one another. Had they gone out alone, they may have succeeded in seeing people saved, but how would people understand what they were being saved into? The gospel is a lived message, and only one who is living in it alongside others can share it with the true depth it merits.

The Barnabas/Paul church-planting team was made up of people that aimed at gathering together more people. They replicated their way in which they too were formed. They brought what they'd been taught. They carried with them a display that not only gave information away but also satisfied the hearers intrinsic need for becoming and belonging.[6] Anthropologists Sherwood Lingenfelter and Marvin Mayers comment, that by nature, our task as people of mission to those who need to hear of the mission of God is an example of Christ, creates a drastic personal reorientation.[7] Humanity needs to realize that our deepest poverty enters not only through a lack of belief, but through our disconnection from each other and from God.

Church planting ensures that people hear and respond to the message of the gospel as it brings people together. Belief leads to believers congregating as true faith is confirmed. In Pauline theology, there is great stress placed upon the "household of God,"[8] and in Acts 13:43 we see believers continuing on with Paul and Barnabas. Justin Martyr would say that the first sign of true conversion is that people instantly had a concern for the body of Christ. Here's Justin's depiction of the familial nature of early worship:

> We hold our shared church service on Sunday because it is the first day of the week. In our churches, the rich among us come to the aid of the poor, and we always stick together... everyone in the city or countryside gathers together, where the memoirs of the apostles or the writings of the prophets are read for

as long as time allows. When the reader has finished, the leader of our community gives a sermon in which he instructs us and urges us to imitate these good teachings. Next, we stand together for prayers... bread and wine mixed are brought, public prayers are offered, and an "Amen" is offered by the congregation... the deacons distribute the elements as well to those who were absent. There's a giving of the offering in whatever amount seems appropriate to them. The money goes to the widows, the orphans, the needy, the sick, those in prison, and anyone else who may land in our congregation.[9]

Justin Martyr wisely associates compassion and care as being consistent with true salvation. The reason why his association is vital is that in Scripture salvation is not solely a one-off event. It's a journey. It requires constant help along the way. In 1 Peter 1:3-5, Peter states, "Praise be to the God and Father of our Lord Jesus Christ! In his great mercy, *he has given us new birth* into a living hope through the resurrection of Jesus Christ from the dead, and into an inheritance that can never perish, spoil or fade. This inheritance is *kept in heaven for you*, who through faith are shielded by God's power until the coming of the *salvation that is ready to be revealed* in the last time" (italics mine). Christ not only catches us at the moment of salvation and new birth, but he keeps us as a sign of his power. Justification is the sign of initial new birth, but sanctification is the sign of keeping on. Genuine faith moves toward glorification. Salvation completes us. Peter speaks about final salvation as being a joy revealed to us at the end of time.

Salvation births us as a baby, sees us through our teenage years, into adulthood, and into old age as we mature and grow. No one can do the process alone!

The mission of God and the expansion of his kingdom was and should always be seen not as a cycle of "getting people into heaven," but rather as a mission that continues helping people grow in their manner of walking with the Lord and becoming like him. His deliverance not only catches us; it also keeps us and completes us.

Steps 1–5 of the Pauline cycle (see figure 7:1) almost perfectly describe how God catches us, whereas steps 6–10 tell us more about how God keeps us. He surrounds us with all the resources necessary to confirm our faith, to consecrate leadership, to commend believers, to continue relationships, and finally to start the whole process over again in forming new teams to plant new churches. Laurence J. Peter suggests that when most churches begin walking through steps 6–10, they promote faithful members while failing to really focus on their character, competency, or Christlikeness. An individual elevated to a level above one's capability becomes frustrated and unproductive.[10] Thus, influence is not just about a person's skill level or place in the organism; it is about helping the person understand his or her role within the world-wide body of Christ.

True Christian maturity in Paul's cycle forms only when a person adjusts to a life lived together in family. Overseers of great responsibility emerge not merely from people who excel in ability, but more often from people who excel in relational love for the whole. Even after Paul planted churches in various places, he still shepherded them with the utmost care and compassion, as did John, Peter, and others. Many of the epistles and pastoral letters are loving responses of deep emotional feeling accompanied by well-intentioned rebukes to issues residing in each church.

As the church grew, shepherds and equippers emerged and relationships deepened. The natural rhythm was to keep multiplying. Even through spontaneous expansion, they retained their accessibility to the apostles. They felt reciprocal affection toward them. It is very clear that the local churches turned to the apostles for direction and insight as less a formality than a stance of relationship and family.

People with needs or questions usually turn to someone they know, like, and respect. People turn for counseling to someone whom they feel is competent, who observes professional ethics, and who knows God.[11] Paul's listening is reflective and participatory. He's deeply committed to the churches' maturation and governance.[12] Many sought his counsel in structuring their family activity as carried out by fathers and mothers, uncles, aunts, or grandparents. They also sought Paul's instruction within the cultural structure as well.

All the synergy of the early church's life together culminated in one thing: the word increasing. The whole aim of the early church was the expansion of God's people. Every man, woman, and child, when rightly understood, viewed themselves as being on mission toward equipping, expanding, resourcing, training, releasing, and multiplying God's beloved.

The mission of forming families is different from building church entities. Michael Todd Wilson and Brad Hoffmann in their book *Preventing Ministry Failure* discuss many aspects necessary to maintaining a healthy mission, but the three things they stress to the greatest degree are rest, recess, and renewal.[13] God's mission is restful first and foremost because it is so repetitive. We don't have the stress of trying to figure things out, craft mission and vision statements, and invent new ideas. We rest because Paul's cycle is so clear and enjoyable. Second, the mission of God is restful and renewing for the very fact that we don't lead anything. Jesus is the leader of his church. He's the cornerstone. He's the builder. The foundation, walls, subfloor, and interior design of God's family are all being erected around us by the hands of the Trinity, and we are on mission most when we stop to marvel. Worship. Enjoy beauty. Revel in life together. Eat and Drink. Reminisce and remember. Jesus often found places of solitude for prayer and contemplation (Lk. 5:16), and churches and ministries must be led to do the same. Personal vitality, creativity, and perseverance are direct results of spiritual renewal.[14]

As we consider our mission to multiply the people of God, we are encouraged to do so under the sabbath, the shalom, and the peace of God.

USING AND ABUSING SPIRITUAL "GIFTS"

If I've succeeded in convincing you that every believer in God's family is called to church planting—people building—then I hope you're asking, "What's my role?" To answer the question, let's revisit the idea of spiritual ministries.

I've grown quite disgusted today with how spiritual gifts have been dumbed down to nothing more than superpowers, personality tests, or pieces in a chess game that serve only to run a particular pastor's pet fancy and inflated vision. Across the board, I feel like our view on spiritual ministry has gone way out of whack. In evaluating ministry on the coattails of speaking about church planting, I've grown particularly tired of one phrase I often hear coming out of the majority of church leaders' mouths: "I want to help you discover where we can use your gifts here at _(fill-in the Church name)_."

Such a phrase is uttered only once a crucial shift has happened in how we view God's gifted body. It indicates that people are no longer going to be cultivated, but their DNA, makeup, and demonstration of church life together will be fitted into slots predetermined by those in leadership. The homes and people orbit the church central and are used to build up that entity. This model of church consumes people and trains people to consume.

God has already given us the way for all members of the church to function. The Great Commission. The proper way to see that body of Christ continues to multiply beyond the cult of personality and stage is to flip the front and back door of the house. The family-home life of the community is where the uniqueness and personality of the people are best pastored, cultivated, and awakened. It's where God invests all his time, resources, and energy. It's even where he derives all of his kingdom language. Family. Out of the family fabric, the true kingdom voice emerges.

With the above thinking in place, central gathering place that springs up for the church now serves rightly as the satellite. The gathered event of worship expresses and captures the voice of the people. It puts on display the people's personality. People no longer consume, but they see themselves as vibrant producers within the kingdom of God. They begin to automatically link their vocation, their talents, and anything they bring to the expansion, the expression, and the vibrant flourishing of God's home.

The paradigm-shift I'm proposing simply changes everything, particularly how we view the spiritual gifts. Consider for a moment how many of the overt displays of "spiritual gifts" today produce spectacles, not servants. New Wave spiritual teaching tells us to keep searching for the next endowment of power for ourselves. Give me, give me, give me! We have assumed that the overwhelming generosity of God is like a supernatural PEZ dispenser doling out sweet after sweet to satisfy our belly. The gifts have made us into individual-ability-alcoholics. We've become addicts of the flesh rather than catalysts for vibrant service, sacrifice, love, and obedience to Jesus. To make matters worse, today spiritual gifts are portrayed as being for individual uses, not for the advancement of the whole church.

Gifts are seen as something that makes us into superheroes, not servants. The Corinthian church fell into this lie. They were a church full of people looking to make an idol out of something or somebody. In 1 Corinthians 1, Paul identifies a few types of Christians that were emerging. We will refer to these developing Christian-flavored people as the star-struck (1:10-17), the stoic (1:20), the debater (1:20), the Jew and the Greek (1:22), and the nobleman believer (1:26). The star-struck Christians were making celebrities out of the apostles. Some of them were following Paul, others Cephas, and others Apollos. Rather than welcoming the hero worship from these people, Paul responds by asking, "Is Christ divided? Was Paul crucified for you? Or were you baptized in the name of Paul?" (1:13). Paul's point: Why are you putting people on a pedestal?

There were also perceived "wise" Christians. Some of these may have been

Stoics, sober-minded ones who believed that emotions are destructive. Some may have been Epicureans, who believed that simplicity and pleasure were the greatest goods. No doubt some Jewish scribes—highly educated people who were akin to our modern lawyers—were also converted. Finally, there was the nobleman. They were likely the prosperity Christians, believing that health, wealth, and prosperity is the name of the game. As you can see, the early church attracted many whose beliefs or central aims did not reflect the nature of Jesus.

Things haven't changed much. We live in an age where there are self-proclaimed, falsely inaugurated superheroes everywhere. Spiritual gifts are the cape they wear. They flourish because we are always trying to make someone into a functional god that can save us, make our lives better, or just numb our pain a few seconds. Sadly, spiritual gifts have been assigned the task of serving our idol worship rather than to us become like our God.

What hero worship naturally results in is locations. Stadiums. Spot over Spirit. In the Old Testament, locations were of extreme importance. Israelites from all over Israel and Judah made pilgrimages three times a year for the Feast of Weeks, the Feast of Booths, and the Passover. Many of our Psalms (Ps. 120–134) are called Psalms of Ascent and were sung during people's pilgrimages to Jerusalem. The spot of the temple and Jerusalem were considered sacred—places for God's presence and restitution.

When Jesus came, he observed many of the feasts, pilgrimages, and special Jewish celebrations common to the Old Testament. After Jesus' ascension, however, the spot of enlightenment or presence changed. Jesus took up residence in two locations. The first location is at the right hand of the Father as a resurrected man in a fully renewed—but still skin and bones—spiritual body, interceding in heaven. The second location Jesus now inhabits in Spirit is the hearts of humankind through salvation and the regeneration of the Holy Spirit.

Why is all this important? Today, even the language in much of our song lyrics in churches worldwide speaks as if we are summoning God's presence. Holy Spirit power-seekers travel the globe on pilgrimages to find the next superhero, super healer, or location where God's spirit is "being poured out." Unfortunately, the mentality of spot over Spirit has overwhelmed the conversation of spiritual gifts and ministries.

When the emphasis is placed upon people, locations, and situations as grounds for Spirit empowerment, it really undermines one person. Jesus!

Consider the ministries that succumb to the above mentality, and you'll notice that often times their ministries subtly start to try and "act out" the ministry of Jesus. People will try to attempt to intercede 24/7. That's Jesus' job. People will begin to claim to summon or send the Holy Spirit's presence. That's Jesus' job. People will seek gift after gift, experience after experience, and this demonstrates a devaluing of Christ's once-for-all sacrifice.

The poisonous perspective on God's gifting results in an equally unsettling demeanor. I've experienced the phenomenon all over the world. Their posture seems confident, but it is simply loud and even abrasive. It causes me to wonder if this was the demeanor of our King Jesus. His posture was one that was so gentle. He neither extinguished a flickering candle nor broke a bruised reed.

Neither the posture nor the results desired in spiritual gifting today matches that of the disciples and apostles. When they utilized their gifting, it often brought on them great persecution and even death. Today, such ecstatic experiences are sought as a means to better one's life. It's a complete shift in perspective.

We must also notice the way in which modern spiritual gift seekers replicate. They make all of the gifts, particularly tongues, normative when in Acts there's only a handful of actual attestations to tongues accompanying salvation. When tongues did accompany salvation, it was when the gospel transferred from Jerusalem, to Judea, then to Samaria, and the ends of the earth. God replicated the Pentecost experience so that all cultures previously separated from the Israelite family knew that they'd all been grafted in by the same sign. For the Jews, this multiplication of tongues in other places was more a sign of their judgment. It was a sign that they were rejecting God, and so his gospel was unleashing elsewhere. He invited them through the sign to come along and not get left behind.

The sign of tongues served as an authenticating tool. Most of the signs were given to point the way to the destination. Therefore, they dissipate in the writings of the rest of the New Testament. The diminution does not suggest that they stopped, but merely that the apostles were authenticated in the same way Jesus was, and that you and I can base our faith on the foundation of the apostles (N.T.) and prophets (O.T.) in order to become like Jesus.

The gifts are not meant to make spectacles, superheroes, or spots more sacred. Yet this is how we often use them. We elevate things to places of worship and thus distort their purpose. A new paradigm changes our posture. If spiritual ministry is activated through an enabled body, then our gifts don't single us out as individuals; they graft us in. It's the community that stands out. We are called to warm the community with the love of Jesus, invigorating it with the power of the Spirit and making it fresh and exciting with the salt of the Christian difference.[15] We are to the world a family that is actively serving, not seeking spectacle; a community of servants, not superheroes—a community where the emphasis is placed on the Spirit in his people over and above the spots where we meet.

As I end this chapter, I challenge you to think about the fact that you're a church planter. Let it sink in. I want God to bring to mind your ministry within God's mission. God will use your spiritual ministry in whatever sacred or secular vocation you're in to share the gospel, see people saved, and bring people back to God. Consider yourself called and equipped. You've been singled out by the Holy Spirit and in-dwelt by him. There's no turning back now.

28

SYNERGETIC WORSHIP & MISSION

G od's S.ignature Mission is profoundly unified. His purpose is to be a holy God dwelling amidst a holy people. If we don't accept God's mission, we will undoubtedly arrive at either of two possible solutions, which are conveyed in figures 7.2 and 7.3. I call these two possible solutions divergent and emergent worship and mission. First, take a look at figure 7.2.

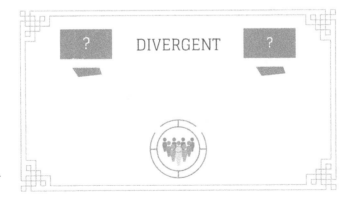

Fig. 7.2

The graphic attempts to show people deciding upon their own course and own object of worship. People are amazing in their capacity to arrive at the oddest conclusions, so I've conveyed what they might journey toward through the use of a question mark. We are obviously welcome to try and outbid God on what is the best avenue for worship. We are allowed to give in to the inspiration of our imprisoned will and follow lesser loves, but all it brings is divergence. We move away from each other and from the embracing dance, or *perichoresis* of the Trinity (as shown in the circle).

In the divergent model, there can only be division. It's the culmination of postmodern thought. Racial division, cliques, denominations, political parties, preference, and any one of a million other things that can and will divide us is the only logical result. When we make something ultimate in our own life, we will naturally hold everyone else ultimately to it. The catch-22 is that because we're imperfect, our objects of worship and our missional course will always be jagged and never straight. Divergence leads us on a journey of separation, aloneness, false hope, and a life aimed at the smoke and mirrors that we design for ourselves.

Figure 7.2 assumes that we're making an item or a destination of our own fancy the goal of our affections and mission. Figure 7.3 attempts to show what happens when we make each other the ultimate source of our worship:

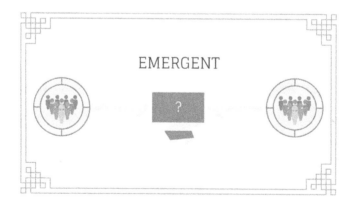

Fig. 7.3

Emergent worship and mission attempts to show what we will to do to draw closer to one another while refusing to accept that there's any truth. Call it tolerance. We will prioritize full acceptance of one another over commitment to truth. To accomplish this, we will make room for all kinds of lies to prevent our divergent beliefs from impairing our friendship.

For example, the atheist who believes there is no god and the pantheist who believes that everything is god will unite on the basis that one truth is as good as another. There's only one problem. Both can't be right. It logically can't work.

Tolerance breaks down when one person's truth intersects another person's truth in an adverse way. For example, let's say my neighbor believes that lust, adultery, and stealing are okay, and I believe they are not. We can live in a lie that each of us is correct only until that neighbor breaks into my house, sexually assaults my wife, and steals my property. Now we have a problem. I'm either going to hold my truth over my neighbor's head and judge him by it, or he'll hold his notions over mine and insist that he's free to do whatever he pleases with my family and possessions.

Either way you slice it, someone is left to assert the superiority of his truth. The question that remains is, which truth is absolute?

When Jesus says in John 14:6, "I am the way, the truth, and the life. No one comes to the Father except through me," he is pointing to himself as the absolute for all truth. Since everyone can't be right, we must conclude that either Jesus is right or we are right when we act on our own truth. Which is it? We can't have it both ways. If we believe we all can make truth, then we have to compliment Hitler in the same breath that we hail Mother Teresa.

Our human contradictions of tolerance are logically inconsistent. Humans are constantly clawing to get back to each other, and we're desperately inventing ways to do it. But our devices don't work. We seek unity in each other and so we conclude that unity is found in race, sexual orientation, preference, celebrity, clique, hairstyle, culture, class, and whomever looks like us. At the foundation, we're making ourselves god. We get to assess what's true. We define righteousness though we can't even live in congruence to our own construct.

Emergence is seen in every level of culture past, present, and future, and it always has one thing in common: It is timely but never timeless. The flavor of the century always passes and possibly morphs into a faint whisper of what it was.

The Trinity's S.ignature Mission claims a perfect unity that can help both the idolater of places and things and the idolater of persons to explore better thinking. In figure 7.4 we see a graphic of what some have called convergent worship. Take a look.

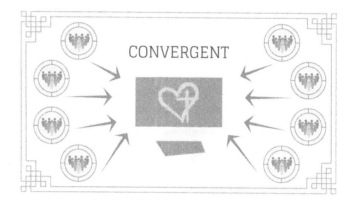

Fig. 7.4

The apostle Paul suggests to us in 1 Corinthians 2:2 that the centerpiece for human reasoning is "Jesus Christ and him crucified." Jesus claims this about himself. Convergent Worship takes this seriously. What's depicted in the graphic above is that Christ and his work on the C.R.O.S.S. is the central place toward which everyone is moving in affection. The surrounding people represent the masses. You can fill in each people group with any meaning you like. They could represent countries, cultures, and tribes. They could represent male, female, and the thirty-two Baskin Robbins flavors of sexual orientation. They could represent class, political affiliation, hobby, fame, revenue, vocation, educational placement, etc. The thing this graphic demonstrates is that when we gather around the cross, it neutralizes everything. It lays the proud low and elevates the lowly. The cross demonstrates to the greatest in the world that though they claim themselves great, they would never dare stoop to die for someone else, let alone a vile sinner. The cross demonstrates to the most humiliated of creatures that the universe's Savior sees them and cares for them.

Convergent worship encourages us to bring all of our biases and differences to the C.R.O.S.S. and allow God's way of relating, doing things, ordering of life, program for training, and mission to confront everything about us. The cross suggests that all of our differences need to answer to God, not each other. Jesus clearly lays out the truth of life, and we need to all pay the piper. We need to question amongst ourselves and provide an answer only to Jesus as to whether we are doing what he has asked us to do—to reveal his image to the world. If by submitting to Jesus as the perfect ultimate we discover holes in our own thinking, morals, and worldview, then we take up our cross, follow him, and are transformed through the renewing of our minds. Convergent worship is a very helpful way to think about worship because it takes the problem out of the center ring and asks the right question first: Does that square with Jesus?

Many of you reading this as Christians may be resounding with a hearty "Amen"—as you should. However, there's still a disconnect. I've been all around the world in every denominational and cultural setting you can possibly imagine, and though every orthodox Christin agrees that Jesus and the work of the cross is central, our methods and preferences continue to divide us. We build denominations, para-churches, contemporary and traditional hymn services, seeker- and believer-aimed productions, and the like. We may be courteous enough to sit in a room with each other and make small talk over whom is at the center of all of life and even pray in unity, but once discussion begins about the practical aspects of living out the Christian mission and our worship, we divide. We simply won't have the conversation.

It seems that once we answer the Jesus question, we never again let God's nature into any other topic. If we're talking about church structure, we turn instantly to systems theory and what the latest research says. When we start a business, we turn to economics. When we start talking about marriage and human life, we go straight to politics. When we talk about gender and male and female roles, we use human analogies and try to debunk logic with better logic. I'm absolutely astonished that we rarely ask; "Well, what is the Trinity like?"

I've heard pastors fight vehemently over whether the church is led by a senior pastor or by multiple leaders. I've seen respectable people refuse to love across the aisle just because one is a Democrat and the other is a Republican. I lived in the South for seven years and heard the way people differentiated between churches. They would say, "Oh, that's the black church" or "Oh, that's the church that's not Baptist." They'd say it as if that other church was some kind of poison. People were willing to separate over color and denomination. When I was thrown into these messes, I listened time and again to the logic, the stats, the theologies, the by-laws, the preferences, the research, blah, blah, blah. You know what I never have heard? "What is the Trinity like?" As people slammed fists and screamed for senior leadership, never once did people deal with the fact that not even our God is a senior leader. He's a senior plural. We! When racial and feminist activists seek to right the wrongs inflicted on them, many scream in blame, rage, and intimidate and override anyone who expresses another viewpoint. Never once has someone discussed the strength of submission as seen in the Trinity. The racist and feminist only see vice. Never once has the one screaming over skin color stopped to think about the fact that the personhood of the Trinity allows not only for deeper uniqueness and dignity beyond just skin, but God teaches us that forgiveness is a more healing posture for gaining justice than revenge.

As I've stood in the midst of conflict over many of these issues, do you know what I've done? First, I didn't confront anyone. I didn't join in the lunacy. My viewpoint could only add more fuel to the fire. I merely sat quietly in the midst, pictured in my mind the Triune God in the center of whatever difference we were having out, and when I finally spoke, I pointed at the being of the Trinity and said, "Tell me what *he* is like." I allowed the Trinity to speak for himself. In a community of those who worship the God of the Bible, this approach works with any issue.

When people erupt and say, "Let's abort babies" while others say, "Let's not," I simply say, "Which option best reveals the Trinity's value for life, not death?" Some may buck and say that I've implied that I'm pro-life, and I am. But I urge them to reach for something far deeper. I attempt to be pastoral before taking a position. I've seen situations where a mother and baby were both as good as dead unless one of them was sacrificed for the other. At that moment, my answer to the question wasn't so black and white. I had to look at the Trinity and ask "Lord, what would bring the most life out of the situation?" There have been times, in moments of difficult suffering, as with the cross of Jesus, that God's answer is—sacrifice brings more life. I've also seen situations where someone cried out "Death to the baby!" when their teenager had been raped. They shook their fist, screaming "Life for my daughter," while Christians in their midst said urged deeper thought. Long story short, that baby was spared and grew up to be a pastor.

If you really want to get down to brass tacks about life, take a look at how the Scripture refers to Jesus. The angel came to Mary and acknowledged Jesus as a person right before Mary became pregnant. The angel affirmed the idea of human life even before conception. The Greek word used to reference Jesus in the womb is the same word used to refer to him when he's running around as a twelve-year-old. Clearly, the Bible's view of personhood is answered not in logic, but in looking straight at what God is like.

My point in all of this is that there's a better way to unify people across denominational, political, racial, gender, and class lines. Solutions do not begin by arguing about the problem or by attacking another person. Deep resolve comes when we first answer the worship question. Again, every issue is a worship issue. Every virtue and vice simply reveal the object of one's worship. We must first expose the virtue or vice that is supreme in any given situation. We must first determine into whose image we are intending to grow. Then we can move forward with better ways of thinking and doing. The deepest questions in life are not answered by debate; they are handled by the personhood of our God. Living worship—united in nature,[1] love,[2] mission,[3] and fellowship.[4]

Convergent worship is helpful, but not complete. It brings us together around the object of our worship, but it doesn't succeed in deploying us into mission. Synergetic worship and mission will do this for us. Look at figure 7.5.

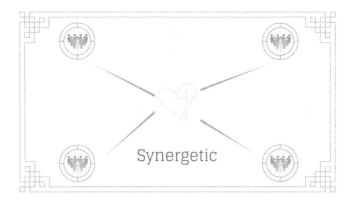

Fig. 7.5

Synergy is the interaction or cooperation of two or more people, organizations, substances, or other agents to produce a combined effect greater than the sum of their separate effects. For synergy to happen in churches, it assumes the realities of divergent, emergent, and convergent worship are working together. Synergy assumes that we all tend to travel different paths (divergence), and yet somehow we're all seeking a way back to each other (Emergence). Yet synergy not only requires that people converge to the center to discuss what is most pertinent to all human life—the personhood and work of the Trinity—but it then spins us back out onto the world as a unit. Synergy has centripetal and centrifugal force. It spins in and out. It gathers and it scatters. It's like a deep breath in and a strong breath out. Synergy requires that we not only look like Christ in what we believe to be true about him (orthodoxy), but it requires that we look like Christ in how we act his image out (doxology).

Rhythms of Inward and Outward Transformation

Let's consider synergy more deeply through the lens of the Garden and the temple imagery in the Old and New Testaments. Synergetic motion to worship and mission has forever been God's desired reality. Let's begin with creation's pattern for worship as shown in figure 7.6 just a few paragraphs down.

Earlier, we looked quite extensively into how the original creation was conceived of as a cosmos temple. Eden is portrayed as a "city on a hill" in which God dwells, and out from God's presence flows the life of rivers into the Garden. Eden is the overarching Holy of Holies. In the Garden, God did not dwell behind a curtain but with humankind. He walked with Adam and Eve. The Garden was full of lush trees, the lamps of the sun, moon, and stars, the animals, and all the things we associate with beautiful landscapes. The Garden was akin to God's inner courts. Later when Solomon erected the temple for worship, the inner courts were full of garden-like imagery, from a lampstand that looked like a tree and had perched upon it lights that pointed to the celestial lights in our universe's sky, to the vaulted ceilings that were named for the enormous expanse of the sky.

Adam served as God's priest in stewarding all time, resource, and energy in a manner that would best honor and glorify God's purposeful intentions.

On the outside of the temple and outside the Garden lay the uninhabited wilderness or the outer courts. It symbolized all that was unsuitable for the flourishing of human life. Adam was tasked to take the civilization of the

Garden and expand it in commerce, family, love, and all manner of making in order to see that humanity both flourished and multiplied.

To the left and right of the temple sat the basins, or "seas," surrounded by animals and fruits to symbolize the wild. The whole temple looked like a mini cosmos. A diorama. Some of you remember making those in school.

Notice the trajectory of the Garden. The arrow in the graphic indicates that Adam and Eve dwelled in the house and the presence of God and were sent out.

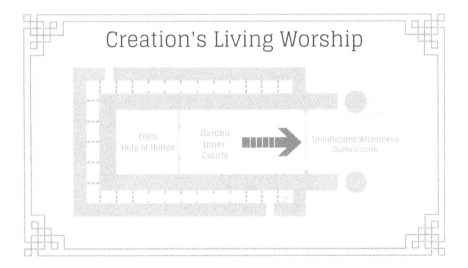

Fig. 7.6

The trajectory of the Temple was much different from that of the Garden. The original trajectory of the Garden was outward. From his original position in the Garden, Adam was to affect the world. But because of sin, humanity was kicked out of God's presence. Since then, we've been forever trying to get back in. The trajectory of the temple reflects the result. It is a place where worshipping people go inward rather than outward. Everyone to this day is still trying to reach immortality. Some try and do it through works, surgeries, or sacrifices. Others do it through incantation, meditation, and fancies of reincarnation. No matter the method, the gap between our mortality and and our craving for immortality exists. We all feel it. As shown in figure 7.7, the arrow is reversed. God's people were being gathered in once again from the places where they had fled.

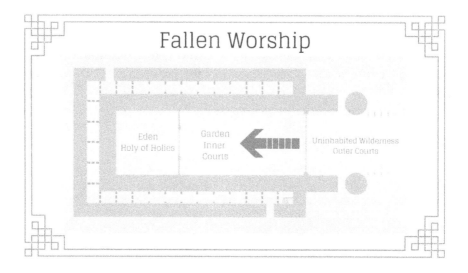

Fig. 7.7

Every civilization in all of history has felt the reversal of God's arrow for worship and mission. We all feel the reality that in some way we're cut off from something we're forever trying to get back to. In Ezekiel 31:3-6 we get a glimpse into how this reality of separation played out in the dynasties of Assyria. Likewise, in Daniel 4:10-12 for Babylon, and how earlier civilizations like Egypt and even Israel attempted to remedy the gap:

> Assyria is portrayed in the passage as growing to envelop the earth in the way that Eden should have done. However, the way Assyria accomplished the growth was unjust and sinful. Therefore, her world-encompassing tree had to be cut down in judgment, just as was Eden's. Daniel 4:10-12 depicts virtually the same, though more abbreviated, picture of Babylon's world dominance. She is portrayed as a huge tree in which "was food for all." The tree was "visible to the end of the whole part" and the branches spanned the earth so that all "the beasts of the field found shade under it, and the birds of the sky dwelt in its branches." Like Assyria, the tree is cut down in judgment because of the pride and sinful disobedience to God.

The point of Ezekiel's portrayal of Assyria is to apply it to the Egyptian kingdom and to foretell its same doom (Ez. 31:2, 18). The application of this world-expanding garden picture to Egypt is intriguing in light of a fascinating nature of Egyptian religion ... The Egyptians themselves believed that the first hill of creation (i.e., their version of Eden) had been located in Egypt and that all of creation had expanded out from their country. Accordingly, their temple, which contained a profusion of garden-like scenes, symbolized such a cosmic expansion. They believed that their kingdom should dominate and cover the world in imitation of the original creation ...

Ezekiel 17 and 19 depict Israel with the same image of the cosmic tree that began to grow high from a garden but then was cut down ... it is possible that Israel's repeated tendency to build idolatrous altars on "every hill and [under] every leafy tree" (Ez. 20:28; so likewise 1 Kgs. 14:23; 17:10, Jer. 2:20; 3:6) was a sinful and perverted attempt to replicate the conditions of Eden for which only judgment could come.[5]

The temple alludes to humanity's attempt to crawl our way back out from the muck and the mire and scrape our way back into garden civility at the base of Eden's holy hill. The temple gives us a visual that demonstrates the impossible climb. The canyon between us and our Creator is vast. It's as far as imperfection is from perfection. It's as far as death is from life. The only hope of bridging such a gap is for someone to die, conquer death, and mend the cliff of incompleteness once again. An altar was needed.

God strategically placed in the outer courts of the temple an altar. The altar was for sacrificing animals and burning offerings. Each day, each season, and each festival was marked by the sight of billowing smoke and the smell of burnt animal flesh. The stench of death filled the air constantly to remind the people as they put their hands to plow, their feet to the road, and their minds to matter, that all their acts were covered in sin. Death. And yet a different image emerged on the horizon. A hope. The altar allowed the people a place to come and confess their sins. They could then wash in the basins and get clean to symbolize their purification from filthiness. God was giving them a way to come back into his presence again.

But not fully yet. In those days, only the priests could enter the inner courts on behalf of the people. As the high priest would walk past the altar and basin and into the inner courts, he was greeted with three primary things that symbolized all that the people had lost and would regain through their sacrifice: the lampstand, the shewbread, and the incense. These objects, sitting under the vaulted sky of a garden-like solarium, would remind the priest and the people of God's faithfulness to feed them his word[6] (as symbolized in the shewbread), light their paths by the illumination of the Holy Spirit,[7] and make their lives like prayerful fragrances of sweet incense.[8]

But the gap still remained in part. Humanity in total could not commune with God without a mediator. We could not yet get inside to God's presence. The Holy of Holies.

Inside the Holy of Holies was a box known as the ark of the covenant. Contained within the box were three things: the tablets on which the Ten Commandments were written (representing God covenant with Moses—Ex. 20), the golden pot with manna (representing God's provision for Israel in the desert—Ex. 16), and the rod of Aaron that had budded (representing the authority of the priestly leadership—Nm. 17). In these particular items are represented the story of God and his people in Israel. The symbols tell the story of how God protected Israel through the law, how God provided for Israel in the manna, and how God empowered Israel through the Aaronic leadership. Each item in the ark points to the glory of God. Each item tells one story to which he's the answer. Humanity could never lead, provide, and obey like God, so for the Holiest of Holies to dwell with man, God himself would have to come down once for all.

The New Testament writers pick up temple and tabernacle imagery to call people's attention back to the intentions of the Garden-temple. They actively write in a manner that causes us to remember all that was lost in the artistry of Solomon's Temple, and how a new creation begins in Christ.

The apostles begin their logic with the Holy of Holies. Their logic moves in the exact reverse to the Old Testament's starting point. Christ is acknowledged as being higher than Aaron. Only Jesus can make a sacrifice that is good for all time for the forgiveness of sins (Heb. 5:4). Wilfrid Stott points out that when the New Testament author of Hebrews refers to Christ's sacrifice he "invariably uses the present tense, showing its continuous character" (5:1,3; 8:3a,4; 9:7; 10:1,2,8), whereas, "in contrast with this, when he speaks of Christ's offering he invariably uses the *aorist*—the completed past tense with present implications" (8:3b; 9:14,28; 10:12).[9] What all this speech communicates is that through Christ's one-time sacrifice, he perfected and obliterated the worship/sacrifice system of the temple. All requirements for worship are now satisfied in the past, present, and forever future. The work was done by our worship leader. King Jesus.

Christ's sacrifice is for all time. He has now entered the true tabernacle of heaven in two ways: (1) as seated, and (2) as interceding.[10] He sits in rest because sin and death lay in waste. He also sits as our high priest poised in power; interceding for his saints as they come to fully realize the victory that he has already procured. He has established a new covenant. He fulfilled all the law in himself. His provision is ours.

By ascending into the arms of the Father and taking the seat on high, Christ has effectively lifted earth back up to heaven. The throne in his kingdom is the new Eden. All the earth is God's garden-footstool, and the inner courts of his presence are in the hearts of every man, woman, and child that believes in Jesus as Lord and Savior.

Figure 7.8 attempts to show the new-creation rhythm of worship and mission as it plays out through Christ's temple-body—his church. You and me! Notice how the arrow is again reversed, but this time there are arrows facing both directions:

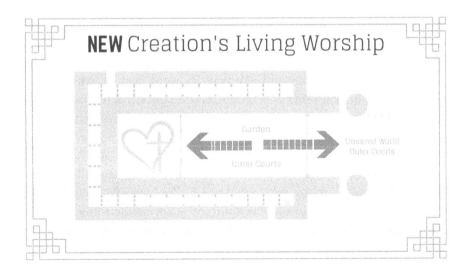

Fig. 7.8

NOTE that there's a by-play between coming in and going out. There's a rhythm that repeats. It's like breathing in and then exhaling out. It's liturgy. A repetitive form. The purity of heaven is colliding with the perversion of our sinful world and gently breathing into it a new life.

Today, people draw near to God internally via the same rhythm of the temple. We come near to Jesus by his gathering hands. We come near to his altar and basin. As we approach his holiness, we are gripped like Isaiah with shame at how unclean we are. Christ's very nature requires that we see our humanity for what it is. Seeing God as he is truly revealed unveils the nature of man. Imperfect. When compared to Christ, we are nothing but the scum of the earth, as Paul says. We confess our sins. But as we do, something different overwhelms us. Assurance of pardon. Forgiveness. As we approach the altar, we see that on it lies a flowering lily, and no longer a dead Savior. He has risen! He's alive. He's conquered death. We can rejoice in victory, but a true rise of victory is only felt afresh as we first plummet to the depths over and over again of who we once were without Jesus. The gospel preaches to us over and over again. First the bad news. Then the glorious news.

We stand tall. We walk confidently. We've confessed our sins, our inner shames, our burdens, and all the dark that clings to us. Jesus blood pours over us. He's the wellspring of life. He wells up within us like the bubbling basin. He cleanses us. Our response is thankfulness. In our heart's we enter his Garden-Kingdom. His life enters us, residing in our very chests, and we find rest in him.

At his feet, we hear his word. We pray his words and his will, and we celebrate his life amongst friends at the provision of this table. It is in the Word that God correctly describes himself to man. And from seeing and savoring him, songs saturated with truths spring forth from our hearts. Just as a fussing baby is soothed by a nurse's lullaby or beasts of burden are pacified by the wayfarer's tune, so God's Word, when set to music, lightens the load of carrying its spiritual truths into our hearts.[11] We sing. We respond. We celebrate. He is the bread of life, his Spirit the lamp, and he within us is the fragrance. We present ourselves as living sacrifices, holy and acceptable to God—this is our spiritual worship (Rom. 12:1).

But wait ... something glorious has changed. The arrow stops. It reverses. When Jesus died, the veil covering the holiest place was torn. God no longer saw fit to confine his glory to one space, but he unleashed himself on the four corners of the cosmos. He's the second and last Adam, and in him, we are freed to go out. We're commissioned to be sent. We are commanded and privileged to take all the inner peace we've found in the civility and beauty of Christ's garden and go and share it with a warring world.

God's rhythm of worship breathes in every time we draw near in gathered worship, and it breathes out every time he sends us out in scattered worship. When he inhales, we get closer. We see his face and his nature. We see our corruption in comparison. He comforts us, cleanses us, and brings us gently closer to "taste and see that he is good." The movement is inside-out. As we go out, we're armed with the Word, prayer, and the fragrance of God, as we tell the message of how his death (the altar) makes people clean (the basin). There's a movement of Synergy. A spinning circle. We spin in on each other rather than away. We collide at the Savior. We gather there with each other and with the Lord in a meal within our hearts, eating and drinking in celebration of Christ's life and death.

The emphasis in gathering is not for gathering's sake. The emphasis of Jesus and the apostles is placed more on scattering. Most of life happens in dispersion. In the field. Synergy unites and then explodes outward. It's a bomb. It doesn't throw shrapnel at itself, as some ingrown churches do—only to the destruction of themselves. It throws shrapnel outward. It hurls the word of God into the air like a sword that cuts deep into the bone and marrow of people's hearts, revealing to them true grace. Grace is a different kind of shrapnel. Its assault is aggressively healing, killing our self-entitling, self-glorifying, self-protecting, autonomously deified ego, and gently revealing the cowering orphan underneath all our make-believe armor. God's loving pursuit scoops up the lost one and brings him back home.

The emphasis of worship in the New Testament is on pursuit. The pursuit of people. The filling of people. A kingdom not made by human hands. Saved souls. Worship spills out of filled people into the filling of all things. God's pursuit of his glory and our pursuit of him and each other. Worship is synergetic. It's taking God's sense of embrace into the everywhere. It doesn't collapse in on itself like a dying star. Loving worship is self-forgetful and on mission. We ingest God's perfection, his leadership, and his provision in closeness. He arms us with his word, prayer, and a sense of the table, of home, and of family, and he commissions us to be a fragrant offering to the world. He lays the message of the altar and basin in our hands as we go into the outer courts and the unsaved world. We are tasked to tell the world the good news of the gospel, which first includes the bad. We tell them of the horror of the altar. We tell them of their violation of God's law. We tell them the truth of how we've murdered Jesus; how we've destroyed beauty. We've vomited up perfection only to swallow our own dirty finger. As the weight of shame crouches tireless at a door like a stone laid across our chest, the altar now whispers the good news: "Jesus is risen." He's cleaned death's table. He offers life to us. Shame lifts. Our naked soul parades around freely with the ability to fully know and be known by our Trinitarian family.

29

THE TRINITY ANSWERS MISSION

Trinity Worship and mission was planned and orchestrated before history even began. The Godhead determined that their mission was going to be the C.R.O.S.S. and good news of Jesus. The good news is more than a message. It's about a holy God living in and amongst a holy people. It's about our God producing in us the relationship, reasoning, order, education, and mission of the life of God. His way. His truth. His life. Every facet of the C.R.O.S.S. displays the missional unity and focus that the Father, Son, and Holy Spirit have in working together for a common goal of wrapping us up into the swells of their image.

The image of our one[1] God is best revealed in the Son of God,[2] who claimed to be the exact representation of the Father. Jesus was proclaimed as the one anointed with the Spirit of God;[3] a King.[4] This King came from the seed of Abraham, Isaac, and Jacob.[5] He hails from the tribe of Judah.[6] He is the ultimate warrior who indeed crushed the serpent's head,[7] thus fulfilling the prophecy made to Adam in Genesis. Jesus completes the story. Jesus completes the Old Testament.[8] Jesus' image proclaims the year of Jubilee and liberty to all those captive[9] to any element of this fallen world. He came to serve, preach good news to the poor, and bind up the broken-hearted.[10] With Jesus came his reign in the hearts of man. He is the God-man supreme who is tender and compassionate, sinless, and who lives to bear the utmost penalty for the guilty verdict due us.[11] He brings light into a dark world that has no understanding of God, and to a people that have completely turned away from God.[12] He lives to extend his love to the sinner and to restore us back to a fruitful life of abundance.[13]

MISSIONAL CONCLUSIONS

Under the full weight of all that we've discussed in this book, *Trinity Worship*, we now arrive at a place of conclusion. First, consider how our discussion of mission can influence our discussion in a variety of other areas in our life. Figure 7.9 claims that though we are united in mission under our Triune God, we will always remain diverse, and must also be reforming, repenting, and recalibrating back to God's original intentions for his image-bearing family:

Signature Mission ... How God Leads

REFORMING DIVERSITY	Anthropological (origin, nature, & purpose of humanity)
	Soteriological (nature of salvation)
MISSION & VISION	Teleological (end & aim to human function)
	Experiential (power that is transformational)
	Doxological (praise & glory being the aim of all logic)
RHYTHMS	Incarnational (servant personhood of Christlikeness)
	Ecclesiological (identity, purpose, & structure of the church)
	Angelogical & Demonological (nature & ministry of angels & demons)

Fig. 7.9

For brevity's sake, I'm not going to delve into every facet in figure 7.9, but let's bring some of the subjects above together for some final points:

- **Teleology, Experience, Doxology:** Satisfaction in Him
- **Anthropology & Soteriology:** Trinity Family, Marriage, Kingdom Family

- **Rhythms of Incarnational Ecclesiology:** Tri-Missional Circles

What is the aim and function of the human mission? We've answered the question. Our most satisfying end is found in what brings God the most glory. In thinking and acting upon the Trinity, we experience the power of transformation in the whole scope of human nature, society, and creation. We enjoy our end and aim of human function in the responsive celebration and rest that results from a correct paradigm of thinking. As in football, we must have an end zone before we can score a touchdown. We find our end zone in God's nature, and that is our ultimate goal—our doxology.

Play Ball!

Soteriology is identical.

Many have tried to sum up mission and salvation as a personal experience that only pertains to one's sin and is preserved through isolated quiet times. The Trinity's nature speaks anything but. We can't describe God's mission using language that is foreign to God himself! We're added into something. Baptism. We die in the water of individualism and when we're pulled out from the waves, we are recalibrated to a new way of life. The best way to learn God's design for our own personal growth in mission and worship is within and around marriage and family.

There is one symbol that helps us visualize soteriology and mission more than any other. That symbol is found in the human sexual act. Sex is an ejaculation of one into another. The sperm enters an egg and makes a child. The individual sperm has its own life as it squiggles around, and the egg is dead and dormant if something doesn't act upon it to awaken it. The potential of life to emerge in the egg depends on the sperm reaching its destination. This intermingling is not just science. It's romance. Kissing is an exchange of fluids and an intertwining of breath whereby two persons begin to inhale and exhale in and from one another. Through the dance and intertwining of the flesh, birth happens. New life.

I don't want to associate God's work in salvation and in multiplying the family of God entirely with sex—thus making the Trinity's love into something sexual (which it absolutely is not). I do, however, want us to make the connection. Jesus makes the connection. He says that salvation is being "reborn." God's unity with the human heart is not unlike the man and woman becoming one. God's Spirit exhales into our hearts. Our hearts are dormant and dead until acted upon and awakened by his freeing wind. Through the intertwining of the supernatural and our human hearts, birth happens. New life.

Sex is missional. Salvation is missional. Sex is life passed from one to another. The result of sexual union is the multiplying of families. Children. We must not make God perverse in likening the dance of spiritual life identically to that of sexual procreation, but we must also resist the trap of making sex meaningless. God created sex as a symbol of something. He desired it to point to something beyond just the exchange of fluids. I believe that the symbol of sex demonstrates to us on a level we can understand, the very enjoyment, oneness, and multiplication power that comes from a kingdom-family resting within the Trinity's wings.

We must associate the physical act of "making love" with God's act of salvation in bringing us into his love if we are to truly understand human identity and the reality of what God saves us into. Sex is always linked with the idea of family, and only a perverted culture would try to take that link away.

Though I'm absolutely not implying that the church has anything in common with a sexual orgy, the idea that we and God are intertwined with each other is thoroughly scriptural. Paul says we are "in Christ" 270 times, and Christ is "in us" 70 times. The Bible places emphasis not on us being internal with one another, but on us being internal to Christ. As believers, we are "in God." By some stretch of the imagination, we are spiritually internal to God. Believers are best described and understood as a subset of all of God's oneness, as we are indwelled internally by the Spirit within our hearts. Somehow, what we are in is also in us. Believers are bonded to one another and internal to one another—not by anatomy, but by the Spirit of God. All in all.

Therefore, I do believe wholeheartedly that the life that exists in and between the members of the Trinity can be a model for church life. This is why I believe that the best representation and experience of God's image can be captured in the marriage, the family, the meal, and the home.

On that note …

Let me now examine the final bullet point above regarding what I call the rhythms of incarnational ecclesiology as seen in tri-missional circles. That's a mouthful. If, in fact, the life of the Trinity is best represented in a face-to-face dance (*perichoresis*), then why shouldn't our environments of family closeness follow suit? Why shouldn't our discipleship models orbit the table? Why shouldn't our metaphors for salvation illumine the embrace of the family? Why should we settle for buildings that over the last 2,000 years have visibly grown central, larger, and sterile with platforms and pulpits that are increasingly further from and higher above the congregation? Why should we continue settling for models of ministry that actually reinforce and communicate division? Why should we continue to try and shape our life together around methods that cloud the meaning of words, titles, and theological concepts in Scripture? The worship environment should explain meaning, not cloud or complicate it.

Into our confusion, God speaks simpler creativity. He has already given us the original idea toward which we can work backward. As he congregates in a missionally relational "circle," so should we. What we circle around and toward is the Bread of Life. The meal is the artistic symbol that captures the worship and mission of God! No other method or model speaks quite as loudly and clearly. No other invention postures us quite so correctly.

In the Lord's Supper, the need of everyone is acknowledged and met. Believer and unbeliever alike dines together in friendship and learns from one another. The believer learns afresh from the unbeliever of their unsaved state before salvation in Christ—thus sustaining humility and reverence as he grows in Christ. The unbeliever learns of the invitation and the necessity of salvation.

Not only did Jesus raise a cup and loaf in order to claim that his blood and body secured his kingdom rule; he also left that rule and authority to us with very helpful guidelines. His meal is not only a place of community; it's also a place of authority. His authority is pressed out through his people in the same manner as the titles and tendencies found in the Old and New Testament. Let's look at figures 5.1 and 5.2 again:

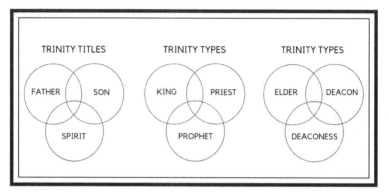

Fig. 5.1

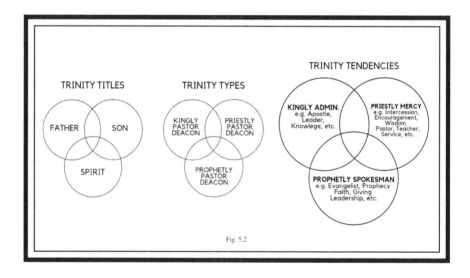

Fig. 5.2

THE TRINITY IS IN PURSUIT. And pursuit never stops. It's eternal. It's a forever mission to capture our attention and involve our head, hands, and heart:

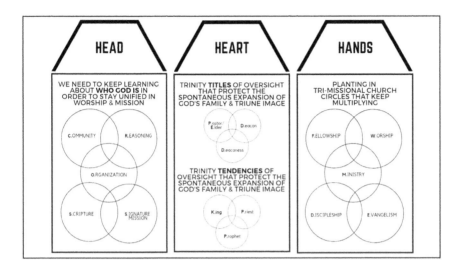

Fig. Ap2b

As SEEN in the HEAD section of figure Ap2b, God wants us to unite and advance as a unit. He doesn't want our thoughts to be built around personality, preference, denomination, or creed, but around knowledge of who he is. His nature is always pleasantly the same. Unchanging. God commissions us in the HEART section of figure Ap2b with title and tendency to go and make. Create. Work. Innovate.

We don't meditate in mind and make with matter and meaning just for the thrill of doing something new. Our invention goes in reverse. All that we do points the world back to our origins and the way life was intended to be. We take our unique design and proclivity and intentionally link it to objectives that benefit the church—the body of Christ. Ministry results. Planting churches. The works of our HANDS may not directly associate with planting churches on mission, but everything we do indirectly has the same end. We are not to grow our own kingdoms, but rather work toward the hands of his kingdom.

The figures above may appear too idealistic. In a world that is increasingly criminalizing and demonizing authentic closeness, belief in Christ, and faithfulness to the kingdom of God, the gospel of the C.R.O.S.S. seems almost an impossibility. Nonetheless, the gospel is about the good news. Hearing the message and living it out is not possible in our natural state. But we serve a supernatural God who is perfectly capable of putting on display his

C.ommunity—*the way he relates*, his **R**.easoning—*the way he does things*, his **O**.rganization—*the way he orders life*, his **S**.cripture—*the way he teaches and desires us to learn*, and his **S**.ignature Mission—*the way he leads*, in spite of any objection or opposition.

The only question remains; "Will you join him?"

30

CIRCLE RESOURCES

For Information & Growing Resources on
Planting C.R.O.S.S. Churches through Circles ...

GO TO: WWW.GARDENCITYPROJECT.COM

ALSO: SEE OUR APPENDIX FOR ADDED ASSESSMENT &
PLANNING TOOLS

PART VIII
APPENDICES

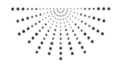

APPENDIX 1: PPK ASSESSMENT

There are many personality and gift assessments out there, such as DISC, Myers-Briggs, SHAPE, 4-Colors, Enneagram, etc. The PPK is not a personality assessment to label or quantify you. Generally, most tests focus first on building a case for *who* you are before establishing a case for *whose* you are. By emphasizing the finding of one's identity in yourself before first understanding your origins in God, most tests limit your identity to humanistically misdirected assumptions, research, or theology. They focus attention on how you function—your image. This assessment is different. We focus our attention on how the Trinity functions—his image. As we understand him, only then can we truly understand ourselves.

So ...

This assessment is about you thinking deeply about God! What is he like? How is he one, and three? How does he do things? How does he order life? How does he shape belief or carry out purpose and calling?

No matter how you score, your role will ultimately reflect God's image, not your own. You will need to look unto him in how to serve in your role, so as to show forth his glory, not your own!

In the PPK Assessment, we will look at the five ways in which the Scripture broadly shows that the Trinity is united. We use the acronym C.R.O.S.S., for we believe the center of the human story is based around the life, death, and resurrection of Jesus. To make anything else central in our focus is problematic. Therefore everything comes back to his work in life, death, resurrection, ascension, and consumption. His work is for our benefit. The acronym follows the same wording as it does in this book:

C.ommunity

R.easoning

O.rganization

S.cripture

S.ignature Mission

The words above provide a way to categorize the way the Trinity appears to be broadly united in Scripture. Like him, we also are to experience the flourishing that comes with being united by his love within and with others as we extend that love outwardly. This acronym in no way attempts to limit God or the Trinity. His nature is beyond our comprehension, but within Scripture we are given ways to understand his likeness in the person of Jesus. This PPK Assessment is a comprehensible tool to evaluate his incomparable image in a manner that is practically helpful. We hope this study will encourage your theologically guarded imagination to be enraptured into the joy of the Trinity and to contemplate the richness of who he is and who we are in him.

In looking at these five ways in which the Trinity is united, we can uncover tidbits of what Jesus meant when he prayed that we "may be one as He and the Father are one." We can then determine the ways in which we can best do the following: relate in community and fellowship; reason in our life of worship; organize in our ministry; learn and discover truth in our discipleship, and serve and lead others in our calling and evangelism.

Similarly, as God is Father, Son, and Holy Spirit, we see three roles appear in the Old Testament through which humanity attempted to carry out (or image) this tri-perspectival likeness of God on earth—in kings, priests, and prophets. In the Old Testament, there were always kings who operated most in the governing realm, priests who operated and functioned in the worship/spiritual realm, and prophets who guarded God's people in righteousness and truth. Our goal is not to pigeonhole the Godhead into these predetermined roles, for we can see that Jesus is named as all three in Scripture

—the King, Priest, and Prophet. But though the members of the Trinity at times appear to share the same functions, they seem to serve predominantly and primarily in one of these three roles.

The same is true for us. To some extent, you may contain a bit of all three of the PPK tendencies. Yet God most likely has equipped you for a role of service that dwells primarily in one of these roles. This is where this assessment is also different. It doesn't get you thinking about your life in terms of your one personality, but it helps you think in "one-another" language. Yes, you are an "I," but like the Trinity, you are inseparable from the community and the "we" of God's family and likeness because you are made in God's image.

For Access to the Fillable PPK Assessment

Go to www.gardencityproject.com/gcp-circles to begin.

APPENDIX 2: USING THE PPK PLANS

U SE **PPK** TO **THINK** ON **WHO GOD IS** AND ON **GOD'S STORY:** The Scripture reveals how God's leadership structure has always been "triune." We know that the Godhead is three persons—Father, Son, and Holy Spirit. God, as a Three-in-One "us," is the originator, creator, and foundation for all of life.

In I Samuel 8:1-5, humanity grew weary of God's invisible triune theocracy. They demanded that Samuel provide them with a physical king. Though this grieved God, he indulged the people's desire and tasked Samuel to anoint this new king. The life of Samuel was pivotal in Israel's history. Even as a child, Samuel was given his own ephod, a garment normally reserved for a priest as he ministered before the Lord in the tent of meeting at Shiloh where the ark of the covenant was kept (1 Samuel 2:18; 3:3). He was known as a *priest*. He was also known as a *prophet*, as he anointed the first two kings of Israel. He was also the last in the line of Israel's judges (their role of the *kingly* leader) and was considered by many as the greatest judge (Acts 13:20).

Samuel represents the first human authority accountable as a prophet, priest, and king. When the people had grown weary of God's leadership, he allowed humanity to settle for imperfect human regimes. However, through Samuel, he still intervened to guarantee that earth's leadership structure would still remain triune. God still commissioned priests in the cultic realm to carry out spiritual duties on behalf of the people, kings to delegate his decrees and politics for the people's benefit, and prophets to speak his message of truth and warning to the people. This structure remained, though fractured and sinful, until the time when Christ came and redeemed these three roles—declaring himself to be the only perfect prophet, priest and king.

Though these three **titles** in proper belong to Christ, their **tendency** remains in humans for the carrying out our specific roles in more priestly, prophetic, or kingly ways. In his death and resurrection, Christ has not done away with these tendencies, he's merely redeemed them and made available even more **types** and ministries through those that are filled with his Spirit.

In the New Testament church, God's leadership style is still tri-partite, in that elders, deacons, and deaconesses are clearly the three that are to oversee the church for its own protection, shepherding, and growth in truth and maturity. The father, mother, and children, on the other hand, are still what constitutes a family structure. Despite the specificity of their titles, all leaders will tend to carry out their roles of ministry and service in either a more priestly, prophetic, or kingly way. As reminders of these tendencies, let's look again at figures 5.1 and 5.2.

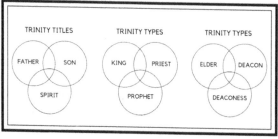

Fig. 5.1

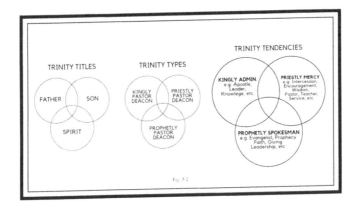

Fig. 5.2

Use PPK to Think on Who and Whose You Are in God's Story: Our unity finds its source individually and collectively in God's triune nature, and he not only calls us to be like him as human beings, but also to do like him. It is in who we "be" that we have our identity and psychological, mental, spiritual, and emotional health, and it is in what we do that we actualize God's DNA and image. He summarizes what we are to do in the Great Commission. In Matthew 28:18-20 Jesus says:

All authority in heaven and on earth has been given to me. Go therefore and make disciples of all nations, baptizing them in the name of the Father and of the Son and of the Holy Spirit, teaching them to observe all that I have commanded you. And behold, I am with you always, to the end of the age.

He calls us into his one-of-a-kind mission by saying go. The nature of that mission is to teach and make disciples by proclaiming and living out all that is true. By living in a Christian manner, we create Jesus culture wherever we go. His presence always with us enables us to order and reason all of life around God's nature in both our ministry and our worship. Both the beginning and the end-result in all of our living is family fellowship. People are baptized into the community to begin their life in God, and forevermore we model the life of God together as a family from the beginning through eternity. The simplicity of how we are to love the Trinity with all our head, heart, and hands is seen in figure AP2a:

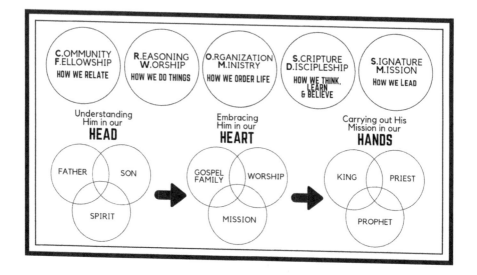

Fig. AP2a

The Church Gathered & Scattered. Where to Go from Here with PPK and Circles:

- Use the PPK to assess the *imago Dei* (image of God) uniqueness of yourself or those meeting in your community-family churches, or what we call *circles*. Whether a circle is informally brought together to create, or formally meets to plant churches or something more intentional, this can help everyone better learn about themselves, others, and God. PPK helps people to bring to the circle their distinctiveness in a way that best serves the community and creativity of the circle as a whole.
- Use the Descriptions (see Appendix 3–5) as added tools to help you as a group work well together, form healthy plurality in leading your circle forward, and to continue multiplying health groups that are led in triune-pod teams. These descriptions will help each person to learn how to best grow and exercise their tendencies alongside others. Whereas most assessments aim at defining you as an individual, this assessment focuses on shaping the entire community together.
- Each circle can determine what its mission and demographics will

be. A circle's purpose and form should largely reflect the makeup of those within the circle and those the circle intends to engage around them. A community can use the Circle Idea Generator as an aid to help in planning and shaping their circle in spiritual and creative growth whenever they meet. And the different plans can be used for those in the group to engage each person's tendencies (prophetic, priestly, or kingly) in planning, development, and strategy. All the tools for forming circles are available at www. gardencityproject.com/gcp-circles.

Together we safely know God. Become Like God. Follow God and serve God. With head, heart. hands.

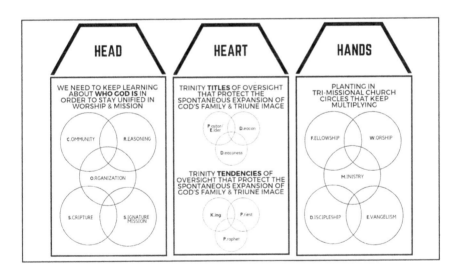

Fig. AP2b

33

APPENDIX 3: CROSS PROPHET

An In-Depth Look at the Prophet "Type!" *In the following Appendices, we will look at the prophet as a "Function" and see how "Prophet-tendency" people relate to Priestly or Kingly-tendency people.*

DISCLAIMER ONCE AGAIN: It should be stressed before we move any further that the Prophet, Priest, King wording does not give you a "Title,"— like you're a (P)rophet on par with the OT Prophets. Scripture is very clear that elder/pastors, deacons, saints, and ministers are correct "Titles" for the people of God in the NT. However, the PPK assessment describes your "Tendencies." Whether you have the title of pastor, teacher, parent, son, daughter, engineer, CEO, accountant, mechanic, manager, employee, or you serve in some capacity in the over 270+ spiritual ministries listed in the New Testament (**See Appendix 7**), you have a "Tendency" in how you carry out your "Title"; whether it be in a more priestly, prophetic, or kingly way. Knowing your tendencies can make you more effective in building up the body of Christ in a manner that best reflects, images, and glorifies Christ.

Secondly, we must remember that in the New Testament, every believer is called a prophet,[1] a priest[2] and a king.[3] These names are gifted to us in Christ as "identities" that affirm our value, worth, and placement within his kingdom.

Therefore, we cannot avoid becoming more priestly, more kingly, or more prophetic, simply because we see ourselves as weak in one particular area. God has gifted us with his identity in these areas and expects us to become rounded in our approach to kingdom life. However, the fact still remains that we may lean toward a specific "tendency" in how we approach our role in his kingdom, and thus we need to combine our gifts with the gifts of others in the body to help us grow in our approach. We are all to become like Jesus and Jesus displayed the full likeness of the Triune God. We are to bear his image. Though we may play a role within the cosmos, church, or culture as an individual, we can still learn from and exhibit the other traits of those in God's community.

The Prophet

HOW THE PROPHET WORKS TOGETHER WITH THE PRIEST

TENDENCIES OF A PROPHET

COMMUNITY
A prophet prioritizes what the Body believes.

REASONING
A prophet thinks prescriptively in command.

ORGANIZATION
A prophet focuses on what is right.

SCRIPTURE
A prophet learns only what is significant.

SIGNATURE MISSION
A prophet sees precept and truth.

PROS & CONS WITH PRIESTS
IN THE HOME, WORK, & MINISTRY

A prophetly type's bold, confrontational, brave, exact, and uncompromising nature in the face of the suffering caused by sin, exhorts the priestly type in courage, faith, and the strength that truth has in rescuing and training people for righteousness.

However, priestly types can naturally be soured by a prophetly type's proneness toward individuality, abrasiveness, seriousness, and intensity in attacking problems and incorrect belief with little regard for the emotions of a person.

WORKING TOGETHER IN HARMONY

To seek unity with the priest, the prophet must study not only what is right, but grow in his wisdom as to the correct timing of truth's application for admonishment, encouragement, rebuke, and teaching. The priest must be willing to understand the threatening nature of evil, sin, and disobedience, and must welcome the prophet's urgency; while also being bold enough to bring a more patient, compassionate, and loving approach to the sharing of the truth.

 **A KING**
Emphasizes Policy

 **A PRIEST**
Emphasizes People

 **A PROPHET**
Emphasizes Precepts

The Prophet

HOW THE PROPHET WORKS TOGETHER WITH THE KING

TENDENCIES OF A PROPHET

COMMUNITY
A prophet prioritizes what the whole **believes**.

REASONING
A prophet thinks **prescriptively** in **command**.

ORGANIZATION
A prophet focuses on what is most **right**.

SCRIPTURE
A prophet learns only what is **significant**.

SIGNATURE MISSION
A prophet sees **precept** and **truth**.

PROS & CONS WITH KINGS
IN THE HOME, WORK, & MINISTRY

A prophetly type's bold, confrontational, brave, and uncompromising nature in the face of the suffering caused by sin exhorts the kingly type in the necessity of recognizing a higher path and divine method for truth in governing.

However, kingly types can naturally be soured by a prophetly type's exhaustive detail, inability to act without being exact, nit-picking criticism, and narrow short-sightedness.

WORKING TOGETHER IN HARMONY

To seek unity with the king, the prophet must recognize the king's nature to be the "gas" of the car, and his own nature to be the "brakes." Both are needed for safe driving. Kings must learn to consult the prophet for detailed truth, and prophets must learn to consult kings for the bigger picture; lest they each fall prey to losing sight of the forest because of the trees. They must both realize together that **message** and **method** both preach with equal power.

A KING
Emphasizes Policy

A PRIEST
Emphasizes People

A PROPHET
Emphasizes Precepts

34

APPENDIX 4: CROSS PRIEST

An In-Depth Look at the Priest "Type!" *In the following Appendices, we will look at the priest as a "Function" and see how "Priest-tendency" people relate to Prophetly or Kingly-tendency people.*

DISCLAIMER ONCE AGAIN: It should be stressed before we move any further that the Prophet, Priest, King wording does not give you a "Title,"—like you're a (P)rophet on par with the OT Prophets. Scripture is very clear that elder/pastors, deacons, saints, and ministers are correct "Titles" for the people of God in the NT. However, the PPK assessment describes your "Tendencies." Whether you have the title of pastor, teacher, parent, son, daughter, engineer, CEO, accountant, mechanic, manager, employee, or you serve in some capacity in the over 270+ spiritual ministries listed in the New Testament (**See Appendix 7**), you have a "Tendency" in how you carry out your "Title"; whether it be in a more priestly, prophetic, or kingly way. Knowing your tendencies can make you more effective in building up the body of Christ in a manner that best reflects, images, and glorifies Christ.

Secondly, we must remember that in the New Testament, every believer is called a prophet,[1] a priest[2] and a king.[3] These names are gifted to us in Christ as "identities" that affirm our value, worth, and placement within his kingdom.

Therefore, we cannot avoid becoming more priestly, more kingly, or more prophetic, simply because we see ourselves as weak in one particular area. God has gifted us with his identity in these areas and expects us to become rounded in our approach to kingdom life. However, the fact still remains that we may lean toward a specific "tendency" in how we approach our role in his kingdom, and thus we need to combine our gifts with the gifts of others in the body to help us grow in our approach. We are all to become like Jesus and Jesus displayed the full likeness of the Triune God. We are to bear his image. Though we may play a role within the cosmos, church, or culture as an individual, we can still learn from and exhibit the other traits of those in God's community.

The Priest

HOW THE PRIEST WORKS TOGETHER WITH THE KING

TENDENCIES OF A PRIEST

COMMUNITY
A priest **enjoys** free-flowing relationship.

REASONING
A priest thinks **emotively** in story & **promise**.

ORGANIZATION
A priest acts on what prioritizes **connection**.

SCRIPTURE
A priest learns best in **tangible experience**.

SIGNATURE MISSION
A priest sees how **people** are the **purpose**.

PROS & CONS WITH KINGS

IN THE HOME, WORK, & MINISTRY

A priestly type's ability to listen, encourage, empathize with, create spontaneously among, and rejoice in the dreams and ideals of another motivates the kingly type in parenting, in marriage, in ministry, and vocationally to feel support.

However, a priestly type measures support and success via connection not stats; love not analytics; people as purpose, not people for the sake of purpose; and they prioritize the **biography** of living life together with others over and above the mere assembling of the facts as in a documentary.

WORKING TOGETHER IN HARMONY

To seek unity with a king, a priest must value a king's network in bringing people together, his ability to collect facts on how people are best served, and his innate sensitivity to being thoughtful for the whole. The priest must train the king in compassion, the "grey areas" of dealing with people, and the art of relaxing in relationship, but must welcome the king's order, ingenuity, and understanding of authority.

A KING
Emphasizes Policy

A PRIEST
Emphasizes People

A PROPHET
Emphasizes Precepts

The Priest

HOW THE PRIEST WORKS TOGETHER WITH THE PROPHET

TENDENCIES OF A PRIEST

COMMUNITY
A priest **enjoys** free-flowing relationship.

REASONING
A priest thinks **emotively** in story & **promise**.

ORGANIZATION
A priest acts on what prioritizes **connection**.

SCRIPTURE
A priest learns in **tangible experience**.

SIGNATURE MISSION
A priest sees how **people** are the **purpose**.

PROS & CONS WITH PROPHETS

IN THE HOME, WORK, & MINISTRY

A priestly type's ability to listen, encourage, empathize with, create spontaneously among, and rejoice in the dreams and ideals of another, validates, affirms, and gives the prophetly type meaning behind his/her fight for truth.

However, a priestly type often seems too soft, narrow, compromising, patient, and overly gracious to others to a prophetly type's manner of applying the truth. The prophet can thus exasperate the priest with his/her forthright, determined, urgent, and often insensitive approach to dealing with sin and error.

WORKING TOGETHER IN HARMONY

To seek unity with a prophet, a priest must be ever-increasing in his/her understanding of how Scripture portrays unity within the judgment and wrath of God, alongside the goodness, grace, and mercy of God's character. A priest must welcome command, and teach compassion to the prophet, and the prophet must remember that the **manner** one uses to deliver the truth in love is as important as the **message** itself.

A KING
Emphasizes Policy

A PRIEST
Emphasizes People

A PROPHET
Emphasizes Precepts

35

APPENDIX 5: CROSS KING

An In-Depth Look at the King "Type!" *In the following Appendices, we will look at the king as a "Function" and see how "Kingly-tendency" people relate to Priestly or Prophetly-tendency people.*

DISCLAIMER (last time, I promise): It should be stressed before we move any further that the Prophet, Priest, King wording does not give you a "Title,"—like you're a (P)rophet on par with the OT Prophets. Scripture is very clear that elder/pastors, deacons, saints, and ministers are correct "Titles" for the people of God in the NT. However, the PPK assessment describes your "Tendencies." Whether you have the title of pastor, teacher, parent, son, daughter, engineer, CEO, accountant, mechanic, manager, employee, or you serve in some capacity in the over 270+ spiritual ministries listed in the New Testament (**See Appendix 7**), you have a "Tendency" in how you carry out your "Title"; whether it be in a more priestly, prophetic, or kingly way. Knowing your tendencies can make you more effective in building up the body of Christ in a manner that best reflects, images, and glorifies Christ.

Secondly, we must remember that in the New Testament, every believer is called a prophet,[1] a priest[2] and a king.[3] These names are gifted to us in Christ as "identities" that affirm our value, worth, and placement within his kingdom. Therefore, we cannot avoid becoming more priestly, more kingly, or more prophetic, simply because we see ourselves as weak in one particular area. God has gifted us with his identity in these areas and expects us to become rounded in our approach to kingdom life. However, the fact still remains that we may lean toward a specific "tendency" in how we approach our role in his kingdom, and thus we need to combine our gifts with the gifts of others in the body to help us grow in our approach. We are all to become like Jesus and Jesus displayed the full likeness of the Triune God. We are to bear his image. Though we may play a role within the cosmos, church, or culture as an individual, we can still learn from and exhibit the other traits of those in God's community.

The King

HOW THE KING WORKS TOGETHER WITH THE PRIEST

TENDENCIES OF A KING

COMMUNITY
A king stuctures relationship.

REASONING
A king thinks logically and descriptively.

ORGANIZATION
A king acts on what prioritizes security.

SCRIPTURE
A king learns in conceptual "Big Ideas."

SIGNATURE MISSION
A king sees how systems accomplish vision.

PROS & CONS WITH PRIESTS

IN THE HOME, WORK, & MINISTRY

A kingly type is persuasive, thoughtful, systematic, intentional, conceptual, and fantastic at the **how-to's** of life. Priestly types resonate and work well with them in parenting, marriage, vocation, and serving because the kingly type is intentional and careful.

However, a priestly-type is more concerned with the **who**. They **enter into** people's journey naturally, and a kingly-type's tendency to **work on** the community or family in a more detached manner can cause a priest to resist any feeling of law and order, and even control.

WORKING TOGETHER IN HARMONY

To seek unity with a priest, a king must walk amongst the people in order to apply concepts, directions, and solve problems in a concise, sensitive, and fluid manner, ensuring the growth of people's safety amongst trusting and thriving relationships.

● **A KING**
Emphasizes Policy

● **A PRIEST**
Emphasizes People

● **A PROPHET**
Emphasizes Precepts

The King

HOW THE KING WORKS TOGETHER WITH THE PROPHET

TENDENCIES OF A KING

COMMUNITY
A king stuctures relationship.

REASONING
A king thinks logically and descriptively.

ORGANIZATION
A king acts on what prioritizes security.

SCRIPTURE
A king learns in conceptual "Big Ideas."

SIGNATURE MISSION
A king sees how systems accomplish vision.

PROS & CONS WITH PROPHETS
IN THE HOME, WORK, & MINISTRY

A kingly type is persuasive, thoughtful, systematic, intentional, conceptual, and fantastic at the how-to's of life. Prophetly types take comfort in the king's value for intellectual pursuits, and their ability to see and order the big picture.

However, a prophetly type is most at home in the why of the details. They are concerned with what is right above how to get somewhere. This can lead the king and prophetly type to differ in assessing issues and problems, along with the will, avenue, and timing of God.

WORKING TOGETHER IN HARMONY

To seek unity with a prophet, a king must take time to consider, ponder deeply, and demonstrate how an overall plan, structure, description, or concept, relates to, upholds, interacts with, and ensures the preservation of God's truth above all else. Both must acknowlege how both content and context work together.

A KING
Emphasizes Policy

A PRIEST
Emphasizes People

A PROPHET
Emphasizes Precepts

APPENDIX 6: TRINITARIAN DIVERSITY

Throughout this book, we've discussed how the Trinity relates in C.ommunity, how the Trinity does things in R.easoning, how the Trinity orders life in O.rganization, how the Trinity teaches us to learn in S.cripture, and finally, how the Trinity leads in their S.ignature Mission. Deeper contemplation of the Trinity's C.R.O.S.S.-unity will lead to more timeless, timely, and unified ways of thinking, acting, and feeling across all realms of study. The Trinity is truly united in their paradigm of truth and way of life, even amidst all that makes them distinct. Learning to think upon the Trinity first and foremost in all things will bring greater peace to all the ways in which humanity seeks to divide, and will at the same time allow our differences to flourish in a manner that equips and builds up the whole into the glory of Christ. Below are the images used to summarize each chapter of this book. I've included them all in this appendix to encourage all those reading this book to continue on in trinitarian contemplation in your realm of culture, craft, trade, and influence.

C.ommunity ... How God Relates

IMAGE OF GOD	Anthropological: (the origin, nature, & purpose for humanity)
IDENTITY	Psychological: (affecting of the mind, will, motivation, & emotions)
	Biographical: (account of a person's life)
FAMILY OF FAMILIES	Sociological: (origin, development, & organization of human society)
HOUSEHOLD OF GOD	Covenantal: (agreement cut between God & man, & upheld by God)
	Ecclesiological: (identity, purpose, & ontology of the church)
SACRAMENTS & MEALS	Sacramental: (visible signs of kingdom family & inward grace)
LOVE ONE ANOTHER	Kingdom Ethics & Virtue

R.easoning ... How God Does Things

PHILOSOPHY FOR ALL OF LIFE	Ontological (the nature of existence & our identity within)
	Philosophical: (rational investigation of truths)
	Dialectical (dialogue as a community buidling education)
	Value System (the family is the center where vice or virtue is forged)
ECCLESIOLOGY	Historical (involved in time past, present, & future)
	Christological (identity, purpose, & ontology of the church)
	Presuppositional (proof leading to belief, faith, or adherence)
	Sacramental: (visible signs of kingdom family & inward grace)
	Agricultural and Creational: (seasons, land, seed, & blessing)

O.rganization ... *How God Orders Life*

MULTIPLICITY	Structural (the way we order all things) Judicial (laws, statutes, truths, & morality)
TRINITARIAN MUTUAL SUBMISSION	Theology Proper (the personhood of the Trinity) Theology Ancillary (the support of image-bearers)
ADMINISTRATION	Economic Efficiency (Rationing of time, talent, & treasure)

S.cripture ... *How God Teaches & We Learn*

STORY	Grammatical & Performance Bibliological (nature & function of Scripture)
BELIEF	Confessional & Creedal (historical acknowledgment of truth) Apologetical (a defense of one's beliefs)
KERYGMA & DIDACHE	Proclamational & Embodied Community (forthtelling & sharing) Doctrinal & Doxological (foundational beliefs that are correct) Educational (how we learn & teach)
COMPLETE	Eschatological (beginning & end to the consummation of creation)

Signature Mission ... How God Leads

REFORMING DIVERSITY	Anthropological (origin, nature, & purpose of humanity) Soteriological (nature of salvation)
MISSION & VISION	Teleological (end & aim to human function) Experiential (power that is transformational) Doxological (praise & glory being the aim of all logic)
RHYTHMS	Incarnational (servant personhood of Christlikeness) Ecclesiological (identity, purpose, & structure of the church) Angelogical & Demonological (nature & ministry of angels & demons)

APPENDIX 7: SPIRITUAL MINISTRIES LIST

B elow are concrete examples of ministries in the letters of Paul. This resource is helpful in demonstrating how many gifts tests have limited what the Scripture deems spiritual ministry to be. Not only have gifts tests limited spiritual service to the confines of the church entity only, it has further caused us to divorce spiritual service from our roles in cultural society in all facets of the home, work, and play. If we read the gifts lists that Paul includes in the manner he intends—as small, subset examples of ministries that are infinitely numerous—we can begin to talk about all realms of culture, vocation, and service as having worshipful and spiritual formation implications.

PROCLAMATION OF THE GOSPEL

Rom. 1:9; 15-16; 14-15; 1 Cor. 1:21-23; 2:1; 4; 9:14-18; Gal. 1:11-12, 16; 4:13.

PASSING ON APOSTLES TEACHING

1 Cor. 15:1; 2 Thes. 2:15; 2 Tm. 2:2.

APOSTLESHIP

Rom. 1:1; 1 Cor. 9:1-5; Gal. 1:17-19; Eph. 3:1-13.

PRAYER AND PETITION

Rom. 1:9-10; 1212; 1 Cor. 14:15; Col. 4:12; Phlm. 4.

ENCOURAGEMENT, STRENGTHENING, REFRESHING

Rom. 1:12; 1 Cor. 16:17-18; 2 Cor. 7:13; Col 4:11.

GENEROUS FINANCIAL GIVING TO BELIEVERS AND UNBELIEVERS

Rom. 12:13; 15:25-27; 1 Cor. 13:3.

OVERSEEING AND CHURCH DISCIPLINE

1 Cor. 5:3-5; 2 Cor. 10:6; 13:2; 2 Thes. 3:14-15; Ti. 3:10.

HOSPITALITY

Rom. 12:13; 1 Cor. 16:6; 1 Tm. 3:2.

BAPTIZING

1 Cor. 1:14-17

CHURCH PLANTING

Rom. 15:20-21; 2 Cor. 10:14, 16.

CHURCH MEETINGS

Rom. 16:5; 1 Cor. 16:19; Phlm. 2.

FINANCES IN MISSIONS

1 Cor. 9:14

REMINDING BELIEVERS OF TRUTH

1 Cor. 4:17

LEADING BY EXAMPLE AND MODELING

1 Cor. 4:16; 1 Thes. 1:5-7.

TEACHING

Gal. 6:6; Col. 1:28.

MEDIATING IN CONFLICT

1 Cor. 6:5; Phil. 4:2-3; Phlm. 8-21.

TONGUES

1 Cor. 13:8; 14:1-33, 39-40.

SIGNS AND WONDERS

Rom. 15:19; 2 Cor. 12:12; 1 Thes. 1:5.

PROPHECY

1 Cor. 13:2, 8-9; 14:1-6; 1 Tm. 1:18.

KNOWLEDGE

1 Cor. 1:5; 13:2, 8-9.

FAITH

1 Cor. 13:2

USING PSALMS, HYMNS AND SPIRITUAL SONGS TO TEACH AND ADMONISH

ONE ANOTHER

Eph. 5:19

MINISTRY IN AND TO PRISONERS

Phil. 2:25-30; 2 Tim. 1:16-17.

CARRYING AND DELIVERING MONEY TO THE CHURCH

Phil. 4:18; 2 Cor. 8:19.

CORRECTING FALSE DOCTRINE

Gal. 1:6-9; Col. 2:8-23; 1 Tm. 1:3-7; Ti. 1:9-13.

EVALUATING PROPHESY

1 Thes. 5:21; 1 Cor. 14:29.

MENTORING

2 Tm. 2:2—appointing elders; Ti. 1:5—helping the weak; 1 Thes. 5:14.

PUBLIC READING OF SCRIPTURE

1 Tm. 4:13

EVANGELISTS

2 Tm. 4:5

WOMEN TEACHING YOUNGER WOMEN (MEN TEACHING MEN)

Ti. 1, 2—administering help to orphans and widows; 1 Tm. 5:9-10—preaching; 1 Tm. 5:17; 6:2.

DEFENDING THE FAITH

2 Tm. 4:16

HELPING TRAVELING MISSIONARIES

Ti. 3:13

MIRACLES, HEALINGS

1 Cor. 12:9-10

HELPS

1 Cor. 12:29

SERVING

Rom. 12:8

MERCY

Rom. 12:8

WORDS OF WISDOM OR KNOWLEDGE

1 Cor. 12:8

LEADERSHIP

Rom. 12:8; 1 Cor. 12:28.

EXHORTATION

Rom. 12:8

DISTINGUISHING SPIRITS

1 Cor. 12:10

OTHER:

- Planting or watering (1 Cor. 3:6-8; 9:11)
- Commercial: managing what was entrusted to one as a steward (1 Cor. 4:1; 9:17; Eph. 3:2; Ti. 1:7).
- Military: serving as a soldier (1 Cor. 9:7; 2 Tm. 2:3-4).
- Familial: serving in the furtherance of the gospel like a child serving his father (Phil. 2:22).
- Architectural: doing the work of a builder (Rom. 15:20; 1 Cor. 3:10-15).
- Domestic: serving as a slave of Christ (Rom. 1:1; 1 Cor. 7:22; 2 Cor. 4:5; Gal. 1:10; Eph. 6:6; Phil. 1:1; 2 Tm. 2:24; Ti. 1:1).

ENDNOTES

2. IMAGO DEI

1. Lewis, C.S. *Mere Christianity*, Bk. III, chap. 10.
2. Erickson, M. J. *Christian Theology*, 2nd ed. (Grand Rapids, MI: Baker Books, 1998).
3. Ibid, p. 533.
4. Ibid, p. 533.
5. Ibid, p. 534.
6. Gen. 1:28-29
7. Gen. 1: 27; "male and female He created them." Each gender, in relationship with one another, intentionally reflects the Trinity's friendship and relational nature.
8. Gen. 1:27

3. UNITY & GLORY

1. Cyril of Alexandria, *Commentary on John*, 1, Chap. 9.
2. Augustine, *On the Trinity*. IV, Chap. 12.

4. THE FALL

1. Ware, B. A. *Father, Son and Holy Spirit: Relationships, Role and Relevance* (Wheaton, IL: Crossway Books, 2005), p. 75.
2. Elwell, W.A. *Evangelical Dictionary of Theology* (Grand Rapids, MI: Baker Books, 2001).
3. *Humanist Manifesto II*, 1973.
4. Owen, J. *A Display of Arminianism* (Edmonton: Still Waters Revival Books, 1989) Kindle Locations 809-810.
5. Mt. 23:37; Jhn. 7:17; Rom. 7:18; 1Co. 9:17; 1Pt. 5:2 Phlm. 14.
6. 1Pt. 1:2
7. Mt. 6:25-34; Col. 1:15-16.
8. Woofolk, A. *Educational Psychology*, 5th ed. (New York: Longman, 1994).
9. Yount, W.R. *Created to Learn* (Nashville, TN: B&H Publishing Company, 2010).
10. Skinner, B.F. *The Technology of Teaching* (New York: Appleton-Century-Crofts, 1968), p. 110.
11. Biehler, R. F. and Snowman, J. *Psychology Applied to Teaching*, 7th ed. (Boston, MA: Houghton Mifflin Company, 1993), p. 346.
12. Elwell, W.A., p. 1275.
13. Edwards, J., p. 149.
14. Elwell, W.A., p. 1275.
15. Edwards, J. *Religious Affections* (Philadelphia: G. Goodman Printer, 1821).
16. Gregory of Nazianzus, *The Fifth Theological Oration—On the Spirit*, in *Christology of the Later Fathers*, ed. Edward R. Hardy, p. 211.

5. THE FATHER

1. Mt. 16:17; Mark 13:32; Lk. 22:29-30.
2. Barr, J. "Abby Isn't 'Daddy," *Journal of Theological Studies* 39, no. 1 (1988). p. 28-47.

8. THE TRINITY IN THE OLD TESTAMENT

1. Deut. 4:35, 6:4, 10:14; Psa. 96:5, 97:9; Isa. 43:10, 44:6-8, 44:24, 45:5-6, 45:21-23, 46:9, 48:11-12; Jhn. 17:3; 1Ti. 2:5; Rev. 1:8.
2. Mt. 3:16-17; 11:27; 17:1-9; 27:46; Jhn. 1:18; 14:16-17.
3. Jms. 1:17
4. Heb. 13:8
5. Letham, R. *The Holy Trinity: In Scripture, History, Theology And Worship* (Phillipsburg, NJ: P&R Publishing, 2004), Kindle Locations 238-241.
6. Six synopses paraphrased from *Shane Wood's* talk entitled *"A Peculiar Organization of Thought."* Accessed August 15, 2018 from https://www.shanejwood.com/the-book-of-revelation/.
7. Gen. 3:9-19
8. Gen. 9:1-8
9. Gen. 9:1-8
10. Gen. 18
11. Exo. 3:1-17
12. Psa. 18:7-15; Exo. 19:16. **See also** Exo. 20:18; Job 37:5; Psa. 29:3-9; 77:18; 97:4; Isa. 30:27-33; Amo. 1:2; Hab. 3:11; Zec. 9:14; Rev. 11:19.
13. Isa. 29:5-6. **See also** Jdg. 5:4-5; Psa. 77:18; Hab. 3:6.
14. Ex 3:2. Fire represents the purity, holiness, and awe of God. **See also** Exo. 13:21; 19:18; 24:17; Lev. 9:24; Num. 14:14; Deut. 4:11-12; 5:4,22-26; Jdg. 13:20-22; Psa. 97:3; Joel 2:30.
15. Exo. 19:18. See also Exo. 20:18; Psa. 144:5; Isa. 6:4; Isa. 30:27; Joel 2:30; Rev. 15:8.
16. Exo. 16:10. Clouds and smoke convey the mystery and transcendence of God. God speaks to Moses from the cloud: Exo. 19:9; 24:15-16; 33:9; 34:5; Duet. 31:15; Lev. 16:2; Num. 9:15-22; 14:14; 1Ki. 8:10-11; Eze. 1:4; 10:3-4

    See also the transfiguration of Jesus Christ: Mt. 17:5; Mk. 9:7; Lk. 9:34-35; Rev. 14:14-16.
17. Josh. 5:13-15
18. Isa. 6:1-5
19. Psa. 18:8-16
20. Amos 6:1-4, 8:1
21. Jer. 1:11,13
22. Ezek. 1-8
23. Zech. 1 & 6
24. Num. 24
25. Gen. 16:7-13. See also Gen. 18:1-22; 32:24-30; Jos. 5:13-15.
26. Isa 6:1. John interprets this verse to refer to Jesus Christ (Jhn. 12:41). See also Eze. 1:26; 10:1; Dan. 7:9; Rev. 4:2; 20:11.
27. Isa. 6:2; Eze. 1:5-18; 10:9-13; Rev. 4:6-11.
28. Eze. 10:4. See also Exo. 16:10; 24:16; 40:34-35; Lev. 9:23-24; Num. 14:10; 1Ki. 8:11; 2Ch. 7:1-3; Psa. 29:3,9; 97:2-6; Eze. 11:22-23.
29. Isa. 30:27. See also Num. 12:9-10; Psa. 18:13-15.

30. Exo. 19:16; 20:18-20; Isa. 6:5.
31. Isa. 6:8; Eze. 1:28-2:1.
32. Num. 12:5-8
33. Heb. 1:4
34. Heb. 2:14-18
35. Heb. 3
36. Heb. 4-5
37. Heb. 10
38. Heb. 6
39. Heb. 8
40. Heb. 7
41. Heb. 9
42. Heb. 12
43. The Bible emphasizes the pre-existence of the Son, his equality as a Son with God, and identifies Jesus with the Yahweh of the Old Testament (Col. 1:13-17; 2:9; Jhn. 1:18; 6:39-41; 20:28; 1Ti. 2:13; 2Pt. 1:1; Isa. 6; Heb. 1:10-12; Psa. 102:25-27).
44. Jhn. 14:19
45. Deut. 32:6; Isa. 63:16; [twice] 64:8; Jer. 3:4, 19, 31:9; Mal. 1:6, 2:10.
46. 2Sa. 7:14; 1Ch. 17:13; 22:10; 28:6; Psa. 68:5; 89:26.
47. Exo. 4:22-23; Deut. 1:31; 8:5; 14:1; Psa. 103:13; Jer. 3:22; 31:20; Hos. 11:1-4; Mal. 3:17.
48. Exo. 4:22-23; Hos. 11:3-4.
49. Isa. 9:6
50. Mic. 5:2-5
51. Dan. 7:14
52. Gen. 3:15
53. Warfield, B. B. "The Spirit of God in the Old Testament," in *Biblical and Theological Studies*, ed. Samuel G. Craig (Philadelphia: Presbyterian and Reformed, 1952), p. 127-56.
54. Gen. 1:2; Psa. 33:9; 104:29-30.
55. Eze. 37:8-10
56. Num. 27:18, Judg. 3:10, 1Sa. 13:16, Exo. 31:3.
57. Isa. 63:11-12; Hag. 2:5; 1Sa. 19:20, 23.
58. Isa. 11:2-3; 42:1; 61: 1.
59. Jhn. 8:28-29
60. Gen. 1:2, Psa. 33:6b.
61. Jhn. 3:16, 6:38.
62. Rev. 5:6
63. 2Ti. 3:16-17
64. Jhn. 16:12-14
65. 1Cor. 1:18

9. TRINITARIAN HISTORY

1. Tertullian, Ag. Prax, chap. 9.
2. Macleod, D. *Shared Life: The Trinity and the Fellowship of God's People* (Ross-shire, Scotland: Christian Focus Publications, 2005), p. 37.
3. Cyril of Alexendria, *On the Unity of Christ,* pg. 52.
4. Ferguson, E. *Church History: From Christ to Pre-Reformation*, vol. 1 (Grand Rapids, MI: Zondervan, 2005).
5. Ibid, p. 75.

6. Macleod, D. *Shared Life: The Trinity and the Fellowship of God's People* (Ross-shire, Scotland: Christian Focus Publications, 2005), p. 44.
7. Ferguson, E., 2005.
8. Christopher, H. A. *Learning Theology with the Church Fathers* (Downers Grove, IL: IVP Academic, 2002), p. 61.
9. Macleod, D., p. 99-133.
10. Anderson, J. N. D. *The Word's Religions* (Downers Grove, IL: InterVarsity, 1963).
11. Qur'an 17:111; 19:88-92.
12. Christopher, H. A., p. 85.
13. "Hypostatic Union" in the *Westminster Dictionary of Christian Theology*, ed. A. Richardson, Denzinger, ed. Bannwart, p. 148.
14. Zizioulas, J. *Being as Communion* (St. Vladimirs Seminary Press, 1997), p. 18.
15. Hardy, E. R. *Christology of the Later Fathers.* (Philadelphia: Westminster Press, 1954), pp. 329-330.
16. Christopher, H. A., p. 54.

10. BIBLICAL WORSHIP

1. Gen. 3:7-24
2. Gen. 9:1-17
3. Gen. 15; 17:3-8.
4. Deut. 9:9-15; Exo. 34:27-28.
5. Psa. 89:3-4
6. Leonard J. E. *I Will Be Their God: Understanding the Covenant* (Chicago, IL: Laudemont Press, 1992).
7. Frame, J. M. W*orship in Spirit and Truth* (Phillipsburg, NJ: P&R Publishing, 1996), p. 1.
8. Stapert, C. R. *A New Song for an Old World: Musical Thought in the Early Church* (Grand Rapids, MI: Calvin Institute of Christian Worship Liturgical Studies, 1998), Kindle Locations 243-244.
9. Bartholomew, C. G., & Goheen, M. W. *The Drama of Scripture: Finding our Place in the Biblical Story* (Grand Rapids, MI: Baker Publishing Group, 2004).
10. Frame, J.M., p. 23.
11. Ware, B.A., p. 51.
12. Eph. 1:9-12
13. Jhn. 6:38; 4:34; 5:23-24, 30, 36-38; 6:44; 7:28-29; 8:16-18, 42.
14. Jms. 1:17
15. Rom. 8:31-32
16. Jhn. 6:37-65
17. Jhn. 14:16
18. Mt. 11:25-27
19. Luk. 2:49; Jhn. 2:16.
20. Mt. 3:17, a conclusion of Psa. 2:7 and Isa. 42:1.
21. Jhn. 6:27
22. Jhn. 4:21-24
23. Jhn. 5:30, 36; 6:38-40; 8:16-18, 26, 49.
24. Jhn. 17; Mt. 6:9.
25. Jhn. 14:16, 26; 15:26.
26. Heb. 13:8
27. Eph. 1:20-23

28. Eph. 1:22
29. Mt. 16:18
30. Psa. 146:1-2; Mt. 1:21; Tit. 2:11-13; Phi. 3:20; 2Ti.1:10; 2Pt. 1:1.
31. Jhn. 14:1
32. Jhn. 5:21
33. Jhn. 1:1-18; Col. 1:15-20.
34. Jhn. 5:26-29
35. Jhn. 5:22-30. The "Son of Man" description in Dan. 7:14; Mrk. 8:38; 1Th. 3:13; 2Co. 5:10; 2Th. 1:7-10.
36. Job 26:11-14; Psa. 89:9; 107:23-30; Mt. 14:26, 33.
37. Jhn. 15:16
38. Mackintosh, H. R. *The Doctrine of the Person of Jesus Christ* (Edinburgh: T & T Clark, 1912), p. 27.
39. Mt. 24:36
40. 1Ti. 2:5
41. 1Co. 15:24-26
42. 1Co. 15:24-28
43. Phi. 2:5-11; 2Ti. 2:11-13. In Rev. 5:8-10 we find *hymns* explicitly addressed *to* God rather than just about Him.
44. Jhn. 14:16
45. Acts 5:3
46. Eph. 4:30
47. 1Th. 5:19
48. Acts 7:51
49. Mt. 12:31-32
50. Rom.1:4
51. Isa. 11:2
52. Rom. 8:2; Rev. 11:11.
53. Isa. 11:2
54. Heb. 9:14
55. Jhn. 14:17; 15:26.
56. Jhn. 14:17
57. Jhn. 14:26
58. 1Pt. 1:11; Gen. 1:2; 1Pt. 4:14; Mt. 10:20; Gal. 4:6; Lk. 1:35.
59. Jhn. 15:26
60. Acts 1:8
61. Ware, B., p. 119.
62. Col. 3:9-10, 1Th. 5:23-24.
63. Chapell, B. *Christ-Centered Worship* (Grand Rapids, MI: Baker Academic, 2009), p. 17.
64. Poythress, V. S. *Symphonic Theology* (Phillipsburg, NJ: P&R Publishing, 1987).
65. Temple, W. *The Hope of a New World* (White Fish, MT: Kessinger Publishing, 2005), p. 30.
66. Witvliet, J. D. *Worship Seeking Understanding* (Grand Rapids, MI: Baker Academic, 2003), p. 33.
67. Webber, R. *Ancient Future* (Grand Rapids, MI: Baker Books, 2008).
68. Bartholomew, 2004.
69. Aristotle, *Politics*, 1340a.

11. TYPES OF COMMUNITY

1. Much of the information listed on the different types of groups comes from "Small Group Models," *Christianity Today Archives*. Accessed August 24th, 2018 https://www.small-groups.com/build/models/.
2. Jhn. 14:6
3. Eph. 4:15

13. ONE ANOTHER

1. Mk. 9:50; 11:31.
2. Zec. 7:9; 8:16-17; Jas. 4:11
3. 1Pt. 4:9
4. 1Th. 4:18, 5:11; Eph. 4; Heb. 3:13; 10:24-25.
5. Gal. 5:13, 6:2; Col. 3:13; 1Pt. 4:8, 10; 1Jn. 4:7, 11.
6. Eccl. 4:10
7. Isa. 13:8; Jer. 7:5; Mt.18; 1Tm. 6; 1Co. 6:1.
8. Mt. 18
9. 2Chr. 25:21; Jas. 5:16.
10. Eph. 5:21; Rom.12:10; 15:5; 2Co. 13:11.
11. Jhn. 17:23
12. Rom 12:5; 1Co. 12:8, 25.
13. Gen. 11:3
14. Rom. 15:14
15. Jhn. 17
16. Gal. 3:27-29
17. 1Pt. 4:9; Rom. 14:5, 13; 15:7; Eph. 4:2, 32.
18. Mt. 9:20
19. Mt. 25:14-30
20. Prv. 11:24, 13:7.
21. 1Co. 6:17
22. Mt. 5:18, 30; 6:24.
23. Mt. 19:17
24. Mt. 23:9
25. 1Co. 12:18; Rom. 5:12-19.

15. OUR TEMPLE HOME

1. Sailhamer, J. *Genesis Unbound* (Sisters, OR: Multnomah Books, 1996), p. 38-40.
2. God hovers over waters even before creating the waters on day 2—just a thoughtful sidetone that alludes to our idea of the new things old.
3. Sailhamer, p. 64.
4. Ibid, p. 64.
5. McGee, J.V. "The Tabernacle: God's Portrait of Christ." *Thru the Bible Radio Network* (2002), http://www.thruthebible.org/atf/cf/%7B91e2424c-636c-40c2-9c55-890588e90ece%7D/The%20Tabernacle.pdf (accessed, May 1, 2012).

6. Beale, G.K. *The Temple and the Church's Mission* (Downers Grove, IL: InterVarsity Press, 2004), p. 32.
7. Ibid, p. 34.
8. Jhn. 1:1
9. Beale, p. 34.
10. Ibid, p. 39-40.
11. Brooks, W.E. "The Perpetuity of Christ's Sacrifice in the Epistle to the Hebrews," *Journal of Biblical Literature, LXXXIX* (June, 1970): 207.
12. Guthrie, G.H. *The NIV Application Commentary* (Grand Rapids, MI: Zondervan, 1998), p. 328.
13. McGee, 2002.
14. Hughes, P.E. "The Blood of Jesus and His Heavenly Priesthood in Hebrews." *Part II, The High-Priestly Sacrifice of Christ,* Biblioteca Sacra 130, no. 519 (J-S, 1973): 195-212.

16. A FAMILY OF FAMILIES

1. Cotton, J. *A. Practical Commentary ... Upon the First Epistle Generall of John* (London, 1656), p. 189.
2. Ware, 2005.
3. Yauk, D. *Authority: Every Human's Journey From Slave to Free* (Fort Collins, CO: Garden City P&P, 2016).
4. Peter Leithart in his book *The Four: A Survey of the Gospels*, asserts that Matthew's Gospel patterns itself after the structure of the Old Testament in order to show us that Jesus is Israel. The Gospel begins by establishing Jesus as the new creation (Mt. 1:1; Gn. 2:4; 5:1). Matthew traces Jesus through Abraham (Mt. 1:1-17; Gn. 12-26), Joseph the dreamer (Mt. 1:18-25; Gn. 37), and correlates the nations in the time of Joseph to the Magi in the time of Jesus (Gn. 38-50; Mt. 2:1-12). Like Pharaoh, Herod, himself a Jew (an Edomite—demonstrating that Israel had indeed become so perverse they'd become Egypt), sought to kill children to get to Jesus (Mt. 2:13-15; Ex. 1-2). Jesus is thus portrayed as the New Moses in Matthew 3–4, and his five discourses in Matthew 5–7 parallel the Sinai revelation. Matthew 10 bears similarity to the preparation of the tribes to enter the land in Deuteronomy, and is followed by references of Joshua, David and Saul in Matthew 11–12, and ends with the Parables of the Kingdom (Mt. 13), which allude to Solomon Wisdom literature. Matthew 14–18 is filled with imagery and allusion to 1 & 2 Kings, and the ministries of Elijah and Elisha in 19–28 allude to the ministry to the Southern Kingdom of Israel (Mt. 19:1) and the reign of Joash, followed by the ministries of Jeremiah and Ezekiel.

17. THE LORD'S SUPPER

1. Yauk, D. *Reconsidering the Lord's Supper* (Fort Collins, CO: Garden City P&P, 2018).
2. Plutarch, *Quaest. cone.* 612D; 614 A-B.
3. Cole, R. L. *Love-Feasts: A History of the Christian Agape* (London: Charles H. Kelly, 1916), p. 73.
4. You as the reader may also find it interesting to consider Dave Yauk's research on the worship leader in *Reconsidering the Liturgy and the Worship Leader*. In the historical days of the early church, those called *benefactors* were the image of what Paul and Jesus would have deemed "worship leaders." The hosts of meals and the curators of the culture were the ones capitalizing on, shaping, and forming people's view of what is to be honored and

worshipped. The framework of Jesus and Paul was much broader than our slender view of worship today.

5. Streett, R. A. *Subversive Meals: An Analysis of the Lord's Supper Under Roman Domination During the First Century* (Eugene, OR: Pickwick Publications, 2013), p. 239-240.
6. Ibid, p. 250.

18. LITURGY & RHYTHMS

1. Yauk, D. *Reconsidering the Worship Leader and Liturgy* (Fort Collins, CO: Garden City P&P, 2017).
2. Some of this outline was taken from the thoughts of Bryan Chapell in *Christ-Centered Worship: Letting the Gospel Shape our Practice* (Grand Rapids, MI: William B. Eerdman's Publishing, 2009).

20. PPK HOUSEHOLD

1. Gen. 1:27; 5:1-2.
2. In Acts 2:41 both men and women believe and are baptized.
3. Gal. 3:27-28 says, "For as many of you as were baptized into Christ have put on Christ. There is neither Jew nor Greek, there is neither slave nor free, *there is neither male nor female*; for you are all on in Christ Jesus" (italics mine).
4. 1Co. 11:3
5. Eph. 5:21-33; Gen. 2:20-22.
6. Col. 1:18
7. Eph. 5:23
8. Keller, T. *The Meaning of Marriage* (New York: Riverhead Books, 2011), p. 195.
9. Lewis, C. S. *The Business of Heaven* (New York: Harvest Books, 1984), p. 169-170.
10. Grudem, W. *Systematic Theology* (Grand Rapids, MI: Zondervan, 1994), p. 463-464.
11. Gen. 3:1
12. Gen. 2:15-17
13. Rom. 5:15
14. The names of the twelve apostles are these: The first, Simon, who is called Peter, and Andrew his brother; and James the son of Zebedee, and John his brother; Philip and Bartholomew (Nathanael); Thomas and Matthew the tax collector; James the son of Alphaeus (James the Less), and Thaddaeus (Judas, son of James); Simon the Zealot, and Judas Iscariot, the one who betrayed Him. (Mt. 10:2-4).
15. 1Tm . 3:1-7
16. Col. 3:18-20
17. The word is used to speak of Jesus submitting to his parents (Lk. 2:51), demons submitting to the disciples (Lk. 10:17), submission to government (Rom. 13:1), the universe being subject to Christ (1Pt. 3:22), Christ being subject to the Father (1Co. 15:28), church members submitting to church leaders (1Co. 16:15-16), wives submitting to husbands (Col. 3:18), servants submitting to masters (Ti. 2:9), and Christians submitting to God (Heb. 12:9).
18. Grudem, p. 466.
19. 1Sa. 8:19-22
20. 1Sa. 10:24
21. 2Chr. 19:6; Psa. 2:10-11; Jhn. 5:27.
22. Gen. 14:3

23. Exo. 6:13; Eze. 1.
24. Jhn. 2:3
25. 2Sa. 24:3
26. 2Sa. 24:21
27. 1Kgs. 1:47
28. 2Sa. 7:5-17
29. 2Sa. 6:14
30. 2Sa. 7:2; 1Chr. 22; 1Kgs. 5-7.
31. 1Kgs. 8:12-21, 62-66; 2Chr. 5; 7:1-11.
32. Dan. 1-3, 1 & 2 Kgs.
33. Isa. 56:7
34. Isa. 35:4-6; Mt. 11:4-5; 35:4-6.
35. Psa. 8; 2Kgs. 9:13
36. Rev. 19:11-16
37. Heschel, A. *The Prophets* vol. 1 (New York: Harper, 1969), p. 25-26.
38. Duet. 18:15-22
39. Jer. 1:9; Isa. 6:5-10; Jhn. 8:26.
40. Num. 12:6; Jhn. 5:19-20.
41. Duet. 18:16-19
42. 2Sa.12:1-12
43. Jhn. 4:19
44. Eph. 2:20
45. Col. 2:2; 1Ti. 3:16.
46. Eph. 1:9, 3:6, 9, 5:32.
47. Jhn. 16:8
48. Psa. 139:7-10
49. Lk. 1:35
50. 1Co. 2:10-11
51. Heb. 9:14

21. CHURCH POLITY

1. Acts 14:23
2. Ti. 1:5
3. Stewart, A. C. *The Original Bishops* (Grand Rapids, MI: Baker Academic, 2014), KL 4098.
4. 1Ti. 3:1-7
5. 1Ti. 3:2; Ti. 1:9.
6. 1Co. 11:1
7. Ti. 2:7
8. Stewart, Kindle Location 3868.
9. Aristotle, *Pol.* 1255B.
10. Leaney, A. R. C. *The Rule of Qumran and Its Meaning: Introduction, Translation, and Commentary* (London: SCM, 1966), p. 189.
11. Stewart, KL 3006-3009.
12. Liebmann, H. "Zur altchristlichen Verfassungsgeschichte," in *Kleine Schriften I,* ed. Kurt Aland, TUGAL 67 (Berlin: Akademie-Verlag, 1958), p. 144.
13. Stewart, KL 1593.
14. Strabo, *Geogr.* 14.2.5.
15. Stewart, KL 7838.

16. We discuss in our section on S.ignature Mission how a collective viewpoint in regard to the spiritual "gifts" forms a healthier way of doing life together. When we see ourselves as the body, and we minister as one, we prioritize serving not spectacle, making servants, not superheroes, and we emphasize the filling of the Spirit rather than the sacredness of spots or location (defined in later chapters).

22. A BRIEF ON GOVERNANCE

1. Hall C.A. *Learning Theology with the Church Fathers* (Downers Grove, IL: IVP Academic, 2002), p. 175.
2. Psa. 135:5-7; Mt. 5:45; Lk. 8:25.
3. Psa. 104:21-29
4. Dan. 2:24; 4:24-25; Isa. 10:5-12; Acts 17:26.
5. Prv. 16:33; Est. 4:14; Jhn. 1:7.
6. Acts 2:23
7. In Luke 4:1-13, notice that Jesus ends the devil's efforts to tempt him by exclaiming, "you shall not put the *Lord your God* to the test" (italics mine). Jesus asserts that he is Satan's Lord. Satan has no right and power to offer Jesus' provision, power, or protection to anyone, and yet he masquerades as if he does. Satan's attacks are but a slight-of-hand, a magic trick, and an allusion. Satan is so full of pride that he believes he has power, even though he has nothing beyond what's been allowed him by God.
8. Isa. 45:7
9. Mt. 5:45
10. Psa. 23; Jhn. 10.
11. Jhn. 3:16
12. Jhn. 10
13. Gen. 20:6
14. Rom. 1; Acts 14:16.
15. Gen. 32-50
16. Job; 1Co. 10:13.
17. Jhn. 9:1-12
18. 1Co. 13:7
19. Chrysostom, *Homilies on the Acts of the Apostles* 15, NPNF 11 (Peabody, Mass.: Hendrickson, 1994), p. 99.

23. THE TRINITY ANSWERS ORGANIZATION

1. Edwards, J. *Works,* 13, p. 220-221 (no. 37).
2. William Bradford: History of Plymouth Plantation, c. 1650.
3. Supply and demand is the concept where if supply of anything grows, prices drop, and if supply decreases, prices rise. No matter the scenario, we measure transport down to what it will do to the individual and the local economy. Products are dictated by desires, wants, and felt needs. Our desires of worship are driving the economy. Answering the worship question changes the whole nature of what may gain value and what may lose value.
4. Cost and benefits is basically a pros-and-cons list. If you see a jacket you want to buy, you weigh not only the cost, but how it will make you look and what it will do for your image. The concept of cost and benefits goes much deeper into human identity and worship than the dollars spent.

5. Opportunity costs. When you take an opportunity, say choosing a job, you're giving up other things. Opportunity costs us something. What we miss in these decisions is that worship and our view of the "good life" is subconsciously underlying what may make us choose something and leave another thing. Answering the worship question is essential to making good decisions, assessing true opportunity, and weighing costs rightly in what it will ask of us—particularly in how it will weigh against God's essentials of families, meals, home, and Jesus.

6. The diamond water paradox is a concept fascinated with the fact that a commodity like water is more a necessity, but diamonds, for instance, have more value in terms of market dollars. If diamonds were suddenly to disappear, we might be upset, and a few industries would go down for sure, but we would survive. If we lost water on the other hand, everything would dive into chaos. This economic principle helps us consider how we prioritize and measure value. It helps us drive down to the essential needs of humanity and, I would dare say, exposes how we've complicated the human experience, and how we can work to simplify.

7. Incentives are kind of like a bribe. If you do something you get something. Money is not the only commodity either. Consider how ticket vendors incentivize a concert by slowly making tickets harder to get so you'll buy quickly. Consider the incentive of the gym. It's enticement is not in the money but in what it will make us look like, the health it may provide, or the triathlon it may help us conquer. What motivates someone to give a kidney? The incentive is not just in the money; it's in the helping of others. People change their behavior in response to incentives constantly seeking to improve their lives in light of new conditions.

8. Money supply looks at how many actual printed dollars are floating around out in the global space. By printing less and more bills, the whole world can actually change. It shows us that money is an illusionary commodity with value that is actually quite vapid, and yet we serve it as slaves. Jesus said we cannot serve two masters. We can worship God, or money, but not both.

9. Interest rates are expressed normally as an annual percentage of the total amount borrowed. Interest exists because debt exists. The world actually encourages us to take on debt of all kinds, whereas Jesus work hard to owe nothing to anyone except for love. Debt or lack of debt are more questions of worship and whose kingdom we're building than about mortgages, cars, and school loans.

10. Inflation is simply the increase of overall prices of products and services in the economy.

11. Job availability has two sides. One, there are less or more jobs available as people's desire to work has gone up, so employment fluctuates in states of rise and decline. Two, there is more or less work available, and people's desire to work has gone down; which means there's more incentive, worldview, belief, and worshipful reasons not to provide, show honor, or serve with dignity than there are reasons to go out and work as God's commanded us to.

12. There's no such thing as free in economics. There's no such thing as "free lunch." You're paying for free things through hidden costs, or someone else is paying for them in unpaid labor, long hours, or in some other link in the chain of distribution. Everything requires some that are serving those being served.

24. HERMENUETICS

1. Yauk, D. *Reconsidering Singing* (Fort Collins, CO: Garden City P&P, 2018).
2. Historical epic largely fills Genesis and the first half of Exodus, Numbers, Joshua, Judges, Ruth, 1 and 2 Samuel, 1 and 2 Kings, 1 and 2 Chronicles, Ezra, Nehemiah, Esther, Jonah, and possibly Acts.

3. The last half of Exodus; also Leviticus, Deuteronomy.
4. Job, Proverbs, Ecclesiastes.
5. Psalms, Song of Solomon, Lamentations.
6. Isaiah, Jeremiah, Ezekiel, Daniel, Hosea, Joel, Amos, Obadiah, Jonah, Micah, Nahum, Habakkuk, Zephaniah, Haggai, Zechariah, Malachi.
7. Daniel, Revelation, Gospels (Matthew, Mark, Luke, John), and possibly Acts.
8. Romans, 1 and 2 Corinthians, Galatians, Ephesians, Philippians, Colossians, 1 and 2 Thessalonians, 1 and 2 Timothy, Titus, Philemon, Hebrews, James, 1 and 2 Peter, 1, 2, and 3 John, Jude.
9. Synecdoche, hyperbole, irony, ellipsis, euphemism, dysphemism, anthropomorphism, personification, parables, etc.
10. 2Ti. 3:16-17; 2Pt. 1:20-21; Mt. 5:18; Jhn. 16:12-13.
11. 1Pt. 3:19
12. Mt. 8:23-27
13. Gen. 3:15
14. Hos. 10:12
15. Rev. 22:2
16. Eze. 31
17. Jer. 1:11-12
18. Utley, B. *Ezekiel 17.* https://bible.org/seriespage/ezekiel-17. (Accessed Nov. 12, 2014).
19. Acts 5:30
20. Psa. 1:3
21. Psa. 52:8
22. Eph. 3:17
23. Mt. 7:17-19
24. Mt. 24:14
25. McKnight, S. *Kingdom Conspiracy: Returning to the Radical Mission of the Local Church* (Grand Rapids, MI: Baker Publishing Group, 2014).
26. Jhn. 18:36
27. McKnight, p. 99.
28. Yauk, D. *The Tempo of Discipleship* (Fort Collins, CO: Garden City P&P, 2015).
29. Yauk, 2015.

25. CREATIVE TRANSFORMATION

1. Marr, B. *How Much Data We Create Every Day? The Mind-Blowing Stats Everyone Should Read.* https://www.forbes.com/sites/bernardmarr/2018/05/21/how-much-data-do-we-create-every-day-the-mind-blowing-stats-everyone-should-read/#3c9d64ba60ba. (Accessed November 20, 2018).
2. Robinson, K. *How Schools Kill Creativity.* https://creativesystemsthinking.wordpress.-com/2015/04/26/ken-robinson-how-schools-kill-creativity/. (Accessed November 20, 2018).
3. Sherman, C. *The Art of Writing and Speaking in the English Language* (England: The Old Greek Press, 1905).
4. Robinson, 2018.
5. Mason, C. as quoted in *Personal Reflections on the Gentle Art of Learning* by Karen Andreola (Charlotte: Mason Research Company, 1998), p. 29.
6. Yauk, D. *The Tempo of Discipleship* (Fort Collins, CO: Garden City P&P, 2015).
7. Yauk, 2015.
8. Andreola, p. 114.

9. Crouch, A. *Culture Making: Recovering Our Creative Calling* (Downer Grove, IL: InterVarsity Press, 2009), p. 23.

26. THE TRINITY ANSWERS SCRIPTURE

1. Textual Criticism: concerned with establishing the original or most authoritative text.
2. Philosophical Criticism: concerned with the study of biblical languages and their accurate use of vocabulary, grammar, and style of that period.
3. Literary Criticism: concerned mostly with the genres that lie within the text itself that might help one derive a date of its authorship and function.
4. Historical Criticism: concerned with interpreting biblical literature in the context of other historical writings.
5. Traditional Criticism: concerned with oral traditions as they precede and influence written text.
6. Form Criticism: concerned with classifying a written material (i.e., as hymn or parable)
7. Apologetical Criticism: concerned with cross-referencing apparent contradictions, addressing raised questions, and uncovering intended meaning.
8. Exegetical Criticism: concerned with maintaining the original meaning of the texts.
9. Redaction Criticism: concerned with studying how final documents were assembled by final authors or editors.
10. Bruce, F.F. *The Epistle To The Hebrews* (Grand Rapids, MI: Eerdmans, 1990), p. 145.

27. EVERYONE IS A CHURCH PLANTER

1. Redman, R. *The Great Worship Awakening* (San Francisco, CA: John Wiley and Sons Inc., 2002), p. 175.
2. Grudem, W. *Systematic Theology: An Introduction to Biblical Doctrine* (Grand Rapids, MI: Zondervan, 1994), p. 857. Summarized in Mark Driscoll and Gerry Breshears' book *Vintage Church: Timeless Truths and Timely Methods*, (Wheaton, IL: Crossway, 2008), p. 37.
3. Leithart, P. *The Four: A Survey of the Gospels* (Moscow, ID: Canon Press, 2010), p. 178-179.
4. Based on a graphic in David J. Hesselgrave's, *Planting Churches Cross-Culturally* (Grand Rapids, MI: Baker Academic, 2007), p. 281.
5. Taylor, J. "The Marks of Leadership," *Christianity Today 8* (January 3, 1964): p. 5.
6. Yount, W. R. *Created to Learn* (Nashville, TN: B&H Publishing, 2010), p. 449.
7. Lingenfelter S. G. & Mayers, M. *Minstering Cross-Culturally: An Incarnational Model for Personal Relationships* (Grand Rapids, MI: Baker Academic, 2003).
8. Bruce, F. F. *The Apostle of the Heart Set Free* (Grand Rapids, MI: William B. Eerdmans Publishing, 1977), p. 255.
9. *First Apology* 14 ANF 1:167, (slightly adapted for use).
10. Peter, L. J. *The Peter Principle* (New York: Bantam, 1970), p. 19-27.
11. Narramore, C. M. *The Psychology of Counseling* (Grand Rapids, MI: Jossey-Bass, 1993), p. 14-17.
12. Wilson M. T. & Hoffman, B. *Preventing Ministry Failure* (Downers Grove, IL: IVP Books, 2007), p. 201-211.
13. Ibid, p. 178.
14. Ibid, p. 179-181.
15. Ibid, p. 65.

28. SYNERGETIC WORSHIP & MISSION

1. Mt. 5:6; 1Pt. 2:2; Psa. 42:1.
2. 1Jn. 4:20; Jhn. 17:26.
3. Isa. 42:1; Mk. 1:10-11; Acts 2:22.
4. 1Jn. 1:7; Phil. 1:5; 1Co. 12:7; Gal. 6:2.
5. Beale, G. K. *The Temple and the Church's Mission* (Downers Grove, IL: InterVarsity Press, 2004), p. 129.
6. Jesus is referred to as the Word (Jhn. 1:14), the Bread (Jhn. 6:35), and the one who modeled a ministry of the word for both hurting and healing (Heb. 4:12).
7. Psa. 119:105; Isa. 30:21.
8. 2Co. 2:14-15; Phil. 4:18; Rev. 8:3-4; Mk. 4:4-14.
9. Stott, W. "The Conception of 'Offering' in the Epistle to the Hebrews," *New Testament Studies, IX* (October, 1962).
10. Hughes, P. E. "The Blood of Jesus and His Heavenly Priesthood in Hebrews." *Part II, The High-Priestly Sacrifice of Christ,* Biblioteca Sacra 130, no. 519 (J-S, 1973): pp. 195-212.
11. O'Donnell, D. S. *God's lyrics: Rediscovering Worship Through Old Testament Songs* (Phillipsburg, N.J: P & R Publishing).

29. THE TRINITY ANSWERS MISSION

1. Jhn. 1:1; Eph. 1:3-14; Col. 1:15-19; Rev. 1:18.
2. Psa. 2:7; Mt. 3:17.
3. Isa. 11:2; 61:1; Psa. 45:7-8; Mt. 3:16.
4. Psa. 2:6
5. Gen. 12:3; 21:12; 28:14; Luk. 3:34; Gal. 3:16; Heb. 11:17-19.
6. Gen. 49:10
7. Gen. 3:15; Gal. 4:4.
8. Mt. 5:17
9. Isa. 7:14; 58:6; 61:1-2; Psa. 72:10-11; Mic. 5:1.
10. Luk. 4:18-19; Mt. 20:28.
11. Isa. 6:9-10; 40:11; 42:2; 53:9.
12. Jhn. 12:46
13. Jhn. 3:16; 10:10.

33. APPENDIX 3: CROSS PROPHET

1. All can prophesy (Acts 2:16-21), all can discern truth as led by the Holy Spirit (1Jhn. 2:20,27), all can admonish and encourage one another (Col. 3:16; Heb. 3:13), all can instruct (Rom. 15:14), and all can live a life that brings others to salvation (1Co. 9:19-23; 10:31-11:1)
2. All of us are a royal priesthood (1Pt. 2:9) having access to God through Christ (Heb. 4:14-16). We are daily offerings and sacrifices unto Him (Rom. 12:1-2), worshipping him (1Co. 14:26), and doing good as we share with others (Heb. 13:16).
3. All believers rule and reign with Christ (Eph. 2:6) in a kingdom of selected leadership (Acts 6:1-6) which are elected by the people in order to lead the whole unto maturity (Eph. 4:11-13). The kingship of every believer gives them power to fight and defeat the world, the flesh

and the devil (Eph. 6:11-18; Jas. 4:7; 1Jhn. 2:27; 4:4; 5:4), and enables us all to participate in the royalty of Christ (1Pt. 2:9).

34. APPENDIX 4: CROSS PRIEST

1. All can prophesy (Acts 2:16-21), all can discern truth as led by the Holy Spirit (1Jhn. 2:20,27), all can admonish and encourage one another (Col. 3:16; Heb. 3:13), all can instruct (Rom. 15:14), and all can live a life that brings others to salvation (1Co. 9:19-23; 10:31-11:1)
2. All of us are a royal priesthood (1Pt. 2:9) having access to God through Christ (Heb. 4:14-16). We are daily offerings and sacrifices unto Him (Rom. 12:1-2), worshipping him (1Co. 14:26), and doing good as we share with others (Heb. 13:16).
3. All believers rule and reign with Christ (Eph. 2:6) in a kingdom of selected leadership (Acts 6:1-6) which are elected by the people in order to lead the whole unto maturity (Eph. 4:11-13). The kingship of every believer gives them power to fight and defeat the world, the flesh and the devil (Eph. 6:11-18; Jas. 4:7; 1Jhn. 2:27; 4:4; 5:4), and enables us all to participate in the royalty of Christ (1Pt. 2:9).

35. APPENDIX 5: CROSS KING

1. All can prophesy (Acts 2:16-21), all can discern truth as led by the Holy Spirit (1 Jhn. 2:20,27), all can admonish and encourage one another (Col. 3:16; Heb. 3:13), all can instruct (Rom. 15:14), and all can live a life that brings others to salvation (1Co. 9:19-23; 10:31-11:1)
2. All of us are a royal priesthood (1Pt. 2:9) having access to God through Christ (Heb. 4:14-16). We are daily offerings and sacrifices unto Him (Rom. 12:1-2), worshipping him (1Co. 14:26), and doing good as we share with others (Heb. 13:16).
3. All believers rule and reign with Christ (Eph. 2:6) in a kingdom of selected leadership (Acts 6:1-6) which are elected by the people in order to lead the whole unto maturity (Eph. 4:11-13). The kingship of every believer gives them power to fight and defeat the world, the flesh and the devil (Eph. 6:11-18; Jas. 4:7; 1Jhn. 2:27; 4:4; 5:4), and enables us all to participate in the royalty of Christ (1Pt. 2:9).